Mark Dawes, Ruth Matthews,
Andrew Roberts and Geoff Thwaites

Cambridge International AS & A Level
Thinking Skills

Coursebook
Third edition

CAMBRIDGE
UNIVERSITY PRESS

CAMBRIDGE
UNIVERSITY PRESS

University Printing House, Cambridge CB2 8BS, United Kingdom

One Liberty Plaza, 20th Floor, New York, NY 10006, USA

477 Williamstown Road, Port Melbourne, VIC 3207, Australia

314–321, 3rd Floor, Plot 3, Splendor Forum, Jasola District Centre, New Delhi – 110025, India

103 Penang Road, #05-06/07, Visioncrest Commercial, Singapore 238467

Cambridge University Press is part of the University of Cambridge.

It furthers the University's mission by disseminating knowledge in the pursuit of education, learning and research at the highest international levels of excellence.

www.cambridge.org
Information on this title: www.cambridge.org/9781108441049 (Paperback)

First published 2005
Second edition 2013
Third edition 2018

20 19 18 17 16 15 14 13 12 11 10 9 8 7 6 5

Printed in Great Britain by CPI Group (UK) Ltd, Croydon CR0 4YY

A catalogue record for this publication is available from the British Library

ISBN 978-1-108-44104-9 Paperback
ISBN 978-1-108-44110-0 Cambridge Elevate Edition (2 years)

This book represents a third edition of Thinking Skills: Critical Thinking and Problem Solving. This edition has been revised to bring it into line with the new Cambridge International AS & A Level Thinking Skills syllabus. Much of the original material in the Critical Thinking sections of this book has been written by John Butterworth, who was a co-author on the first two editions.

．．

Contents

Introduction

This Coursebook has been designed primarily to prepare students for the Cambridge International AS & A Level Thinking Skills. It builds on the successful first and second editions and takes account of teachers' feedback.

Thinking skills courses develop students' ability to synthesise information, data and critical comment to creatively produce their own critical thinking and problem solving. As well as providing full coverage of the CI syllabus, this Coursebook prepares students for other tests and examinations that assess the transferable skills of solving problems, critical thinking and reasoning, for example the TSA and BMAT assessments.

The Coursebook takes a 21st century approach to skills-based learning; one which helps to develop critical and investigative thinking, and informed and disciplined reasoning. It aims to develop a specific set of intellectual skills, independent of subject content and responds to a need for more mature and sophisticated ways of thinking. Beyond that, it will provide the tools to better understand, analyse and make a reasoned response to questions, problems and issues in the widest sense. Debate, investigative thinking and informed reasoning are encouraged. The Coursebook will, therefore, equip students not just for thinking skills assessments but also for academic study at A Level and beyond, for preparation for professional careers, and for life as an reflective, engaged global citizen.

The Coursebook is supplemented by a Teacher Resource. Each chapter has the following features.

> **Learning objectives**
>
> *This chapter introduces the idea of a problem and considers some simple examples to help you identify the key information that is required to solve problems and apply some simple problem-solving strategies.*

Learning objectives outline what students will have covered and understood by the end of the chapter.

A **chapter introduction**, where appropriate, identifies any content sections that are not required by the CI AS & A Level Thinking Skills syllabus but are relevant for readers who want a broader exposition of the thinking skills.

Chapter content explores the Problem Solving or Critical Thinking topic and the related skills. The skills are demystified for the student, and put into a real life context.

> Reading through this chapter and attempting the activities will help you identify different types of claim. It will also introduce you to some of the techniques used in critical thinking.
>
> **Cambridge International**
>
> If you wish to focus on preparing for Cambridge International AS and A Level Thinking Skills, you should work through Section 14.1 Claims and statements and Section 14.3 Fact, falsity and opinion and then attempt the end-of-chapter questions.
>
> You will need to be able to recognise claims and assess the likelihood of the content of a claim being true irrespective of its source.

> **EXAMPLE ACTIVITY 1.1**
>
> Imagine that you have to work out the best way to fit a number of rectangular packages into a box. Which of the four categories of skill identified above would be relevant to solving the problem?

Example Activities are questions or tasks students can attempt either individually or as a group. A commentary is provided to show what is required, in a scaffolded manner.

Activities are questions or tasks without a commentary for students to test their skills and progress. Activities apply skills to realistic scenarios and develop the ability to understand and engage confidently in problem solving or reasoningt. Within the Problem solving section, Combining your skills Activities provide practice in combining the problem-solving skills developed over several chapters in order to tackle more challenging exam-style questions. Suggested answers to Activities are given in the Teacher Resource.

> **ACTIVITY 1.1**
>
> Imagine you are going to book tickets for a concert. List the pieces of information you need and the processes that you need to go through in order to book the tickets and get to the concert. In what order should you do them? First list the main things, then try to break each down into smaller parts.

> **Summary**
> Having read this chapter you should be able to:
> - identify the information that is important in solving a problem
> - identify an appropriate method to solve the problem.

Summary points at the end of each chapter outline what students have learned.

End-of-chapter questions enable students to practise synthesising the skills developed in the chapter. Suggested answers are in the Teacher Resource.

> **End-of-chapter question**
>
> You want to buy a new mobile phone. You will use it for texting, making a few phone calls and keeping in touch with friends and family on social media. You have found two phones:
> - a 'Mobes4U' phone that costs $36 if you sign a two-year contract with the company
> - a 'Pay'N'Go' phone that costs $50 but you are not tied to a contract.
>
> **a** What other pieces of information should you consider before you decide which phone to buy?
> **b** Explain how you would use the information to make a decision.

> **Exam-style question**
>
> Nazim is planning to cook curries and sell them. He will take orders for parties. He will cook the curry and rice beforehand, then put the cooked food in serving dishes that will keep it hot. Nazim will pay his friend Raj, who has a van, to make deliveries and to fetch the serving dishes back after the party.
>
> Nazim's first order is for a party of 27 people. He has a recipe using vegetables, chick peas, onions and tomatoes. He is now trying to work out the right quantities of spices. For 15 people he would normally use 100 g of spices, made up of ginger (20%), turmeric (25%), coriander (35%), and cumin seeds (20%).

Exam-style questions at the end of each chapter are in the style students will see in the CI AS and A Level examinations. Suggested answers are in the Teacher Resource.

> **Appendix A: Mapping of Coursebook coverage of Thinking Skills tests and qualifications**
>
> – Content is not relevant
> * Content is partly relevant
> ** Content directly relevant

Appendix A sets out a mapping grid that highlights relevant content against the more widely used thinking skills assessments.

Problem Solving	What do we mean by a problem	Selecting and using information	Processing data	Working with models	Solving problems by searching	Finding methods of solution	Trends in data	Transforming data	Summarised data	Identifying features of a model	Necessary and sufficient conditions	Changing the scenario of a problem
Chapter	1	2	3	4	5	6	7	8	9	10	11	12
CI AS and A Level Thinking Skills[1]												
Paper 1	**	**	**	**	**	**	**	**	**	*	**	**
Paper 2	–	–	–	–	–	–	–	–	–	–	–	–
Paper 3	**	**	**	**	**	**	–	**	**	*	**	**
Paper 4	–	–	–	–	–	–	–	–	–	–	–	–
TSA[2]	**	**	**	**	**	**	**	**	**	*	*	*
(Singapore) K & I[3]	–	–	–	–	–	–	–	–	–	–	–	–
IBO TOK[4]	–	–	–	–	–	–	–	–	–	–	–	–
BMAT Section 1[5]	**	**	**	**	**	**	**	**	**	*	*	**
BCAT[6]	–	–	–	–	–	–	–	–	–	–	–	–
LSAT[7]	*	*	*	–	*	*	*	–	*	*	**	*
CCTST[8]	–	*	–	*	–	–	–	–	–	–	*	*

Part 1
Problem solving

Chapter 1
What do we mean by a 'problem'?

Learning objectives

This chapter introduces the idea of a problem and considers some simple examples to help you identify the key information that is required to solve problems and apply some simple problem-solving strategies.

1.1 Routine activities or problems

There are many things that we automatically do every day and would not consider to be 'problems'. For example, consider the action of making a cup of instant coffee – if you analyse the processes you need to go through, they are quite complicated. Just the list of items you need is quite long: a cup, a teaspoon, a jar of coffee, a kettle, water – and milk and sugar if you take them. Having found all these items, you fill the kettle and boil it; use the teaspoon to put coffee into the cup; pour the boiling water into the cup, just to the right level; stir; add milk and sugar; then put all the things you used away again. We could, if necessary, break this down even further, for example by explaining in detail what needs to be done to boil the kettle.

Although this is complicated, it is an everyday task that you probably do without thinking (assuming that you drink coffee that is, although the same principle applies for making tea or preparing your breakfast). To continue the coffee example, if over the years you have made many cups of coffee, you may have tried adding different quantities of coffee granules, milk and sugar to work out the strength of coffee that you prefer. Once you have established this, you simply make the coffee to your preferred specifications from that point onwards.

When you encounter something new, even a task which is no more complicated than others that you have previously completed, the processes required to complete the task may need considerably more thought and planning. Experience of similar problems is often helpful, however: when trying a new type of hot drink you may be able to more readily work out what the best combination of ingredients is for you.

Problem solving takes place when you are required to perform a task that you have not previously completed. These tasks may be very similar in nature to ones that you have done in the past or may be completely new. Experience of a wide range of different problems and their solutions is therefore very useful in developing problem-solving skills.

> **ACTIVITY 1.1**
>
> Imagine you are going to book tickets for a concert. List the pieces of information you need and the processes that you need to go through in order to book the tickets and get to the concert. In what order should you do them? First list the main things, then try to break each down into smaller parts.

1.2 What skills are needed to solve problems?

There are a range of different skills that can be required to solve problems, which can be divided into the following categories:

1 Understanding the problem that needs to be solved

Information might be presented in a range of different forms, using tables or diagrams in addition to text. Different pieces of information will be related to each other in many different ways, which might be explained through a simple mathematical model.

Being able to identify the appropriate pieces of information, and understand how they are related to each other, is necessary if the solution to a problem is going to be found.

2 Processing the information that is available to solve the problem

Reaching the solution to the problem may require some simple mathematics to be performed, based on the relationships that exist between the different pieces of information. There may also be certain criteria that need to be met – for example, a maximum weight that can be transported over a bridge in one journey.

Processing the information allows deductions to be made which lead to the solution to the problem.

3 Analysing data and representing it in different ways

Presenting information in a different way often allows different insights to be gained about the data that is available. Recognising patterns that exist in data can be very helpful for solving problems.

When considering problems that involve objects that can be moved into different positions and orientations, it can be very useful to be able to identify key features that confirm that the shape is unchanged.

4 Developing a problem that has already been solved to consider more complex situations that might occur

Many problems are solved by first considering much simpler versions of the problem. Once simplified versions of problems have been solved, it is important to be able to look at how that solution helps with the solutions to more complicated problems.

In addition to these problem-solving skills, there are a number of mathematical skills which are needed – many tasks will require some simple arithmetic and, as mentioned above, some familiarity with methods for representing data, such as bar charts and pie charts, is very useful.

EXAMPLE ACTIVITY 1.1

Imagine that you have to work out the best way to fit a number of rectangular packages into a box. Which of the four categories of skill identified above would be relevant to solving the problem?

Commentary

This problem involves mainly categories 1 and 2, but could involve some of category 4 as well:

1 Understand the problem that needs to be solved:

The dimensions of the box and the packages need to be known. Once these have been worked out you also need to think about the different orientations in which the packages could be placed into the box. You might make an initial assumption about the best orientation, which may turn out later to be wrong.

2 Process the information that is available:

Once you know the relevant dimensions, some appropriate calculations should enable you to work out how many boxes can be fitted in for each orientation.

4 Consider more complex situations:

If we know how to solve the problem in situations where all of the packages are the same shape and size then similar methods may help in situations where there is more than one shape of package.

If you had to solve the problem, you would need to be systematic and have some sort of strategy. In the case of problems such as this one it may also be difficult to be confident that you have the best solution – what if the best solution that you have found leaves a gap and the volume of the gap is larger than the volume of the box, how can you be sure that a different arrangement would not have managed to pack an extra box?

With some problems the method of finding an answer might be quite clear. With others there may be no systematic method and you might have to use trial and error from the start. Some problems will require a combination of both methods or can be solved in more than one way.

The example below is a simple problem; you can give either a simple answer or a more complicated one, depending on the degree of detail you consider necessary.

EXAMPLE ACTIVITY 1.2

Luke has a meeting, in a town that is 50 miles away, at 3 p.m. tomorrow. He is planning to travel by train from the town where he lives to the town where the meeting is, walking to and from the station at both ends.

List the pieces of information Luke needs in order to decide what time he must leave home.

Commentary

Let us start by thinking of everything that Luke does from leaving his house to arriving at the meeting:

1 He leaves his house.

2 He walks to the station.

3 He buys a train ticket.

4 He goes to the platform.

5 He boards the train when it arrives.

6 He sits on the train until it reaches its destination.

7 He leaves the train.

8 He walks to where his meeting is to be held.

We can construct the pieces of information that he needs from this list. They are:

1 The time taken to walk from his house to the station.

2 The time needed to buy a ticket (including the time waiting in a queue).

3 The time to walk to the platform.

4 The train timetable.

5 The time taken to walk from the station to where the meeting is being held.

EXAMPLE ACTIVITY 1.3

Suppose that we are given the following additional information:

It takes Luke 15 minutes to walk to the station and will take him 20 minutes to walk to the meeting. The trains leave the station every 30 minutes from 9 a.m. and the train journey takes a total of 50 minutes. Luke estimates that it will take him 10 minutes to buy his ticket and walk to the platform.

What time should Luke leave home in order to get to his meeting on time?

Commentary

We could choose a start time based on when we *think* Luke should leave home and then work out what time Luke would arrive, but a better strategy would be to work out when Luke should leave by working backwards from the meeting start time.

The sections of the journey can be considered one at a time. The start time of one activity is always the time by which the previous activity must have been completed.

Section of journey	Must be completed by	Time required	Latest start time
Walk to meeting	3:00 p.m.	20 minutes	2:40 p.m.
Train	2:40 p.m.	50 minutes	1:30 p.m.
The latest train that arrives by 2:40 p.m. must leave no later than 1:50 p.m., and the 1:30 p.m. train is the latest such train.			
Walk to station, buy ticket, walk to platform	1:30 p.m.	25 minutes	1:05 p.m.

Of course, you could do the whole thing by guesswork, but you might get it all wrong and, more to the point, you cannot be confident that you will have got it right.

1.3 Selecting a problem-solving strategy

In the sense we are using the word in this book, a 'problem' means a situation where we need to find a solution from a set of initial conditions. In some cases, as in the example above, the method for solving the problem is not difficult to work out once you have identified the information that is important.

In order to solve problems we must use the information that we are given in a certain way. The way in which we use it may be quite straightforward; it may for example be simply a matter of searching a table for a piece of data that matches given conditions. In other cases, instead of searching for a piece of data, we may have to search for a method of solution. The important thing in either case will be to have a strategy that will lead to the solution.

Imagine you are going out and can't find your house keys. Finding them is a problem in the sense meant by this section of the book.

- One method (and sometimes the quickest) is to run around all the *likely* places to see if they are there.

- After the likely places, you start looking at the *less likely* places, and so on until they turn up or you have to resort to more systematic methods.

There are two systematic ways of searching.

- The first (using experience) involves thinking carefully about when you last came into the house and what you did: this can be the quickest method.

- The other (which in mathematical terms is often known as the 'brute force' method) involves searching every room of the house thoroughly until they are found. This is often the most reliable method but can take a very long time and most people will use it as a last resort.

When people are solving problems similar to the one identified above, they may use any one or more of these methods. One of the prime skills that you need is to make a good judgement of which method is the most appropriate one to use in each particular situation.

In any problem, you will be presented with some initial pieces of information – these may be in the form of words, a table of numbers, a graph or a picture. You will also know what question it is that you need to answer. The first thing to do is to identify which pieces of information are most likely to be useful in proceeding to the solution and to try to work out how these pieces of information may be used. In many situations much more information than is needed is available and identifying which of it is redundant (not needed for the solution to the problem) is an important part of the problem-solving process.

The example below is relatively easy. It is not difficult to find a way of approaching the problem, and the necessary calculations are clear and simple.

EXAMPLE ACTIVITY 1.4

Julia has been staying in a hotel on a business trip. When she checks out, the hotel's computer isn't working, so the receptionist makes a bill by hand from the receipts, totalling $471. Julia thinks she has been overcharged, so she checks the itemised bill carefully.

Room:	4 nights at $76.00 per night
Breakfast:	4 at $10.00 each
Dinner:	3 at $18.00 each
Telephone:	10 units at $1.70 per unit
Bar:	Juices and soft drinks totalling $23.00
Laundry:	3 blouses at $5.00 each

It appears that the receptionist miscounted one of the items when adding up the total. Which item has Julia been charged too much for?

Commentary

Although this example is simple, it illustrates many of the methods used in solving problems:

- Look at the data provided. Identify which pieces are relevant and which are irrelevant. In this case all of the information is relevant to the solution as we will need to know how much Julia should have been charged.

- Make an intermediate calculation before you can reach the answer. In this case it was necessary to calculate the value that the bill should have been in order to identify where Julia had been overcharged. The sum of the charges on the itemised bill is $453, so Julia has been overcharged by $18.

- Search the data for a piece of information that helps to solve the problem. In this case, we need to find an item on the bill that could cost $18 (either singly or for some number of them). The only item on the itemised bill for which this is true is dinner, so Julia must have been charged for one extra dinner.

This is an example of using a systematic procedure to solve the problem.

The example below, whilst still being relatively simple, involves a slightly different type of problem where the method of solution is less obvious.

EXAMPLE ACTIVITY 1.5

The SuperSave supermarket sells Sudsy washing-up liquid for $1.20 a bottle. At this price they are charging 50% more than the price at which they buy the item from the manufacturers. Next week SuperSave is having a 'Buy two, get a third free' offer on this item. The supermarket does not want to lose money on this offer, so it expects the manufacturers to reduce their prices so SuperSave will make the same actual profit on every three bottles sold.

By how much will the manufacturers have to reduce their prices?

Commentary

There are several pieces of information that we will need in order to solve this problem.

1 How much do SuperSave normally buy a bottle of Sudsy washing up liquid for?

   To make a 50% profit on the sale of each bottle, SuperSave must pay 80¢ for each bottle (two-thirds of the price for which they sell it).

2 How much profit do SuperSave normally make on the sale of three bottles of Sudsy washing up liquid?

   The profit is 40¢ for each bottle, so the profit is normally $1.20 on three bottles.

3 How much would SuperSave need to pay for three bottles in order to make this profit under their new offer?

   Under the offer, SuperSave would only be paid $2.40 for three bottles, so need to pay just $1.20 for three bottles.

4 By how much do the manufacturers need to reduce the price?

   The price needs to be reduced to 40¢ per bottle, which is a reduction of 40¢ per bottle (or half of the normal price).

In fact, it is possible to deduce that the manufacturers would have to reduce the price to half the normal price without knowing that SuperSave's normal selling price is $1.20:

1 Since the amount that SuperSave must pay for the bottles is two-thirds of the price for which they sell it, the profit that SuperSave make on the sale of three bottles must be the price for which they sell one bottle. Additionally, SuperSave currently buy three bottles for the same price at which they sell two.

2 Once the offer is in place, customers will only be paying for two bottles when they buy three. To make the same profit on the sale of three bottles, SuperSave will therefore need to have bought the three bottles for the price at which they sell one.

3 The price that SuperSave pay for bottles must therefore have reduced to half of its previous value.

There are other ways in which the solution could be found. For example, it would be possible to choose a value for the reduction, see whether it would give the required result and then adjust it accordingly. The systematic approach is more efficient however (unless you are lucky enough to choose the correct value on your first guess).

ACTIVITY 1.2

Match the key terms (1–7) with the correct definition (A–G).

Note: you will not be asked to give definitions in the problem-solving exam, but it will help you develop your problem-solving skills if you understand these key terms.

Key terms	Definitions
1 Data	A Using logic, mathematics or a systematic process in order to work out a way to do a task that you have not done before.
2 Problem-solving	
3 Information	B Plan for how to achieve something.
4 Redundant	C Involving a method, plan or step-by-step process to do something.
5 Systematic	
6 Strategy	D Way of solving a problem, or finding the best way to achieve a desired result, by trying one thing or another until something succeeds.
7 Trial and error	
	E Knowledge, facts or news about a person, situation or event.
	F Facts, numbers and statistics used to calculate, plan or analyse something.
	G Information that is not useful or necessary.

Summary

Having read this chapter you should be able to:

- identify the information that is important in solving a problem

- identify an appropriate method to solve the problem.

End-of-chapter question

You want to buy a new mobile phone. You will use it for texting, making a few phone calls and keeping in touch with friends and family on social media. You have found two phones:

- a 'Mobes4U' phone that costs $36 if you sign a two-year contract with the company
- a 'Pay'N'Go' phone that costs $50 but you are not tied to a contract.

a What other pieces of information should you consider before you decide which phone to buy?

b Explain how you would use the information to make a decision.

Exam-style question

Nazim is planning to cook curries and sell them. He will take orders for parties. He will cook the curry and rice beforehand, then put the cooked food in serving dishes that will keep it hot. Nazim will pay his friend Raj, who has a van, to make deliveries and to fetch the serving dishes back after the party.

Nazim's first order is for a party of 27 people. He has a recipe using vegetables, chick peas, onions and tomatoes. He is now trying to work out the right quantities of spices. For 15 people he would normally use 100 g of spices, made up of ginger (20%), turmeric (25%), coriander (35%), and cumin seeds (20%).

a What weight of turmeric must Nazim put in a curry for 27 people?

b The food has been ordered to arrive at the party at 7:30 in the evening. Nazim knows he needs 30 minutes to prepare the vegetables. The curry takes 2 hours to cook and the rice takes 20 minutes. Putting the food in the dishes takes 10 minutes and putting the dishes in the van is another 10 minutes. Raj's journey to the party will take 25 minutes.

What is the latest time Nazim can start preparing the food?

c Nazim is buying rice. The supermarket sells 10 kg of basmati rice for $15.45. Today they have a 'buy 3, get the 4th free' offer. The wholesaler also offers 50 kg sacks of rice for $59.00.

Based on price, which rice should Nazim buy?

d Nazim wants to calculate the prices he should charge to customers to make sure he can make a profit. State three pieces of information that he needs.

Chapter 2
Selecting and using information

Learning objectives

This chapter describes some of the forms in which data may be presented and considers the way in which the relevant information can be selected from different representations of data.

2.1 Understanding information in various forms

Before attempting to solve any problem it is important to be able to identify the pieces of information that are relevant. In some cases, the information will be provided simply as a passage of text and many such examples will be seen in the coming chapters. In this chapter we shall consider some of the other ways in which information may be presented.

2.1.1 Tabular information

Tables can be used to show information such as summaries of surveys, specification sheets or transport timetables.

EXAMPLE ACTIVITY 2.1

The table below shows the prices that a supplier charges for exercise books. For each size of book the price per book depends on the total number in the order.

Table 2.1

		Number ordered				
		0–49	50–99	100–199	200–499	500 +
Size	Small	$1.20	$1.00	$0.90	$0.80	$0.75
	Medium	$1.50	$1.20	$1.10	$1.00	$0.90
	Large	$2.00	$1.50	$1.30	$1.25	$1.20

How much would it cost to buy 300 medium exercise books?

Commentary

Tables are a very useful method for displaying information clearly and so it is easy to see that the correct price per book is $1.00 when 300 are bought. The total cost is therefore $300.

ACTIVITY 2.1

Amira is a businesswoman who wants to give $3 000.00 to a local school so that every pupil can start the school year with new books and stationery.

There will be 240 pupils in the school at the start of the school year.

Amira wants every child to have:

- a pack of pencils – cost $0.73
- a ruler – $0.20
- one text book – $10.00
- two small exercise books – refer to the table of the supplier's prices in the example above.

The headteacher says this would cost more than the amount that Amira will give to the school. Amira does not agree.

Who is right? Explain your answer.

Note: In this Activity you will need to select what information to use, not just use the obvious.

2.1.2 Graphical information

Graphs are used in science and business to provide information in such a way that it can be absorbed quickly and easily. For example, a graph may show variables, such as temperature, over time; financial data may be shown in bar charts.

EXAMPLE ACTIVITY 2.2

The graph below shows monthly temperatures for Bangladesh. The average temperature was recorded for each day of the year. The lower end of each bar shows the lowest average temperature recorded for any day during the month and the top end of the bar shows the highest average temperature recorded for any day during the month.

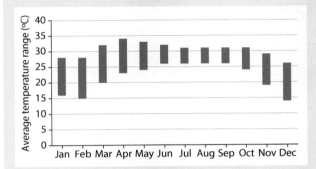

What is the difference between the lowest average temperature and the highest average temperature during the year?

Commentary

There are two skills involved here. Firstly, one must understand the verbal description of what the graph shows. Then, based on the question, one must interpret the graph in the required way.

In this example, the lowest average temperature for any day of the year was 14°C (in December) and the highest average temperature was 34°C (in April). Therefore, the difference is 34 – 14 = 20°.

ACTIVITY 2.2

Refer to the graph of monthly temperatures for Bangladesh. In which month is the greatest difference between lowest and highest average temperatures?

2.1.3 Pictorial information

Pictures, for example in the form of engineers' or architects' drawings, can be used not only to show what something looks like, but to also give information about relative sizes and positions.

EXAMPLE ACTIVITY 2.3

The picture below shows a tiled floor where 24 individual tiles with different printing on them are used to make up the overall pattern.

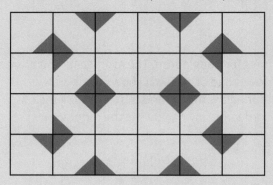

How many different patterns of tile are needed to make up the overall pattern?

Commentary

Solving this requires a systematic evaluation of the picture. We not only need to identify the apparently different tiles, but also to look at how tiles can be used in different orientations.

It is useful to consider a way in which the different tiles can be identified so that comparisons can be made easily. In this case each of the corners of a tile is either empty or contains a triangle. There are therefore up to five different types of tile that could be used:

- A tile with no triangles in any corner.
- A tile with a triangle in just one corner.
- A tile with triangles in two corners – there are two possibilities:
  - the two corners containing triangles are adjacent to each other.
  - the two corners containing triangles are opposite each other.
- A tile with triangles in three of the corners.
- A tile with triangles in all four corners.

In the picture given, three of the types of tile are used: the one with no triangles in a corner, the one with just one triangle and the one with triangles in two opposite corners.

In this simple example, it is fairly easy to identify the types of tile without the need to categorise them. However, for more elaborate patterns finding a way to identify the tiles easily may be more important.

ACTIVITY 2.3

Now imagine you have the following tiles:

- Seven tiles with no triangles in any corner.
- One tile with a triangle in just one corner.
- One tile with triangles in two opposite corners.

How many ways can you arrange them to make a square of nine tiles?

2.1.4 Diagrammatic information

Diagrams come in a wide range of forms: flow charts, maps, schedules, decision trees and many other types can summarise numerical and spatial information.

EXAMPLE ACTIVITY 2.4

The map below is a simple representation of the only roads joining four towns.

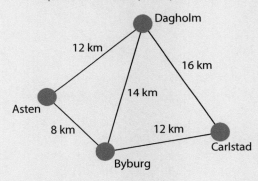

I live in Asten and wish to visit a friend in Carlstad. I will travel through Byburg on the way to visit my friend and then return home via Dagholm.

How much longer is my journey home compared to my outward journey?

Commentary

The lengths of the two journeys need to be identified from the diagram:

On the outward journey I will travel to Byburg (8 km) and then on to Carlstad (12 km), so the total distance will be 20 km.

On the homeward journey I will travel to Dagholm (16 km) to visit my sister and then to Asten (12 km), so the total distance will be 28 km.

The journey home will therefore be 8 km longer than the outward journey.

ACTIVITY 2.4

Refer to the map in the example above.

I need to collect a parcel in Byburg on my way home. What is my shortest route home?

2.2 Understanding what information is required to solve the problem

Sometimes selecting the relevant information requires identifying the key pieces of information, as the example below shows.

EXAMPLE ACTIVITY 2.5

Grunfling is an activity held in Bolandia, where competitors have to contort their faces into the most extreme shapes. Several Bolandian villages have a grunfling competition each year. Each village puts up a champion grunfler who demonstrates his or her skills, then the villages vote one by one. (They are not allowed to vote for their own grunfler.) Each village awards eight votes to their favourite, four to the second, two to the third and one to the fourth. Clearly, tactical voting is important, so the order of voting is changed every year. This year, the villages vote in order from most northerly to most southerly. The results before the last two villages have voted are shown (in voting order).

Table 2.2

Fartown	6
Waterton	5
Blackport	6
Longwood	24
Gigglesford	12
White Stones	9
Martinsville	24
South Peak	4
Riverton	13
Runcastle	17

Which villages could still win the competition?

Commentary

There are three important pieces of information that need to be identified:

1 The scoring system means that any one village could receive, at most, 16 more votes (if both of the remaining villages were to vote for them).

2 Since Riverton and Runcastle are not allowed to vote for themselves, they can only achieve 8 more votes each.

3 Some of the villages will not score any more points, which means that any village that can reach a score of more than 24 could still win.

Given these pieces of information, any of the villages that have already voted and have a score of at least nine (25 votes needed minus the 16 votes that could still be awarded) could still win the competition – that is Longwood, Gigglesford, White Stones and Martinsville.

The two villages that are still to vote would need to have a score of at least 17 (25 – 8) to still have a chance to win the competition – that is just Runcastle.

There are therefore five different villages that could still win the competition.

ACTIVITY 2.5

Refer to the information about the grunfling competition.

Longwood has been thrown out of the competition for buying votes and Gigglesford has suddenly withdrawn. The judges have decided that the votes for the remaining villages will stand. The votes that Longwood had been awarded will be distributed equally between the six villages at the bottom of the table.

Riverton awards eight votes to Waterton, four to Fartown, two to White Stones and one to Runcastle.

How could Runcastle vote tactically to ensure they achieve the best possible result?

Summary

Having read this chapter you should be able to:

- understand information presented in tabular, graphical, pictorial or diagrammatic form

- identify the relevant information that is needed in order to solve a problem.

End-of-chapter question

Jasmine is preparing to go to university. She lives in Lakeside and could attend either the Western University or the University of Technology.

a What is the shortest distance that Jasmine could travel to get to university?

b What is the longest distance that Jasmine could travel to get to university?

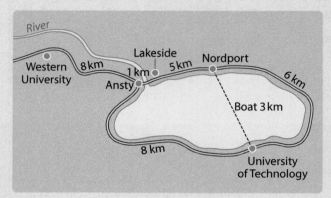

Exam-style questions

1   The charts show percentages of sales income for the types of food items sold by two local shops last week.

SavvySaver's income from food sales was $25 000. Meggamart's income from sales was $50 000.

Which shop had the larger income from sales of tinned food?

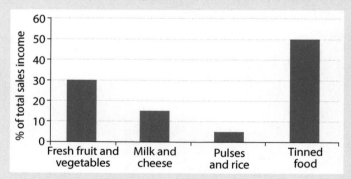

a SavvySaver income from food sales

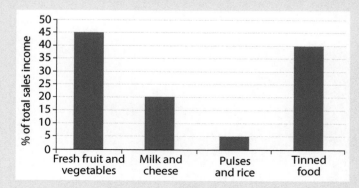

b Meggamart income from food sales

2 Clara is a fashion designer. She is designing a pattern for a shirt fabric. The design is made up of small squares. There is a decorative pattern against one or more sides of each small square. The small squares will be arranged in a block of four that will be repeated to make the larger overall design. Within the block of four, there will be:

- one square containing one pattern
- one square containing two patterns
- one square containing three patterns
- one square containing four patterns.

One possible way of arranging the designs in the each of the small squares is shown below.

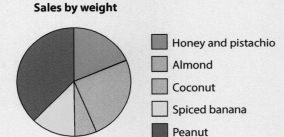

What is the total number of different small squares that can be created?

3 Matiz makes sweets. He sells them in 250 g boxes. The charts show his sales for his different types of sweet for the last month.

Sales by weight

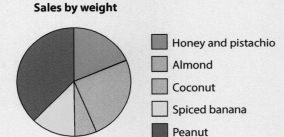

- Honey and pistachio
- Almond
- Coconut
- Spiced banana
- Peanut

Sales by income

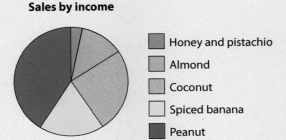

- Honey and pistachio
- Almond
- Coconut
- Spiced banana
- Peanut

Which type of sweet is:

a the most expensive?

b the cheapest?

19

4 The chart shows numbers of patients admitted to the emergency department.

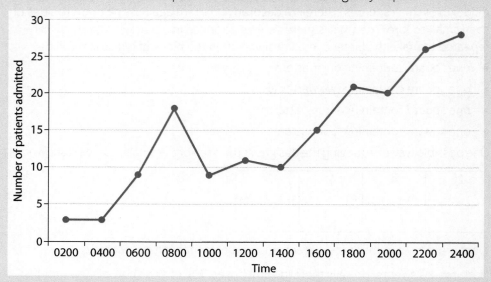

The department manager is planning how many nurses should be on duty. Nurses work either 0600 to 1400 (early), 1400 to 2200 (late), or 2200 to 0600 (night).

Based on numbers of admissions:

a when should most nurses be on duty?

b when are fewest nurses needed?

Chapter 3
Processing data

Learning objectives

The previous chapter considered the different ways in which data could be presented. This chapter looks at how the data can be processed by performing simple calculations as part of the method to solve problems.

3.1 Processing information to solve problems

In the previous chapter we looked at different ways in which data could be presented and how to select the relevant data to solve a given problem. In each of the examples it was not necessary to do much more than to identify one or two pieces of the data. In many cases more processing of the data is required once the relevant pieces of information have been identified.

3.1.1 Problems involving simple calculations

Problem-solving situations may often involve commonly known formulas to be applied. For example, in problems relating to speeds, distance and time, the formula speed = distance travelled ÷ time taken is likely to be required.

A simple example of this is illustrated below.

EXAMPLE ACTIVITY 3.1

Luiz and Bianca are brother and sister and go to the same school. Luiz walks to school using a footpath, a distance of 900 m, and he walks at 1.5 m/s. Bianca cycles to school along the roads, a distance of 1 500 m, and she cycles at 5 m/s. They both plan on arriving at school by 8:55 a.m.

Who leaves home first and by how much?

Commentary

The skill in this question is to use the correct pieces of information appropriately and at the right time in the calculation. There are five relevant pieces of data (the two distances, the two speeds and the fact that they arrive at the same time). It is quite clear that the method of solution is to calculate each of the journey times.

Luiz walks 900 m at 1.5 m/s, so this takes him 900 ÷ 1.5 = 600 seconds (ten minutes).

Bianca cycles 1 500 m at 5 m/s, which takes her 1 500 ÷ 5 = 300 seconds (five minutes).

As Luiz takes five minutes more, he must leave home five minutes earlier.

The information in this example could be presented in a number of different ways. For example, it would be possible to summarise all of the information in a table as shown below:

Table 3.1

Name	Length of route (m)	Speed (m/s)	Arrival time
Luiz	900	1.5	8:55 a.m.
Bianca	1 500	5	8:55 a.m.

Although this is not necessary to solve the problem, it can be useful to summarise the information in tables or other representations in order to help find the solution.

ACTIVITY 3.1

Refer to the information about Luiz and Bianca.

Today Bianca wants to get to school before Luiz.

Luiz leaves 15 minutes early. He has arranged to walk to school with his friend Rafael.

Rafael lives five minutes' walk away from Luiz. Rafael always takes five minutes to get ready before he leaves his house. The walk to school usually takes 20 minutes from Rafael's house, but Luiz and Rafael speed up to three metres per second.

What time should Bianca leave home to get to school before Luiz?

3.1.2 Problems based on a more complex set of information

EXAMPLE ACTIVITY 3.2

In an inter-school hockey knockout competition, there are initially 32 teams. Teams are drawn by lots to play each other and the winner of each match goes through to the next round. This is repeated until there are only two teams left, who play each other in the final, and the winner gets a cup.

Matches have two halves of 20 minutes each. If the teams are level at the end of normal play, two extra 10-minute periods are played. If it is still a draw, teams take penalty shots at goal to decide the winner.

Chorlton High were eventually knocked out in the semi-final (without extra time). In one of the earlier rounds they had to play the two extra periods before they won.

For how long in total had Chorlton High played when they were knocked out?

Commentary

There is a considerable amount of information given here, and the text needs to be read carefully to ensure that all of the relevant information is identified.

Firstly, we need to know how many matches Chorlton High played:

- 32 teams played in Round 1 and half of them (16) went through to the next round.
- So 16 teams played in Round 2.
- Eight teams played in Round 3 (the quarter finals).
- Four teams played in Round 4 (the semi-finals).
- There were then only two teams left in the final.

Therefore, Chorlton High must have played in four rounds in total.

Now we need to work out the total amount of time that they had played:

- Each round had 40 minutes of play: $4 \times 40 = 160$ minutes.
- One round included extra time: an additional 20 minutes.

The total amount of time was therefore $160 + 20 = 180$ minutes, or 3 hours.

ACTIVITY 3.2

The winning team in the hockey competition was Newport College. They played extra time in Round 1 and in the final.

a For how long in total had Newport College played at the end of the final?

b How many games were played in total by all teams?

ACTIVITY 3.3

Rajesh is cooking a meal for some friends. This will involve roasting a chicken, which takes two hours' cooking time plus 15 minutes resting on removal from the oven. The oven takes 15 minutes to warm up. He will also cook some rice (30 minutes soaking plus 15 minutes cooking), broccoli (five minutes to prepare and five minutes to cook) and a sauce (10 minutes to prepare and 15 minutes to cook).

What should be the timings of events if the friends are to eat at 7 p.m.?

Summary

Having read this chapter you should be able to:

- perform simple calculations to deduce new information
- identify the sequence of calculations required to solve more complex problems.

End-of-chapter questions

1   The petrol usage of a number of cars has been measured. Each car started with a full tank, then made a journey (all journeys were over similar roads). After the journey the tank was filled to the top, the amount of petrol needed to fill it being recorded. The results are shown below. Put the cars in order of their petrol efficiency (km/litre), from lowest to highest.

Table 3.2

Car	Length of journey (km)	Petrol used (litres)
Montevideo	120	10
Stella	150	16
Riviera	200	25
Roamer	185	21
Carousel	230	16

2   The table below shows information about different crisps or chips that are sold as healthy snack foods.

Table 3.3

Snack (chips or crisps)	Nutrition information per pack				
	Weight of pack (grams)	Calories	Carbohydrates (grams)	Fat (grams)	Protein (grams)
Chickpea chips	24	110	16	4	2.5
Lentil bites	30	87	20	8	2
Potato crisps	28	150	16	9	1
Spicy vegetable bites	27	105	17	7	2
Sweet potato chips	25	140	12	8	3

Which snack should you pick if you want:

a   the lowest number of calories in a pack?

b   the healthiest snack in terms of weight of fat per 100 g?

c   the healthiest snack in terms of calories per 100 g?

Exam-style questions

1 Jane's journey to work involves three separate stages:

- A walk of 0.5 kilometres to the train station at a constant speed of 5 km/hour.
- A train journey of 40 kilometres at a constant speed of 80 km/hour.
- A bus journey of 6 kilometres at a constant speed of 30 km/hour.

   a How long does Jane's journey to work take?

   b Today the road was closed and the bus took a detour via a completely different route. The journey took 20 minutes longer than usual.

   How much further than the usual bus route was the detour?

2 There are nine teams in the women's football league. Each team plays every other team twice per season: once at home and once away.

   a How many matches did each team play during the season?

   b How many matches were played in total during the season?

   c Away sides lost 32 matches last season. Of the other matches, ten more were drawn than were won by the away side.

   How many matches were drawn last season?

3 The most popular ride at the South Coast theme park is the Supersplash water attraction. It takes 4 minutes to load the passengers into the boats, 5 minutes for the ride, then one minute at the end to unload them. There are 6 boats, each holding 50 people. There is a five-minute gap between boats starting and finishing the ride.

   The number of people joining the queue each hour on the first day of the summer holidays is shown below.

Morning			Afternoon						
9–10	10–11	11–12	12–1	1–2	2–3	3–4	4–5	5–6	6–7
240	400	900	750	1 000	1 200	. 900	300	240	100

   How long can you expect to wait for a ride if you join the queue at exactly 1 p.m.?

4 Elizabeth's recent holiday involved her flying around the world from London. She stopped in Tokyo, Auckland, San Francisco and finally returned to London. The schedule for her journey is set out below.

Table 3.4

Journey	Departure time	Time at destination at departure time	Local arrival time
London – Tokyo	Sun 13:00	Sun 21:00	Mon 08:30
Tokyo – Auckland	Tue 16:00	Tue 19:00	Wed 04:00
Auckland – San Francisco	Thu 12:00	Wed 17:00	Thu 07:00
San Francisco – London	Sat 06:00	Fri 22:00	Sat 10:00

How much time did Elizabeth spend flying?

Adapted from Cambridge International AS & A Level Thinking Skills 9694 Paper 11 Q3 June 2016

Chapter 4
Working with models

Learning objectives

This chapter explains how models of situations can be used to help with the solution to problems by finding the outputs that are predicted or the inputs that would be required to achieve a particular outcome.

4.1 What is a model?

The most obvious and familiar use of the word '**model**' is that of a replica of an object, for example a car, at a smaller scale. In the context of problem solving the word is used in a wider sense. Models can be pictures, graphs, descriptions, equations or computer programs, which are used to represent objects or processes. These are sometimes called 'mathematical models'; they help us to understand how things work and give simplified representations that can enable us to do 'what if?' type calculations.

Architects, for example, use a wide range of models. They may build a scale model of a building to let the client see it and to give a better impression of how it will look. Their drawings are also models of the structure of the building. In modern practice, these drawings are made on a computer, which will contain a three-dimensional 'walk-through' picture on the screen.

4.2 Simple models

This chapter deals with the recognition and use of appropriate models. A simple example of a model can be seen in the way that various bills are calculated. For example, the amount of a quarterly electricity bill can be described as:

A standing charge of $30, plus 10¢ per unit of electricity used.

This can be shown algebraically as:

$c = 30 + 0.1\,u$

where c is the amount to pay (in dollars) and u is the number of units used.

The model has two parameters that can be adjusted to give different structures for the electricity bill:

- the standing charge
- the amount to be paid per unit of electricity used.

If the electricity company were to decide to change to monthly billing without changing the overall amount that the customer pays then they would adjust the model by changing the standing charge to $10. If the cost to the company of producing the electricity were to increase, they might decide to pass the additional cost on to the customer by increasing the amount to be paid per unit of electricity.

28

> **EXAMPLE ACTIVITY 4.1**
>
> The length of time for which a candle will burn is determined by the amount of wax that is used. Aman makes her own candles. The amount of wax that she used for each candle is 4 g for every hour that it needs to burn for, plus an additional 2 g.
>
> Aman wants to make two types of candle: some that will burn for seven hours and some that will burn for 12 hours. She uses 400 g of wax to make equal numbers of each candle.
>
> How many candles of each type will Aman make?

Commentary

The model that Aman uses for the amount of wax to use is similar to that of the electricity bill described above: there is a fixed amount (2 g), plus an amount for each hour that the candle must burn (4 g).

Using the model we can calculate that the amount of wax needed for a candle that will burn for seven hours is 2 + (7 × 4) = 30 g.

Similarly, the amount of wax needed for a candle that will burn for 12 hours is 2 + (12 × 4) = 50 g.

One candle of each type therefore requires a total of 80 g of wax.

Since Aman is using 400 g of wax she will be able to make five of each type of candle.

ACTIVITY 4.1

Aman wants to colour some wax using three different colours to make 15 candles that will each burn for 24 hours. How much wax does she need in each colour?

4.3 Other types of models

Not all models are of a type that could be expressed as a formula. In some cases the model may simply be a set of rules that will be followed.

EXAMPLE ACTIVITY 4.2

A robot is programmed to apply the following instructions in order to move through a maze:

- If it is possible to move forwards then move one space forwards.
- If it is not possible to move forwards then keep turning right until it is possible to move forwards again.

The robot is placed in the square at the bottom left of the maze (marked R on the diagram).

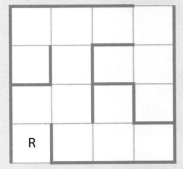

How many of the squares will the robot move through before leaving the maze?

Commentary

In order to explain the order in which the squares are visited it would be useful to have a number that can be used to reference each square. The diagram below shows how each square will be referred to in the explanation that follows.

1	2	3	4
5	6	7	8
9	10	11	12
R	14	15	16

Applying the model is then simply a matter of following the instructions as described:

- Move one square forwards (to square 9).
- Turn right and move one square forwards (to square 10).
- Turn right and move one square forwards (to square 14).
- There will now be two right turns before the robot can again move forwards.
- The robot will then move forwards through squares 10, 6 and 2.
- Turn right and move forwards (through squares 3 and 4).
- Turn right and move forwards (through squares 8 and 12).
- There will now be two right turns before the robot can again move forwards.
- The robot will then move forwards through squares 8 and 4 and then leave the maze.

The robot will therefore visit a total of 10 squares (its starting square, 9, 10, 14, 6, 2, 3, 4, 8 and 12) before it leaves the maze.

ACTIVITY 4.2

Refer to the information about the robot and the maze.

a What happens if you want the robot to get back through the maze to point R by following the same rules as before?

b What does this show about using models?

4.4 Complex models

A more complicated example of a model would be the type that governments set up to simulate their economies. These usually consist of large numbers of equations and associated data and are implemented on computers. They can predict (with varying success) things such as what will happen to the inflation rate if interest rates are raised. Such models are gross simplifications because there are too many variables contributing to the condition of a national economy and all factors can never be included.

Scientists also use models, for example in predicting population growth. Such a model, for example to predict fish stocks in fishing areas, can be invaluable as it may be used to control quotas on fish catches to ensure that fishing does not reduce stocks to unsustainable levels.

In the following activity you are asked to use different models to compare calculations.

EXAMPLE ACTIVITY 4.3

The current structure of income tax collection in a country is that the first $2 000 of annual earnings are tax-free (this is called the tax threshold), then 20¢ of tax is charged on every dollar earned over this (this could also be described as a 20% tax rate).

The government is determined to reduce the tax burden on lower-paid people and intends to bring in a new system, which will mean that the threshold for paying tax will rise to $10 000. They intend that those who earn $26 000 will pay the same amount of tax as under the old system.

What will be the tax rate on earnings over $10 000?

Commentary

The model of tax used here is quite simple and has two parameters:

- the tax threshold (the amount of earnings that are tax-free)
- the tax rate.

In order to find the answer to the question, we must first calculate the tax that a person earning $26 000 pays under the current system:

Tax will be paid on $26 000 – $2,000 = $24 000

The amount of tax will be 24 000 × 20¢ = $4 800

We must now calculate the tax rate that would lead to the same amount of tax paid under the new system for earnings of $26 000:

Tax will be paid on $26 000 – $10,000 = $16 000

To achieve $4 800 in tax, the rate will need to be $4 800 ÷ $16 000 for every $1 earned, which is a tax rate of 30%.

As shown above, the calculations can be summarised as a series of calculations deduced from the description of the model. Models can take a variety of forms, and may also be represented in the following ways, among others.

4.4.1 The algebraic model

It is also possible to express the problem algebraically so that the solution can be found by solving an equation:

Having worked out the amount of tax to be paid on earnings of $26 000 under the current system, the tax rate, r, under the new system would have to satisfy the following equation:

$$4 800 + (26 000 - 10 000) \times r$$

Solving this equation requires the same steps as were used in the solution presented above.

Algebraic methods are not usually required to solve problems – but are helpful in that they provide a clear way to express the solution. As shown above, the solution can be expressed as an explanation of the steps taken, if preferred.

4.4.2 The graphical model

Another way in which a model can be expressed is through a graph. The graph below represents the current tax structure of the last activity.

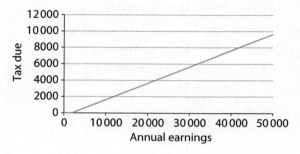

If the new system were added to this graph then the sloped section would need to start at $10 000 on the x-axis and meet the line for the current system at the point where earnings is equal to $26 000.

ACTIVITY 4.3

Next year the tax rate will rise to 35%. The government raises the amount to be paid by people earning $26 000 to $4 900. What must the tax threshold be set at?

ACTIVITY 4.4

Combining your skills

This past Cambridge International A Level question will give you practice in combining the problem-solving skills you have developed in Chapters 1–4 in order to tackle more challenging questions.

Alan is organising a business dinner for 46 people at the local hotel. Two kinds of table are available: round tables can seat six people and square tables can seat eight people. He wants to seat all of the people so that there are no empty spaces at any table. He works out that there are two different combinations of round and square tables that will do this.

a   What are the two possible combinations of round and square tables that will work?

Dinner is a buffet and is charged at $50 for a round table and $60 for a square table. Alan telephones the hotel to make the arrangements, but they inform him that they have only four of each kind of table. Alan realises that he can no longer seat all the people so that there are no empty spaces at any table.

b   Which combination of round and square tables will enable him to seat the 46 people for the lowest possible cost?

Alan considers not inviting two people, in order to bring the total down to 44 people.

c   How much would Alan have to pay to seat 44 people?

There are additional charges for two extra items which Alan wants: drinks and table decorations. The costs are shown in the table below. Alan can choose, for each item, to pay a price per person or a price per table or a price for the whole room.

Table 4.1

	Per person	Per table	Whole room
Drinks	$4	$20	$130
Table decorations	$1	$7	$50

d   If Alan chooses the cheapest way to pay for each item, how much money could he save on drinks and table decorations altogether by inviting 44 people rather than 46?

The hotel now insists that Alan must choose the same payment method (price per person, price per table or price for the whole room) for both items.

e   If Alan chooses the cheapest way overall, how much could he save on drinks and table decorations altogether by inviting 44 people rather than 46?

Cambridge International AS & A Level Thinking Skills 9694 Paper 31 Q1 June 2017

Summary

Having read this chapter you should be able to:

- understand what is meant by a model
- use a model to perform calculations and to make predictions
- calculate the appropriate input values for a model that would generate a particular outcome.

End-of-chapter questions

1   Amber works in a sales department. Her basic salary is $1 000 per month. She also earns commission on all sales that she makes.

    a Use the graph below to calculate the percentage commission that Amber is paid on the sales she makes in a month.

    b How much commission does Amber receive when she has made sales of $40 000?

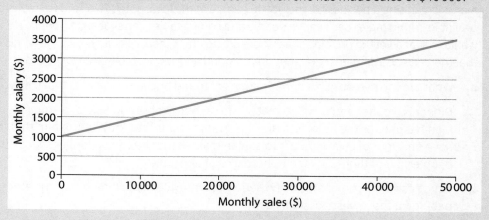

2   The following recipe makes a cake that serves 12 people.

- You need 300 ml strong tea, 500 g dried sultanas, 125 g brown sugar, 250 g flour, 5 g cinnamon, and one egg or milk.
- Soak the sultanas in the tea for two hours, then mix in all the other ingredients.
- Bake in an 18 cm square tin for one hour and 15 minutes at an oven temperature of 170 °C.

    a You want to make the cake recipe for 32 people. You have a 15 cm square tin, a 20 cm square tin, a 25 cm square tin and a 15 × 18 cm rectangular tin. Which combination of tins should you use to get as near as possible to the right volume?

    b How much tea should you use in the cake that will be cooked in the 25 cm tin?

    c You have found some guidance on adjusting oven times and temperatures:

        'Square cakes: The bigger the cake, the lower the temperature needed and the longer the cooking time. For every extra 1 cm in the size of the cake tin add five minutes to the cooking time. This means that a 15 cm square cake needs 5 minutes longer than a 14 cm cake. For every full 15 minutes extra time, lower the oven temperature by 10°.'

        What temperature and time should you use for the 25 cm cake?

Exam-style questions

1   Taxiwhizz is a private taxi hire company.

- It charges $2.50 when the passenger is picked up, then $0.45 for every complete kilometre travelled. If the taxi has to wait, for example because it is stuck in traffic, the charge is $1.50 for every five minutes it is not moving.
- If there are more than two passengers, there is a charge of $2.00 per extra passenger. Items of very large luggage are charged at $2.50.

- If the taxi journey starts between midnight and 6.00 a.m., 30% is added to the total cost of the journey.

Klement, Markus and Sybille have booked a taxi to go home after a party. The taxi is booked for 12.30 a.m. but it waits 12 minutes till Markus gets in. The journey is 17 km.

What is the cost of the taxi?

2 Sukhjit wants new furniture. He has asked a carpenter to give a quotation for making the furniture. The carpenter says it would take two days to build the furniture and he would charge $18 per hour for labour. A day is eight hours' work. The carpenter also charges the cost of any materials he buys plus 25%. His quotation is $713.

   a Sukhjit wants to compare this quotation with the cost of buying flat-pack furniture and assembling it himself. How much is the carpenter paying for materials?

   b The carpenter could reduce his quotation if his apprentice did some of the work. In this case, the carpenter's work would take one day, but the apprentice is slow and his work would take 1.5 days. The apprentice's work is charged at $8 per hour.

   How much less would Sukhjit pay if the apprentice did some of the work?

3 Doctor Which is a time traveller but her time machine has a fault. It is travelling forward in time at two times the rate of time (as humans understand time). The time machine cannot be stopped. Doctor Which can programme the time machine to travel five years forwards in time, or to travel two years backwards in time, or she can do nothing and continue to travel at twice the speed of time. Right now she is at 31 December 2042. If she can quickly program the time machine to travel to the year 2056, then Oylkann, the engineer, will be able to make repairs.

How should Doctor Which program the time machine so it gets her to 2056? On what date should Oylkann expect Doctor Which to arrive?

4 The diagram shows a room where a robot cleaner is being tested. The squares each indicate a section of the floor that the robot cleans as it moves.

Dock ↓	2	3	4	5	6	7
↓8	9	10	11	12	13	14
15	16	17	18	19	20	21
		22	23	24		
		25	26	27		
		28	29	30		

The robot's sensors enable it to work out the shortest route it can take to clean the whole room. It can turn left or right but not reverse. When it has finished it returns to its docking station, marked 'Dock' on the diagram.

What route can the robot take that will enable it to clean the room and return to its docking station, while the fewest possible squares are covered more than once?

Chapter 5
Solving problems by searching

Learning objectives

This chapter considers one method which can be applied to solve a wide range of different problems – searching the set of possibilities for a solution.

5.1 When is searching an appropriate method?

The chapters so far have introduced the basic concepts which are used when solving problems. Many problems involve choosing the best option from within a small selection of possibilities. In the simplest of cases the problem might be to find the options that satisfy a certain set of criteria or that give the most efficient option, as the following example shows.

EXAMPLE ACTIVITY 5.1

John needs to buy a collection of books for the course that he is studying. The individual prices of the books are $30, $35 and $45. There are three different bookshops that John could go to in order to buy the books, each of which will offer different discounts:

- The first shop sells all of the books at 10% less than the usual price.
- The second shop gives a discount of $10 on any purchase of $75 or more.
- The third shop gives a discount of 20% on any book that normally costs more than $40.

John will buy all of the books at the same shop and will choose the shop that gives him the cheapest price.

How much will John pay for the books?

Commentary

In this case there are three different options offered and the task is to find the cheapest one. The three different prices need to be considered one at a time:

- At the first shop the total discount will be 10% of $110 (the total price of all of the books), so John would save $11.
- At the second shop the discount will be $10 as the total cost of the books is more than $75.
- At the third shop the discount will be 20% of $45 (as only the $45 book will receive a discount), so the discount will be $9.

John's best option would be to go to the first shop, and he would pay a total of $99.

ACTIVITY 5.1

John knows he will need four more books priced at $10, $15, $22 and $23 for next term.

- When he bought the books in the first shop he was given a loyalty card. For every full $10 that he has spent he will get $1 he can use when he buys more books. However, the first shop has reduced its discount to 5%.
- The second shop has changed its discount offer to $9 off any purchase totalling $60 or more.
- The third shop has changed its discount offer to 15% off any book that normally costs $20 or more.

John still wants to buy all four books from the same shop. What is the cheapest amount he could pay for them?

5.2 Searching in a systematic way

There are many similar situations in which searching would be a suitable method for solving a problem. Some other examples are:

1 What is the smallest amount of money that cannot be made using up to four coins?
2 Which combination of products should be manufactured in a factory in order to make the greatest profit?
3 Which route should I choose to reach my destination as quickly as possible?

Each of these questions involves considering a set of different options and then choosing the best one. We will consider a few examples to see how such problems can be approached.

> **EXAMPLE ACTIVITY 5.2**
>
> Amir wishes to buy some gifts to give to a friend. The gifts that he has found cost $4, $6, $9 and $14. Amir has only $25 to use to buy the gifts and he wants the amount that he spends to be as close as possible to $25, without going over.
>
> What are the prices of the gifts that Amir will buy?

Commentary

One way to approach this question is to make a list of all of the possible total amounts that Amir might pay. It is important to make sure that all of the possibilities are found. The table below shows one way in which that might be done.

Table 5.1

$4							
$6	$10 ($4+$6)						
$9	$13 ($4+$9)	$15 ($6+$9)	$19 ($10+$9)				
$14	$18 ($4+$14)	$20 ($6+$14)	$24 ($10+$14)	$23 ($9+$14)	$27 ($13+$14)	$29 ($15+$14)	$33 ($19+$14)

On each row the first value is the price of the gift being considered and the others are the result of adding that price to any of the values on any of the higher rows. The highest value in the table which does not exceed $25 is $24. The $24 was calculated by adding $10 and $14 and the $10 was calculated by adding $4 and $6. Amir will therefore buy the gifts priced at $4, $6 and $14.

This method of finding all of the possible solutions to the problem is called an 'exhaustive search' and often requires an efficient system for recording the possibilities as they are found.

Searching is not the only method that could be used to solve this problem – you might also note that the total price of the gifts is $33 and so Amir must choose not to buy gifts with a total price of more than $8. The lowest priced way to do this is to omit the $9 gift.

Searches become longer very quickly – even adding one extra gift will mean that there are far more possibilities to be considered.

EXAMPLE ACTIVITY 5.3

Suppose there is an additional gift that Amir could buy that costs $19 and that Amir is now willing to spend up to $30 on the gifts. What will be the total cost of the gifts that Amir will buy now?

Commentary

The addition of one more gift has doubled the number of possible combinations that need to be considered, so there are far more options to consider in this case. For this reason exhaustive searches are usually only useful for searches over a small set of options. This example is also less easily tackled by the other approach suggested – the total value of the gifts is now $52, so if we consider the value of gifts that Amir does not buy the total will need to be at least $22.

If we search from the most expensive present:

Any one gift chosen alongside the $19 gift will reach $22 or more, so the cheapest option is to use the $4 gift, making a total of $23. Since that is only $1 more than the minimum, the only way a better solution could be found would be if exactly $22 could be made and this is not possible.

Amir will therefore spend a total of $29. The set of gifts that is identified by the method above is those that cost $6, $9 and $14, but another set (the $4, $6 and $19 gifts) would also achieve the same total.

ACTIVITY 5.2

The map shows the main roads between different areas of Hinchester.

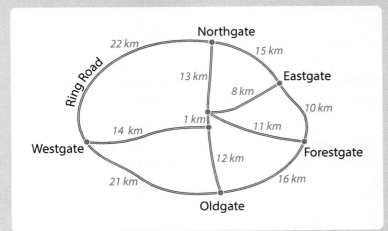

Buses start at Westgate and go around the Ring Road in both clockwise and anti-clockwise directions to arrive back at Westgate. Buses also travel from Northgate to Oldgate and back. The bus fare is priced according to the distance travelled.

What would be the shortest bus journey from Westgate to Forestgate?

5.3 Selecting an appropriate search method

If the number of possibilities to be searched is large it can be difficult to check through all of them by hand (although computers can be very useful in doing this if no better way can be found). There are some useful methods which can be used to make searches more efficient, whether being conducted by hand or by a computer, as the next example will show.

EXAMPLE ACTIVITY 5.4

In a sports league, teams score points for each of the matches that they play. Each match results in either a win, a draw or a loss. A team scores five points for each win, two points for each draw and zero points for each loss. One team has played 30 matches this season and scored a total of 113 points.

What is the greatest number of matches that this team could have drawn in the season?

Commentary

There are a large number of different ways in which 30 match results can be divided into wins, draws and losses, but it is not necessary to consider them all to solve this problem. If we start by considering a particular number of wins, then the number of draws and losses that are needed to achieve the correct score can be calculated:

Ten wins would score 50 points and so a further 63 points would need to be scored from the draws (as losses score no points). Since 63 is not a multiple of two there is no way to achieve this.

Eleven wins would score 55 points and so a further 58 extra points would need to be scored from the draws. This would need 27 draws, but that gives a total of 38 results which is more than the 30 matches that the team has played.

Now that we have an understanding of the structure of the problem we can quickly explore the options that are needed. We can see that the number of wins must be odd, so the maximum number of wins is 21 (giving 105 points), which would require four draws in addition.

We can consider the other possibilities by noticing that for every two wins that are removed, five draws must be added to maintain the same score. The other possibilities are therefore:

19 wins and nine draws, which is still less than 30 matches.

17 wins and 14 draws, but this is a total of 31 matches and so is not valid.

The greatest number of draws is therefore nine.

5.4 Identifying the most efficient solution

In the above example there were two particular features of the method that made the search more efficient:

- Rather than thinking of the cases as being made up from three different numbers (wins, draws and losses) it was realised that there would never be more than one set for any given choice of the number of wins (and it is quite easy to work out what this set is in each case).

- Rather than starting from the beginning with each new set, a method for deducing a new set from one that has already been found was devised (i.e. that the same total score could be achieved by changing two wins for five draws).

In some cases it is possible to complete the search for several possibilities at the same time, as the final example shows.

EXAMPLE ACTIVITY 5.5

Coins are available in denominations of 1¢, 5¢, 25¢, and $1. What is the smallest amount of money that cannot be made by a combination of at most ten coins?

Commentary

At first this sounds like a daunting task, but it can be solved quite quickly if we are careful about the way in which we consider the options.

1 First, we will consider the amounts up to 5¢ and work out how many coins are needed to make each total:

    1¢ = 1 coin   2¢ = 2 coins   3¢ = 3 coins   4¢ = 4 coins   5¢ = 1 coin

    Any amount between 6¢ and 9¢ will be made most efficiently by taking a 5¢ coin and then the appropriate number of coins from the cases above for the remaining amount.

2 We can extend this idea by noticing that all coins, apart from the 1¢ coin, are multiples of 5¢, so for any amount we can consider the most efficient way to achieve the greatest multiple of 5¢ less than what is needed and then add on the required number of 1¢ coins. The smallest amount of money that cannot be made by a combination of at most ten coins must therefore be made using four 1¢ coins.

3 Once we know that there are four 1¢ coins for the amount of money that we are looking for, we can apply the same reasoning to the 5¢ coins to deduce that there must be four of them in the set.

4 Since that identifies eight coins that make up the amount of money that we are looking for there must be three further coins if the amount cannot be made from ten or fewer coins.

    The smallest amount must therefore be made of four 1¢ coins, four 5¢ coins and three 25¢ coins – a total of 99¢.

In this example, searching by checking each number in turn would take a very long time, but recognising the common factors between the numbers allows the possibilities to be checked much more quickly in groups.

41

ACTIVITY 5.3

Roxanne has a small business making and selling jewellery. She is planning which items to make to sell at a craft fair. She will sell no more than three different designs and she wants to make as much profit as possible. She has only five days to make the items.

The table below shows Roxanne's costs for materials and labour, her prices to customers, her estimate of how many of each item she might sell at the craft fair, and the number of days she would need to make enough items to sell.

Table 5.2

Design	Cost for materials and labour per item	Price to customer	Estimated sales figure	Number of days to make estimated sales figure
Silver ring	$15.50	$25	10	2
Pendant with gemstone	$13	$28	6	2
Necklace	$15	$30	8	3
Bracelet	$45	$65	3	1
Pair of earrings	$11.50	$20	20	4

Which three designs should Roxanne make to sell at the craft fair?

ACTIVITY 5.4

In a community centre quiz evening, teams were awarded five points for a correct answer, no points for no answer, and minus two points for an incorrect answer. The teams marked their own score sheets. I arrived late and the scores after seven questions were shown on the board as follows:

Table 5.3

Happy Hunters	28
Ignorant Idlers	18
Jumping Jacks	16
Kool Kats	12
Lazy Lurkers	−1

a One team was clearly not even clever enough to calculate their score correctly. Which one was it?

b Which other scores between −14 and 35 are also not possible when seven answers have been checked?

Summary

- Searching is an effective method for finding solutions to certain types of problems.
- An 'exhaustive search' involves finding all of the possible cases that need to be considered.
- In some cases, searches when there are a large number of possibilities can be done more quickly by:
  - choosing the starting point for the search carefully
  - recognising some feature of the problem that allows some of the possibilities to be eliminated
  - identifying a feature of the problem that allows other solutions to be generated from one that has already been found
  - using a pattern that can be spotted to check groups of possibilities at the same time.

End-of-chapter questions

1 I recently received a catalogue from a book club. I want to order seven books from their list. However, I noticed that their price structure for postage was very strange:

Table 5.4

Number of items	Cost of post and packing
1	45¢
2	65¢
3	90¢
4	$1.20
5	$1.50
6 or more	$3.20

I decide, on the basis of this, that I will ask them to pack my order in the number of parcels that will attract the lowest post and packing charge.

How much will I have to pay?

2 Jasmine has been saving all year for her brother's birthday. She has collected all the 5¢ and 20¢ coins she had from her change in her piggy bank. She is now counting the money by putting it into piles, all containing $1 worth of coins. She notices that she has a number of piles of different heights.

If 5¢ and 20¢ coins are the same thickness, how many different heights of $1 pile could she have?

Exam-style questions

1 The notice below shows admission prices to the Tooney Tracks theme park.

Table 5.5

Adult	$12
Child (aged 4–16)	$6
Child (aged under 4)	Free
Senior citizen	$8
Family ticket (for 2 adults and 2 children)	$30
– Additional child 4–16 or senior citizen	$5
– Additional adult	$10
Family ticket (for 1 adult and 2 children)	$20
– Additional child 4–16 or senior citizen	$5
– Additional adult	$10

Maria is taking her three children aged 3, 7 and 10 and two friends of the older children (of the same ages) as well as her mother, who is a pensioner.

What is the least it will cost them?

2 The diagram shows a children's hopscotch game. The winner has to land on any four squares so that the numbers will add up to 40.

Which two numbers must the child land on in order to score 40?

Chapter 6
Finding methods of solution

Learning objectives

In the last chapter one particular method of finding a solution to a problem (searching through the options) was introduced. This chapter considers some alternative strategies that can be used in cases where searching is either impossible or would be too time-consuming a method.

6.1 Intermediate stages in problem solving

The examples so far have been relatively simple problems with a very simple method for reaching the solution. For many problems however, the primary skill required is to develop a method of solution. In most cases the method for finding the solution is likely to require identifying some intermediate steps that need to be taken.

When tackling a new problem, it can be very useful if you have seen a problem of a similar sort before, which you know how to approach – this is where experience in tackling problem-solving questions can be invaluable. If the problem is completely unfamiliar then there may be a number of different ways in which the problem can be approached. Whether you are familiar with similar problems or not, it is important to realise quickly if your approach to the problem is proving unsuccessful.

One strategy that can help to solve problems when you are not clear how to proceed is to analyse the problem by:

- organising the information you are given (possibly by making a sketch or putting the data into a table)
- identifying the pieces of information that you think are important
- simplifying (rejecting unimportant information)
- deciding which pieces of information could lead to the answer.

This may be illustrated as in the diagram below. Here, the calculation steps are represented by the arrows. Not all of these processes are used in all problem solutions.

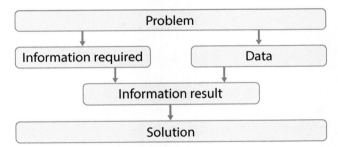

6.2 Drawing conclusions from relationships between data

The following activities consider a range of different problems and look at how the method of solution may be found.

EXAMPLE ACTIVITY 6.1

Sam sells sandwiches in a shop that he owns. Unfortunately, he did not check his stock carefully last night and has arrived at the shop this morning to find that he has only got enough bread to make 30 sandwiches. He can contact his usual supplier, who will be able to deliver the bread in three hours for the normal price. Alternatively, the supplier will deliver the bread in one hour if Sam is willing to pay an additional $10. Sam's other option is to buy the bread from the supermarket next door, but that will cost $20 more than the price that he usually pays.

Sam normally expects to be able to sell 20 sandwiches every hour, but customers who cannot get a sandwich when they come into the shop will not wait. When the ingredients are bought at the normal price, Sam makes a profit of $1 for each sandwich that he sells.

Which option for getting his bread should Sam adopt in order to maximise his profit?

Commentary

We need to compare the effect that each of the options has on the profit. Firstly, there is no advantage in paying extra to get the bread now as Sam has enough bread to last for more than the first hour anyway. The only comparison that is needed is therefore between getting the delivery in three hours or paying the additional $10 for a one-hour delivery.

In three hours Sam would expect to sell a total of 60 sandwiches and make a profit of $60. Taking the one-hour delivery to ensure that he has enough bread to make these sandwiches will reduce the profit to $50.

If he does not pay the extra $10 then he will only be able to make and sell 30 sandwiches in the first three hours and only have a profit of $30.

Since the timing of the delivery will have no effect on the sales for the rest of the day, Sam should pay $10 for the delivery in one hour to maximize his profit.

ACTIVITY 6.1

Lee wants to join an online science society.

A subscription for a year runs from January to December and costs $110. A six-month subscription runs either from January to June or from July to December and costs $57.50. Membership paid for on a month-by-month basis starts on the day payment is made but always ends on the last day of the same calendar month. The monthly fee is $10.

Today is 21 February. What is the cheapest way for Lee to be a member of the science society from today until he goes to college at the end of September next year?

EXAMPLE ACTIVITY 6.2

Amy and her brother David live 400 km apart. They are going to have a week's holiday by exchanging houses. On the day they are starting their holiday, Amy leaves home at 8 a.m. and David at 10 a.m. They both drive at 120 km/h on a motorway that travels directly between their houses.

At what time do they pass each other on the road?

Commentary

We have already seen examples which involve journeys where the information features speeds at which people travel (for example, Luiz and Bianca's journeys to school in Chapter 3). We are therefore already familiar with solving problems involving the relationships between speed, distance and time. The difference in this case is that we do not know immediately the distances that they are travelling, so we need to calculate that first before we can continue. We also need to consider the effect of their different starting times.

We could begin by representing the information in a diagram (as timelines for Amy and David):

Table 6.1

	8 a.m.			10 a.m.	???	
Amy	Leaves home	Travelling	...	Travelling	Amy and David pass each other	...
David	At home		Leaves home	Travelling		...

One approach to solving the problem would be to take the following steps:

- Step 1: The difference in the starting times can be eliminated by considering how far Amy will have travelled by 10 a.m. In two hours she will travel a total of 240 km. Therefore, at 10 a.m. we know that Amy and David are 160 km apart.

- Step 2: Since they are driving at the same speed as each other, they must meet halfway between their positions at 10 a.m., which means that they both travel an additional 80 km.

- Step 3: Since they are travelling at 120 km/h. this will take 40 minutes. Amy and David will therefore pass each other at 10:40 a.m.

The different steps can be viewed as filling in more details on the timeline:

Table 6.2

	8 a.m.		10 a.m.		10:40 a.m. (Step 3)	
Amy	Leaves home	Travels 240 km (Step 1)	160 km from David's house (Step 1)	Travels 80 km (Step 2) taking 40 minutes (Step 3)	Amy and David pass each other	...
David	At home		Leaves home			...

6.2.1 An algebraic solution

There are usually a range of different approaches that can be taken to solve problems – in the solution above, a sequence of simple steps needs to be taken in order to reach the final solution to the problem. While it is not required for any of the problem solving at this level, algebra can be a very useful tool when solving problems. An alternative solution to this problem might look like this:

Suppose that Amy and David pass each other t hours after 10 a.m.

The total amount of time that Amy has been travelling will be (t+2) hours and so she will have travelled 120(t+2) *km.*

The total amount of time that David has been travelling will be t hours and so he will have travelled 120t *km.*

Since the total distance is 400 km,

$$120(t+2) + 120t = 400$$
$$240t + 240 = 400$$
$$240t = 160$$
$$t = \frac{2}{3}$$

Since they pass $\frac{2}{3}$ of an hour after 10 a.m., the time must be 10:40 a.m.

ACTIVITY 6.2

Amalia and Zelda are keen cyclists. They are doing a 70 km time trial.

Amalia sets off at 10 a.m. She cycles at 20 km/hour until she reaches halfway, where there is a steep hill. It takes her 20 minutes to cycle up the hill at 15 km/hour. At the top is a café where Amalia stops for 20 minutes for tea and cake. She then continues at 25 km/hour until she reaches the end of the time trial.

Zelda sets off 45 minutes after Amalia. She cycles without stopping at a constant speed of 30 km/hour.

At what time does Zelda pass Amalia?

6.3 Making inferences about patterns in data

EXAMPLE ACTIVITY 6.3

Petra's electricity supply company charges her a fixed quarterly sum plus a rate per unit for electricity used. In the most expensive quarter last year (January to March), she used 2 000 units and her bill was $250. In the least expensive quarter (July to September), she used 600 units and her bill was $138. She is now adding extra insulation to her home which is expected to reduce her overall electricity consumption by 25%. What can she expect her January to March bill to be next year (if there are no increases in overall tariffs)?

Commentary

The first thing to recognise is that we have been presented with a model. Since both bills include the same quarterly charge, the difference in the two bills ($250 – $138 = $112) must be the price for 1 400 units of electricity.

One unit of electricity therefore costs $112 ÷ 1,400 = 8¢.

We could now work out the quarterly charge, but there is no need as this will remain the same for the next bill. The only difference is that Petra expects to have used 500 units less than before, so her bill should be $500 \times 8\text{¢} = \$40$ less than the January to March bill last year.

Petra should expect her bill to be $\$250 - \$40 = \$210$ for January to March next year.

6.3.1 An algebraic solution

Again, an algebraic approach is also possible; we could express the model algebraically as we saw in Chapter 4. In this case the equation will be:

$$C = M + Ru$$

where c is the charge for a particular bill for which u is the number of units used. Unlike the examples we have looked at so far in this book, where the parameters were known, here we have not been told what the fixed monthly sum (M) or the rate per unit (R) are, although we do know that they are the same for the two bills we have been told about.

Our intermediate step is therefore to find the values of these two parameters. From the information that we know, we could write down a pair of simultaneous equations which we can then solve to find the values of M and R. The two equations would be:

$$250 = M + 2{,}000R$$

$$138 = M + 600R$$

Notice that one approach to solving this pair of simultaneous equations would be to subtract the second one from the first, leading to $112 = 1{,}400R$.

This is exactly the same as our first deduction when using the non-algebraic approach – the algebra is simply providing a way to clearly express the steps that we are taking.

ACTIVITY 6.3

Bruce's mobile phone provider charges $10 per month for 250 minutes of phone calls and unlimited texts. In the past three months he has made about 550 minutes of calls every month. He pays 50¢ a minute for calls when he has used more than 250 minutes.

A different provider will charge $7 per month for 200 minutes of phone calls and unlimited texts. When he goes over 200 minutes of calls he will pay 20¢ per minute.

How much would Bruce reduce his phone cost by over the next 12 months if he changes provider and still uses the same number of minutes per month?

Summary

Having read this chapter you should be able to:

- compare the effects of a range of options that could be taken

- identify steps that need to be taken in order to reach the solution to a problem.

51

End-of-chapter questions

1   The votes have recently been cast at the local elections. Voting is carried out using the alternative vote system. This means that each voter ranks the candidates in order of preference. Votes are initially counted on the basis of all voters' number one ranking. The candidate with the least votes is excluded and the votes of those people who placed him or her as number one are reallocated using their second preferences. The process then continues until a winner is established. The results of the first count are shown below. How many candidates still have a chance of winning?

Table 6.3

Patel	323
Brown	211
Walsh	157
Ndelo	83
Macpherson	54
Gonzalez	21

2   There are 16 students in Miss Pilbeam's tutor group. They have all been allocated a locker. Each locker should show its number but the numbers have worn away. Miss Pilbeam has started painting new numbers but has not yet finished. The diagram shows how the lockers have been numbered so far.

16	3		
		11	8
		7	
4			1

'How do we know which locker to use?' ask the students. 'Easy', says Miss Pilbeam. 'The numbers in any row will add up to 34. So will each of the four columns and the two diagonals. The centre four adjacent squares add up to 34 too'.

Copy the diagram and write in the missing locker numbers.

Exam-style questions

1   Jack buys small tins of tomatoes every week. They usually cost 50¢ each. Last week, however, Jack saw that the shop was selling six large tins of tomatoes plus a bag of pasta for $7.50. He worked out that the pasta was normally $2. Jack decided that he could use one large tin of tomatoes instead of two small tins so he bought 18 large tins of tomatoes together with three bags of pasta.

This week, however, the small tins of tomatoes are on offer at $1.60 for a pack of four.

How much more did Jack pay last week for tinned tomatoes than if he had bought them this week?

2 Five students, Alec, Bryn, Igor, Molly and Suzy, took an exam. The exam was marked out of 30.

- The highest mark awarded was 26.
- The lowest mark was 7.
- The average (mean) mark was 16.
- Molly achieved 8 marks more than Bryn.
- Igor got exactly three times the mark that Alec achieved.

What mark did each student achieve?

3 A word game involves making words from random letters. Letters in a word can score 1, 2, 3, 4 or 5 points.

- STALE scores 15 points
- CHEAT scores 15 points
- CHEST scores 19 points
- CHASE scores 16 points

How many points is CHALETS worth?

4 Five friends have a meal at a restaurant. At the end of the meal one of them pays the bill for all five. Later they try to work out how much each of them should pay according to what they ordered.

The bill is confusing. It reads:

- 1 starter + 1 main course + 1 salad = $16
- 1 main course + 1 dessert = $13.25
- 1 main course + 2 salads + 1 dessert = $20.25
- 2 main courses + 2 salads = $23.00

How much did each item cost?

5 Jack is in the supermarket. He needs to buy 30 litres of lemonade for a children's party. There are 4 brands on the shelf, all of which normally cost $2.75 for a 2-litre bottle. This week, however, each of the brands has a different special offer, as follows:

- Fordowne $2 off when three 2-litre bottles are purchased
- Imp   20% off all 2-litre bottles
- Swish   Buy four 2-litre bottles, get another one free
- Tiara   2.5-litre bottle for the normal price of a 2-litre bottle

a Which brand of lemonade should Jack buy to keep the cost as low as possible?

b Refer to the information above about the offers on lemonade brands. What combination of brands of lemonade would reduce the cost even further?

Part a Cambridge International AS & A Level Thinking Skills 9694 Paper 11 Q5 June 2016

Chapter 7
Trends in data

Learning objectives

The concept of modelling was introduced in Chapter 4. This chapter looks at identifying and explaining patterns and trends in data by adapting models to fit different situations.

7.1 Identifying trends in data

While models describe the relationship between a number of variables, they often do not take into consideration every variable involved. The most important features to be modelled can often be determined by looking at trends in the data. Trends in data can also be helpful in identifying when something may have changed. In the simplest case this may be as simple as recognising when something happens to change a steady pattern, as the example below shows.

EXAMPLE ACTIVITY 7.1

At the office where Joe works the swipe-card system logs the time at which employees enter and leave the building. For the last two weeks the times at which Joe arrived at work are shown in the table below.

Table 7.1

Week	Monday	Tuesday	Wednesday	Thursday	Friday
1	08:30	08:35	08:52	08:48	08:31
2	08:55	08:31	08:12	08:31	08:32

On several days Joe's journey to work had been affected by roadworks which had increased the amount of time that it took for him to travel to work. The roadworks took place over seven consecutive days.

Identify the days on which the roadworks were taking place and explain how they might have resulted in Joe's arrival times at work.

Commentary

We can see from the table that Joe's journey to work usually results in his arriving at about 8:30, but there are three days where the arrival time is about 20 minutes later and one day where it is about 20 minutes earlier. As is often the case when looking for a general trend in some data, we are not concerned with the small fluctuations around these times – it is only the larger jumps that we need to worry about.

Given that the first late arrival was on the Wednesday of week one, it is likely that this is the day on which the roadworks started. Joe was later than usual for the first two days, but may then have adjusted the time at which he left home so that he could arrive at the normal time.

Joe was again 20 minutes later than usual on the Monday of week two, so perhaps he assumed that the roadworks would have finished over the weekend and left at his normal time. He then adjusted his departure time from Tuesday. On Wednesday, when the roadworks had finished, he still left home at the earlier time and so he arrived at work approximately 20 minutes earlier than usual.

In this example we are providing an explanation for the fluctuations in arrival time based on the fact that there were roadworks affecting the journey. There may be many other plausible explanations that could be given.

ACTIVITY 7.1

The table below shows supermarket sales income over a ten-week period. A sales promotion takes place during week ten.

Describe the pattern in the sales figures. Explain the factors that may cause the pattern and any variations in the pattern.

Table 7.2

Month	Month 1				Month 2				Month 3	
Week	Week 1	Week 2	Week 3	Week 4	Week 5	Week 6	Week 7	Week 8	Week 9	Week 10
Sales in $1000	974	705	532	1149	969	711	536	1410	967	912

7.2 Fitting models based on observed patterns

Once a pattern has been identified there are often a range of explanations that might be given and these may be applied in the form of a model.

EXAMPLE ACTIVITY 7.2

Nikul runs exercise classes at his local gym, and gets there each day by train and bus. Classes start at different times each day, but his first class of the day is always either at 9:00, 9:30 or 10:00. He always gets to the railway station 45 minutes before he is due to start teaching and the train journey takes 20 minutes, after which he takes a bus to the gym, which takes 10 minutes. Trains leave every 20 minutes, starting on the hour, and the buses also leave at regular intervals. Some days Nikul finds that he gets to work five minutes early. On all the other days he finds that he gets there five minutes late.

What possible departure times for the buses could explain the times that Nikul arrives at the gym?

Commentary

On a day on which Nikul's first class starts at 09:00 he will arrive at the station at 08:15. That means that he will get the 08:20 train and be waiting for a bus from 08:40. We don't know whether this is a day where he is late or early, but it is straightforward to consider both cases:

- If this is a day where he is five minutes early then there must be a bus at 08:45.
- If this is a day where he is five minutes late then there must be a bus at 08:55 (and no buses between 08:40 and 08:55).

On a day on which Nikul's first class starts at 09:30 he will get to the station at 08:45. This means that he will have to wait for the 09:00 train and will be waiting for the bus from 09:20. There is no way that this could be the day that he is 5 minutes early, so there must be a bus at 09:25 which gets him there five minutes late.

→

Since train times repeat every hour, the case for 10:00 must be the same as for 09:00, but with one hour added to the times.

Since we know that there are some days on which Nikul arrives five minutes early, they must be on at least one of the days where his first class starts on the hour. Therefore there must be a bus either at 08:45 or at 09:45.

The most obvious explanation is therefore that there are buses every 20 minutes (running at 5, 25 and 45 past the hour), meaning that Nikul is five minutes early when his class starts at 09:00 or 10:00 and five minutes late when the class starts at 09:30. It could also be the case that the buses run more regularly than this, as buses running every ten minutes (at 5, 15, 25, 35, 45 and 55 past the hour) would also give the same outcomes. The important features are that there are buses at 25 and 55 minutes past the hour with no buses in the preceding five minutes.

ACTIVITY 7.2

Karen gets to the bus stop each morning just in time to catch the 8.15 bus to work. On some mornings, Karen is waiting for the bus when her colleague Elsa drives past. Elsa always stops and gives Karen a lift to work.

Karen prefers having a lift from Elsa to taking the bus. She realises that on mornings when she has got the bus, Elsa has arrived at work before her. Karen writes down the following log:

Week 1 Monday	Got bus at 8.19
Week 1 Tuesday	Got bus at 8.16
Week 1 Wednesday	Lift from Elsa at 8.12
Week 1 Thursday	Lift from Elsa at 8.13
Week 1 Friday	Got bus at 8.16
Week 2 Monday	Got bus at 8.21
Week 2 Tuesday	Lift from Elsa at 8.11
Week 2 Wednesday	Lift from Elsa at 8.12
Week 2 Thursday	Lift from Elsa at 8.10
Week 2 Friday	Got bus at 8.15

What does Karen's log tell us about:

a the time Elsa drives past?

b the time the bus arrives?

At what time should Karen get to the bus stop if she wants a lift from Elsa?

7.3 Deducing values for one or more parameters

Identifying trends in a set of data is the first step in creating a model to describe the data. In simple cases the structure of the model to be used might be known, but exact values of the parameters need to be worked out. The next example is of such a situation.

EXAMPLE ACTIVITY 7.3

My company regularly uses a taxi service to take staff to the airport. If there are several passengers needing to travel from our town at similar times, they combine this into a single journey. They divide the total cost by the number of passengers and invoice each passenger separately. The distance is always the same and the time only varies by a small amount, but I do not know how they work out the charge for the journey. The charges made for some recent journeys are shown in the table below:

Table 7.3

Number of passengers	1	2	3	4	5
Charge per journey per passenger	$40.00	$19.98	$14.68	$12.03	$10.38

There are a number of different charging structures they could use. All taxis charge a fixed price per kilometre and per minute of journey time. In addition they may charge a fixed hire fee and an additional charge depending on the number of passengers carried.

What is the charging structure used by this taxi company? What limitations are there to the conclusions we can derive?

Commentary

In order to work out the charging structure used by the taxi company we must first work out the total cost of each of the journeys by multiplying the charge per customer by the number of passengers. This gives us the following values:

Table 7.4

Number of passengers	1	2	3	4	5
Total cost of journey	$40.00	$39.96	$44.04	$48.12	$51.90

Apart from slight variations in the overall costs, the price is roughly $40 for journeys with either one or two passengers and then an additional $4 for each extra passenger. We can therefore conclude that the charging structure used by this taxi company must have the following features:

- $40 for a journey of this type for up to two passengers
- an additional $4 for each additional passenger carried.

The additional charge depending on the number of passengers carried can therefore be deduced exactly, but since all journeys were over the same distance and approximately the same amount of time, there is no way to work out the exact way in which the $40 is reached.

ACTIVITY 7.3

The table shows the prices at the Superfit sports and health centre.

Table 7.5

Sport/activity	Adult	Child up to 16 years	Family (2 adults and 2 children)
Swimming pool	$3.00	$1.60	$7.50
Spa (1 hour)	$8.00	$4.20	$20.00
Gym (1 hour)	$5.00	$2.60	$12.50
Exercise class (1 hour)	$2.60	$1.40	$6.50
Climbing wall (1 hour 30 minutes)	$9.00	$4.70	$22.50

What is the charging structure used at Superfit?

ACTIVITY 7.4

Combining your skills

This question will give you practice in combining the problem-solving skills you have developed in Chapters 1–7 in order to tackle more challenging questions.

Chocco-O-La makes luxury chocolates. The cost of making a box of chocolates depends on the cost of the materials, production and packaging.

Chocco-O-La cannot control the cost of raw materials, which depends on cocoa bean prices. Packaging costs have increased by a consistent percentage each year. Chocco-O-La calculates its selling price by adding a fixed percentage onto the total cost price.

The table below shows some costs and prices for 100 boxes of chocolates over the last three years.

Table 7.6

	Raw materials $	Production $	Packaging $	Total costs $	Selling price $
Year 1	695.00		150.00		1700.00
Year 2		530.00		1418.00	1772.50
Year 3	725.00	500.00	156.06		

a   Calculate the missing figures in the table.

Chocco-O-La is trying to speed up production. The chocolate moulding machine breaks on most days. When this happens production stops until the machine is repaired.

Chocco-O-La has two people who can carry out machine repairs. Jordan has done the job for ten years. Les is new and is still finding out how to do the job. Each works two days then has two days off. They don't both work on the same day.

The table below shows the production time lost over two weeks.

Table 7.7

	Production time lost in minutes						
	Monday	Tuesday	Wednesday	Thursday	Friday	Saturday	Sunday
Week 1	10	98	165	15	32	89	154
Week 2	17	21	78	121	23	18	76

b Which days was Jordan working, and which days was Les working?

c What other conclusion could be derived from the data?

Summary

Having read this chapter you should be able to:

- identify patterns within sets of data

- give plausible explanations for changes in the patterns within a set of data
- identify parameters for models based on a set of data.

End-of-chapter question

Manisha recently went on holiday to Outlandia. She used her mobile phone once each day to call home. In Outlandia calls are charged by the minute. Calls made during the day are charged at twice the cost of calls made during the evening or night. All Manisha's calls lasted less than 10 minutes.

The Outlandia Phone Corporation's bills customers as shown in Manisha's bill below:

Total amount due: $63.00

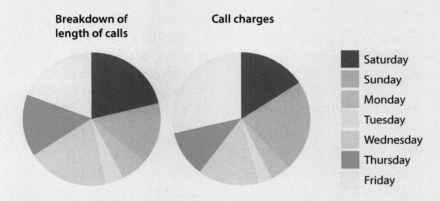

Breakdown of length of calls

Call charges

- Saturday
- Sunday
- Monday
- Tuesday
- Wednesday
- Thursday
- Friday

Which days were the ones when Manisha made calls during the day?

Exam-style questions

1   Lara travels to work every day by train. There are two trains every hour from her local station to the main station. The first is the express. The second, the stopping train, calls at several small stations between Lara's station and the main station.

Lara writes down all her journey times because she can claim money back from the train company if the train is more than 30 minutes late.

Lara's journey times over a two-week period are shown in the table below.

Table 7.8

	Week 1					Week 2				
	Monday	**Tuesday**	**Wednesday**	**Thursday**	**Friday**	**Monday**	**Tuesday**	**Wednesday**	**Thursday**	**Friday**
Train departs	0810	0810	0825	0810	0825	0815	0829	0810	0810	0825
Train arrives	0831	0831	0857	0831	0857	0836	0928	0831	0831	0857

a   On which days did Lara take the express train?

b   On which days did Lara take the stopping train?

c   On how many days can Lara claim money back from the train company?

61

2 A small company works from Monday to Friday. They have decided to provide biscuits for staff to eat at the afternoon break. There are seven members of staff. Avtar never eats biscuits. The others all have one biscuit. Lydia sometimes has an extra biscuit, or even two extra.

The choice of biscuits is chocolate digestives, which have 16 in a packet, or jammy dodgers, which have 22 in a packet.

a What is the minimum number of packets of biscuits that must be bought to ensure there are enough to last for the next four weeks?

b Lydia gives up biscuits completely after the first week. What is the shortest possible period that the remaining biscuits will now last?

3 Ms Ahmed teaches English at Level 1 and Level 2. She also teaches Critical Thinking. In a single class the number of students is always between 15 and 25. English Level 1 and Level 2 students may attend the same class. Ms Ahmed is paid $32 per hour. She has 1 hour per week with each group of English students and 4 hours per week with each group of Critical Thinking students. There are 183 students for Level 1 English and 110 students for Level 2 English. There are 31 students for Critical Thinking.

What is the total amount that Ms Ahmed earns per week?

4 Peter's Pizzas sell pizzas in three sizes: Small, Medium and Large. The types of pizza are grouped into three categories: Basic, Standard and Luxury. The cost of making each type of pizza is shown in the table below.

Table 7.9

	Basic	Standard	Luxury
Small	$0.60	$0.80	$1.20
Medium	$0.90	$1.20	$1.80
Large	$1.60	$2.50	$3.00

In order to set his prices, Peter assumes that it will cost him $1.50 to make any delivery, regardless of the number of pizzas to be delivered.

He does not want to make a separate charge for delivery of pizzas and wishes to set the prices so that he will make a profit of at least 20% overall on any delivery.

He has therefore worked out that the lowest price he could charge for a Small Basic pizza is $2.52 and the lowest price he could charge for a Large Luxury pizza is $5.40.

a What is the lowest price that Peter could charge for a Medium Luxury pizza?

Peter also wishes to offer special deals when buying more than one pizza. He wishes to make two offers: a percentage discount on the sale of three pizzas or more; and an offer in which, for any order of two or more pizzas, the cheapest pizza is reduced to half price. In either case he still wishes to make a profit of at least 20% overall on any delivery.

b If the prices are still set as before, what is the greatest percentage discount (to the nearest 1%) that Peter can offer on orders of three pizzas?

c What price should Peter now charge for each Large Basic pizza so that he will still make a 20% profit on a delivery of two such pizzas if the second one is half price?

Peter decided to set the discount at 10% for an order of three pizzas or more. He also decided to set the price of a Large Standard pizza at $5.20.

d   If a customer placed an order for two Large Standard pizzas and one other, cheaper, pizza, what price would the other pizza have to be so that the two offers resulted in the same overall cost for the order?

Unfortunately, Peter forgot to specify that only one offer could be used for any order. He received an order for three Large Standard pizzas, and the customer claimed that one of the pizzas should be half price and that there should also be a 10% discount on the order.

e   If Peter does apply both offers to this order, what will be his overall profit?

Cambridge International AS & A Level Thinking Skills 9694 Paper 31 Q1 June 2016

Chapter 8
Transforming data

Learning objectives

This chapter considers the different forms in which a set of data can be represented, and explores how shapes change their appearance when they are rotated.

8.1 Alternative representations of data

Humans are very good at making links between different views of real things. For example, if a cat is curled up asleep it is a very different shape from a cat that is running, or one that is sitting up and looking at you, yet even children easily recognise that these are all the same type of animal.

This becomes more difficult when the representations are more abstract, yet it is still important. In particular, in statistics we use different representations of data. Sometimes this involves simplifying the data to a few key numbers (such as finding the mean or the range of the data), while at other times we might put the data into a table, or draw a bar chart or a pie chart perhaps. These different representations might be useful for particular purposes, or we might be given the representations (perhaps in a newspaper) and need to work with what we have got.

If we have two classes that are studying the same subject and each class takes the same test we will have two sets of marks. If we want to compare the two classes we could try to look at all of the marks, but it will be difficult to understand what is going on. We might make it easier if we put the two sets of data in ascending order, but this will still be difficult. If we work out the mean score for each set then we will have two numbers we can compare and this is easy to do: the class with the higher mean did better on average. We might also be able to compare the two classes if the results are grouped and then displayed in bar charts, but drawing pie charts is unlikely to be useful.

Note that whatever we do with the data won't tell us which teacher is 'better' or which class has worked harder. There could be all sorts of reasons why the class that got the lower mean mark might not be considered to have underachieved. They might have had lower marks in a similar test at the start of the course, they might not have studied the subject for as long, they might not have had as many lessons each week, or their teacher might have been unwell for part of the year. Can you think of any other reasons?

EXAMPLE ACTIVITY 8.1

Here are the most popular first languages spoken across the world, according to the CIA World Factbook.

Mandarin Chinese (893 million people), Spanish (425 million), English (337 million), Arabic (264 million), Hindi (264 million), Portuguese (205 million), Bengali (190 million), Russian (168 million), Japanese (124 million), other languages (4 453 million).

These figures are from 2016 and refer to the *first* language (a lot more people speak or understand these languages too).

What does this tell us?

Commentary

At the moment the information as it is presented is quite difficult to understand. Perhaps it would be easier to understand if we used percentages:

Mandarin Chinese (12.2%), Spanish (5.8%), English (4.6%), Arabic (3.6%), Hindi (3.6%), Portuguese (2.8%), Bengali (2.6%), Russian (2.3%), Japanese (1.7%), other languages (60.8%).

→

We could represent this information in many different ways:

- We could add it to a map (but this would be difficult to interpret because some languages are spoken as a first language in many countries but not everyone in a single country shares the same first language).
- We could try to use the actual numbers.
- We could draw a bar chart (but the bar for 'other languages' looks like it might be rather big).
- We could draw a pie chart (but some of the sections will be very small and difficult to see).

What if we wrote it as a list?

Mandarin Chinese (12.2%)

Spanish (5.8%)

English (4.6%)

Arabic (3.6%)

Hindi (3.6%)

Portuguese (2.8%)

Bengali (2.6%)

Russian (2.3%)

Japanese (1.7%)

Other languages (60.8%).

This is now easier to understand.

A common way of using percentages is to say 'if the world consisted of 100 people...'

In this situation, if there were 100 people in the world (and if they represented the whole world) then:

Table 8.1

First language	Number of first language speakers
Mandarin Chinese	12
Spanish	6
English	5
Arabic	4
Hindi	4
Portuguese	3
Bengali	3
Russian	2
Japanese	2
Other languages	61

There are still some difficulties with this method of representing the information (What happens when you add up the number of people? Why is that unexpected? What is going on?), but this might be the clearest way of doing it.

We can see that while there are nine languages that are very popular, over $\frac{3}{5}$ of people speak a different language as their first language.

The CIA World Factbook has the following information about the ages/genders of people across the world (2016 est.):

0–14 years: 25.44% (male 963 981 944/female 898 974 458)

15–24 years: 16.16% (male 611 311 930/female 572 229 547)

25–54 years: 41.12% (male 1 522 999 578/female 1 488 011 505)

55–64 years: 8.6% (male 307 262 939/female 322 668 546)

65 years and over: 8.68% (male 283 540 918/female 352 206 092)

If the world were 100 people, how many of them would appear as each age and gender?

8.2 Relationships between features of an object

We sometimes need to be able to visualise what is going on in a particular situation. One way to do this is to have a mental image and to manipulate that image. Another is to draw out the scenario and to manipulate that diagram.

8.2.1 Manipulating a mental image

EXAMPLE ACTIVITY 8.2

Here is a square piece of clear plastic with a capital letter A on it:

Here is the same piece of plastic, after it has been rotated:

A	A	A	A
The original	Rotated 90° clockwise	Rotated 180°	Rotated 270° clockwise

It is also possible to *reflect* the original piece of plastic to form each of the other versions. Can you see how?

Commentary

If we reflect the initial letter in the diagonal shown here then it turns:

Reflecting the original piece of plastic in a horizontal line turns:

Reflecting in the other diagonal turns

ACTIVITY 8.2

1   In a similar way to the letter A, it is possible to reflect this capital letter B to form all of the rotations. Show how.

2   The letter F cannot be reflected to form any of the rotations. Explain why not.

3   What is special about the shapes that can be reflected to make their rotations?

8.2.2 Manipulating a diagram

Sometimes we will need to draw out a diagram to help.

EXAMPLE ACTIVITY 8.3

My tablet computer can fit 20 apps on the screen. When I hold the tablet in a landscape orientation there are five apps going across and four going downwards. When I rotate the tablet so it is portrait there are four apps going across and five going downwards. The icons then shuffle themselves so they are in the same order, reading from the top left of the screen. Which two icons stay in the same spot on the screen?

Commentary

An initial idea is that the first icon stays in the same place, but a moment's thought shows that this isn't the case. Some diagrams are helpful:

1	2	3	4	5
6	7	8	9	10
11	12	13	14	15
16	17	18	19	20

1	2	3	4
5	6	7	8
9	10	11	12
13	14	15	16
17	18	19	20

Let's rotate the second diagram:

4	8	12	16	20
3	7	11	15	19
2	6	10	14	18
1	5	9	13	17

Now we can see that icons 7 and 14 are the only ones that stay in the same place on the screen.

ACTIVITY 8.3

A piece of jewellery is made by putting four pieces of coloured glass (**R**ed, **Y**ellow, **G**reen, **B**lue) together in a square:

R	Y
G	B

Using these four colours in different orders, how many different pieces of jewellery can be made?

(It will be the same if we can reflect or rotate it.)

8.3 Identifying features from different types of representation

Sometimes experience of solving one problem can help with another. We might also find it useful to identify the key piece of information.

EXAMPLE ACTIVITY 8.4

The shapes from the game *Tetris* are sometimes called 'tetrominoes'. There are five different tetrominoes:

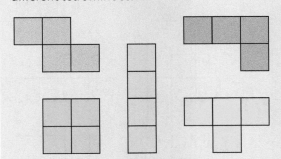

In some of them it is possible to write in the numbers 1 to 4 so that consecutive numbers are not in adjacent squares (horizontally or vertically). In which of the above shapes can't this be done?

Commentary

In the solution below three of the shapes (green shape A, blue shape B and purple shape C) have been numbered in what is essentially the same way. Even though they are different shapes they are actually similar to each other because the squares are in a line. It is also interesting that if you start with the number 1 on one end in these three shapes you can't then complete the numbering, so the number 1 has to go in one of the middle spaces.

→

A

3	1	
	4	2

B

3
1
4
2

C

3	1	4
		2

D

1	
	2

E

	X	

The red shape (D) cannot be done. We can put 1 anywhere (the four corners are the same because we can just rotate the square). The number 2 must go diagonally opposite. Now there is no legitimate place to put 3.

In the yellow shape (E) the square marked with a cross is the problem. It touches all of the other squares.

ACTIVITY 8.4

Now try placing the numbers 1 to 5 on the 12 pentominoes below, following the same rules. Try to identify quickly which ones cannot be done.

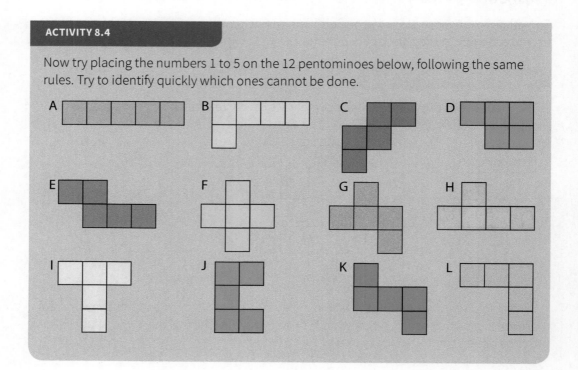

ACTIVITY 8.5

1 Complete the following 3-by-3 grid so that the numbers 1, 2 and 3 appear exactly
once in each row and in each column.

	2	
1		

2 Here are some more 3-by-3 number grids that have already been completed. What
similarities are there between all three of the grids?

A

1	2	3
3	1	2
2	3	1

B

3	1	2
2	3	1
1	2	3

C

3	2	1
2	1	3
1	3	2

ACTIVITY 8.6

This is a diagram of a phone SIM-card holder.

It is a rectangle shape but with a corner cut off. This is so the SIM card can only go into
the holder one way round.

a If the SIM card were a complete rectangle, how many ways could it be inserted?

b If it were a square, how many ways could it be inserted?

c How many ways could it be inserted if it were a square with a corner cut off? Explain
your answers.

d It is possible to make a triangular SIM card that can only fit one way. Draw one such
triangle and explain why it will only fit one way.

Summary

This chapter examined how we often see (and receive) information in different formats and need to be able to change between these formats easily to solve problems. This is important because:

- one representation is often easier to understand or more useful in a particular situation
- one representation might be misleading
- a problem might be easier to solve if we represent it in a different way.

End-of-chapter questions

1 Here are some instructions to guide you from point A to point B:

S L S S R S S

'S' means 'go straight ahead for one block'

'L' means 'turn 90° to the left'

'R' means 'turn 90° to the right'

S L S S R S S is shown on this map:

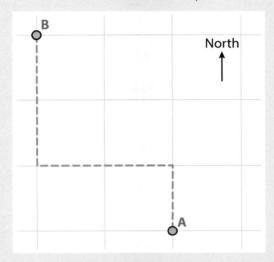

a Look at the following routes. Explain which one is the odd one out.

Route 1) S L S S R S S

Route 2) S S L S R S L S

Route 3) S L S L S R S R S S S

b On the map you always start facing northwards and are only allowed to go to the north or to the west. What do you notice about all of the permitted routes?

c What is the shortest set of instructions that will take you from A to B?

2 All of the numbers from 1 to 9 are put into the grid so all the rows, all the columns and the two diagonals each add up to 15. The numbers 1 and 5 have been put in already.

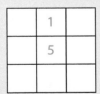

There are two possible numbers that can go in the bottom left corner. What are they?

3 The table shows the results of a questionnaire, asking the five colleges in a town the proportion of students taking 1–4 A Level subjects.

Table 8.2

College	Percentage of students taking number of A Levels shown			
	1	2	3	4
Abbey Road	13	25	42	20
Barnfleld	5	18	55	22
Colegate	24	36	28	12
Danbridge	16	18	61	5
Eden House	10	14	48	28

The local newspaper added the numbers together and divided by five to work out the percentages for the whole town.

a Why doesn't this work?

They then drew a graph but had forgotten to include the data for one of the colleges.

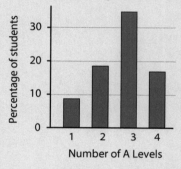

b Which college did they forget?

4 I have to remember a four digit number when I withdraw money from a cash machine. The first and last digits are the same and the middle two digits are the square of the first digit. Only two different digits are used. What could my four digit number be? Write down all of the possibilities.

Exam-style questions

1 A student has researched the costs that make up the price of fuel in different countries. The amounts are given in the local currencies and these all have different exchange rates.

Table 8.3

	Sudaria	Idani	Anguda	Boralia
Crude oil	0.70	18.68	0.40	0.50
Refining	0.02	4.67	0.02	0.02
Wholesale	0.09	3.63	0.05	0.14
Retail	0.06	2.08	0.06	0.05
Tax	0.50	22.84	0.80	0.34
Total	1.37	51.90	1.33	1.05

Last night she drew a pie chart for one of the countries but did not label it and cannot remember which country it was for. Which country is it?

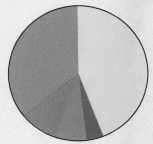

2 Roger's cleaning company calculates its prices for cleaning buildings in the following way:

- There is a fixed charge of $20.
- $0.50 is charged for every square metre of floor area in the building.
- An additional $10 is charged for every room in the building.

In this question assume that all rooms in buildings have a floor area that is a whole number of square metres.

a What would be the price for Roger's company to clean a building containing 5 rooms and having a total floor area of 50 square metres?

Trevor is planning to set up a cleaning company, but only wants to calculate his prices based on the floor area to be cleaned. He will not have a fixed charge or add any extra to the price for the number of rooms.

b What should he charge per square metre of floor area to match the price of Roger's company for a building containing five rooms and having a total floor area of 50 square metres?

Trevor has decided to set his charge at $1.50 per square metre to be cleaned.

c If a building has six rooms and would cost the same to clean with either company, what is the total floor area?

Trevor also intends to offer an 'Express' service in which he will have three cleaners clean the building, rather than just one. He wants to set the price for this service so that he earns twice what he would from the standard service, after paying his cleaners. Trevor pays each cleaner $0.90 per square metre to be cleaned.

d How much should Trevor charge per square metre of floor area for the 'Express' service?

As soon as Trevor announced his prices, Roger's company reduced their prices by making the extra charge per room just $5. One of the bookings that Trevor had received was cancelled because Trevor's price at the standard rate had been cheaper, but was now $15 more expensive than Roger's price.

e i What is the minimum number of rooms that could be in such a building?
ii What is the floor area of a building with this minimum number of rooms?

Trevor decided that he would offer to clean the smallest room in any building with more than three rooms for free. This meant that Trevor's price for the job that he lost was now cheaper again.

f What is the maximum number of rooms that there could be in this building? Justify your answer.

Cambridge International AS & A Level Thinking Skills 9694 Paper 32 Q3a–f June 2015

Chapter 9
Summarised data

Learning objectives

This chapter explores how data from different sources can be combined in the solution of a problem and how, having been given the summary of some data, information about the original scenario can be deduced.

9.1 Summarising data

We are used to seeing data being represented in different forms. This might involve calculating averages or drawing graphs of particular types. There might be more than one sensible way to do this, as illustrated in the examples that follow.

EXAMPLE ACTIVITY 9.1

In a particular forest there are two varieties of mushrooms growing close together. One variety of mushroom is edible, while the other is poisonous. A fungus expert has this information about the heights of mushrooms and the diameters of their caps (all measurements are in cm):

Table 9.1 Edible and poisonous mushrooms

Edible mushroom		Poisonous mushroom	
Diameter	Height	Diameter	Height
5.3	7	7.2	10.4
7.2	8.3	4.7	3.2
4.6	5.8	6.7	11.3
7.8	9	5.4	5.7
8.3	10	4.6	4.4
6.1	7.5	7.6	11.6
9.4	10.4	6.3	9.6
8.7	9.5	6.3	8.3
5.5	6.6	6	7
3.6	5.4	5.1	4.9
7.3	9.1	6.3	9
3	4.6	5.7	7.7

(**Note:** this data only refers to these two varieties of mushroom in this one particular forest. You will not be able to use this data to decide whether any mushrooms you find elsewhere are likely to be poisonous or not.)

A student finds five more mushrooms in the same forest and measures them:

Table 9.2 Measurements of mushrooms

Mushroom	Diameter	Height
A	3.5	4.8
B	6.7	10.5
C	6.2	7.5
D	5.8	8.2
E	7.2	5.5

For each mushroom, can the student tell whether it is likely to be edible or not?

Commentary

One way to tackle this problem is to draw a graph. Here we have two pieces of information about one thing (for each mushroom we know its diameter and its height), so it would be appropriate for us to draw a scatter graph to display the data provided by the expert:

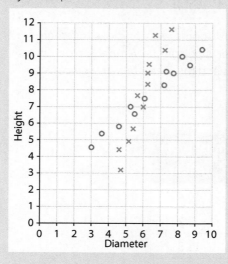

The edible mushrooms are shown as circles, while the poisonous ones are crosses. There appears to be a strong positive correlation for each type, because we can see a general pattern for each one.

Now we can plot the new mushrooms on the graph too:

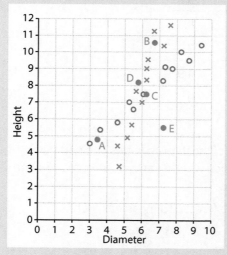

Mushroom A lies on the line for the edible mushrooms, while mushroom B is in amongst the data for the poisonous mushrooms.

Mushroom C has dimensions that are almost exactly the same as another of the edible mushrooms, but it also lies very close to the line for the poisonous mushrooms. Mushroom D appears at first glance to be a poisonous one, but if we removed the crosses from the scatter graph then D wouldn't be out of place amongst the edible mushrooms. This idea of mentally removing one or other set of data is a useful one in helping to decide where the new mushrooms belong. We cannot easily tell which type of mushroom C and D are. It would be wise not to eat either of them!

Mushroom E is an outlier. It isn't close to either of the lines of data. Perhaps it is a different type of mushroom entirely, or maybe there is greater variation in the sizes of mushrooms than our limited amount of data has shown us. On this basis we cannot say for certain that it is edible.

In some Physical Education lessons a teacher explored the value of warming up before undertaking exercise. At the start of a lesson the students measured their 'standing long jump' distance. They stood with their feet together, behind a line. Then they jumped forwards, keeping their feet together. Another student measured where their feet landed.

After that they carried out their usual warm-up activities and then measured their standing long jump again to see whether it had changed.

Here is the data for a class of Grade 6 students (aged 11 or 12 years old) and a class of Grade 10 students (aged 15 or 16 years old), with all distances given in metres.

Table 9.3

Grade 6		Grade 10	
Before	After	Before	After
1.19	1.4	1.52	1.75
1.49	1.54	1.6	1.82
1.24	1.2	1.76	1.98
1.3	1.38	1.8	
1.7	1.88	2.02	2.28
1.2	1.18	1.32	1.55
1.45	1.5	1.98	2.11
1.48	1.5	1.56	1.94
1.36	1.4	1.3	1.61
1.32	1.44	1.74	2.1
1.52	1.56	1.58	1.9
1	1.12	1.5	1.72
1.28	1.1	1.38	1.72
1.23	1.48	1.96	
1.36	1.36	1.86	2
0.96	1.2	1.74	1.95
1.6	1.61	1.3	1.7
1.8	1.7	1.32	1.74
1.38	1.32		
1.4	1.6		

1 What problems are there with the data?

2 What do you notice about the data?

3 What is the value of the warm-up on the performance of the two classes?

Commentary

1 To start with, it was important to match up the data. One line in the table must show the 'before' and 'after' measurements for the same student, otherwise we won't be able to make the comparisons we want.

There are other possible problems with the data. Some of the data has been recorded to two decimal places, while some is given with only one decimal place. We don't know whether the numbers with one decimal place should be followed by a zero (so 1.6 should be recorded as 1.60 because it was 1 metre and 60 cm), or whether some students found it difficult to measure the distance accurately (so they gave a vaguer number), or whether the instructions given by the teacher were not clear and the students used different degrees of accuracy.

There are 74 pieces of data and 25 of them are given to only 1 decimal place. This is more than a third of them, so we can probably discount the idea that all of these should be followed by a zero (because we would expect about a tenth of them to end in a zero in this way).

There are two gaps in the Grade 10 data. Perhaps two students were injured during the lesson and couldn't do the second jump, or maybe they had to leave the lesson early. We will need to ignore their first jump as well in our analysis.

2 In the data you might notice the following:

- there are more students in the Grade 6 class
- some Grade 6 students jumped further before warming up, whereas all of the Grade 10 students improved
- some of the Grade 6 students jumped further than students four years older than them, both before and after warming up
- mostly the older students jumped further than the younger students. It would be a mistake to assume that this is a causal relationship, though. It might not be the case that being older makes you jump further, but instead it could be that older children are taller and that being taller helps you jump further.

3 An easy type of analysis to carry out is to find the mean of the jumps (ignoring the first-jump data for the two students in Grade 10 who don't have data for their second jump).

Table 9.4

Grade 6 mean		Grade 10 mean	
Before	After	Before	After
1.36	1.42	1.59	1.87

This shows us that on average both classes improved after the warm-up and that the Grade 10 students improved by 28 cm on average, which is more than the 6 cm improvement in the Grade 6 students' jumps.

→

Here are scatter graphs of the two sets of data:

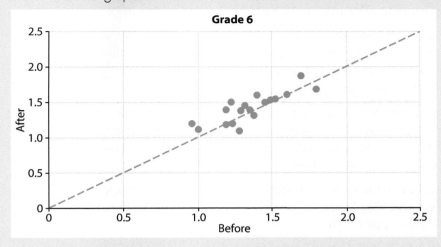

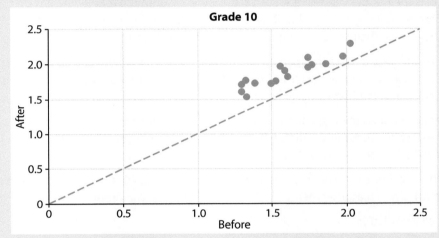

The lines are not lines of best fit. These show where the before and after jumps are exactly the same. Points above this line represent pupils whose second jump was better than their first, while points below the line show pupils whose first jump was better.

This helps us to see that some of the Grade 6 students did not improve after the warm-up, whereas all of the Grade 10 students improved.

Because more of the Grade 10 data is closer to the top right-hand corner of the graph this shows that Grade 10 students tended to jump further than those in Grade 6.

The data tells us that these Grade 10 students found the warm-up to be much more useful than the Grade 6 students did. We can make some guesses as to why, but we can't tell for certain.

Maybe the Grade 10 lesson was early in the day and the Grade 6 lesson was in the afternoon. Perhaps the Grade 6 lesson was immediately after a break, so the students might have been running around and have been a little warmed up already. There might be lots of other reasons for this difference too.

9.2 Working backwards: data

Sometimes we will have some raw data and will need to summarise and analyse it.

On other occasions we might have some data that has already been summarised in some way. This might make it easier to analyse (as in the example and activity above) or might make it more difficult. Sometimes we can reconstruct some of the original data from the summary we have been given.

If we know that the mean height of a group of students is 155 cm, we know that 155 cm is somewhere in the middle of the heights. This single piece of information might be useful if we want to compare this group to another group, but it doesn't tell us how many people there are, whether the heights are all close together, how tall the smallest person is, and so on.

If we also know that there are 10 people in the group then we now know that the total of all of their heights is 1 550 cm (which is 15.5 m), because to work out the mean we add up the numbers and divide by how many there are.

The median is the middle value of a set of data. If we know that the median height of the group is 158 cm then that tells us that if we put everyone in order of their heights then the height in the middle (halfway between the height of person 5 and person 6) will be 158 cm.

The mode is the piece of data that occurs most. If the mode of the heights is 160 cm then we know that at least two people have this height and that there are more people with a height of 1.6 m than there are with any other height.

The difference between the biggest and smallest pieces of data is called the range. If the range of the data is 28 cm then we know that the difference between the heights of the shortest and the tallest people is 28 cm.

We are going to explore whether it is possible for a set of five positive whole numbers to have the numbers 4, 5 and 6 as their mean, median and mode (in some order or other).

1   First of all we will try:

- mean = 4
- median = 5
- mode = 6

There are five numbers, so it might be useful for us to draw out five lines or five boxes:

_ _ _ _ _

What does each piece of summary data tell us? The mean of the five numbers is four, so their total is 20. The median is five, so the middle number is five. The mode is six, so the number six appears the most.

We will assume that the numbers are in increasing order and will put in the median: _ _ 5 _ _

The number 6 appears the most, so there must be two of them and they have to appear to the right of the 5: _ _ 5 6 6

We have used the median and the mode (but know that the first two numbers must be different from each other and cannot be 5 either). So far these add up to 17. The mean tells us they add up to 20, so the first two numbers are one and two.

Here is the full answer: 1 2 5 6 6

2   What happens if we change the order of the original statements?

- mean = 5
- median = 4
- mode = 6

This time we know, from the median and the mode: _ _ 4 6 6

The total so far is 16 and the mean tells us that this time the total must be 25. The first two numbers need to add up to nine, but this isn't possible because they both have to be smaller than four.

That means it is not possible to have a set of five integers with these summary figures.

3 Let's make another change:

- mean = 6
- median = 5
- mode = 4

The median and the mode give us: 4 4 5 _ _

The total (from the mean) is 30. The final two numbers need to add up to 17 and must both be bigger than five (to ensure the mode will be four).

This time there are three possible answers:

4 4 5 6 11

4 4 5 7 10

4 4 5 8 9

ACTIVITY 9.1

Which of the following sets of summary data could be genuine?

Which of them could describe more than one set of data?

The numbers are always whole numbers greater than zero and there are five of them each time.

1 mean = 4, median = 5, range = 6

2 mean = 4, mode = 5, range = 6

3 median = 4, mode = 5, range = 6

4 mode = 4, median = 5, range = 6

5 median = 4, mean = 5, range = 6

6 range = 4, median = 5, mean = 6

A shampoo advert claims that 85% of people said that it made their hair look shinier. In the small print of the advert it says that 120 people were asked.

Is it possible for this to be true? It is, because $\frac{102}{120}$ = 85%, so 102 people said their hair looked shinier, while 18 said it didn't.

If we are told 43% of people liked their shampoo, could five people have been asked?

$\frac{1}{5}$ = 20%, $\frac{2}{5}$ = 40%, $\frac{3}{5}$ = 60%, so it isn't possible to get to 43%.

Could six people have been asked?

$\frac{2}{6}$ = 33%, $\frac{3}{6}$ = 50%, so we can't get 43%

(**Note:** throughout this chapter numbers have been rounded to the nearest whole number where appropriate.)

What about seven people?

$\frac{2}{7}$ = 29%, $\frac{3}{7}$ = 43%. It is therefore possible that only seven people were asked. There are lots of other possibilities (such as multiples of 7), but 7 is the smallest number of people that could have been asked.

83

ACTIVITY 9.2

1   What is the smallest number of people who could have been asked, if the percentage who liked the shampoo was each of the following?

   a 75%   **c** 22%   **e** 83%

   b 90%   **d** 15%   **f** 29%

2   $\frac{17}{99}$ = 17% (when rounded to the nearest whole number). $\frac{97}{99}$ = 98%. What is the only whole number percentage that cannot appear if 99 people were asked if they liked the shampoo?

ACTIVITY 9.3

Here are two graphs from the Office for National Statistics about changes to the ways different types of transport are used in Great Britain.

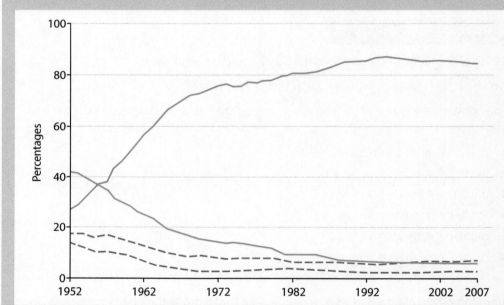

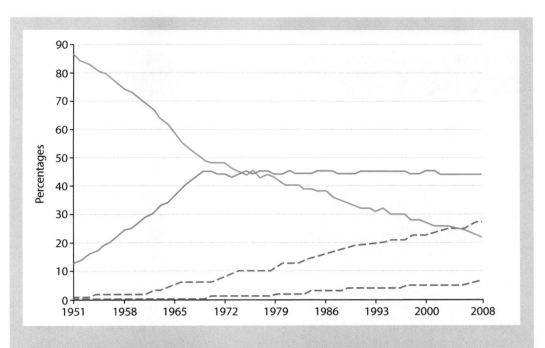

One of these graphs had the title 'Households with regular use of a car', and the four lines were labelled (in some order):

- 3 or more cars
- 1 car
- 2 cars
- 0 car

The other was titled 'Passenger transport: by mode' and the four lines were (in some order):

- Bus and coach
- Car and van
- Rail
- Other

Is it possible to work out which title goes with which graph and to label the lines correctly?

9.3 Working backwards: numbers

Sometimes we will have some numerical problems to solve and will be given clues that will enable us to do this.

These might involve contexts that are considered to be 'real' ones (such as working out a passcode from numerical clues) or might involve a scenario that is explained to you. You won't necessarily be familiar with the background to the scenarios or be interested in them, but that shouldn't be an issue.

EXAMPLE ACTIVITY 9.3

In a soccer tournament four clubs play each other once each. This means there are six matches altogether. The winner of each match gets three points, the loser gets no points and if it is a draw then both teams get one point. A league table is created showing the number of points each club amassed, the number of wins, draws and losses and the number of goals they scored and conceded.

Table 9.5

Team	Won	Drawn	Lost	Goals scored	Goals conceded	Points
Dynamo	3	0	0	4	1	9
Mustang	1	1	1	5	1	4
Galaxy	1	1	1	1	1	4
Clash	0	0	3	1	8	0

Even if you are not a soccer fan you can still read the table. But is it also possible to work out the score and the result of every match?

Commentary

A first glance shows us that Dynamo won all of their games and Clash lost all of theirs. Mustang and Galaxy both had one victory (they must have beaten Clash) and one loss (they must have lost to Dynamo); they also are the only teams to have a drawn match, so they must have drawn when they played each other. The matches and the results therefore are:

Dynamo beat Mustang

Dynamo beat Galaxy

Dynamo beat Clash

Mustang drew with Galaxy

Mustang beat Clash

Galaxy beat Clash

Now let's look at Dynamo's goals. They scored four goals and conceded one while winning three matches, so their results must have been 1–0, 1–0, 2–1 (with their goals appearing first).

Galaxy scored one goal and conceded one goal while winning one game, losing another and drawing a third. The only possible way for them to have done that is for the scores to be 1–0, 0–1, 0–0.

Let's update the list of matches:

Dynamo beat Mustang (1–0 or 2–1)

Dynamo 1–0 Galaxy

Dynamo beat Clash (1–0 or 2–1)

Mustang 0–0 Galaxy

Mustang beat Clash

Galaxy 1–0 Clash

Mustang scored five goals and conceded one and because their draw against Galaxy didn't use any of these goals we know that they must have lost 1–0. This means they won 5–0.

We can therefore fill in the rest of the results.

Dynamo 1–0 Mustang

Dynamo 1–0 Galaxy

Dynamo 2–1 Clash

Mustang 0–0 Galaxy

Mustang 5–0 Clash

Galaxy 1–0 Clash

Finally, we can check that the table makes sense by looking at Clash and their goals (this is the only part of the table we haven't yet used). According to our results Clash lost all three games, scoring one goal and conceding eight.

ACTIVITY 9.4

Here are two similar tasks:

1 Using all of the digits 1, 2, 3, 4 and 5 once each, make a one-digit number that is divisible by one, then put a digit on the end to make it into a two-digit number that is divisible by two, then put another digit on the end to make it into a three-digit number that is divisible by three, then put another digit on the end to make it into a four-digit number that is divisible by four. When the final digit is put on the end it should make a five-digit number that is divisible by five.

2 Use all of the digits 1, 2, 3, 4, 5 and 6 to make a similar set of numbers, where the final six-digit number is also divisible by six.

One of these questions can be answered and the other one cannot. Explain!

ACTIVITY 9.5

In elementary school, children learn their multiplication tables. They often recite them in order ('1 times 5 is 5, 2 times 5 is 10', and so on) but are then tested on them with the tables all mixed up.

Here are the first nine statements from one of the tables. Digits have been replaced with letters and the order has been mixed up. Work out which letter stands for each number.

$Z \times W = FG$
$G \times W = M$
$R \times W = GM$
$W \times W = FL$
$L \times W = GW$
$M \times W = ZG$
$F \times W = W$
$E \times W = ZL$
$Y \times W = GJ$

Summary

This chapter explored how data from different sources can be combined in the solution of a problem and how, having been given the summary of some data, information about the original scenario can be deduced.

You should now be able to:

■ solve more complicated problems
■ combine information from different sources to help you solve problems
■ work out information about the original scenario from a summary you have been given.

End-of-chapter questions

1 Morse code is a way of turning messages into collections of dots and dashes. I am learning how to transmit Morse, so I am still very slow. The table below shows the amount of time it takes me to tap out each letter. In the right-hand columns letters are shown, along with the number of times they usually occur in 1,000 letters of written English.

Table 9.6

	Morse Code	Time (seconds)
A	● —	0.5
B	— ● ● ●	0.9
C	— ● — ●	1.1
D	— ● ●	0.7
E	●	0.1
F	● ● — ●	0.9
G	— — ●	0.9
H	● ● ● ●	0.7
I	● ●	0.3
J	● — — —	1.3
K	— ● —	0.9
L	● — ● ●	0.9
M	— —	0.7
N	— ●	0.5
O	— — —	1.1
P	● — — ●	1.1
Q	— — ● —	1.3
R	● — ●	0.7
S	● ● ●	0.5
T	—	0.3
U	● ● —	0.7
V	● ● ● —	0.9
W	● — —	0.9
X	— ● ● —	1.1
Y	— ● — —	1.3
Z	— — ● ●	1.1

Letter	Frequency
E	127
T	90
A	81
O	75
I	69
N	67
S	63
H	61
R	60
D	43
L	40
C	28
U	28
M	24
W	24
F	22
G	20
Y	20
P	19
B	15
V	10
K	8
J	2
X	2
Q	1
Z	1

a Which letters have been given a set of Morse code symbols that means messages will take too long to send?

b Why might this have happened?

2 In a class the students are divided into groups. On an English exam the mean score for three of the groups was:

Group A – mean score 18/20

Group B – mean score 15/20

Group C – mean score 14.5/20

For each of the following statements write down: True / False / Can't tell. Explain your answers, providing examples and calculations where necessary.

a At least one student in Group B got more than 15 marks.

b At least one student in Group B got 15 marks or more.

c There are more students in Group A than in Group B.

d The best score in the class was achieved by a member of Group A.

e All of the students in Group A did better than all of the students in Group B.

f If exactly two of the four students in Group A got full marks then the lowest possible score in Group A was 13.

g If there are four students in Group B then it was possible that someone scored zero marks.

h If there are four students in Group C then it is possible that the scores were consecutive numbers.

i If there are four students in Group B then it is possible that the scores were consecutive numbers.

j If there are five students in Group C then it is possible that the scores were consecutive numbers.

3 Emily and Helen have gone travelling and will stay in a different hostel each night for five nights. Each hostel costs a whole number of dollars.

- Monday's hostel cost 20% more than Tuesday's.
- On Tuesday they paid $\frac{3}{4}$ as much as they did on Thursday.
- The cheapest night was $14.
- Wednesday's accommodation cost $10 more than Thursday's.
- Tuesday's hostel was half the price of Wednesday's.

Did they spend more or less than $100 on accommodation?

4 In a school there can be at most 30 children in a class. There are 25 lessons in a week and each teacher can teach up to 22 lessons. There are 1 327 children in the school. What is the smallest number of teachers that are needed?

5 A recipe for 12 cupcakes requires:

200 g flour

4 eggs

150 g sugar

You have got 10 eggs, 365 g sugar and 600 g flour. How many cupcakes can you make?

6 An online retailer has the following delivery charges per item.

- $8 for next-day delivery.
- $5 for three-day delivery.

a If you pay $28, how many items did you order?

b If you pay $39, how many items did you order?

Exam-style questions

1 **a** A passcode is made up of five digits. Work it out from the following information.

- The fourth digit is three times the second digit.
- The third digit is six times the fifth digit.
- All the digits are different.
- The first digit is one less than the fourth digit.

  b Another passcode is also made up of five digits. Work it out from the following clues.

- The product of the first and second digits is equal to the product of the fourth and fifth digits.
- The digits in positions one and five are both multiples of three.
- The digits are all different.
- The largest digit is seven.
- Two of the digits are the same as their position number.

2 Five teams play in a hockey tournament. Each team plays every other team once.
So far:

- Team A has played four games
- Team B has played three games
- Team C has played four games
- Team D has played two games
- Team E has played three games.

  a Which teams still need to play each other?

  b How many matches will there be altogether?

3 In a football league, teams get three points for a win, one point for a draw and zero points for a loss.

  a One of the teams has 23 points. What is the smallest number of games they could have played?

  b Another team has 20 points. They have won, drawn and lost the same number of games. How many games have they played?

  c Another team has 10 points. They have won more games than they have drawn. How many games have they drawn?

Chapter 10
Identifying features of a model

Learning objectives

This chapter considers the different types of features that can affect how a model is created and how a problem is represented. It will also address how a model can be adjusted to take particular features into account.

10.1 Different types of representation

A common form of representation is a graph. If information has been presented in this way then we need to know what the x-axis and the y-axis stand for, what the gradient of the line means, whether the points where the line meets one of the axes has meaning and what happens when two lines cross.

EXAMPLE ACTIVITY 10.1

This graph shows two journeys carried out by remote control cars. One car is red and the other is blue. The horizontal axis shows time elapsed and the vertical axis shows the distance away from a particular place. The cars travel in a straight line.

What can you tell about the journeys of the two cars?

What do the gradients of the two lines tell us?

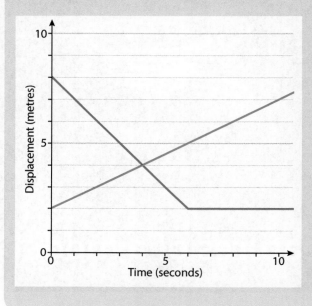

Commentary

The red line has a gradient of $\frac{1}{2}$. This means that for each second that elapses the red car's distance away from the initial point increases by $\frac{1}{2}$ a metre and the speed is therefore $\frac{1}{2}$ metre per second. When the time is zero seconds the red line is at the two metre point, indicating that it starts by being two metres away from the place where the measurements are being carried out. The equation for this graph is $s = \frac{1}{2}t + 2$ (where the displacement is shown using the letter s and the time using t).

The blue line has the equation $s = -t + 8$. The gradient is -1, and this tells us the blue car's speed is 1m/s but in the opposite direction from the red one. The '+8' shows that it starts eight metres away from the measuring point. After six seconds the blue car stops and remains two metres away from the measuring point. On the graph the blue line is horizontal, which has a gradient of zero, and this makes sense because the speed is zero.

After four seconds the two cars are both the same distance away from the measuring point and this is shown by the two lines crossing on the graph.

ACTIVITY 10.1

What do the graph and images tell us about trends in the use of smartphones in the USA?

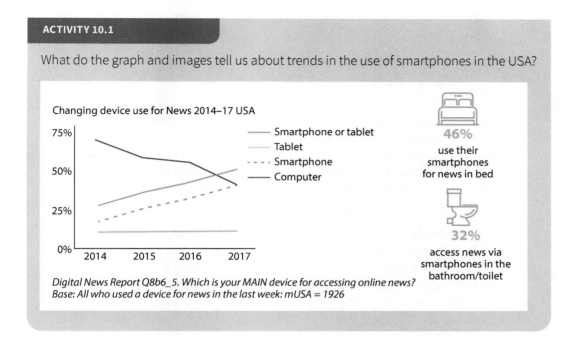

Digital News Report Q8b6_5. Which is your MAIN device for accessing online news?
Base: All who used a device for news in the last week: mUSA = 1926

10.2 Features of a model: non-standing representations

Some graphical representations of information are not the usual sort of graphs that you might have studied in school. These are sometimes referred to as 'infographics' and may combine different types of information in a way that is easy to understand and which may also be rather beautiful.

EXAMPLE ACTIVITY 10.2

A key part of driving safely is knowing how much of a gap to leave between you and the vehicle in front of you. The distance you need to leave is known as the 'stopping distance' and this is shown in the following diagram.

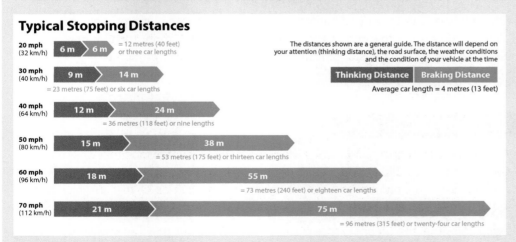

1 Can you work out what each part of the diagram tells us?

2 What is the stopping distance at 35 mph?

Commentary

The left hand side gives the speed the driver is travelling at, in mph and in km/h. The stopping distance is then shown as a type of bar chart, with the bars split into two sections.

The blue part is known as the 'thinking distance'. This is the distance the car travels in the time it takes for the driver to react to what has happened on the road and to realise that they need to push their foot down on the brake pedal. This reaction time is the same at every speed but the car travels further when it is going faster. The number of metres this takes is written on the blue part and we can see from the numbers and from the lengths of the blue bars that it increases by the same amount each time.

The red part is the 'braking distance'. This is the distance the car travels after the brake pedal has been pressed, while the brakes are slowing the car down. Again, the numbers of metres are shown on the red bar, but this time they don't increase in a linear way. At higher speeds the braking distance is much greater. For example, when we double the speed the thinking distance doubles but the braking distance is almost multiplied by four.

Table 10.1

Speed	Thinking distance	Braking distance
30 mph	9 metres	14 metres
60 mph	18 metres	55 metres

Next the total stopping distance is given in metres, in feet and in a number of car-lengths. The last of these is perhaps easier to visualise.

It is worth bearing in mind that these are approximate stopping distances and assume the road is dry, the car is small and well maintained and the driver is alert and not unwell. A larger, heavier car being driven at night in the rain may well need a much longer stopping distance. In these non-ideal conditions the model that is used for stopping distances in this diagram might turn out to be wrong by a significant amount.

This might lead us to believe that the graphic is actually rather approximate, so it would be fine for us to estimate the stopping distance at 35 mph, and that may be a sensible thing to do. The stopping distance at 35 mph is therefore something between 75 feet and 120 feet.

ACTIVITY 10.2

A European newspaper featured an article about the amount of food that was sold just before a national holiday, and tried to put the big numbers it used in context by telling its readers that the number of carrots that were purchased was 3.5 million which was 'enough to stretch around the world 11 times'.

If you know that the circumference of the Earth is 40 000 km, how can you work out that the author of the article made a mistake?

ACTIVITY 10.3

This is a quick pencil-and-paper game for two players.

Write down the numbers from one to nine.

Player 1 circles a number using a pen. Player 2 then chooses any number that hasn't been circled and puts a circle around it, using a pencil. Player 1 can then choose any unused number and circles that with their pen.

The winner is the first player who circles three numbers that add up to 15.

For example, if you have circled 2, 4, 8, 9 you would win because 2 + 4 + 9 = 15.

If you have 2, 3, 4, 6 you don't win because you don't have *three* numbers that add up to 15.

Play the game a few times against someone else. Can you find a strategy to help you win?

10.3 Adjusting a model

In many scenarios we will not have a definitive set of data or rules to follow and will need to make some decisions about how to create an appropriate model. Sometimes we will need to decide between a very simple model and one that is more complicated. There are pros and cons to both types of model. A simple model is likely to be easier to set up and to use but may turn out to be overly simplistic and could give results that are inaccurate. A more complicated model may be more accurate but will also be more difficult to use.

One way to deal with this sort of situation is to start with a simple model and to adjust it.

EXAMPLE ACTIVITY 10.3

Some printers use cartridges (boxes of ink that cannot be refilled and which are slotted into the machine), while other types of printer can easily be refilled using bottles of ink.

The cheapest printer in a local computer store costs $30. It requires two ink cartridges, one for black ink, which prints about 190 pages, and one for colour, which prints about 165 pages. The cartridges are sold for $11 (black ink) and $15 (colour), or you can buy both together for a total of $24.

The cheapest printer that can be refilled using bottles of ink costs $180. It uses four colours of ink (black, magenta, yellow and cyan), each of which costs $10. The four bottles will, in total, print about 6 500 pages.

1 Which printer is better value?

2 Which printer would you buy? Give reasons and calculations to support your decision.

Commentary
The easiest way to compare the printers is to imagine printing the same number of pages on each one.

Printer 1 (cheapest printer)
We would pay $24 for the pair of cartridges. Suppose we use up both cartridges at the same time. $24 gets us 190 pages of black and 165 pages of colour printing, a total of 355 pages.

Printer 2 can print 6,500 pages, which is about 18 × 355. To print 6 500 pages on Printer 1, we need 18 × $24 for the cartridges, plus $30 to buy the printer. This is a total of $462 for 6 500 pages.

Printer 2 (cheapest printer that uses ink bottles)
The ink costs $40 for the 4 bottles and the printer itself costs $180. That is a total of $220 to print 6,500 pages.

Comparison
The next 6,500 pages that are printed will cost $432 using Printer 1 and only $40 using Printer 2.

Another benefit of Printer 2 is that it is possible to refill each ink colour separately, so if you use lots of yellow you only need to refill that colour. With Printer 1 you have to replace the colour cartridge as soon as one colour runs out, even if the other colours could last longer.

We might need to adjust this model. Maybe you only want to print in black ink and won't ever need colour: that would make Printer 1 cheaper, because the black cartridge prints 190 pages, so we would need 34 of them to print 6 500 pages, and these cartridges are cheaper ($11 each). The black cartridges will cost $374 for 6 500 pages, which is still more expensive than Printer 2.

ACTIVITY 10.4

Under what circumstances might someone buy Printer 1, the cheapest printer in the computer store? After all, it works out more expensive if you print 6 500 copies.

Perhaps a printer has a particular lifespan? If Printer 2 would only print 6 000 pages before it wore out and needed to be replaced, then Printer 1 would be cheaper. If this were the case, how many pages of printing would make both printers (including paying for ink) cost the same amount?

ACTIVITY 10.5

Combining your skills

This past Cambridge International A Level question will give you practice in combining the problem-solving skills you have developed in Chapters 1 – 10 in order to tackle more challenging questions.

There are five identical car parks at the Nambassa festival, each taking hundreds of cars, but there is only one exit, where each car has to stop to hand in a badge. Since everyone tries to leave at the same time there are queues.

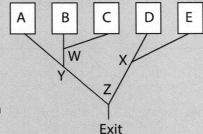

At each junction cars will merge alternately: one from one branch and then one from the other. Assume that car parks all start with the same number of cars, and ignore the small number of cars on the tracks. It takes one hour for everyone to leave.

a **i** The first car to exit came from car park C and the second from car park D. From which car parks did the next seven cars come from? List them in order.

    ii Which three car parks empty long before the others?

b Peter wanted to rearrange the tracks so that the total time to clear all the car parks is reduced. Explain why this will not be possible.

Terry is concerned that people using some car parks will complain that some other car parks emptied long before theirs did. To avoid this, he is considering arranging for cars to merge two to one, instead of alternately, at some of the junctions. By doing this he hopes to make the earliest emptying of any car park as late as possible.

c Determine which junction(s) should be two to one, and which branch is which, to achieve Terry's aim. Explain your reasoning for junction Z.

Lorraine suggested that it might be better if the track from C were moved over to join the one from D. Peter pointed out that, although she was not sure whether he meant before or after junction X, it would not make any difference because it would simply be equivalent to relabelling the car parks.

d **i** Draw a different layout for the tracks, with no more than two tracks merging at any junction, which is not equivalent to relabelling the car parks.

    ii How long would it take before one of the car parks becomes empty in your new layout, if cars merge alternately at all junctions?

Cambridge International AS & A Level Thinking Skills 9694 Paper 31 Q2 June 2016

Summary

This chapter examined how we can use different representations to help us to understand and improve on a model and how we can identify particular features of the model from those different representations.

It also helped to explore how a model can be made more accurate but at the risk of increasing the complexity.

End-of-chapter questions

1 On a square grid (like the 3 × 3 grid shown below), start in the top right-hand corner and go diagonally across the squares to make a path.

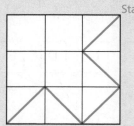 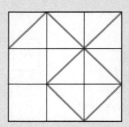

Start

The first path has length five. The second path is not allowed because it joins back up to itself.

   a What is the longest path that can be made on a 3 × 3 grid?

   b What is the longest path that can be made on a 4 × 4 grid?

2 A tin of 'barista-style coffee' costs $5 and will make 40 cups of coffee. In a coffee shop a black coffee is $1.50.

   a How much will I save by buying a tin of coffee and making my own?

   b Why might I still want to buy a cup of coffee from the coffee shop?

Exam-style questions

1 I have four discs that have numbers on each side. They look like this:

   I drop the discs on the table and add up the numbers.

   a What is the smallest total I could get?

   b What is the biggest total I could get?

   c Why do you always get an even number?

2 Design three discs (as in question 1) using six different numbers between 10 and 20 so the total you get will always be an odd number.

3 The price of an aeroplane ticket changes, depending on how full the flight is and how close it is to the departure day. One airline prices its tickets as follows:

   A ticket for today costs $356. For each day in the future the price of the ticket is half way between yesterday's price and $100. This stops when the price is $101 – after that all prices are $101.

   a What will be the price of a ticket to travel in two days' time?

   b When will a ticket cost $108?

4 The price of a cup of coffee in a shop (before sales tax has been added) is $2.10.

Here is the breakdown of the cost:

Table 10.2

Profit	35¢
Rent	75¢
Wages	65¢
Cup/lid/etc	15¢
Coffee beans	10¢
Milk	10¢

What should the cost of a cup of coffee be if the following changes happen?

a the rent on the shop increases by 20%

b wages rise by 10%

c the profit on each cup is doubled.

The farmers who grow the coffee get 20% of the cost of the coffee beans (the rest pays for transport, storage, etc).

d If the farmers' payments are doubled, what is the new cost of the cup of coffee?

5 A gym has different membership options:

$600 per year or $60 per month. Alternatively, you can pay $11.50 per visit.

a If I go to the gym once a week, what is the cheapest membership type for me?

b If I go to the gym eight times in a month, how much will monthly membership save me compared to paying per visit?

c If I go to the gym seven times each month, how much will annual membership save me compared to paying per visit?

6 In a supermarket there is a coupon on each tin of baked beans that will give you 15¢ off the next tin you buy. A single tin of beans usually costs 80¢. If I buy a tin of beans, tear off the coupon, go and use it to buy another tin, tear off that coupon, etc., how many tins could I buy with $10?

Chapter 11
Necessary and sufficient conditions

Learning objectives

This chapter introduces the concepts of necessity and sufficiency, and methods for identifying whether statements are necessary or sufficient.

11.1 Necessary and sufficient

Do you have enough information to answer a question? Do you have to have that particular piece of information? These are two key ideas when solving problems, and it is important to use the correct vocabulary when answering questions.

If you have enough information then what you have is **sufficient**.

If a piece of information is required then it is **necessary**. In this case there may be more pieces of information that are also necessary.

EXAMPLE ACTIVITY 11.1

I am thinking of a particular four-sided shape. How can I tell whether the shape is a rectangle?

If you ask a student this question they might say the following things:

1 It must have four angles.
2 The opposite sides must be parallel.
3 The opposite sides must be the same length.
4 The diagonals must be the same length.
5 The angles must be right angles.
6 The diagonals must cut each other in half.
7 It must have two lines of reflection.
8 It must have two longer sides and two shorter sides.

Which statements are true and which are false?

Commentary

Some people are surprised to hear that statement 8 is false, but that is the case. It doesn't matter whether there are two longer sides and two shorter sides or whether they are all the same length, even though when they are the same length we could also call the shape a square.

In that case we might also question the truthfulness of statement 7. All rectangles have *at least* two lines of symmetry, but if it is a square (which means it is still a rectangle) then it will have two extra lines of symmetry.

All of the other statements are true. This means they are *necessary* conditions for a four-sided shape to be a rectangle. In other words, in every rectangle statements 1 to 6 are true.

Let's look at a few of these in greater detail. If we know that statement 1 is true then that isn't very interesting or helpful. We know that a four-sided shape has four angles and the shape doesn't have to be a rectangle.

If, as statement 2 suggests, we know that the opposite sides of a four-sided shape are parallel then the shape must be a parallelogram. It might be a rectangle, it might be a rhombus and it might be a square but we don't know for certain which of these it is.

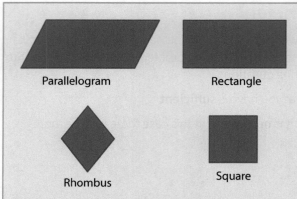

Parallelogram

Rectangle

Rhombus

Square

Statement 5 is different. If the four-sided shape has four right angles then it must be a rectangle (it could be a square, but this is still a type of rectangle). This means that statement 5 is a *sufficient* condition for a four-sided shape to be a rectangle. If we know that statement 5 is true then the shape must be a rectangle.

What about the other statements? Are they necessary or sufficient conditions?

On their own, statements 3, 4 and 6 are all necessary conditions. For example (for statement 3), a rhombus has opposite sides that are the same length, but this doesn't have to be a rectangle. If we know it is a rectangle then the opposite sides are certainly the same length. It is a necessary condition.

If we know that both of statements 4 and 6 are true then the four-sided shape must be a rectangle. If a four-sided shape has diagonals that are the same length and which cut each other in half then it has to be a rectangle. The previous sentence is therefore a sufficient condition.

ACTIVITY 11.1

Write down some statements about isosceles triangles (where two of the sides of the triangle are the same length). Which ones are necessary conditions and which are sufficient conditions?

11.2 'All'

Sometimes, when we use the word 'all' it can refer to necessary or sufficient conditions.

For example, take the sentence 'all cats are animals'. Being a cat is a sufficient condition for being an animal. If you tell me a particular thing is a cat then I know it is an animal. On the other hand, being an animal is a necessary condition for being a cat.

Two things arise from this statement. Firstly, 'all cats are animals' is not the same as 'all animals are cats'. It is entirely possible for an animal to be a dog, or a mouse and not to be a cat. Secondly, while being a cat is a sufficient condition for being an animal, it is not a necessary condition. There are other things that aren't cats that are also animals.

EXAMPLE ACTIVITY 11.2

A famous example of a task that links with this idea is the *Watson Selection Task*.

Peter Watson was a psychologist and developed this in 1966.

There are four cards, all of which have a number on one side and a colour on the other side. They are placed on the table like this:

Which cards do you need to turn over to check whether the following statement is true?

'If there is an even number on one side of the card then the other side is red.'

Spend a minute thinking about this.

Commentary

Most people answer that you need to turn over the 8 card and the red card. Can you see why this is incorrect?

Let's go through each card in turn:

- '3' isn't an even number, so we don't care what is on the other side. There is no need to turn this one over.

- '8' is an even number, so if the statement is true we need to check that there is red on the back of the card.

- The red card is more difficult. We don't need to turn it over, because having an odd number on the back of this one isn't a problem, in the same way that having red on the back of the 3 is fine too.

- We do need to turn the brown card over. If there is an even number on the back then the statement is false, so we need to check this.

It might help to rephrase the original statement using 'all'.

'If there is an even number on one side of the card then the other side is red' would then become 'all cards with an even number on one side are red on the other side'.

In the same way that there are animals who are not cats, there might be cards with red on one side that do not have an even number on the back.

ACTIVITY 11.2

We can further link the above idea with necessary and sufficient conditions. If we have cards with the fronts and backs of each card as shown here, which of the below statements are true?

front:

| 1 | 2 | 3 | 4 | 5 | 6 |

back:

| A | C | A | A | A | B |

1   Having B on one side is necessary and sufficient for having 6 on the other side.
2   Having A on one side is a necessary condition for having an odd number on the other side.
3   Having A on one side is a sufficient condition for having an odd number on the other side.
4   Having an odd number on one side is a necessary condition for having A on the other side.
5   Having an odd number on one side is a sufficient condition for having A on the other side.
6   Having C on one side is necessary for having an even number on the other side.
7   Having C on one side is sufficient for having an even number on the other side.

11.3 Necessity, sufficiency and problem solving

We can use the idea that information can be necessary or sufficient to help us to solve other problems.

EXAMPLE ACTIVITY 11.3

I am a runner. If you want to work out how long a particular run took me, you could ask me outright! Alternatively, if I tell you the distance I ran and the speed I ran it at then you could work out how long it took me.

1   Are these pieces of information necessary or sufficient for answering the question?
2   Instead of this I could have told you the rate at which I ran (for example: four and a half minutes per km). What other piece of information do you need to be able to work out how long the run took me?

Commentary

In the first scenario the distance is a necessary piece of information and the speed is a necessary piece of information. Taken together they are sufficient for working out the time the run took.

In the second scenario the rate is a necessary piece of information. We also need the distance.

ACTIVITY 11.3

In some countries you must pass a test to get a full driving licence that will allow you to drive a car. You also, in many countries, have to be 16 or older.

If you live in a country where drivers have to pass a test and have to be aged 16 or older, which of the following statements are necessary if you want to drive a car?

Statement 1: Have a full driving licence
Statement 2: Own a car
Statement 3: Pass a driving test
Statement 4: Be 16 years old or older

ACTIVITY 11.4

Do each of the following sentences involve necessary or sufficient conditions?

a In order for your motorbike to work you need to put fuel in it.

b To pass your A level you have to turn up to the exam.

c To get a good mark you must hand in your homework.

d For you to be able to buy a chocolate bar the shop must be open.

e Strawberries need water to grow.

f You have to be fit if you want to run a marathon.

ACTIVITY 11.5

Combining your skills

This question will give you practice in combining the problem-solving skills you have developed in Chapters 1–11 in order to tackle more challenging questions.

Ennid, Kate, Marcie and Parminder are friends who are trying to find a house to rent together.

They each need a bedroom and they want a shared kitchen and living room. They could pay up to $1000 a month in total, but want to pay less if they can. They would prefer to live within 10 km of the city centre.

Kate is a wheelchair user so she needs her bedroom and a shower room to be on the ground floor. Kate would also like to be able to park her car off the road. Parminder wants storage for her bike.

The friends have drawn up a list of the houses they have seen so far. Which house would be most suitable for them?

$\longrightarrow$

105

Table 11.1

	Rent	Bedrooms	Kitchen	Living room	Bathroom	Distance from city centre	Other
Wisteria Cottage	$1000/month	4	Yes	Yes	On first floor	10 km	Park off road
18 Grove Road	$950/month	3 plus suitable room on ground floor	Yes	Yes	On first floor	6 km	Small garage and off-road parking
77 Mead Close	$235/week	3 plus suitable room on ground floor	Yes	Yes	On first floor and shower room on ground floor	5 km	Shed storage
21 West Avenue	$1100/month	4	Yes	Yes	On first floor	9 km	Lift to first floor
91 North Boulevard	$950/month	3 plus suitable room on ground floor	Yes	Yes	On first floor and shower room on ground floor	11 km	Large garage
The Lawns	$1200/month	3 plus suitable room on ground floor	Yes	Yes	On first floor and shower room on ground floor	4 km	Garage and store
3 The Lea	$1250/month including utilities	4 plus suitable room on ground floor	Yes	Yes	On first floor	3 km	Off-road parking
38 Station Street	$975/month	3 plus suitable room on ground floor	Yes	Yes	On first floor	1 km	Park on road. Shed storage

Summary

Having worked through this chapter you should now:

- understand the concepts of necessity and sufficiency
- be able to identify whether particular statements are necessary or sufficient
- understand and be able to use appropriate vocabulary when answering questions.

End-of-chapter questions

1 In the year 2016, 470 billion plastic bottles were sold across the world. For each of the following questions either answer them or state that they will require further information:

   a How many bottles were sold each minute?

   b How many bottles were sold per person?

   c How many water bottles were sold in the year?

   d How many bottles will be sold in 2026?

   e How many bottles were sold per second on average?

   f The population of Switzerland is 0.11% of the population of the world. How many bottles were sold in Switzerland?

2 A friend of mine has joined the million miles club. This means he has flown over one million miles with a particular airline. He always flies from London to Los Angeles and back again. Is this information necessary and/or sufficient for us to work out how many flights he has taken?

3 Adele's album '25' was released near the end of 2015. In the USA the album sold 8 million copies in 2015 which, according to a news article, was 130 copies per minute.

   a What date was the album released?

   b We do not have enough information to work out how many copies the album sold in 2016. Explain why.

4 In the UK car owners have to pay an annual tax to use their car on the road (this varies according to the size of the car and its level of pollution). On average motorists pay £166 per year. I want to work out how much this works out to be per mile. What information do I need to enable me to do this?

5 I have got 12 coins that are all either 1¢, 5¢ or 10¢. I have at least two of each coin. There are more 1¢ coins than 5¢ coins, and more 5¢ coins than 10¢ coins.

   At the moment you can't work out how much money I have got. Which of the following pieces of information is sufficient (along with the things you already know) for you to work out how much money I have?

   - There are four 4¢ coins.
   - There are three of one of the types of coin.
   - The 5¢ coins are, altogether, worth the same as the 10¢ coins.
   - There is an odd number of two of the coins.

6 There is a bag of red, blue and green counters. I take a handful of the counters. It turns out that I have grabbed 17 counters, that there are more red ones than blue ones and that there are half as many green counters as blue counters. You cannot tell how many of each colour I have got. Which additional piece of information will be sufficient to tell you what I have got?

   - There are at least two of each colour.
   - Fewer than half of the counters are red.
   - The number of red counters is not a multiple of three.

Exam-style question

The Science Fiction book club has monthly meetings between October and May. There are no meetings in December and April.

Each month the meeting is about a different genre. The secretary is organising next year's programme of meetings and has arranged for people to talk on different dates. Unfortunately he has now lost the draft programme, but he still has his notes:

- Robot fiction must come before Space Exploration and after Post-apocalyptic fiction.
- Science Mysteries must be immediately before Scientific Romance.
- Feminist SciFi cannot be meeting 2.
- Post-apocalyptic fiction is meeting 4.

In which month will the meeting genre be Alien Invasion?

Chapter 12
Changing the scenario of a problem

Learning objectives

This chapter explores what types of changes can be made to a problem, what the effects of these changes are likely to be and within what sort of range answers are likely to lie.

12.1 Changing scenarios

A problem usually involves a scenario of some kind. Making changes to this scenario might make very little difference to the way the solution is worked out or the problem is dealt with. For example, if you fill a car up with fuel there is one price at the service station for the type of fuel you use, and it doesn't matter how much you buy. If you put four times as much fuel in your car then you will pay four times as much for it.

On the other hand, sometimes a change in the scenario can lead to bigger differences. If in your local supermarket you can buy a single bottle of water, or you can buy a pack of six identical bottles, it is often significantly cheaper for you to buy the pack of six.

Sometimes it is difficult to know what the effect of a change will be. If a new supermarket opens near to where you live, will the prices in the existing and in the new supermarket be lower because they will be fighting each other for customers? Or is there a minimum point below which it doesn't make economic sense to lower prices further? Or will the two supermarkets sell slightly different products, rendering direct comparisons impossible? Perhaps they will advertise price reductions on certain items to entice shoppers to go there but will then increase other prices to compensate (sometimes supermarkets sell certain products at a loss to encourage shoppers to go there), or maybe they will offer other perks such as free coffee while you shop.

12.2 What types of changes can be made?

Changes can be made to many different parameters, including:

- quantities
- the timescale (to make it longer or shorter)
- prices, including introducing special offers
- tariffs
- the law

as well as other changes.

12.2.1 Changing quantities

This might involve scenarios like buying fuel for your car or bottles of water as mentioned above, but could also apply to other activities with a range of factors to consider.

For example, if an athlete usually runs 5 km but wants to run a marathon (42.2 km), then they will need to approach it in a very different way. They might need to train differently, to run more slowly, to get used to carrying a snack and a water bottle, etc. If they usually run the 5 km race on a running track but the marathon is on a trail (running up and down hills, across fields, etc.) then they might also need to get used to different running shoes.

EXAMPLE ACTIVITY 12.1

Consider the following question:

Abigail runs 100 m in 11 seconds, whereas Ella runs 200 m in 23 seconds. They maintain these speeds for a race of 1 km. Who wins and by how many seconds?

What is the problem with the scenario in this question? Are the numbers in the question realistic?

> **Commentary**
>
> We could easily answer the question (even though this isn't required here). 1 km is 10 × 100 m, so at a constant speed it would take Abigail 10 × 11 seconds to run 1 km. This is 110 seconds, or 1 minute and 50 seconds.
>
> 1 km is 5 × 200 m, so at a constant speed it would take Ella 5 × 23 seconds to run 1 km. This is 115 seconds, or 1 minute and 55 seconds. Abigail therefore wins by 5 seconds.
>
> The problem here is that it isn't realistic for the runners to maintain their speeds over longer distances. Running 100 m in 11 seconds is fast! Maintaining this over a longer distance would be impossible. In fact, the fastest women's 800 m ever (correct up to the middle of 2017) was completed in 1 minute and 53 seconds. It is clearly impossible for Abigail to run 1 000 m in a shorter time than this.

12.2.2 Changing the timescale

This can sometimes involve a direct ratio, for example if you drive twice as long at a constant speed you will go twice as far. But there may be differences even in this simple (and unrealistic) situation. You might, for example, need to stop to buy more fuel, you might need to stop to eat, etc.

12.2.3 Changing prices, including introducing special offers

It is often the case that different people or groups are charged in different ways. For example, in a stationery shop I can buy a pack of marker pens to use on a whiteboard, but schools can buy boxes of 50 marker pens from their suppliers that are far cheaper.

ACTIVITY 12.1

The following table shows the charges for different numbers of cell phones. This is particularly useful where each member of the family has their own phone.

Table 12.1

Monthly cost	1 phone	2 phones	3 phones	4 phones
Company 1	$75	$130	$155	$180
Company 2	$65	$110	$145	$180
Company 3	$65	$125	$145	$165
Company 4	$85	$150	$170	$190

The four companies all have slightly different things included in their plans (for example some have HD video, others have unlimited data), so they are not directly comparable to each other.

a How do the prices change in each of the columns?

b What is the same for all the different payment methods?

12.2.4 Having different tariffs

Why does it cost less for each additional phone?

- If you buy something in bulk it is often cheaper than buying a single item.
- Perhaps it is cheaper for the company because they can issue one bill rather than several separate ones.
- Perhaps competition is lowering prices (when one company makes this offer all of the others have to as well).
- The companies may be looking ahead: when the children in the family become adults they might stay with the same phone company.
- This offer will be used within a family and people of different ages within a family will have different levels of phone use. Some might use lots of data while others text or phone more. Everyone will be on the same tariff, so the company might make money out of some members of the family but lose money on others. As long as they don't lose money overall the company will be happy.

12.2.5 Changing the law

Sometimes changing the law has the effect of changing people's behaviour in ways that are intended by lawmakers. For example, in many countries it is compulsory to wear seat belts if you are in a car. The US National Highway Traffic Safety Administration's research suggests that over 15 000 lives were saved by the wearing of seat belts in the USA in 2007.

Sometimes changes to the law might have unexpected effects. Some people believe that making cycle helmets compulsory results in fewer people choosing to ride a bicycle. There are concerns that the negative effect on health of those who are put off cycling will outweigh the help that cycle helmets might give to those involved in an accident.

12.2.6 Other changes: extrapolation

There are lots of other ways to make changes to a scenario or a problem. A common and important one is extending graphs drawn from the data you have got.

If we have some data that can be shown as a scatter graph or as a time series then we might be able to spot a pattern.

For example, here is a graph of the number of lives saved in the USA each year by the use of seat belts and airbags:

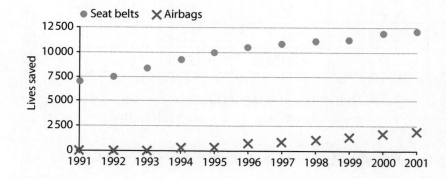

There is an upward trend. We might find plausible reasons why there is this trend. For example, the population of the USA increased during this period, so the number of drivers and cars probably increased too, which is likely to mean an increase in the number of accidents and more people needing to rely on their seat belt or airbag. There might be other reasons too.

Can we assume the line will continue to go up as it moves further to the right? Perhaps. It is possible that the population will continue to increase and that the number of lives saved will increase too. Maybe, though, some of this previous increase was caused by changes in society and in car manufacturing. If there is now a much greater societal pressure to wear seat belts (and if seat belt laws are now enforced more severely) then more lives might have been saved in later years because more people were wearing seat belts. Once 100% of car users are using belts then this increase may stop. Airbags were first fitted to cars in the mid 1970s in the USA and these were the most expensive cars. It is only more recently that they began to be included in mass-market brands of cars, which might explain much of the increase shown on the graph. Again, this effect may not last much longer.

ACTIVITY 12.2 (PART 1)

There are several costs associated with using a light bulb in your home. You need to buy the bulb and then you need to pay for the electricity it uses. Incandescent light bulbs work by heating a filament (a thin piece of wire). The filament gets very hot and this gives off light and also a large amount of heat; the bulbs are usually too hot to touch when they are in use.

Electricity costs about 15¢ per unit. To work out the total cost of the electricity you have used, multiply the cost per unit by the number of kilowatts and then by the number of hours. This means that if you use 1 kilowatt of electricity for one hour you will pay 15¢. A 100W bulb uses 0.1 kilowatts of energy when it is switched on. This type of bulb costs about 80¢ to buy and lasts for about 1 000 hours. How much does it cost to run one of these bulbs over its lifetime?

ACTIVITY 12.2 (PART 2)

In many countries the law is changing so that these types of bulb will be banned for environmental reasons. They are thought to use too much energy and to create too much heat. The alternative is to use other types of bulb that do not get as hot. CFL (compact fluorescent lamp) lights are one alternative. A bulb that gives off the same amount of light as a 0.1 kilowatt incandescent bulb is rated as 0.025 kilowatts. It lasts 10,000 hours but costs $4 to buy.

a What is the difference in cost to run a bulb like this instead of the incandescent bulb?

b How many years will the new bulb last?

c Why might some people be resistant to the idea of changing to the new bulbs?

d What approximations have been used in this question? How will they affect the answers?

ACTIVITY 12.3

Across the whole world, the average time to run a marathon is four hours 21 minutes. This includes elite runners who run a marathon in just over two hours and recreational runners who take much longer. The *Marathon des Sables* is an annual race across part of the Sahara Desert in Morocco. Over six stages the runners run the equivalent of six marathons (although these are not equally spread out) and must carry their food and clothing with them in a backpack.

a Can you estimate the average time to complete the Marathon des Sables?

b What are the differences between this and ordinary marathons?

12.3 Biggest and smallest sensible answers

If we are making predictions or using estimates then our answers are unlikely to be exact. We can often work out the biggest answer we might reasonably expect and the smallest answer that seems likely.

One way to do this is to repeat the calculation you carry out using your biggest estimate and then with your smallest estimate. For example, to estimate the number of bicycles there are in the UK (population 66 million) we could start by estimating the fraction of the population that own a bicycle. Let's assume that this is between $\frac{1}{3}$ and $\frac{2}{3}$ of the population. Many people do own a bike, but not the very old, the very young and those who live in areas where it is difficult to cycle. In addition to this there will be people who decide not to have a bike or who cannot afford to buy one. $\frac{1}{3}$ of 66 million = 22 million and $\frac{2}{3}$ of 66 million = 44 million, so we could say that the number of bicycles in the UK is likely to be between 22 million and 44 million.

EXAMPLE ACTIVITY 12.2

Here is a longer example, based on a true story. American Airlines used to serve salad on their first class flights. An airline employee proposed removing an olive from each salad to save money. How much money might this save the airline this year? What is a reasonable upper amount and a reasonable lower amount?

Commentary

If you were to look up some figures, you would find that in there are currently about 6,700 American Airlines flights per day. We might estimate that about five people have salad on each flight, olives cost $2 per jar and there are about 150 olives in a jar.

To work this out I need to multiply the number of flights by the number of people who have salad, then by the cost of an olive and then by the number of days in a year.

$6\,700 \times 5 \times 2/150 \times 365 = 163\,033.33$

Now let's work out the upper and lower amounts. The number of salad-eaters might be from three to seven. The cost of a jar of olives could be from $1.80 to $2.20.

The upper amount is $6\,700 \times 7 \times 2.20/150 \times 365 = 251\,071.33$

The lower amount is $6\,700 \times 3 \times 1.80/150 \times 365 = 88\,038$

Note that to find the upper amount we take the biggest value for the number of people and the biggest value for the cost of a jar of olives.

This gives an upper amount of $251\,000 and a lower amount of $88\,000 (and it is appropriate to round these values off).

Summary

This chapter looked at how changes can be made to problems and what effects those changes can have. This is useful because we can then easily adapt our answers and approaches to help us to solve more problems.

You should now:

- know what types of changes can be made to a problem
- understand what effect these changes might have

End-of-chapter questions

1   A newspaper published a news story that included a graph:

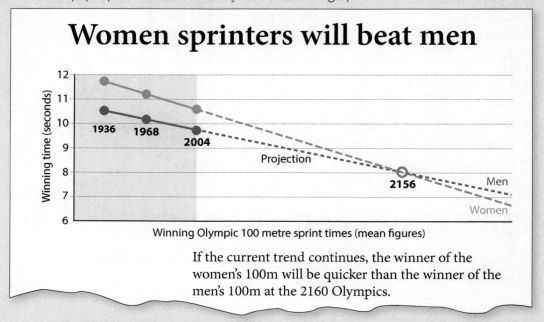

Women sprinters will beat men

Winning time (seconds)

1936   1968   2004

Projection

2156

Men

Women

Winning Olympic 100 metre sprint times (mean figures)

If the current trend continues, the winner of the women's 100m will be quicker than the winner of the men's 100m at the 2160 Olympics.

What is wrong with the graph and the article?

2   Some marathons are always over-subscribed. To enter some of those marathons you can raise sponsorship and try to get a charity place. There are also places reserved for runners who have completed other marathons fairly quickly and who have achieved a particular 'good for age' (GFA) time. The following table shows the GFA times for different age groups (where 'sub' means 'under').

Table 12.2

Men	Time (in hours)	Women	Time (in hours)
Age 18–40	sub 3:05	Age 18–40	sub 3:45
Age 41–49	sub 3:15	Age 41–49	sub 3:50
Age 50–59	sub 3:20	Age 50–59	sub 4:00
Age 60–64	sub 3:45	Age 60–64	sub 4:30
Age 65–69	sub 4:00	Age 65–69	sub 5:00
Age 70–75	sub 5:00	Age 70–75	sub 6:00
76+	sub 5:30	76+	sub 6:30

In 2017 the world record marathon times were:

• Men: 2 hours, 2 minutes and 57 seconds

• Women: 2 hours, 17 minutes and 1 second.

The average time taken for all marathon runners across the world is:

• Men: 4 hours 13 minutes

• Women: 4 hours 42 minutes

• All: 4 hours 21 minutes.

Are the GFA times fair? Explain your assumptions and reasons.

3 At a supermarket there are various ways to buy soft drinks.

Table 12.3

1.75 litre bottle	$1.66
2 × 1.75 litre bottles	$2.50
8 × 330 ml cans	$3.50
24 × 330 ml cans	$7.00
12 × 150 ml cans	$3.50
12 × 330 ml cans	$4.00
500 ml bottle	$1.25
One 330 ml can	$0.70

a Of the different ways of buying soft drinks listed above, are there any that you definitely wouldn't use?

b Which is the best value?

c Under which circumstances might you buy alternatives?

4 Many charities produce wristbands.

a I own four different coloured wristbands. If I wear two of them each day (not bothering about the way each pair is ordered on my wrist), how many days can I wear them for before repeating a combination?

b I buy another one, how many days can I go without repeating myself now?

5 A bar of chocolate has six 'squares'.

It can be broken along the lines to divide it up in different ways.

You can create a piece with four squares and a piece with two squares, or you can create a two, a three and a one. Clearly, the order you break these up in is not important (because breaking it into two, three, one is the same as breaking it into one, two, three or three, two, one).

a How many different ways are there to break the chocolate? List them all.

b How many ways would there be if the chocolate bar had five squares?

117

Exam-style question

Square Deal is a game for two players, played over a number of rounds. In each round both players have a 4 × 4 grid onto which numbered tiles are placed.

There are 34 tiles, numbered as follows:

0 0 1 1 1 2 2 2 2 3 3 3 3 3 4 4 4 4 4 4 5 5 5 5 5 6 6 6 6 7 7 7 8 8

At the beginning of a round the tiles are placed in a bag. The players then take turns to withdraw two tiles at a time from the bag, at random. At each turn, one of the two tiles must be placed on the player's own grid and the other one placed on the opponent's grid. Each player attempts to create rows and columns of four numbers that add up to a total that is a square number, and tries to prevent the other player from doing so. The round continues until both grids are full.

A player's score for the round is the sum of the highest-value row and the highest-value column.

- The value of a row or column that adds up to a total which is a square number is the sum of the squares of the individual numbers.
- A row or column that does not add up to a square number has a value of zero.

For example, in the grid below, two rows add up to totals which are square numbers:

$4 + 1 + 7 + 4 = 16$ and $2 + 5 + 0 + 2 = 9$.

The values of these rows are $4^2 + 1^2 + 7^2 + 4^2 = 82$ points and $2^2 + 5^2 + 0^2 + 2^2 = 33$ points.

There are no columns with totals which are square numbers.

The player's score for this round is 82 (highest-value row) + 0 (highest-value column) = 82 points.

7	3	3	5
4	1	7	4
8	5	2	4
2	5	0	2

The game is normally won by the first player to reach an overall total of 900 points. However, a player whose grid in any round has all four rows and all four columns adding up to totals which are square numbers is said to have made a Square Deal. No points are scored in this round: instead, the player making the Square Deal wins the game immediately.

Russell and Gordon are playing a game of Square Deal. Russell's grid at the end of the first round was as follows:

5	7	0	8
4	6	3	3
1	7	6	2
4	5	8	4

a What was Russell's score in the first round?

In a later round, Gordon had a chance of making a Square Deal on the final turn of the round. He knew that the four tiles still in the bag were 0, 2, 4 and 7, and his grid was as follows:

4	6	3	3
4		5	7
5	1	2	1
3	2	6	5

However, when he took two of the tiles from the bag, the best score that he could make on his own grid was 158 points, made up of 74 points for the highest value row and 84 points for the highest value column.

b Which two tiles did Gordon take from the bag on the final turn of this round? Explain your answer.

c i What is the highest possible score that a player could achieve in a single round?

ii Draw a completed grid that would produce this score.

In the round currently in progress the two grids are as follows:

5	0	3	5
8	6	7	
6		3	1
0	2	5	4

Russell's grid

4	4	2	3
2		7	8
7	1	4	3
5	2		6

Gordon's grid

It is Russell's turn, and he has taken tiles numbered 1 and 5 from the bag.

d Taking into account the four tiles left in the bag ahead of Gordon's turn, explain in detail why Russell should place the 1 on his own grid and the 5 on Gordon's grid and on which squares should the tiles be placed?

Cambridge International AS & A Level Thinking Skills 9694 Paper 31 Q4 June 2017

Part 2
Critical thinking

Chapter 13
An introduction to critical thinking

Learning objectives

This chapter introduces you to the concept of critical thinking. You will learn about the set of attitudes that is essential to informed critical thinking and will have the opportunity to apply them yourself before comparing your conclusions with a worked example.

Claim
- Fact ~matter of fact
- Opinion
~ Hypothesis
~ Prediction

13.1 What makes some thinking critical, and other thinking uncritical?

'Critical', 'criticism' and 'critic' all originate from the classical Greek word *kritikos*, meaning able to judge, discern or decide. In modern English, a 'critic' is someone whose job it is to make evaluative judgements, for example about films, books, music or food. Being 'critical' in this sense does not merely mean finding fault or expressing disapproval, although that is another meaning of the word. It means giving a fair and unbiased opinion of something. Being critical and *thinking* critically are not the same thing.

But if critical thinking just means judging, doesn't that mean that anyone can do it simply by giving an opinion? It takes no special training or practice to pass a judgement. If I watch a film and think that it is boring, even though it has had good reviews, no one can really say that my judgement is *wrong* and the professional critics are right. Someone can disagree with me, but that is just another judgement, no better or worse, you might say, than mine. In a limited sense, this is true. But a serious critical judgement is more than just a statement of preference or taste. A critical judgement must have some basis, which usually requires a measure of knowledge or expertise on the part of the person making the judgement. Just saying 'I like it', or 'I don't like it', is not enough. There have to be some *grounds* for a judgement before we can call it critical.

13.2 Critical Thinking (and critical thinking)

We should also be aware of the difference between 'critical thinking', as a general descriptive term, and Critical Thinking (with a large C and T), which is the name of an academic discipline with a broadly defined content. This book addresses both. It covers the Critical Thinking (CT) component of Cambridge International A Level Thinking Skills and other syllabuses. But it goes well beyond the confines of exam preparation. In fact, having mentioned the distinction, we can largely ignore it. To have maximum value, thinking skills have to be *transferable* from one task or context to others. The aim of this book is to instil a critical approach to reading, listening and reasoning *generally*; and to provide the conceptual tools and skills that enable you to respond critically to a wide range of texts. The Cambridge International syllabus gives the book its *structure* but not its whole purpose.

The objects of critical focus are referred to generically as '**texts**'. The word is used in its broadest sense. In real life a 'text' can be spoken or written or visual: a television programme, for example, or tweet or blog; or just a conversation. In a book, of course, the texts are restricted to objects which can be placed on a page, so that they are often referred to instead as *documents*. Most of the documents that are used in the coming chapters are in the form of printed texts. But some are graphical or numerical; or a mixture of these. Two other generic terms that are used are '**author**' and '**audience**'. The author of a text is the writer, artist or speaker who has produced it. The audience is the receiver: reader, watcher or listener.

However, the audience we are concerned with in these chapters is the **critical audience**, the reader or listener who reflects carefully on what he or she is presented with, and makes an informed and perceptive assessment of it, backed by reasons. Such a person, as already noted, is called a 'critic'. A critical thinker is a critic.

13.3 The objects of critical thinking

Some CT textbooks give the impression that critical thinking is directed only at arguments. This can be quite misleading if it is taken too literally. Arguments are of particular interest in CT, but by no means exclusively so. Information; items of evidence; statements and assertions; explanations; dialogues; statistics; news stories; advertisements . . . All of these and more may require critical responses. What these various expressions have in common is that they all make **claims**: that is, utterances that are meant to be true. Since some claims are in fact *untrue*, they need to be assessed critically if we, the audience, are to avoid being misled. We cannot just accept the truth of a claim passively. Arguments are especially interesting because their primary purpose is to persuade or influence the audience in favour of some claim or other. The critical question therefore becomes whether the argument succeeds or fails: whether we should allow ourselves to be persuaded by it, or not.

Even if the critic is persuaded by an argument, in the sense of accepting its conclusion, there may still be room for reservations about the argument itself. There are good and bad arguments, and a large part of critical thinking is aimed at recognising the difference. A bad argument can be persuasive, and a good argument can sometimes fail to persuade. This is where the discipline of CT becomes interesting, and where it becomes most important to practise.

13.4 Activities

The core activities of CT can be summarised under the following three headings:

- analysis
- evaluation
- further argument.

These recur throughout Part 2 of the book, with different texts and different levels of challenge. As they are fully discussed in the coming chapters there is no need to flesh them out in detail here, but they do need a brief introduction.

Analysis means identifying the key parts of a text and reconstructing it in a way that fully and fairly captures its meaning. This is particularly relevant to arguments, especially complex ones.

Evaluation means judging how successful a text is: for example, how well an argument supports its conclusion; or how strong some piece of evidence is for a claim it is supposed to support.

Further argument is self-explanatory. It is the critic's opportunity to give his or her own response to the text in question, by presenting a reasoned case for or against the claims it makes.

In most CT examinations, including Cambridge International Thinking Skills, these three tasks are set and assessed in roughly equal measure. They are referred to as the three 'assessment objectives'.

13.5 Attitude

As well as being an exercise of skill and method, critical thinking also relates to an attitude, or set of attitudes: a *way* of thinking and responding. For example, here is a fragment from a document. It is just a headline, no more. It belongs to an article on the website of a top British newspaper:

> ## 2029: THE YEAR WHEN ROBOTS WILL HAVE THE POWER TO OUTSMART THEIR MAKERS

Suppose you have just glanced at the headline, but not yet read the article. What would your immediate reaction be? Would you believe it on the grounds that the newspaper would not print it if it were not true? Would you disbelieve it because for so long it has been accepted as fact that, however powerful computers become, they will never think like a human being? Might you even take the cynical view that journalists make claims like this, true or not, just to sell papers, or to cause alarm? According to some we are bombarded by 'fake news' on a daily basis. It is easy to fall into the habit of treating everything with suspicion; believing nothing.

All of these reactions are understandable enough among readers. What they are not is *critical*. They are either passively accepting, or too quickly dismissive. All suggest a closed mind to the question behind the headline.

Critical thinking, by contrast, should always be:

- fair- and open-minded
- active and informed
- sceptical
- independent
- brave.

Most of these attitudes speak for themselves. Without an open mind we cannot judge fairly and objectively whether some statement or story is true or not. It is hard sometimes to set aside or discard an accepted or long-held belief; but we must be *willing* to do it. Nor can we judge any claim critically if we know nothing about it. We have to be ready to take an active interest in the subject matter, and be prepared to investigate and enquire. Hasty, uninformed judgements are not critical. At the very least we would need to read the article before an informed judgement can be possible.

Some degree of scepticism is also needed: a willingness to question or to entertain doubt. Scepticism is not the same as cynicism. For example, it doesn't mean doubting everything that journalists write as a matter of course because you think that they are driven only by the wish to grab the reader's interest, with no regard for fact. Critical appraisal requires each claim or argument to be considered on its merits, not on blanket prejudgements of their authors – however justified those may sometimes seem.

Lastly, critical thinking requires independence and courage. It is fine to listen to others, to respect their beliefs and opinions, to learn from teachers, to get information from books and/or from online sources. But in order to think critically you must also be prepared to take some initiative: to ask your own questions and reach your own conclusions. We get very used to being told or persuaded what to think, so that being faced with choices or decisions can be uncomfortable. The methodology of critical thinking can give you greater confidence in your own judgements, and more skill at defending them. But *exercising* the judgement – using it to form your own views – is ultimately up to you.

13.6 Reasons and evidence

Of course you cannot decide whether to believe a bare statement like the one above purely on its author's own say-so. You need to know the reasons the author has for making the claim. With this in mind, read the following extract from the article to which the headline belonged, then have a go at the example activity below it.

2029: THE YEAR WHEN ROBOTS WILL HAVE THE POWER TO OUTSMART THEIR MAKERS

Computers will be cleverer than humans by 2029, according to Ray Kurzweil, Google's director of engineering.

The entrepreneur and futurologist has predicted that in 15 years' time computers will be more intelligent than we are and will be able to understand what we say, learn from experience, make jokes, tell stories and even flirt.

Kurzweil, 66, who is considered by some to be the world's leading artificial intelligence (AI) visionary, is recognised by technologists for popularising the idea of "the singularity" – the moment in the future when men and machines will supposedly converge. Google hired him at the end of 2012 to work on the company's next breakthrough: an artificially intelligent search engine that knows us better than we know ourselves.

(. . .)

Kurzweil is known for inventing devices that have changed the world – the first flatbed scanner, the first computer program that could recognise a typeface, and the first text-to-speech synthesiser. In 1990 he predicted that a computer would defeat a world chess champion by 1998 (in 1997, IBM's Deep Blue defeated Garry Kasparov), and he predicted the future prominence of the world wide web at a time when it was only an obscure system that was used by a few academics.

For years he has been saying that the Turing test – the moment at which a computer will exhibit intelligent behaviour equivalent to that of a human – will be passed in 2029. "Today, I'm pretty much at the median of what AI experts think and the public is kind of with them," he adds. "The public has seen things like Siri [the iPhone's voice-recognition technology], where you talk to a computer. They've seen the Google self-driving cars. My views are not radical any more."

Supported
– Reasons
– Evidence

125

EXAMPLE ACTIVITY 13.1

How strongly, in your view, does the information in the passage support the headline claim? Does it make you any more or less likely to believe the claim? Give your reasons.

You can work on this individually or in a discussion group of two or more. It is an introductory activity so you are not expected to use any special terms or methodologies.

Commentary

This extract is a piece of journalism. Its headline is a statement, or more specifically a prediction. Because it is a prediction its truth is not known. For that reason we call it a *claim*, rather than a statement of fact. It will not be known until 2030 whether or not the prediction was correct.

The text that accompanies the headline is intended to give the reader some reasons to believe the claim, or at least to take it seriously. The text is therefore a kind of argument. Understanding and evaluating arguments of one kind or another is a major part of critical thinking, as you will find in coming chapters. This particular argument uses two main lines of reasoning to support the prediction: first, that the person who has made the prediction, Ray Kurzweil, is an expert in the field of artificial intelligence; second, that other predictions concerning intelligent machines that may once have seemed impossible, have turned out to be correct and are now not even 'radical'. These reasons are presented as evidence that the event Kurzweil calls 'the singularity' is a reality.

Other experts, Kurzweil says, are divided on the question of when, or even whether, the supposed 'singularity' will happen. Non-experts are divided, too.

How about you? Are you any more or less persuaded by what you have read in this article? Does the evidence support the headline?

Summary

In this chapter the differences between critical and uncritical thinking were introduced.

The chapter also discussed:

- the objectives of critical thinking

- the core critical thinking activities: analysis, evaluation and constructing further argument
- the attitudes that critical thinkers typically show.

Chapter 14
Claims, statements and assertions

Learning objectives

This chapter introduces and explains a number of key terms and concepts used in the discipline of critical thinking. It focuses on the notions of claim, statement, *and* assertion – *the basic elements of reasoning.*

Reading through this chapter and attempting the activities will help you identify different types of claim. It will also introduce you to some of the techniques used in critical thinking.

Cambridge International

If you wish to focus on preparing for Cambridge International AS and A Level Thinking Skills, you should work through Section 14.1 Claims and statements and Section 14.3 Fact, falsity and opinion and then attempt the end-of-chapter questions.

You will need to be able to recognise claims and assess the likelihood of the content of a claim being true irrespective of its source.

14.1 Claims and statements

To make a *claim* is to say something informative; something that is supposedly true. In that respect claiming is close in meaning to the acts of stating or asserting.

We have to say '*supposedly* true' because not all claims are true. Some are based on mistaken beliefs; some are due to careless reporting; some are outright lies. There are some statements, too, that are not straightforwardly true *or* false in any factual sense but are still claims. We'll begin by considering some examples.

(1)   Hungary and Romania share a common border.
(2)   The tide's out.
(3)   The dinosaurs were cold-blooded.
(4)   Water boils at 75°C.
(5)   Torture is wrong under all circumstances.

All five of the above sentences are *statements*. 'Statement' has two meanings here, one for the act of stating something, and another for the kind of sentence that is standardly used to make claims and statements, as opposed to asking questions, or giving instructions, orders, etc.

The two meanings of 'statement' do not cause problems in ordinary conversation but in a more formal discipline, like critical thinking, it is important to distinguish between a sentence (the string of spoken or written words) and what is expressed *by* the sentence – its **content**. Two or more different sentences can be used to express the same content. Instead of (1) you could say: 'Hungary and Romania are immediate neighbours'; for (2) you could say: 'It's low tide' (or 'low water'). You would effectively be making the same claim.

Because statements (also known as grammatical statements) are the standard form of expression for making claims, their content is either true or false. It makes no sense to respond to a question or command by asking whether it is true or false, or to say that you agree or disagree with it. Questions and commands are not expressions of any particular fact, belief or opinion.

[Handwritten margin notes:]

Factual claim
Verify = Prove that something is true
Categorical = Absolutely
Strong vs Weak

Subjective
Vested interest
Value judgement
Beyond reasonable doubt
Justify claim
Vague claim

128

Nonetheless, there are some circumstances in which an instruction or question can be used to make a statement. Take the last of the above examples, (5). The speaker could have made much the same claim by saying: 'How can torture ever be right?' This linguistic device is known as a **rhetorical question**. It is commonplace in persuasive or argumentative contexts, where it can seem more forceful than a plain statement.

Claims and statements can even be made pictorially or symbolically. Signals such as flags are often used at beaches to indicate the state of the tide for the benefit of swimmers and surfers. A flag flying at half-mast means that someone has died. The sign opposite 'states' that there is a double bend ahead.

14.2 Assertion

Claim vs Assertion

Like claims and statements, an assertion is also a claim to truth. Where it differs is in its force – the adjective 'assertive' derives from the same stem. What is implied by an act of assertion is that the speaker knows or is sure of the truth of what he or she is saying. We are therefore more critical when an assertion turns out to be false than we are of a mistaken claim. 'Claim' is a more general, neutral term, for which reason you will tend to find 'claim' used more frequently in critical thinking contexts. Use 'assertion' when it is clear that the author is flatly stating something, and expecting to be believed – even if, in fact, he or she is lying or mistaken.

All assertion = Claim
All claim ≠ Assertion

14.3 Fact, falsity and opinion

A useful distinction can be made between claims to fact, and those which are expressions of opinion. However, it is a distinction that needs some clarification. If we look again at the five examples we can see that although they make statements, there are differences in what they state, or what they are about – their *content*, in other words. Not all content is of the same kind, and the differences can be important to the way in which we evaluate claims.

For example, (1) expresses a fact. More than that, it expresses a known fact, or at least a claim that can be verified, for example by consulting an atlas. Some people might deny the claim is correct, out of ignorance; others might claim that it is true, but without claiming to know it. For those people it would be an expression of opinion even though as *a matter of fact*, (1) is true.

129

Example (2) is also a matter of fact: it is either true or false, and like (1) it can be verified, in this case by going to the beach and checking for oneself whether it is true or not. What is different about (2) is that there is no one claim associated with the sentence. The same sentence can be used over and over to make different specific claims, some true and some false. In philosophy of language, expressions like (2) are referred to as 'type' (as opposed to 'token') sentences.

Another feature of (2) is its **vagueness**. Unless the tide is at its very lowest point, at the precise moment when the sentence is spoken, then strictly speaking the sentence is false. In practice, (2) would usually mean that the tide was 'more out than in', or something of that sort. But would that be a good enough reason to judge that a token use of (2) was true? Precision matters more in some situations than in others. The exact state of the tide can be crucial on occasions: a matter of life and death even. At other times its approximate state is all that the audience needs to know.

Example (3) too is a matter of fact. It has factual content, but unlike either (1) or (2), its content is as yet unverified. Scientists are divided on the matter, with some claiming that the dinosaurs were cold-blooded (like modern reptiles), and others that they were warm-blooded (like birds and mammals). In that sense this claim is nothing more than the expression of opinion, and unless or until there is conclusive evidence one way or the other, it will remain so. This does not mean that statement (3) is neither true nor false. For either the dinosaurs were cold-blooded or they weren't. Scientists may never know the truth, but the truth exists and is there to be discovered, even if it has to wait for the invention of a time machine!

Example (4) is an interesting case. It looks like a straightforward falsehood. It is a well-known fact that the boiling point of water is 100 °C, but that is not the whole truth. It is true at sea level under normal atmospheric conditions, but under different conditions water can boil at much lower temperatures. On Mount Everest, at 8 848 m above sea level, the boiling point of water is around 71 °C. Example (4) is not so much false, therefore, as insufficiently specific. To that extent it has something in common with example (2).

Example (5) is the odd-one-out of the set. It is an expression of opinion, but more than that it is a *matter* of opinion as opposed to a matter of fact. Two people can disagree over the matter, and neither of them is necessarily mistaken. It comes down to what each one thinks or believes to be right, or whether there are circumstance that justify the use of torture. To say that the sentence is true, just means that you assent to it. It can be 'true' in your opinion at the same time as being 'false' in someone else's.

Another way to distinguish claim (5) from the other four is to say that its truth or otherwise is a **subjective** matter dependent upon each individual person (or *subject*) who thinks about the issues. This is in contrast to claims like (1)–(4) whose truth or falsity is **objective** (the *object* being what the claim is about). They are true or false regardless of what anyone thinks or knows.

ACTIVITY 14.1

1   Find or write an example of each of the following:
   • a statement of known fact
   • a claimed fact that cannot be verified or falsified
   • a statement whose content is subjective
   • a vague statement.
2   Give an example of a claim or assertion that is made by means other than spoken or written words.
3   Find an example of a rhetorical question (for example in a newspaper or magazine article).

14.4 Varieties of claim

As well as the broad division into matters of fact and matters of opinion, there are some important categories of claim that it is helpful to recognise and take into account when interpreting and evaluating claims. Some of the main ones follow, with brief descriptions and examples. We shall leave aside simple reports of fact, as these require no further comment.

14.4.1 Predictions

A prediction is a claim that something may or may not happen in the future, or that something as yet unverified will be found to be true. For example, the Meteorological Office might claim, on the morning news:

> (6)   Hurricane Horace will make landfall in the next 24 hours.

If the hurricane does reach the coast within one day of this assertion being made, then it can be said that the prediction (or forecast) was correct. But it cannot be said, even with hindsight, that the prediction was true, less still that it was a fact, because when the claim was made, it was still possible for the weather conditions to change.

Some predictions seem so likely that it is tempting to treat them as facts. If you are playing a game with five dice, and need five sixes on your final throw to win, it is a fairly safe prediction that you will lose. But although the chances of throwing five sixes all at once are low a winning throw is not impossible. On average, five sixes will come up once in every 7 776 (6^5) attempts. The claim that you will lose, therefore, has a high probability of being correct, but it is not a fact. Similarly, if someone said after you had thrown (and lost): 'I knew you wouldn't win', you would be right to reply (as a critical thinker): 'You didn't *know* that: you predicted it correctly.' Prediction and fact are not the same even when the chances of the prediction being correct are vastly higher than in this example.

In short, predictions need to be recognised for what they are and interpreted and evaluated accordingly. Usually this is in terms of probability, and should not be confused with fact.

> **ACTIVITY 14.2**
>
> From your own experience recall two examples of predictions that you have made and/or been affected by. Try to include one that surprised you by being correct, or incorrect.

14.4.2 Hypotheses

A hypothesis is a principle or proposition stated as a basis from which reasoning or a conclusion can be drawn.

Sometimes a 'hypothesis' is described as an educated guess, but it is more than that: a scientific hypothesis is developed from existing knowledge and experience. Scientists use the term 'hypothesis' to mean a provisional supposition which arises from a theory and which can be tested, for example through further research.

> **ACTIVITY 14.3**
>
> Use the internet, newspapers or journals to find examples of recent research based on scientific or other hypotheses.

> **ACTIVITY 14.4**
>
> Discuss and compare the following terms. How similar are they? How, if at all, do they differ?
>
> **hypothesis, guess, hunch, speculation, theory, conjecture**
>
> You can use a dictionary or other resources to assist with the task.

14.4.3 Value judgements

Claims that something or someone is good or bad, beautiful or ugly, deserving or undeserving, and so on are called value judgements, for the obvious reason that they are about quality or worth. It is not a value judgement to observe that dinosaurs had warm blood, or that they were large or (in some cases) carnivorous, since those claims would be factual in kind. It would be a value judgement to say that they were ugly.

An important subset of value judgements concerns matters of right and wrong. Claim (5) is an example of a value judgment of this sort. It makes a moral (or ethical) statement rather than a merely descriptive one that can be assessed as true or false. Most people have such strong feelings of revulsion towards the use of torture that they would regard (5) as *effectively* true, and regard anyone who disagreed as wrong. Nonetheless, (5) is a judgement, not a matter of fact.

Here is another value judgement that is often voiced, in these or equivalent words:

(7)   **The enormous wealth of the top 1% of the population is disgraceful.**

Words like 'disgraceful' are often described as **value-laden**. They contrast with terms like 'enormous', which is plainly descriptive and does not express an explicit judgement. It is not a value judgement to claim that some people earn more in a week than an average worker earns in a lifetime, however wrong that inequality may be judged to be. That statement itself is a matter of fact that can be verified or falsified by comparing the earnings of actual people and doing the maths. It becomes a value judgement when it is claimed that there is something 'excessive', 'obscene', 'shameful', or just 'wrong' about such wealth; or that, on the contrary, it is 'right' for successful and talented individuals to get huge rewards. It might be difficult to justify a claim that the huge pay differentials that exist today are 'right' or 'fair', but in the end it remains a matter of opinion or belief, and people are entitled (at least arguably) to take either side in the debate.

14.4.4 Recommendations

Recommendations (or suggestions) are claims of yet another sort. Here is one:

> (8)   The wages that anyone can earn should be capped to reduce inequality.

A preceive wrong

This may seem quite similar in spirit to (7), the claim that enormous wealth is disgraceful. Both express a similar sentiment, and both are opinions rather than hard facts. However, there is an important difference. Claim (7) expresses a negative judgement about how things are in the world. By contrast the author of (8) is claiming how things *ought* to be, or what should be done in response to the perceived wrong.

Recommendations, like value judgements, are not straightforwardly true or false. Two people – even two people who agree about (7) – may disagree about whether the recommendation to cap wages is the right way to deal with what they see as a wrong. Neither of the two will be factually wrong. If one person says that it is 'true' that high earning should be capped, it just means that he considers it to be a good idea, and vice-versa if another says it is 'false'.

Should = Recommendations

14.4.5 Definitions and descriptions

A definition is a statement about the meaning of a word. Dictionaries are collections of definitions of this sort. But a definition can also be an identifying description of an object or concept. 'A playwright is someone who writes plays' is a definition in both these senses.

Factual claim but arguable

Not all descriptions are definitions, however. 'Shakespeare was a playwright' is a description of someone, but obviously not a defining one, given that there have been countless other playwrights besides Shakespeare. On the other hand, the statement . . .

Relative definitions
↓
Further clearification

> (9)   Shakespeare was the playwright who wrote *Hamlet*.

. . . does, supposedly, define Shakespeare, because only one person matches that particular description. A definition typically has two parts. First the object is described in general terms to establish the *kind* of thing it is – in this case a playwright. Then a further description distinguishes the object from others of the same kind – in this case a particular playwright. Such definitions are known by the rather grand title *genus et differentiam*.

Is a definition a fact? This is an interesting question. If Shakespeare wrote *Hamlet*, then (9) states a fact. But there are some definitions which are not clear-cut. Take the definition of a concept like poverty. One 'official' definition of poverty (at least in the UK) is anyone living on less than 60% of the average nationwide income. This is known as a 'relative definition', because the concept in question is defined by comparison with some other value, here average income. The definition will therefore change in 'absolute' terms as average income rises or falls. Many people would disagree with this definition, or even claim that poverty cannot be defined because what some people regard as poverty, others might consider riches – or at least an improvement on what they have. It is a fact that 60% is the figure claimed by a number of official UK bodies (including the Office for National Statistics) and is used as a basis for some policy decisions; but this is not the same as saying that the definition itself is a fact.

Definitions can be extremely important in arguments, debates or negotiations. How often does a discussion come to a standstill when someone says: 'It all depends on how you define such-and-such'?

These five broad categories are examples of the sorts of claims we read or hear on a daily basis. They are useful descriptions which help us to interpret claims, and will assist in evaluation. It should not be assumed that all claims fall exactly under one or other of the headings. In some cases the categories overlap. There will also be claims that are not obviously covered by any of the labels. These include *complex* expressions such as explanations and arguments, which are the subjects of later chapters. Don't be afraid to categorise a claim in your own words, using your own descriptions of what is being claimed. Human language is extremely versatile, and allows for a great variety of different interpretations.

Simple vs Complex

EXAMPLE ACTIVITY 14.1

How would you describe the type of claim represented by each of the following sentences?

What can be said about the truth or otherwise of each claim?

(10) An international agency should be set up to monitor and control the ownership and use of unmanned aerial vehicles (a.k.a. 'drones').

(11) The tide should be coming in by now.

(12) Educational standards are falling for the first time in ten years. *(Opinion)*

(13) It is time that a cap was placed on the earnings of the most wealthy in society.

(14) There is a black hole at the centre of our galaxy. *(Hypotheses)*

(15) A constellation is a group of stars that form a recognisable pattern in the sky. *(definition)*

(16) Sport is being ruined by big money. *(Opinion)*

Commentary

This activity has given you a first taste of critical analysis and evaluation. What follows in this commentary are some suggested responses to compare with your own.

(10) is a recommendation or proposal. It is not a claim that would ordinarily be described as a fact, even by someone who strongly agreed with it. Its author no doubt holds the view that the rapid proliferation of drones presents a serious risk to the public, and there may be facts that strongly support that view. That does not mean that anyone who opposes the freedom to own and operate drones is in the wrong. Ultimately the issue is a *matter* of opinion, and (10) is an *expression* of opinion.

(11) is a claim to fact, and if the tide is coming in as the sentence is spoken, the claim is true. You probably noticed, however, that the way in which (11) is worded – especially the use of 'should' – gives it the form of a hypothesis or conjecture. Otherwise, why does the speaker not just say, 'The tide *is* coming in now'? The sentence suggests

---

that whilst she does not *know* that the tide is coming in, she has some good reason to *believe* (and therefore *claim*) that it is so. The way in which a claim is expressed, as well as *what* is claimed, can significantly affect how we interpret it and judge it.

(12) is a difficult call. On the surface it is a straightforward claim to fact: either standards are falling or they are not. But precisely because (12) has the appearance of a statement of fact, our critical antenna should be alerted. The trouble is we cannot begin to judge how true or false (12) is without first settling some serious questions, not least what the words mean. 'Educational standard' is a value-laden concept, and a vague one. Are we talking about exam results, or about the quality of thinking and discussion in the classroom? It is a matter of opinion, and a matter of definition, how we measure ups and downs in the quality of education.

(13) is a recommendation, based on a value judgement. It is similar in content to example (8). What makes it a recommendation is that it goes beyond claiming that a situation is good or bad, by suggesting that something should be done about it.

(14) is expressed as a fact, but it is a matter of opinion whether this is true or not. In strict scientific terms it is a hypothesis, not a certain or established fact.

(15) is a definition. It states what a constellation is and in the same breath explains the meaning of the word.

(16) is a value judgement. The key word is 'ruined'.

ACTIVITY 14.4

Discuss each of the following claims with the above examples and comments in mind:

(a) Nitrogen gas is heavier than air.
(b) Colonising other planets must begin within the next century to ensure the future survival of the human race.
(c) Forensic medicine is the application of medical science to crime investigation.
(d) Dogs make better family pets than cats.
(e) Driverless cars will make the roads safer by eliminating human error.
(f) The culling of sharks to reduce the risk of attack on humans is indefensible.
(g) Hawaii is a volcanic island in the Pacific Ocean.

Summary

In this chapter some of the most basic concepts in critical thinking have been introduced and discussed. First and foremost are claims, and their close relatives, assertions and statements.

The chapter also discussed:

■ claims to fact and to knowledge
■ statements of opinion or belief
■ predictions

■ hypotheses
■ value judgements
■ recommendations
■ definitions.

The chapter also introduced the distinction between the contents of claims, and the sentences that are standardly, and non-standardly, used to make claims.

End-of-chapter question

Each of the claims below is a statement or judgement that can be challenged. For each claim:

- Decide whether the claim is true, partly true or untrue and explain why you think this.
- Explain how the claim might be challenged.

(Try not to repeat your reason when you challenge the claim.)

Here is an example:

Claim: Cats make better pets than canaries.

- The claim is partly true.
- *Why I think the claim is partly true*: Many more people have cats as pets than have canaries. This shows that for those owners they make better pets than canaries.
- *Possible ways to challenge the claim*: The claim is a general statement of an opinion. It is not clear what is meant by 'better' pets. Different people want different things from their pet. Cats may not be ideal pets for people who live in apartments or who are allergic to cats. Canaries need less care than cats.

(a) There is too much attention on social media to what so-called celebrities are doing.

(b) The Second World War lasted from 1939 until 1945.

(c) Drinking coffee is bad for you because coffee contains caffeine, which is a stimulant.

(d) The USA puts a greater percentage of its population in jail than any other country in the world.

(e) MIT, Harvard, Cambridge, Oxford and Imperial College London are among the top-ranked universities in the world.

(f) Wearing dark colours will make you look slimmer if you are not very tall.

Chapter 15
Assessing claims

Learning objectives

This chapter progresses from identifying and interpreting claims of different kinds to critically assessing or evaluating them. It introduces a number of key concepts which are essential to the task of evaluation.

Reading through this chapter and attempting the activities will help you to apply criteria in order to assess different claims.

Cambridge International

If you are preparing for Cambridge International AS & A Level Thinking Skills, you should focus on Section 15.4.1 Plausibility and credibility and attempt the end-of-chapter questions.

You will need to use understanding of plausibility to assess the likelihood of the content of a claim to be true, irrespective of the reliability of its source. When you evaluate reasoning you will not generally be expected to challenge claims unless reasoning relies heavily on a very dubious claim.

15.1 Separating truth from fiction

When a claim is made, especially publicly, it is natural to think we are being told the truth. Most of the time we accept claims, especially claims to fact, at face value. For instance, if we read in the newspaper that there has been a plane crash, we are entitled to assume that such an event really has taken place. We don't jump to the conclusion that the statement is false just because we have not witnessed it ourselves. We hear the football results, or baseball scores, and assume they are correct, and not made up to please the fans of some clubs, or annoy the fans of others. We get a weather forecast telling us to expect heavy snow, and we plan accordingly: we don't ignore it just because it is a prediction, and predictions aren't facts. But nor do we ignore the possibility that a prediction might not turn out to be correct.

Assuming that most of what we are told is true or believable is entirely reasonable. Indeed, it is necessary for a normal life, and the functioning of a modern democratic society. If we questioned, or refused to believe, everything we read or heard, life as we know it would come to a standstill. That is why we all have a responsibility to tell the truth; and why people are understandably annoyed if they are told something that is not true.

Everyone knows the story of *The Boy Who Cried 'Wolf!'* or a story like it. The boy has a bad habit of raising false alarms, in particular frightening his community by shouting out that a pack of wolves is approaching the village. At first the villagers run to safety whenever he does this. But after a while they stop believing him, until the day comes when a real wolf appears. By then, of course, the boy has lost all credibility and his for-once-genuine warning is ignored. (You can work out the ending yourself.)

The moral of the story is that truth and trust are both important. People need to be able to rely on what they are told most of the time; and people who speak the truth need others to believe them most of the time. But that does not mean we should respond with blind acceptance to everything that we read and hear. Obviously we cannot assume that just because something has been asserted – in spoken, printed or any other form – it is true, or we have to agree with it. People do make false assertions, not only with intent to deceive, but also out of carelessness or ignorance. Even when there is a core of truth in what someone says, it may be exaggerated, or over-simplified, or a mere approximation, or a rough guess. There are many ways, besides being plainly false, in which a claim may be less than the whole truth.

None of this means that we should start routinely doubting everything. But it does mean we should keep an open and inquisitive mind, and maintain a healthy scepticism.

Naive

Skeptic

15.2 Justification

As you saw in the previous chapter, it is not always possible to *know* whether a claim is straightforwardly true or false. Knowledge requires certainty, or at least near certainty, and certainties are rare. In the absence of certainty, the best evaluation we can give of a claim or belief is to say whether it is *justified*, or *warranted.* These two words mean much the same as each other. A warrant is a right or entitlement. We are entitled to hold a belief, or to make a claim, if there are good grounds – for example, strong evidence – to support it. Without such grounds a claim is unwarranted (unjustified).

At first sight it may seem that truth and justification amount to the same thing: a claim is justified if it is true, and unjustified (or unwarranted) if not. But neither of these is correct. A claim can be true but unjustified if the person making it does not have good reasons to believe it – or in extreme cases may not believe it at all. Conversely, there is a sense in which a false claim can be justified in some circumstances. Someone may make an assertion on the basis of all the information available at the time of making it. If that information gives convincing grounds for the claim, then it is fair to say that it is a justified claim to have made, even if it later turns out to be false on the basis of some new information.

In other words, truth and justification are different. Justification is provided by the reasons that can be found and given for a claim, but truth or falsity belong to the content of the claim itself. We may never know for certain whether the content of a particular claim is true, but we may be able to say that there is sufficient evidence or grounds or support to justify asserting it. Alternatively we may say that a claim is *unjustified*, because there are *not* sufficient grounds or support for it, or because there *are* sufficient grounds to cast doubt on it. This is different from saying that it is actually false.

Judging which of these is the right way to respond to a claim is at the heart of the discipline of critical thinking, and is part of what we mean by 'evaluation'.

> **EXAMPLE ACTIVITY 15.1**
>
> Recall the example in the previous chapter: the claim that the prehistoric dinosaurs were cold-blooded. Two facts are often cited in support of this:
>
> - The dinosaurs were reptiles.
> - Modern reptiles, e.g. snakes and lizards, are all cold-blooded.
>
> You might like to pause here and discuss whether you think the two facts justify the claim that the dinosaurs were cold-blooded before reading on.

> **Commentary**
>
> The two facts give some support to the claim, but only some. They are grounds for the hypothesis that the dinosaurs were cold-blooded insomuch as they add some weight to that side of the debate. If you knew nothing else about dinosaurs, or reptiles, or evolution generally, you might be tempted to accept the grounds as sufficient. But it would be a big step to take. For one thing it would mean assuming that what is true of reptiles now must have been true of reptiles 70 million years ago, and earlier. It is not at all impossible that there were once warm-blooded reptiles running around, including some of the dinosaurs, and that these reptiles became extinct, leaving only the cold-blooded species
>
> →

(handwritten margin notes)
→ Ground for sth being true
Analyse claim in itself

Unjustified > Insufficient support

139

surviving today. Being cold-blooded may have given certain reptiles a survival advantage over the warm-blooded ones. Warm-blooded species use more energy than those with cold blood, and food sources may have become scarce. These possibilities alone mean that the assumption is questionable, though not necessarily false.

So the two facts on their own do not really justify presenting the hypothesis as fact. It could be true, and many scientists consider it more probable than the counter-claim that the dinosaurs were warm-blooded. But there is no proof one way or the other.

ACTIVITY 15.1

Invent a story or scenario in which a claim is made that is true but unjustified.

15.3 Levels and standards

The word 'justified' is not an all-or-nothing term like 'true' or 'certain'. A claim to fact is either true or it is not. It might be objected that some claims are only *partly* true or somewhere in between truth and falsity, like a claim that the tide is out when it would be more accurate to say that it was low. But strictly speaking 'truth' means 'the whole truth and nothing but the truth' and does not allow degrees or approximations.

If speaker and audience really *know* that the content of a claim is true, then naturally it is justified. However, that level of justification is rare since it requires near certainty. Moreover, it applies only to statements of a factual sort. It doesn't apply to predictions and recommendations, or to value judgements; nor to any statements whose truth is questionable or debatable. Since critical evaluation is chiefly concerned with claims that are questionable or debatable – known facts don't need evaluating – what is needed is a set of criteria or standards by which to judge how justified a claim is when its truth is less than certain.

15.3.1 Beyond reasonable doubt

The most familiar example of varying standards of the kind discussed above is in the law. Take a guilty verdict passed in a criminal trial. (A verdict is another special kind of claim.) Under the justice systems of many countries around the free world, a guilty verdict is justified only if it can be proven 'beyond reasonable doubt'. That well known descriptor sets a standard – a high one. So, even if the jury are pretty sure the defendant is guilty, but there is just a small, lingering uncertainty, they must give a verdict of not guilty – or in some countries an 'open verdict' or 'unproven'. It means that on occasions a guilty person will go free for lack of proof, but that is the price for doing everything possible to ensure – not always successfully – that no one who is innocent is punished unjustly.

The standard required for a not guilty verdict is much lower: all that is required to acquit a defendant is that there is *room for doubt* – at least in those societies which apply the principle that a person is innocent until proven guilty. For this reason there is imbalance between the standards that must be met by the prosecution and the defence respectively. This is often expressed by saying that the 'burden of proof lies with the prosecution'.

Explain in your own words what is meant by the phrase: 'the burden of proof'.

15.3.2 Balance of probability

Beyond the criminal courtroom we can find examples of standards that are lower, or less demanding, than the absence of reasonable doubt. In a civil lawsuit, for instance, where both sides are treated more or less equally, a verdict may be justified 'on the balance of probability'. Obviously, it is easier to persuade a judge or jury that a claim is *probably* true than that its truth is beyond reasonable doubt. More generally a claim is described as probable if the reasons to believe it outweigh the reasons to doubt it.

Probability can be expressed mathematically. The standard way to describe it is on a scale from 0 to 1, or as a percentage. Normally we think of probability in connection with events or outcomes – wins, losses, illnesses, accidents and so on. The chance of throwing a six with one throw of a die is 1 in 6 – a probability of 0.17, or 17%. The probability of doing it twice in succession is 0.03, or 3%.

We can also assess certain kinds of claims in probabilistic terms. A familiar example of applying probability to claims can be seen in modern weather forecasting. Suppose snow is forecast. (A forecast, as already noted, is a kind of claim.) Instead of saying straightforwardly that there will be a snowfall in the next 24 hours, a forecaster will often say that there is a 90% chance of snow – or another high figure. This does not mean that the forecast is 90% true, or 90% justified. It means only that a snowfall is likely or, more precisely, that nine times out of ten there is a snowfall when the weather conditions are as they are. Conversely there is a one in ten chance that no snow will fall.

Because of this one-in-ten possibility, a *categorical* claim that snow will fall is not justified, for even if it does snow in the next 24 hours the forecaster could not have known that it would, and in fact knew that it might not. The important word here is 'categorical'. With a categorical claim there are no ifs or buts. A claim might not be true, but it is always presented as the truth, so that there is no getting out of having made the claim it if it turns out to be wrong.

The opposite of a categorical claim is a *qualified* claim. A qualified claim is one that uses words or phrases which add to, or take from, the central claim.

Possibility

Plausible

Credibility

141

Which of the following claims are qualified, and in what way?

(1) It's going to snow tomorrow.
(2) It might snow tomorrow.
(3) It will probably snow tomorrow.
(4) There is a 90% probability (or chance) of snow tomorrow.
(5) It will snow tomorrow for certain.

Commentary

Apart from (1), all of the claims carry some qualification. Claims (2) and (3) do not assert that it will snow, but they raise the possibility, and in the case of (3) the probability. Claim (4) is also a statement of probability, but is much more informative than (3), which is too vague to be really helpful. The word 'probably' on its own can mean practically anything from around 0.5 on the scale to just below 1. By quantifying the probability of snow to around 0.9, (4) makes a stronger claim than either (2) or (3). (If you were planning a journey you might not be put off by (2) or (3), but (4) would at least make you think twice.)

What about (5)? The claim is categorical because it is so definite in what it claims. That would not be wrong, but (5) is also qualified, only in a different sort of way. Not content with stating that it *will* snow, the speaker emphasises the categorical nature of the claim thus making it even stronger. Qualifications, in other words, can work in both directions. Words like 'might', 'probably', 'sometimes' etc. allow for the possibility that the central claim could be false, even if there are reasons to make it. Expressions like 'definitely', 'for certain', etc. do the opposite: they leave no room for doubt.

15.4 How do we judge claims?

We have been considering what it means for a claim to be justified. To recap, a statement of fact is justified in its own right if it is true. That's straightforward, but is not much help in the case of claims and assertions whose truth is in question – that is, if we do not yet know for certain if it is true or not. It is in these cases that the concept of justification is needed. Here are some criteria for judging claims:

A claim has strong justification if:

- it can be shown beyond reasonable doubt to be true
- it can be shown to have exceptionally high probability
- convincing grounds can be given to believe or accept it.

However, do not expect the assessment of claims to be as simple as ticking a box. A claim can rarely be judged to have met any one of these criteria at a glance, given that all three criteria represent a very high level of justification. Even leaving aside the first bullet point, 'exceptionally high probability', and 'convincing grounds' can be very difficult to establish in many cases. It is better to think of these criteria as standards against which to measure a claim's justification. In other words we should think of critical evaluation not as deciding *whether* a given claim is justified, but as *how far* a claim is justified, and whether the level of justification is sufficient reason to accept the claim in the given circumstances.

Often, therefore, we need a range of lesser – though important – standards to apply to claims. Two of these are introduced next.

15.4.1 Plausibility and credibility

A claim is plausible if it is reasonable to think that it could be true. It is plausible that the dinosaurs were cold-blooded. However, it is equally plausible that they were not. The opposite of 'plausible' is 'implausible'. A claim can be implausible if it is far-fetched. It is implausible that the first landing on the moon was a fake, and was secretly filmed

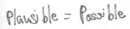
Plausible = Possible

142

somewhere in the United States. There are people who have made the claim, and others who apparently believe it. To them, presumably, it is not implausible. To the majority it is no more than a conspiracy theory that defies common sense.

Of course, some claims that have been widely regarded as implausible have turned out to be true. Many of the latest scientific theories seem highly improbable, especially to a non-scientist. The implications of quantum physics are more like science fiction than science fact. They don't make *ordinary* sense, any more than the solar system made ordinary sense in the Middle Ages.

The point is that plausibility is not enough by itself to justify a claim, or to justify rejecting it either. But this does not mean that it has no value. Questioning the plausibility of a claim can be a useful starting point for evaluation. If a claim seems implausible to you, then it will take stronger reasons than otherwise to overcome your reluctance to believe it. As a fair-minded critic you should then work all the harder to be certain that it cannot be true. Conversely, if a claim seems highly plausible, you should work equally hard to avoid the temptation to accept it at face value and not ignore possible evidence to the contrary

Plausibility and credibility are related in meaning but there are significant differences, too. Plausibility is mostly a feature of the claim itself. It is implausible that NASA would have gone to the trouble of faking the Apollo 11 moon landing. It is also implausible that, if there had been a conspiracy, not one person out of the hundreds of technicians and others involved in the project would have spilled the secret by now. Even if some evidence were found that made it more credible, it would still be an implausible idea. Credibility goes beyond the claim itself. A credible claim is one that is backed by good evidence and/or comes from a reliable source. Plausibility might add to the credibility of a claim, but on its own it does not establish it, and should not be given too much weight.

ACTIVITY 15.3

A story recently circulated about wealthy homeowners in London, and other major cities, excavating beneath their properties to build swimming pools, home cinemas and luxury spas. A British newspaper reported that:

> The mega-basements of the super-rich have even spawned their own urban myth: that many of the JCBs (mechanical diggers) employed in their digging could not practically be retrieved from the bottom of the giant hole, and were simply buried. It is said that newer, deeper excavations have begun to run across them on the way down.

How plausible do you find the 'urban myth' reported in this short extract? What makes it plausible – or implausible – in your opinion? Discuss in groups or pairs.

15.5 Complex claims

Different claims require different approaches, and make different demands on the criteria for evaluation. Some are longer than others, some stronger than others, some more particular or precise than others. These differences must be taken into account when judging claims. We shall start with the difference between simple and complex claims.

Objective = Empirical evidence (sciencetific)

Sentences such as 'The lake is frozen', 'The tide is out', or 'Dinosaurs were reptiles', are *simple* claims, expressed by grammatically simple sentences. The following sentences, by contrast, are complex, each expressing two or more connected claims or statements.

(6) The tide is out and the island can be reached on foot.
(7) The lake is frozen, yet it is not safe to cross.
(8) If the dinosaurs were true reptiles (then) they were cold-blooded.
(9) Sea levels around the world are rising because global warming is melting polar ice.

Note: A simple sentence, when it becomes part of a complex sentence, is called a 'clause'. Words or phrases which express the relation between clauses are called 'connectives'. They include expressions like 'and', 'but', 'because', 'if . . . then', 'although' and 'unless'.

When assessing complex claims we have to take account of the two or more simple claims that make up the whole. We also have to take note of the connective: what it means, and the relation it expresses between the different parts of the complex claim. In the case of (6) the connection is quite straightforward: 'and' indicates that the two conjoined sentences are both being claimed as true. If either of these simple claims is false or questionable, (6) is not justified.

'Yet' is the connective in (7), which is a slightly more complex assertion than (6). Again, the two clauses both have to be true for the whole claim to be true. But the use of the connective 'yet' (or alternatively 'but', 'however', etc.) also suggests that there is something surprising or unusual in this: that the second claim is true *despite* the first being true. The implication is that if the lake is frozen you might expect it to be safe to cross.

Sentence (8) consists of two clauses connected by two words 'If . . .' and '. . . then . . .' (although the 'then' can be omitted, which is why it is in brackets in the example). It is a complex statement, like the others, but is trickier both to analyse and to evaluate. First of all, (8) is not claiming either that the dinosaurs were true reptiles, or that they were cold-blooded. Sentence (8) is what is known as a **conditional** statement. All that is claimed is that *if* the first clause (the if-clause) is true, then the second clause (the then-clause) must also be true. What makes evaluation difficult is that the if-clause can be false without making the whole conditional statement false. A conditional, as a whole, is false only when the if-clause is true and the then-clause false – for instance, in (8), if dinosaurs *were* reptiles but they were *not* cold-blooded. Think about this carefully because many arguments contain conditional statements as part of the reasoning.

Sentence (9) also has more to it than just the two simple claims. It is an explanation, or more precisely a *causal* explanation, as indicated by the connective 'because'. It not only asserts that sea levels are rising and that global warming is melting the ice, but also that the first of these happenings is caused by the second. If we are not satisfied that all three elements are true, then we are not justified in asserting (9).

There is more about conditionals and explanations later in the book.

15.6 Strong and weak claims

Some claims are naturally *stronger* than others. This does not mean that the claim is any more true, or justified, or probable. Strong claims can be false and weak claims can be true. The strength of a claim has to do with how much is being claimed by it, and/or how forcefully it is worded. Why the strength of claims is relevant to critical thinking is because it can be considerably harder to justify a strong claim than a weaker one. Strong claims need strong reasons to support them.

For example, compare these two statements from different newspapers reporting the same story:

(10)   Packs of wild dogs are roaming the streets of Newtown terrorising the residents on a nightly basis.

(11)   Newtown has a problem with numbers of stray dogs periodically creating a public nuisance.

It should be very obvious which of the two is making the stronger claim. Just ask yourself which of the two assertions you would be more likely to believe, in the absence of any additional information. The clear answer is (11). For one reason, if (10) were justified – i.e. not an exaggeration – then (11) would be justified as well, whereas the truth of (11) would not necessarily justify (10).

What makes (11) more credible is that it is restrained and moderated. Statement (10) is more interesting, of course, but the use of expressions like 'packs', 'terrorising', 'wild' and 'roaming', which make it so, also run the risk of exaggeration to the point where the facts do not justify the claim. Statement (11) minimises the risk by its use of 'numbers', 'stray', 'nuisance' – and 'periodically' in place of 'on a nightly basis'.

ACTIVITY 15.4

Compare these two claims:

(a)   Polar bears will be extinct by the middle of the century.
(b)   Polar bears are an endangered species.

One of these claims is *stronger* than the other. Which one is it, and why?

15.6.1 Generalisations

A generalisation is a strong claim that applies widely, or even sometimes universally – meaning in every single case. Consider the following statement:

(12)   Women are better problem-solvers than men.

What makes this a strong claim is that it is a sweeping generalisation. It would be even stronger if it was taken literally to mean that all women are better problem-solvers than any man. Clearly that would be implausible, since it would take just one or two counter-examples to prove it false. However, (12) could be interpreted in a weaker, less sweeping sense, as claiming that in a majority of cases women exhibit better problem-solving skills than men. Even so, it would be classed as a generalisation.

The opposite of 'general' is 'particular'. It would not be a generalisation to select a particular group of women, and compare their thinking skills with those of a group of men. Imagine that two teams – one all-female, another all-male – competed in a problem-solving competition, and the adjudicator concluded at the end that:

(13)   **The women (in the female team) solved more problems than the men.**

This would be a *particular* claim, not a general one, stating that these particular women, on this particular occasion, were superior to the men at the problem-solving tasks that they were set. Claim (13) would be justified if the women won the competition. But no sort of general claim could be made on the strength of (13), especially not (12).

Summary

This chapter has continued to focus on claims and assertions, and introduced the critical activity of assessing claims in terms of justification. It explained that there are levels or standards of justification. These include:

- certainty
- absence of reasonable doubt
- balance of probability
- possibility/plausibility.

The chapter concluded with an examination of three important ways in which claims can be described and compared:

- simple versus complex
- strong versus weak
- general versus particular.

End-of-chapter questions

1 Give an example of a claim that you consider to be:

- justified on the balance of probability
- justified beyond reasonable doubt
- completely justified/certain.

In each case explain why your claim matches the description.

2 Suppose a crime has been committed. The victim (we'll call her Vera) claims that her neighbour (Nick) was the perpetrator, perhaps because she doesn't like him, or perhaps because she wants to see someone convicted, and anyone will do. Other than this she has no reason for making the allegation, and certainly nothing that would count as evidence. But then suppose it is discovered that Nick, just as Vera has claimed, was guilty of the crime! Would the discovery of Nick's guilt justify Vera's accusation?

Explain your answer.

3 On occasions a guilty person will go free for lack of proof of their guilt. That is the price for doing everything possible to ensure that no one who is innocent is punished unjustly.

Discuss the view that the price is sometimes too high.

Chapter 16
Grounds, reasons and evidence

Learning objectives

The main focus of this chapter is on reasons in the form of evidence, and on the criteria for assessing evidence.

Reading through this chapter and attempting the activities will help you to understand reasons in the form of evidence and how to apply criteria in order to judge the value and usefulness of evidence.

Cambridge International

If you are preparing for Cambridge International AS & A Level Thinking Skills, this chapter covers the topic in greater complexity than you need. For Cambridge International you will need to be able to use relevant criteria to evaluate and use evidence. You should focus on Sections 16.1.5 Corrobation to 16.5.8 Applying the criteria and attempt the exam-style question.

16.1 Reasons in the form of evidence

The previous chapter introduced and examined the concept of justification, in particular the justifications we seek for claims and assertions, and ultimately whole texts. A claim is justified if it is known to be true, but that is an ideal situation that is often not achievable. In most cases we must settle for something less than knowledge, namely good *reasons*.

Reasons
→ *Explanation*
→ *Justification*

One point to be aware of here is that 'reason' has two meanings. On the one hand it can be used with the sense of an explanation, to say *why* something is (or is not) so. On the other, it has the justificatory sense of the grounds for claiming something to be so.

Recall the example in Chapter 15:

(1) Sea levels around the world are rising because global warming is melting the polar ice.

Because → Explanation
↓
Cause and effect

Here two assertions are made, one of which is supposed to explain the other. Global warming is claimed as the reason *why* sea levels are rising. This relation is expressed by the connective, 'because'.

Compare this with the following statement:

(2) Global warming must be happening because the polar ice is melting and sea levels are rising.

Must → Certainty
↓
Justification

Superficially there is not a lot of difference between (1) and (2). Again in (2) we see two claims connected by the word 'because'. But this time global warming is not being *explained* by rising sea levels: rising sea levels are being offered as a reason to believe that global warming is taking place. The phrase 'must be' helps us to see that the author is trying to persuade the reader to accept the claim. But even without this clue it is quite obvious that rising seas could not be the cause of global warming, whereas it makes good sense to offer rising sea levels as *evidence* of global warming. It may not be conclusive evidence, but it is supportive.

It can be quite hard sometimes to tell which of these two functions a claim is meant to have – explanation or justification – but the surrounding context will usually provide the clues to enable the right interpretation. It is important to recognise the distinction.

We shall return to explanations in due course; the point of mentioning them here has been simply to draw attention to the distinction. The concern of this chapter is with reasons in the role of evidence or grounds.

16.1.1 Evidence

Providing evidence for a claim is one of the most commonplace forms of reasoning, making it an important topic in the discipline of critical thinking. We are most familiar

149

with evidence in the context of legal hearings and criminal investigation, but evidence plays no less important a part in academic studies, for example in the fields of science and historical research.

Practically anything can be evidence: a footprint, a bloodstain, a written or spoken statement, a statistic, a chance remark, an email, some CCTV footage . . . the list could run to pages. There is good and bad evidence, just as there are good and bad reasons. A bad reason is one that does not justify the claim or action for which it is given. 'My friend told me . . .' is not by itself a good reason to take something as fact.

Judging whether or not a piece of evidence is 'good' depends of course on whether or not it is true, but also on what it is being used as evidence *for*. There is nothing good or bad about a claim that 70% of people questioned said that they believed street crime is on the increase. That is just raw data from an opinion poll. It becomes evidence when it is used as a reason for a conclusion or verdict – that is, when it is used to support or establish another claim. If it were used to justify a claim that street crime really is on the increase, it would be pretty weak evidence, if there was nothing more substantial to back the claim up. On the other hand it would be quite strong evidence for claiming that there is a public perception, or anxiety even, that crime is rising.

From this it can be seen that 'evidence' and 'reason' have an obvious overlap in meaning. Reasons are usually presented as statements, so that you might not want to call a photograph a reason even if it were used in evidence. On the other hand you might say that an incriminating photograph was the reason why, or grounds on which, a jury was persuaded to return a guilty verdict. Despite the overlap there are times when one word is more apt than the other.

Evidence → Reason

16.1.2 Types of evidence

Evidence can usefully be subdivided into two categories: *direct* and *indirect*. Direct evidence, as the name suggests, is first-hand, and immediate. The most direct form of evidence is what we experience with our own senses. If you see something happening in front of your eyes, that is direct evidence – for you, at least – that it has taken place. Of course, there are occasions when we are mistaken or confused about what we see or hear. Also we may misremember some of what we have experienced when we try to recall it later. But it remains true that personal experience is the most intimate contact that we can have with the physical world and what happens in it. It is direct evidence.

16.1.3 Testimony (Individual Testify)

'Testimony' means a given account. A witness statement is testimony. (Here 'statement' means more than a single claim or sentence: it can be a long and detailed report.) So long as it is an account of something that the person has witnessed or experienced *at first hand*, it too can be counted as a form of direct evidence. This is in contrast to what is known as 'hearsay evidence'. The difference is clearly illustrated by the following statements by two witnesses.

W1:   'I know Janet Winters personally, and saw her threaten the receptionist.' (Eye-witness, direct witness)
W2:   'I found the receptionist crying and she said that Janet Winters had threatened her.'

It is obvious why this distinction matters. So long as W1 is telling the truth, and is not mistaken about what she saw, then Winters did threaten the receptionist in some way. W2 on the other hand may also be telling the truth about what she was told, but the receptionist may not be telling the truth. Of course, either of the two witnesses might be lying or mistaken. But in the second case there are two ways in which the evidence may be unreliable; in the first case only one.

ACTIVITY 16.1

There is a well-known party game called 'whispers' in which a message is written on a card and memorised by the first person in a queue. She whispers it to the second, who whispers it from memory to the third, and so on. The last person in the line then writes down what he heard on another card. The cards are then compared. It is a rule that the message cannot be repeated: it must be whispered just once by each player.

As an experiment, set up a version of the game. On completion state what the outcome was, and what conclusions can be drawn from it about 'hearsay evidence'.

It is particularly interesting, and relevant to real-life situations, to play the game using mobile phones.

16.1.4 Circumstantial evidence

By 'circumstantial evidence' we mean a fact, or set of facts, which may be used to support a conclusion or verdict *indirectly*. The facts themselves – the *circumstances* – are not in question. What is in question is what they signify, or permit us to conclude.

The classic example is the so-called 'smoking gun'. A detective rushes into a room after hearing a shot. He sees a body on the floor and a man standing holding a gun with smoke still coming from the barrel, indicating that it has just been fired. The natural assumption is that the man holding the gun has murdered the person on the ground. The detective testifies at the trial, reporting exactly what he has seen. The suspect pleads not guilty because, he says, he too heard the shot and rushed into the room, and picked up the still-smoking gun from the floor where it was lying. The facts – the gun, the smoke, the man holding the gun, the person on the floor – are identical. The interpretations, or explanations for the evidence – the conclusions drawn on the strength of it – are totally opposed.

'A likely story!' you might say to the suspect's explanation. 'Highly implausible.' But in the absence of any other evidence, even the smoking gun is insufficient for a conviction. It is (merely) circumstantial.

16.1.5 Corroboration

Continuing the example from above, if, however, it were also known that the suspect knew the dead man; that in the past he had threatened to kill him; that he owed the dead man money; and/or that he had recently visited a gun shop, then his guilt would be rather more probable. Each of these on its own is another piece of circumstantial evidence, but now the various items *corroborate* each other. Together they provide overwhelming evidence of guilt. In fact, the smoking gun would then be close to proof; the other evidence, without the smoking gun – would be very much weaker. For that reason the expression 'smoking gun' has come to be a metaphor for evidence which would finally settle a case. An investigation may be getting nowhere through lack of conclusive evidence, until the so-called 'smoking gun' turns up in the form of an incriminating email, or revealing photograph, or something of the kind. On its own it would not be proof of the desired conclusion; but on top of other evidence it reduces any lingering doubt to practically zero.

16.2 Example: the student demo

Here is a fictional scenario which will illustrate some of the concepts under discussion:

An unpopular congressman, visiting a university, was greeted by a large student demonstration. As he was stepping out of his car a raw egg thrown from the midst of the crowd struck him on the side of the head and broke, causing abrasions, and staining his expensive shirt. It was followed by a second and third egg. Soon the politician was cowering under a hail of missiles. As the crowd surged forward, he was helped back into the car by security officers and driven away.

A 20-year-old sociology student, Amelia Jackson, was arrested soon afterwards. She had been seen in the crowd, and was caught on surveillance cameras shouting angrily and holding a large placard on a pole.

Jackson was wearing a backpack containing some provisions she said she had bought in the market that morning. Among them was a cardboard egg box with spaces for ten eggs, but with only six eggs in it. She was taken into custody for questioning and later charged with assault, on the grounds that she had thrown one or more objects at the congressman with intent to injure or intimidate.

EXAMPLE ACTIVITY 16.1

Before reading on, note down or discuss your initial response to the above information as evidence to justify charging Amelia Jackson with assault. Would you say she was:

A guilty?

B *probably* guilty?

C probably *not* guilty?

D none of the above?

β

Corroborate = Collective Information

Commentary

The evidence available is entirely circumstantial. There is no *direct* evidence that Amelia Jackson did anything more than attend the demo and express her feelings. No one reports seeing her throw anything, but the accumulation of circumstantial evidence is beginning to look quite serious: first she was present at the scene; second, she was actively demonstrating; third, eggs were among the objects thrown at the congressman; and fourthly – the nearest item to a 'smoking gun' – there were empty compartments in the egg box she was carrying. Do these corroborate each other sufficiently to answer the question above with A, B or C?

Not securely. Verdict B is the nearest a jury could come to incriminating Ms Jackson, whilst D is the safest verdict. Clearly there is insufficient evidence for A: conviction would require evidence that put her guilt beyond reasonable doubt. However difficult it may seem to explain away the empty places in the egg box, it is not impossible that it had nothing to do with the assault on the congressman. Plenty of other people were throwing things: Amelia Jackson may just have gone there to protest, angrily perhaps, but not violently.

→

On the other hand it is very *plausible*, given the circumstantial evidence, that Jackson was guilty as charged. Because of that, C would be a strange conclusion to draw. She is no more likely to be innocent than she is to be guilty.

16.3 The student demo: additional evidence

16.3.1 Amelia's statement

When she was questioned, Amelia stated that she lived in lodgings with two other students and it was her turn to buy food and cook the evening meal. She had bought six eggs so they could have two each. She always bought eggs at a market stall, where they were sold singly. It was cheaper than buying ten; and she took her own cardboard container so that they would not break.

16.3.2 Stallholder's statement

The owner of the stall where Amelia claimed to have bought the eggs stated that he did not recognise her when shown a photograph. But he did make the following statement: 'A lot of the students buy their eggs loose. If they want a box they have to buy ten. I sell loads of eggs that way every day.'

16.3.3 Flatmates' statements

The two students with whom Amelia Jackson shared an apartment were questioned separately, and asked the same three questions. Both gave the same answers:

Q1 'Whose turn was it to cook that day?' Answer: 'Amelia's.'

Q2 'Do you know where Amelia was going when she left the apartment that day?' Answer: 'Shopping. Then to the university.'

Q3 'Was she planning to attend the demonstration?' Answer: 'She didn't mention it.'

16.3.4 Eyewitness account

58-year-old Rajinder Choudhury, a retired headteacher, picked Amelia Jackson out of a police line-up.*

He said:

'She's the one. She was up ahead of me in the crowd, right where the stuff all came from. She jumped up and down, and did a high five with the kid next to her. They were loving it. Then she ducked down and picked something up. The crowd rushed forward then and I lost sight of her, but later I saw her get arrested, and saw her face close up. It was her all right. Later I heard the police were asking for witnesses, so I came forward.'

This is also known as an 'identification parade': a number of people form a line and the witness points out the one he or she claims to have seen. If the suspect is identified in this way, that is a form of first-hand evidence.

EXAMPLE ACTIVITY 16.2

The additional evidence raises a number of further questions.

- First, is Amelia's story plausible, or is it far-fetched?
- Second, is it corroborated by any of the other evidence, and if so how strongly?
- Third, is it seriously challenged by any of the other evidence?

You may wish to re-assess your initial response.

Commentary

Amelia's story is not implausible. Anyone who has been a student, or knows students, would agree that most of them tend to shop as economically as they can, and if eggs can be got more cheaply by taking a container and buying them loose that makes sense. What is more, if there are only three residents in the apartment, then it also makes perfect sense to buy multiples of three, and not ten.

This does not prove Amelia was innocent, but it goes some way towards tipping the balance back in her favour. What is more, there is considerable corroboration from both the stallholder and the other students with whom she shares the flat. Of course the flatmates might be protecting her by answering as they do. They were questioned separately, so the fact that they gave exactly the same answers could mean they were telling the truth. But it could also mean they had prepared what they would say. As far as the stallholder is concerned, he has no reason to say anything which would assist Amelia. Evidently he doesn't even know her.

You may have answered these questions rather differently, but you should at least have registered that the circumstantial evidence against Amelia now looks less threatening. It fits just as well with *her* statement as it does with the charge made against her. What has always to be remembered with circumstantial evidence is that if it can be explained away, and the explanation is not far-fetched, no safe conclusion can be drawn from it. An evaluation of the evidence in this case would not be nearly strong enough to justify a conviction because any number of students, or others, could have bought eggs, and could have thrown them. Amelia is no longer in a special position, but is one of many potential suspects.

What about the 'eyewitness' statement? *Prima facie* (meaning 'on the face of it') this might seem to count *against* Amelia. However, there are a number of weaknesses in Rajinder Choudhury's evidence that should be noted. Firstly, he did not see Amelia actually throw anything; all he saw was her reaction. The claim that she was enjoying what was going on does not mean she actively took part in it. Besides, his identification of Amelia is practically worthless, for reasons which will be discussed shortly. You may also have detected a possible tone of disapproval in his statement, for Amelia or for student demonstrators generally, which could be interpreted as prejudice. He might want her to be guilty, for one reason or another.

16.4 Credibility of evidence

Good reasons backed by evidence can go a long way towards justifying a claim. But to provide full justification the evidence itself must be true. Potentially this looks like a problem for critical evaluation, because that process would go on forever in what is known as a *regress*. If the evidence for a claim has to be true, then evidence for the evidence has to be true, and so on. The melting of the polar ice would be evidence that sea levels will rise – but only if the polar ice really is melting. Scientists are generally in agreement that it is, and we are used to seeing evocative photographs of big white bears adrift on small icebergs. But is this sufficient grounds for the claim that the ice is melting? Is the evidence, in other words, reliable?

For most people the answer would probably be yes, although there are some who claim that the claims about global warming – even if true in the short term – are nothing more than a natural variation in the weather, and would not count as credible evidence that the seas will rise. It is not the business of this book to influence you either way on this or any other issue; only to suggest a methodology for making informed judgements of your own. Obviously, the critic cannot go on indefinitely justifying the evidence for the evidence for the evidence . . . The most we can do, in the example under discussion, is to investigate the evidence to assess its *credibility*. Later we can decide whether it is also supportive of the prediction for which it is given as evidence.

There are two important factors which help to determine the credibility of any piece or collection of evidence. One is plausibility, which was discussed briefly in the previous chapter. In general a plausible claim is better evidence than an implausible one, but as we have seen, plausibility alone is not enough. A second important factor is the *source* of the information that comprises the evidence – where it came from. What we look for in a source of evidence is reliability, the extent to which it can be trusted.

16.4.1 Reliability of the source

The credibility of evidence is affected by the reliability of its source. If the claim comes from a trusted source, we have more grounds for believing it than if we do not know where it came from. 'Source' in this context may be an individual making an assertion; or it may be a book, an article in a newspaper, a website or it may be a publisher. If you have found two conflicting claims, one from a book published by, say, Harvard University Press, and the other from a tweet by some anonymous individual, you would be likely to put your trust in the former rather than the latter. But between these two extremes there are many intermediate levels of assumed reliability.

When deciding the extent to which we can trust a source of information we are looking for qualities such as honesty, knowledge and expertise. There are other qualities, but those are probably the most important. We need the first for obvious reasons: we cannot sensibly trust a known liar. But however honest an author may be, we also have to be assured that he or she is well informed, and expert in understanding the information in question. An honest mistake is no more true than a deliberate lie, even though one may be more excusable in ethical terms than the other.

16.4.2 Judging reliability

Don't imagine that judging who to believe is any easier than judging *what* to believe. Suppose someone says to you: 'Look, I'm telling you the truth and I know what I'm talking about.' This is just a claim like any other. To believe in the source of the claim you have to believe the claim, and to believe the claim you have to believe the source! To avoid going in circles the critic needs a set of objective criteria for judging a source's credibility. There are plenty of options. We examine seven in the rest of this chapter.

16.5 Criteria for assessing evidence

16.5.1 Reputation

A good place to start is **reputation**. Generally speaking a witness or claimant with a reputation for honesty, good education, status in the community, and so on, is a safer bet than someone with no such reputation – or, worse still, a negative reputation. A criminal with a record for fraud is less likely to be believed than a law-abiding citizen with a responsible job; and with good reason. It is reasonable to believe that the probability of obtaining the truth from a reputable source is greater than it is from a disreputable one.

But this is a generalisation. Under certain circumstances it may be more rewarding to consult a convicted criminal than an ordinary law-abiding citizen. If, for example, the subject of inquiry is criminality, a person who has committed crimes and knows the criminal world is likely to be better informed than someone who has no such experience. The risk that the fraudster may lie is balanced by his or her access to direct evidence, and experience of the real world. Ideally, of course, we would hope to find sources that are reputable *and* informed. So, for instance, a qualified researcher who has made it her business to investigate crime and criminal activity, to study statistics, to talk to criminals and law-enforcement officers, to analyse and verify her findings, is arguably the best source of all.

Another point to be borne in mind about reputation is that it may not be deserved. You don't have to read very many newspaper articles before you come across a story of someone who has held a highly responsible position, and betrayed the trust that comes with it. No one's occupation or rank is a guarantee of credibility. Every so often a doctor, or a police officer, a teacher or priest – to say nothing of politicians – will be discovered to have acted dishonestly or stupidly. Conversely, there are countless people with no special status in society who are honest and clever. Reputation is a guideline, but it is no more than that. Cast your mind back to the witness, Mr Choudhury. He was a retired headteacher, and as such would have been expected to be fair-minded and careful with the truth, especially towards students. Yet his testimony was less than wholly reliable. Maybe he was mistaken about what he saw; maybe he was a supporter of the visiting politician and took a dislike to Amelia for showing pleasure at his ill-treatment. Maybe none of these was the case, and he was telling the unvarnished truth. The point is that, although reputation is not irrelevant, on its own it does not guarantee credibility. It is one factor among many.

16.5.2 Perceptual ability

People sometimes claim more than they can reasonably be expected to have seen or heard. Choudhury's evidence is interesting in connection with this. Remember that he identified Amelia. He recognised her in an identification parade as the person he had seen throwing eggs. Here is his statement again:

> 'She's the one. She was up ahead of me in the crowd, right where the stuff all came from. She jumped up and down, and did a high five with the kid next to her. They were loving it. Then she ducked down and picked something up. The crowd rushed forward then and I lost sight of her, but later I saw her get arrested, and saw her face close up. It was her all right. Later I heard the police were asking for witnesses, so I came forward.'

In legal terms Choudhury's identification of Amelia Jackson would be 'inadmissible evidence'. Why? The answer lies in his own testimony. Choudhury did not claim to have seen Amelia actually throw anything. He just said (twice): 'She's the one.' The most that can be taken from his account was that he saw someone showing excitement, and bending down to pick something up. What she picked up the witness does not say, raising the question of how he could even be sure she picked anything up at all.

But there is another weakness in Choudhury's supposedly 'eyewitness' account. Whoever he saw in the crowd, it was from behind; and he lost sight of her in the crowd. He did not see Amelia's face close up until she was arrested. It was that face that he picked out of the line-up. Whether it was the same women as the one he saw from behind in the crowd we can't be sure – and nor, if he were honest, could he. If Choudhury had not seen the arrest, would he have identified Amelia in the line-up? Again, we can't be sure. The credibility of someone as an eyewitness ultimately comes down to their **ability to see** what or who they claim to have seen.

We should really expand this criterion to include not only perceptual ability, but also the ability to apprehend information generally. These are both important factors in assessing certain kinds of evidence. Imagine a witness who claims to have overheard every detail of a private conversation at another table in a busy restaurant. The credibility of the claim could be tested by asking her to sit at the same table and repeat what she could hear in similar, or more favourable, circumstances. If she could not hear the words spoken in the test, she can hardly claim to have heard every detail of the alleged conversation. Her credibility as a witness would come down to her ability to hear what she says she heard, just as Rajinder Choudhury's comes down to his ability to see what he claims to have seen.

ACTIVITY 16.2

At approximately what distance, on average, can a *normal* conversation be overheard in a populated space? At what distance, therefore, would it be unsafe to take an allegedly overheard conversation as reliable evidence?

In small groups, devise and conduct an experiment with the aim of answering this question. Consider some of the problems posed by the question, and explain the measures you took to deal with them, along with your overall conclusion.

16.5.3 Expertise and knowledge

One very obvious criterion of reliability for certain kinds of evidence is the possession of **knowledge and expertise** in the relevant field of inquiry.

knowledge + understanding

A paradigm example is medical expertise. Suppose that during the student protest discussed in the previous chapter a participant had been knocked to the ground by a security guard and later dies. A bystander who was right next to the victim claims his head hit the concrete pavement so violently that his death was no surprise. However, the pathologist who examines the body testifies that injury to the head is slight and there was little evidence of a hard landing. Marks on the body suggest that the man rolled over as he fell and probably protected his head with his arms. Meanwhile the cause of death remains a mystery, and the security guard awaits trial for manslaughter.

ACTIVITY 16.3

Whose testimony is more credible: the bystander's or the pathologist's?

Discuss the above question and decide which factor carries more weight: the expertise of the pathologist, or the perceptual ability of the witness?

16.5.4 Neutrality

Unbiased

As noted at the end of the last chapter, there is a possibility that Mr Choudhury, the headteacher who identified Amelia Jackson, may have formed a dislike for her for some reason. He seems quite eager to point the finger at her, even though he has little hard evidence; and there is something in the tone of his testimony which hints at disapproval. If this were the case, it would further undermine confidence in the evidence. Similarly the bystander who saw a man knocked over by a security guard may have allowed her sympathy for the protesters to influence her testimony, and therefore exaggerated her description of the violence inflicted on the victim. Perhaps she, too, had been pushed around by the security staff, and this was her way of getting back at them. Alternatively she may have known the victim, and wanted someone to be punished for his death. Under any of these circumstances the reliability of her statement would be seriously impaired.

So, as well as being able and informed, a reliable source should, as far as possible, be **neutral** and impartial. Any possibility of bias or prejudice is enough to cast doubt on a source's credibility. A newspaper that has known political affiliations – as many do – might report an event, or give an account of something, in a way that another publication, with different affiliations, flatly contradicts. A third commentator may give yet another version of events, different from either of the others. Any one of the three may be correct, but without any way of judging which one it is, we tend naturally, and justifiably, to place most trust in the one that, as the saying goes, 'has no axe to grind'. Neutrality, therefore, is another essential criterion for assessing credibility.

16.5.5 Vested interest

To protect your interest

One of the main reasons for doubting a source's neutrality is the discovery of a **vested interest** – or **ulterior motive**. Vested interests may take many forms, the most familiar being financial interest. Take, for example, the following scenario: an oil company wants to sink an exploratory well in a region where there is an alleged risk of environmental damage, and possible harm to wildlife. Environmentalists have voiced strong opposition; the oil company has hired a team of 'independent' experts to assess the risks and report on their findings. After some time the team produce a statement that there is practically no risk of contamination or other damage, and the oil company gets the go-ahead. Then, just before the drilling is due to start, two of the experts on the team are found to have substantial shares in the oil industry. Had the report been negative, they would have lost a lot of money; as it stands, they will *make* a lot of money instead.

Obviously the report is discredited, not because it is necessarily false, but because of the vested interest of two of its authors. This is an extreme example, and a stereotypical one. But it is illustrative. Not all instances of vested interest are financial. A scientist who has worked for years on a theory that is threatened by new discoveries might well be tempted to falsify or bury some evidence that would undermine his life's work. At the same time, proponents of an opposing hypothesis might exaggerate the significance of the new discoveries. These conflicts of interest are not unheard of in academic or in professional life. Nor, sadly, are they absent from politics, where electoral advantage may compromise honesty. The general question that we have to ask therefore is this: Does the author of a claim given in evidence have any identifiable motive for making that claim, other than a belief that it is true? If the answer is yes, then truth may not be the author's highest priority.

It is equally important, however, to remember that, just because a person may have a vested interest in some outcome, he or she will not necessarily be untruthful on account of it. There are plenty of honest people, and it must not be assumed that everyone who is called on to give evidence or make a statement will let their own interests get in the way of telling the truth, or giving an honest opinion. There is a danger when starting out in critical thinking to look for the worst in people's testimony, rather than keeping a balanced and open mind. Evidence should be challenged and tested, but not dismissed as worthless simply on suspicion of some ulterior motive.

16.5.6 Corroboration

Each of the criteria that we have so far discussed affects how we judge a claim. Yet none of them, on its own, is usually sufficient to establish the credibility of a claim beyond reasonable doubt. A claim is, by its nature, uncertain, whoever has made it and however plausible it may be. One way in which it can be made more credible is by finding other evidence to **corroborate** it, that is, to back it up. Of all the criteria for assessing credibility, corroboration is arguably the most potent. This is understandable, since it is not a single reason to believe a claim, but a combination of reasons supporting and endorsing each other.

The simplest form of corroboration is agreement between sources – though it must be agreement between independent sources to be reliable. If two or more people make the same claim, or express the same opinion, there is more reason to believe it than if one person alone has made the claim. It is crucial to add the word 'independent' here, because if it is found that one person has influenced the others, the added credibility is cancelled, for they are effectively making a single, joint claim rather than several separate claims which genuinely corroborate one another. You may recall that earlier in this chapter, the police interviewed Amelia Jackson's flatmates separately. The fact that they still gave the same answers added to the credibility of what they said, but there was still the possibility that they had conferred in advance, and anticipated the questions. Indeed, if it is known that they had conferred that would actually *detract* from their credibility, for it would have to be explained why they had conferred. If they were both simply telling the truth, there would be less need to confer.

Corroboration is at its most potent when there is agreement between different kinds of evidence: for example, when statistical evidence bears out what several independent witnesses have said, and the circumstantial evidence all points in the same direction. By the same token, credibility is at its lowest when there is a lack of corroboration, or even disagreement.

16.5.7 Consistency

Last but not least is the criterion of **consistency**. It is related to corroboration insofar as two or more statements can be said to be consistent if they corroborate one another. But consistency does not require any active support or agreement by different sources. A set of claims is consistent just so long as none of them contradicts the others. They can all have the same source. If someone makes a statement to the police consisting of a number of different claims, the credibility of all of them is weakened if there are inconsistencies among them.

For example, suppose a motorist denies having been late for work, and also denies speeding on her way to work, having already admitted her time of leaving home. If it turns out that she could not have driven the distance from home to work without speeding, it is clear that one of her claims at least is untrue. This does not indicate *which* claim was untrue, but it does reveal an inconsistency in her account of the journey. For this reason lawyers routinely look for inconsistencies in the evidence presented by a witness as a way of casting doubt on their reliability.

ACTIVITY 16.4

There is an old party-game called 'alibis' which illustrates the role of consistency in evaluating evidence. Teams of three 'suspects' are required to account for their whereabouts for a given number of hours that they have spent together one afternoon. They are allowed to leave the room for ten minutes to 'cook up' their shared story, which they must do in as much detail as possible. They are then brought back in and questioned, one by one, by the rest of the group who try to catch them out by exposing inconsistencies in their joint testimony. For example: 'Jan says you saw a film: which film? Who was in it? How much were the tickets? Was it dark when you came out of the cinema? . . .' Each conflicting detail, 'don't know', or 'no comment' is a point against the suspects. The team with the fewest points wins.

16.5.8 Applying the criteria

There is a single word that describes exactly how a good critic should use the credibility criteria. The word is 'judiciously', and it means 'with good judgement', to which some dictionaries add 'carefully', 'thoughtfully', 'wisely' and more. The message for critical thinking is clear: don't rush to judgement – especially negative judgement – using the criteria as crude instruments for finding fault. There is a temptation to treat them as a means for point scoring for, or more often against, claims and statements.

Avoid judgements of the kind: 'X has a vested interest in the outcome so he may be (or must be) lying'; or 'Y and Z play golf together so Y can't be reliable'. Likewise, don't assume that because several people all make the same broad claim that it must be believed, or because someone has observed an incident close up that he or she cannot be mistaken. It is more judicious to make your assessments in terms of how far factors strengthen or weaken the credibility of evidence or claims.

It is also important that you remember to distinguish between evaluating claims and evaluating reasoning. This will be covered in a later chapter when evaluating argument is introduced.

Summary

- Claims can be justified by giving grounds, reasons or evidence to support them.
- There is direct evidence, and indirect or circumstantial evidence.
- Evidence is strengthened when it is corroborated by other evidence that is consistent with it.

- The credibility of evidence is affected by the reliability or otherwise of its source.
- Seven reliability criteria were discussed, with examples.

End-of-chapter questions

Read the following passage carefully and answer the questions that follow.

(This task can be completed individually or following group discussion.)

PARTYTIME STAR ACCUSED OF STEALING SONG

by Jan Ewbank, Arts and media correspondent

The superstar band Partytime, and their lead singer Magnolia, came under more fire yesterday when it was alleged that their number one hit, 'If You Knew', was originally written by an unknown schoolteacher who has never received a cent in recognition.

The disclosure came hot on the heels of criticism that Magnolia has cashed in big-time on her much publicised, so-called charity visits to developing countries last year.

Now, if the latest accusations are true, her most famous song isn't even hers to sing. It appears that the tune and chorus of 'If You Knew' were written ten years ago by Sarah Berry. Sarah had worked as a volunteer in Africa before training as a teacher. At college she met Magnolia, then Maggie Coleman.

'The college did a charity concert, and we were both in it', she recalls. 'I wrote a song for it, and Maggie sang it. I didn't think it was all that good, and never gave it another thought afterwards. It was only when I heard 'If You Knew' that I recognised Maggie – and my song.'

Magnolia hotly denies the claim. 'I don't even remember anyone called Sarah Berry', she says. 'I wrote 'If You Knew' because I was fed up of hearing rich people whingeing when there's real hardship and suffering in the world, like we saw in Africa. Whoever she is, she's on the make. If she's got any proof she ought to produce it – or otherwise, shut up.'

Partytime's road manager Paco added: 'I was around when Mags was writing it. It came straight from her heart after the tour. We write all our own songs. People are always coming out of the woodwork accusing stars of plagiarising – you know, stealing their songs – once they're famous. This Berry woman's not the first and won't be the last.'

I visited Sarah in her rented one-room apartment. She dug out an old photograph album and scrapbook. In it was a picture of a very young Magnolia fronting a student band. Under it were the names of the group, including 'Maggie Coleman'. There was also a handwritten song with guitar chords, but no tune. The chorus runs:

'If you'd been to the places I've been / And seen the things that I've seen / You wouldn't be sighing that life is so trying . . .'

Magnolia sings the chorus of 'If You Knew' in front of a big screen showing harrowing images. Her chorus goes: "If You Knew" the things that he's seen / Been to the places she's been / You'd have less to say in your self-centred way . . .'

When I confronted her with this evidence, Magnolia said: 'OK. Maybe this woman did stand on the stage with me once when we were at college. Maybe we sang a song together and some bits of it stuck in my mind. That doesn't mean she wrote it, whatever she pasted in her scrapbook. It's so long ago I just don't remember. As for the tune, that was all mine, and that's what really counts.'

I next visited Professor Jon Rudenko, who has been called as an expert witness in many high-profile plagiarism wrangles. He told me the chord sequence in Sarah's scrapbook would fit the melody line of 'If You Knew', although it would not be impossible for the same chords to fit two quite different tunes. Asked to estimate the odds against two tunes having these same chords by chance, he said: 'Upwards of twenty to one. Not huge. It's quite a common sequence in popular music.'

The jury is out on this one, but whatever the verdict, it's another unwanted smear on Magnolia's already tarnished reputation.

1   Assuming it has been fairly represented by the author, decide how credible the testimony is given by each of the following:

- Magnolia
- Sarah Berry
- Paco
- Jon Rudenko.

Base your assessments on the criteria discussed in this chapter.

2   Identify and assess one or more pieces of circumstantial evidence reported in the article.

3   As a source of information, how reliable do you consider Jan Ewbank's article to be in its reporting of the dispute? On what grounds might someone question its reliability as a source?

4   Imagine you were an informal 'jury' considering the evidence contained in the article. What would your 'verdict' be, and why?

5   Assess the language used by the author Jan Ewbank. Do you consider it to be a fair and neutral report, or judgemental, perhaps even biased? What evidence is there, if any, of partiality towards one side or the other?

Exam-style question

Study the evidence and answer the question that follows.

Research study: findings

The table below shows the probabilities of self-reported criminal activity compared with the average per 1000 people, adjusted for age, ethnicity, first language, unemployment, health, religious affiliation, born overseas, mother's education, mother's age at birth, biological/step/absent father, father ever imprisoned, parents receiving benefits.

	Criminal Damage	Burglary	Robbery	Theft	Assault	Selling Drugs
Unattractive or very unattractive male	+12	+1	+23	+24	+5	+4
Unattractive or very unattractive female	−6	+8	+15	+4	+22	+30
Very attractive male	−1	−1	−10	−6	−6	−21
Very attractive female	−11	−5	0	−3	−20	−6

To what extent does the evidence in the source support the claim that 'very attractive people are less likely than average to commit crimes, whereas unattractive people are more likely to do so'?

Cambridge International AS & A Level Thinking Skills 9694 Paper 23 Q2a and source C June 2012

Chapter 17
Evaluating evidence: a case study

Learning objectives

This chapter looks at two sample texts, and the evidence presented in them. These raise critical questions about the evidence, using assessment criteria and concepts that have been discussed in the preceding chapters.

Reading through this chapter and attempting the activities will help you to practise applying criteria in order to assess the reliability and credibility of evidence.

Cambridge International

If you are preparing for Cambridge International AS & A Level Thinking Skills, this chapter covers the topic in greater complexity than you need. For Cambridge International you will need to be able to assess the credibility of evidence; assess the intrinsic likelihood of the content of a claim to be true, irrespective of the reliability of its source; assess inference from evidence and identify factors which weaken the support the evidence gives to a claim.

17.1 Article 1

> **EXAMPLE ACTIVITY 17.1**
>
> Read the following short text about the history of aviation. Think about what it is saying but also about what it is doing.
>
> How strongly does the information in the article support the headline claim that the Wright brothers were not the first to fly?

handwritten notes (left margin):
- Partly true
- Sources from New York Herald
- Immigrant background
- Back to history over 100 years ago
- More sources will be better

handwritten note (above headline): Clear

WRIGHT BROS *NOT* FIRST TO FLY

Wilbur and Orville Wright made history at Kitty Hawk, USA, December 1903. Or did they?

Many aviation experts and historians now believe that German-born Gustave Whitehead – pictured below with his aeroplane 'No. 21' – beat the Wright brothers into the sky by as much as two or even three years.

In a 1935 article in the magazine *Popular Aviation*, and a book published two years later, author and historian Stella Randolf tells of a steam-powered flight made by Whitehead in 1899, in Pittsburgh, and of signed affidavits from 20 witnesses. One was Louis Daravich, stating that he was present (witness) and accompanied Whitehead on his flight. Randolf tells of two more flights, in 1901 in a plane that Whitehead named 'No. 21', and another in the following year in 'No. 22'.

A headline from the *New York Herald*, dated August 19, 1901 read:

'Gustave Whitehead travels half a mile in flying machine . . .', and quoted a witness who affirmed: 'The machine worked perfectly, and the operator had no problem handling it.'

Whitehead was a poor German immigrant to the United States, who changed his surname to try and fit in, but whose voice was easy to drown out in the debates that followed. The Wrights, by comparison, had influential friends and supporters. The prestigious Smithsonian Institute for Science, in return for ownership of the Wrights' Flyer, agreed not to publish or exhibit anything referring to flights before 1903. The question we should be asking is: Why?

The jury is not so much out. The jury has gone home. Case closed. History suggests it is time to reopen it.

by Jacey Dare

handwritten note: The text is a bit unclear → Slightly confusing

Gustave Whitehead, seen here with his aeroplane 'No. 21', and his daughter

Commentary

Jacey Dare's short article is a paradigm example of a text that needs to be read critically. It is clear from the style of the writing that it is journalistic. Journalists are not always careful in the way they distinguish fact from opinion, or an accurate account from a good story. Some do – and there is no reason to suppose Ms Dare is either careless or untruthful – but it must not be taken for granted that an article in a magazine or newspaper column is invariably well documented and thoroughly researched. Sometimes claims and assertions are made to be provocative, or to make interesting reading. It does not mean that they are false, but it does mean that the claims themselves should not be accepted without question; nor that they should be taken too literally.

Dare's headline claim, on the face of it, is strong (see Chapter 15). Taken literally it is a categorical statement that one of the most widely accepted stories of the twentieth century is fundamentally wrong: that the Wright brothers were not the first to fly a powered aeroplane. The claim is echoed, though a bit more cautiously, in the caption beneath the first photograph. 'Or did they (make history)?' it asks. Since the message is clearly that they did not, or at least that they may not have, made history, this is not a real question. It is what has been described as a rhetorical question, basically a statement. But by presenting it as a question the author is disguising its force so that the reader will not dismiss it as an implausible overstatement.

[handwritten margin note: Assumption = Missing reason]

The overall message of the text is summarised, again more soberly, in the final paragraph, as a claim that the case (against the official version of aviation history) should at least be reopened. The right way, therefore, to interpret what Jacey Dare is doing is challenging an established assumption. A challenge is a kind of claim. It is sometimes called a counter-claim. It is justified if it throws doubt on the supposed fact or opinion that it challenges.

The article then goes on to give some items of evidence for the challenge. This chapter focuses on the strength and credibility of that evidence, and additional evidence, using the criteria discussed in the previous chapter. Two obvious questions need answering in the process: first whether the claims in the article are true, plausible, probable, etc. and, second, whether they provide evidence for the challenge being levelled by the author.

17.1.1 Assessing the claims

As it happens, most if not all of the claims in the first four paragraphs of the article are basically true.

1 There *are* many people who believe that Whitehead flew one or more aircraft successfully before 1903. You only need to look up Whitehead on the internet to see how many supporters he has. Whether they count as 'aviation experts' or 'historians' we will return to shortly, but it is feasible that some are, since they would be the kind of people most likely to be interested in the theory.

   [handwritten margin note: ← Expertise]

2 It is true that Stella Randolf wrote historical books and articles in which she refers to numerous witnesses giving signed statements that they saw Whitehead flying.

3 There really was a story in the *New York Herald* in 1901, reporting a half-mile flight by Whitehead, and quoting a witness as saying that the plane 'worked perfectly'. The supporting photograph of Whitehead with his 'No. 21' is understood to be genuine; and no one disputes that Whitehead built aircraft.

[margin page number: 165]

4 It is a fact that Whitehead was a poor German immigrant, and it is documented that the Smithsonian Institute signed an agreement with the Wright brothers in return for their donating the Flyer.

17.1.1.1 Credibility and reliability

So, if all these four claims are either true or highly probable, are they therefore credible as evidence? As stated in the previous chapter, this question depends in part on the reliability of the sources. We have already raised one of the criteria by which we judge reliability, namely expertise. How many of the sources cited by Jacey Dare qualify as experts? Apart from Stella Randolf, none of them is identified either by name or reputation. You do not have to be an expert to believe something. We have only Dare's word that Randolf and the others have the special knowledge or qualifications that determines whether their opinions on the matter count as reliable evidence. What raises their beliefs above those of the general population? We have no information by which to answer this question.

How about the criterion that was described as 'perceptual ability'? Remember that this should be understood in the much broader sense of being in a position to access information of all kinds. Seeing with one's own eyes, or hearing with one's own ears, etc. is typically held to be the most reliable source of evidence, even though people can and often are mistaken about what they claim to see. But the more removed a person is from the actual event, the more opportunity there is for distortion, error or misrepresentation. Practically all of the evidence cited in the text is second- or third-hand. None is a personal record of a confirmed and dated Whitehead flight, pre-1903. The reader is given a list of people who have reason to think that Whitehead flew: Jacey Dare *reports* that author Stella Randolf *wrote* that Louis Daravich *said* that he flew with Whitehead; and that 20 people wrote affidavits to that effect. Such evidence is inherently weak. It is at best hearsay evidence. In legal terms it would count for very little, and there is no reason for historians to be any less critical in their search for facts. Moreover, both Stella Randolf's article, and her book, were published a full 34 years after the alleged flight of 'No. 21', and the testimony of Louis Daravich was not made public until then either. Why? There are many possible reasons, one being that no one took the matter seriously until then. But another, all-too-plausible reason, would be that it simply wasn't true. Memory is a notoriously unreliable faculty.

Photographic evidence is closely related to seeing: it is a way of recording what one sees, and is often used as evidence. Within limits a photograph is regarded as reliable evidence. There is no reason to think that the photograph of Whitehead with his 'No. 21' is not genuine. As evidence that it flew, however, it is worthless. The Wrights' Flyer, by contrast, is doing exactly what its name implies: flying. 'No. 21' *might* have flown. Some 'experts' have concluded from its design that it was capable of flight, and we shall examine their evidence shortly. But that is not the same as a photograph *showing* it in flight. Had there been such a photograph, Jacey Dare would surely have used it in preference to one that shows the machine stationary on the ground. The clear implication is that there is no photograph of a Whitehead machine airborne – not proof that it did not fly, but lack of proof that it did.

Even the *New York Herald* report – though contemporaneous – is not a first-hand account. It quotes a single unnamed 'witness' but the reporter himself clearly was not there, or he would have given his own account. No single one of the claims would persuade anyone to abandon the official historical account, but added together doesn't the evidence mount up?

17.1.1.2 Selectivity

It does, but only up to a point. What can be said, using a criterion introduced in the previous chapter, is that the evidence is *consistent* with the possibility that Whitehead flew a plane before December 1903. However, that is hardly a surprise. Since all of it is evidence that has been put forward to support the challenge, of course the sum total of it is consistent. By the same token you could say that the different sources all corroborate one another: the so-called aviation experts, Stella Randolf, Daravich and the *New York Herald*.

← consistency

However, corroboration and consistency are of value as evidence only if the sources are neutral and independent; and that they are not selective. Louis Daravich, we are told, testifies in writing that he flew with Whitehead on one or more occasions. His account is corroborated, according to the article, by a further nineteen signed affidavits that were sent to Stella Randolf. This is a significant number but the question that hangs over the witness statements is whether their consistency is due to their having been picked out deliberately to tell a particular story. We do not know the answer to this. The affidavit-writers might all have been members of a Gustave Whitehead fan club who communicate regularly and share their recollections. If so, they could not be described as neutral or independent. It must be emphasised that this does not imply that their statements are untruthful or misleading: only that their value as corroboration is limited. A critical, impartial researcher would need to gather more evidence, and in particular look for counter-claims – for example, statements from people who knew Whitehead well but never saw any of his planes in the air. Corroborating evidence needs to be tested by looking for conflicting accounts. If the search does not yield any contrary evidence, even after a serious attempt to find it, then the corroboration carries more weight.

← With corroboration
↓
contrary evidence

Independent sources
↓
Not collude

Another way to put this is that the witnesses should be representative of the people who were in a position to provide relevant information, not just from those whose testimony supports one side in the debate. There is a fuller discussion of representativeness in Chapter 18 in connection with statistical evidence.

17.1.1.3 Vested interest

One of the most familiar reasons for casting doubt on a person's testimony is that they have an interest in the outcome. Look again at the remark near the end of Dare's article:

> The prestigious Smithsonian Institute for Science, in return for ownership of the Wrights' Flyer, agreed not to publish or exhibit anything referring to flights before 1903. The question we should be asking is: Why?

If this is correct (and there is separate evidence that it is) the question 'Why?' arguably becomes very relevant. There are various possible reasons why no information about powered flight prior to 1903 has been displayed or published by the Smithsonian Institute. One is that there is no evidence to publish, and that is perfectly possible. The Smithsonian has a serious reputation for scientific research – an important factor in judging reliability – so that the absence of information about a Whitehead flight would normally suggest that none exists. Why then, as Jacey Dare asks, would there need to be an agreement by the Institute not to publish or exhibit anything referring to pre-1903 flights? This raises another possible explanation, namely self-interest. The Wrights may have wanted to secure their place in history, by suppressing any competing claims to fame. The Smithsonian, at the same time, wanted the Flyer for its exhibition after it had become famous. It would suit the Smithsonian as well that the aeroplane they had on show was the one that made history. The implications of this are clear: that there are advantages for the parties involved in telling one story rather than any other.

Skeptic ⟷ Naive

167

17.1.1.4 Reputation

Yet again it must be stressed that the existence of potential self-interest for one of the parties in a dispute does not mean that the person's word cannot be trusted. Fortunately, there are many people who respect the truth more than they value their own interests, and who will often sacrifice personal advantage rather than lie or mislead. It is as well that this is so, because if, as a rule, we could not trust people to be truthful we could never believe anything we hear or read.

Here reputation also plays a role in assessing reliability. A reputable source is generally expected to be more trustworthy than the general population, partly because they have earned the reputation but also because they have more to lose if they jeopardise it. [threaten] If it were discovered that the Smithsonian had deliberately suppressed information about a successful flight before the Wrights' at Kitty Hawk, it would seriously damage its valued reputation. It is not just a question of morality. It is actually to the advantage of reputable individuals and organisations to be honest and 'above board', because their reputation is itself of value to them, and it is in their interests to preserve it. The same would apply, perhaps less strongly, to the author of a book (like Stella Randolf) or the editor of a newspaper (like the *New York Herald*). On the one hand these all have a vested interest in challenging the official story, because it will attract readers and sell papers. On the other hand they are unlikely to fabricate evidence, both out of professionalism (we hope), and for fear of being found out. In the extreme case there is risk of being charged with libel.

In other words, vested interest cuts both ways. It does not necessarily motivate a person to falsify evidence. On the contrary, it can often be the very reason why someone takes care to tell the truth. A reputable source of information will want to be trusted in the future. It is not a cast-iron rule in either direction. For the critic there is always a balance to be struck. We should not automatically regard everyone who has something to gain as unreliable. But at the same time we need to retain a healthy scepticism, and be ready to question what we are presented with as fact. We should not assume that the Smithsonian deliberately suppressed information to their advantage. At the same time, we need to be ready to question why they agreed to the Wright brothers' demands.

17.1.1.5 Circumstantial evidence

Last but not least, there is a reference in the article to the circumstances surrounding Gustave Whitehead and the Wright brothers socially. One was a poor immigrant, who had to change his name to be accepted. The others were members of an influential American family. Did this, as Jacey Dare suggests, drown out the voice of one and give unfair 'clout' to the other? This is not a question about the truth of the claim: the difference in their social status is a known fact, but as evidence it is merely circumstantial. It could explain why Whitehead's achievements have never been properly recognised, but it is far from being conclusive evidence that there was an achievement to recognise.

17.1.2 An overstated claim?

Another arguable question mark over Jacey Dare's short article is whether she claims too much. The evidence she provides does not give sufficiently compelling grounds for rewriting the record books. What can be said, however, is that it raises a question mark over the Wright brothers' claim to fame. For even if the argument fails to show that they were *not* the first to fly, it doesn't follow that they *were*. Lack of evidence for something does not prove that it is false, or that the opposite is true.

[handwritten margin notes: Circumstantial evidence → Not supporting argument directly; Hegemony; Necessary]

There is a way, therefore, to be charitable about the document. This is an important word in critical interpretation. Put simply, it means giving the author some benefit of doubt about the meaning of the text, and in particular not taking it too literally. In the present case we need not take the headline as a plain, categorical statement. We can interpret it as doing no more than opening up a debate. On that reading, the wording of the headline is just down to journalistic style. If we understand it as a provocative or 'punchy' title rather than a literal claim, and take the last sentence of the article as the real conclusion, then perhaps Jacey Dare has a more defensible point. Maybe it *is* time to reopen the debate. If that is all she is really saying, then she has a stronger case, although another reader may feel that even that is going too far for the evidence available.

ACTIVITY 17.1

With the help of the discussion above, write your own critical response to Jacey Dare's article. Make reference where relevant to the credibility criteria discussed in Chapter 16.

17.2 Article 2: Further investigation

The article by Jacey Dare is brief, somewhat overstated, and one-sided. The evidence is selective and, above all, it is presented uncritically. No attempt is made to balance claim and counter-claim, or to subject the evidence to analysis and evaluation. The next article is not only much longer and more detailed, with quoted testimonies and reports, it is also much more balanced. In contrast to the Dare article, it is a piece of *critical* writing.

Read the article and make a note of some of the evidence that is cited and analysed by the author. Then carry out Activity 17.2, using ideas and concepts that have been discussed in this and the previous chapter.

GUSTAVE WHITEHEAD: DID HE BEAT THE WRIGHT BROTHERS INTO THE SKY?

by Lee Krystek

1   Although today it is a generally accepted fact that the Wright brothers were the first men to perfect a heavier-than-air craft, it was not always so. Many people believe that early aviation experimenters like Richard Pearse of New Zealand or Preston Watson of Scotland might have a claim to be the first to fly. One enigmatic figure in aviation history whose supporters say he made controlled flights as early as 1899 was Gustave Whitehead, a poor, German immigrant to the United States. Whitehead clearly built a number of aeroplanes before the Wrights were successful in 1903 at Kitty Hawk, but did any of his craft really fly?

2   Whitehead, who Americanised his name from Weisskopf when he immigrated from Bavaria, Germany, was a mechanic by trade who lived and worked in Boston, New York, Buffalo, Tonawanda, Johnstown, Pittsburgh, and finally Bridgeport, Connecticut around the turn of the century. According to at least one biography, Whitehead was fascinated by aviation from an early age and was inspired by the glider flights of Otto Lillienthal to build his own model glider at age 13. Sceptics point out this is surely a mistake or exaggeration since Whitehead was 13 in the year 1887, well before Lillienthal started his glider experiments.

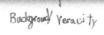
Background Veracity

3 According to an article in the January 1935 edition of *Popular Aviation* written by Stella Randolf and Harvey Phillips, Whitehead made his first flight in a steam-driven aircraft just outside Pittsburgh in the spring of 1899. Two years later, in August 1901, he made another flight with a gas-powered plane (which he designated as 'Number 21') near the town of Bridgeport, Connecticut. In 1902 he made a flight with an aircraft numbered '22' that flew over Long Island Sound. If true, these flights would have meant Whitehead preceded the Wright brothers into the air by at least one, or maybe even three years.

4 Unfortunately there is little information or evidence about the existence of the Pittsburgh flight. The account in *Popular Aviation* tells us that Whitehead hadn't expected the new aeroplane to go as far as it did, and he crashed into a building, destroying the craft:

But as they went onward and upward, steered by Gustave Whitehead at the controls in the front, they exceeded the distance originally planned and found themselves headed for a three-storey brick house. Afraid to attempt to swerve, there was but one hope, namely that they might clear the top of the house. But they failed. Down fell the machine, all but demolished, while the agonised fireman in the back writhed with the pain of a scalded leg. The glasses for indicating water level in the boilers had broken, permitting steam to envelop the man.

[handwritten left margin: Quoting from original publication →]

5 Even the most ardent Whitehead supporters admit that proof of the Pittsburgh experiment is lacking. More evidence is available of the Bridgeport flights, though. The plane Whitehead constructed at Bridgeport was, according to the *Popular Aviation* article:

... a monoplane with a four-cylinder two-cycle motor located forward. Ignition was of the make and break type and Columbia dry batteries were used. The gas tank was gravity-fed and held two gallons of petrol. The body of the machine was constructed of pine, spruce, and bamboo, reinforced with Shelby steel tubing and piano wires. The wing coverings were of Japanese silk, varnished and fastened to the bamboo struts with white tape. The wings spread out behind the two propellers, and were supported with wires running to a central mast. The entire thing weighed approximately 800 pounds. With Mr. Whitehead aboard the weight was increased to about 965 pounds. [handwritten: (Not directly relevant)]

6 On August 14, 1901, or so the story goes, Whitehead made a test flight near the location which was later to become the Sikorsky aeroplane factory. He flew the machine for one and a half miles that day. According to the *Popular Aviation* article the authors interviewed Junius Harworth, who had been a young boy assisting Whitehead. Harworth said he remembered the flight distinctly and in detail.

7 The next January Whitehead was ready with a new machine, which he tested on the 17th. Again *Popular Aviation*:

Gustave Whitehead took his place at the controls of the machine, the men gave it a preliminary push, and it trundled away on its three wheels and was off! The plane performed so admirably that its owner continued his flight for a distance of two miles over the Sound, following the shore line of the beach, although he had intended to make only short flights of not more than half a mile. The men pulled it ashore, and now Gustave Whitehead proposed to fly across the Sound.

8 According to the article Whitehead never made it across the Sound, but turned back, deciding to test the ability to turn the plane instead.

9 As interesting as the assertions in the Randolf and Phillips article were, they were written more than three decades after the incidents depicted and nine years after Whitehead's death in 1927. Evidence more contemporary to the events would be helpful in establishing the truth of the matter. This came in the form of an article in *The Bridgeport Herald* newspaper from August 18, 1901. The author states he witnessed a night test of the plane, at first unpiloted but loaded with sand bags, and later with Whitehead at the controls. Such a news report would seem clinching evidence that the flight had taken place, yet sceptics point out that the story has holes in it. [handwritten right margin: Sceptics: Doubtful]

10 The first is that the aircraft was tested early in the morning before sunrise. With primitive flying technology getting a plane into the air would be dangerous during the day and certainly suicidal at night. Also, the idea that the plane could be tested with no pilot, but only sand-bag ballast seems absurd. Early flying machines were tricky to handle and an unpiloted test inconceivable → oncological

flight would almost certainly have resulted in a crash.

11 Why would a newspaper report a successful flight if it didn't really occur? Though it has virtually disappeared from the mainstream newspaper business, in the 19th and early 20th century hoax journalism was widely practiced. For this reason outlandish stories dating from that period cannot be taken at face value. It would not be inconceivable at all that a reporter looking for a story might have come across Whitehead and his flying machines and decided to say that he actually witnessed a test flight that had never occurred.

hoax
↓
fool people

double negative →

12 How do we know that Whitehead built aeroplanes at all? On that point there is some pretty solid evidence. There are a number of photos showing Whitehead with different flying machines that he'd constructed. Unfortunately none of them show any of his powered machines actually up in the air, though they do confirm that one of his gliders flew. Such a photo of a powered flying machine would have gone a long way toward proving Whitehead's claims.

13 Other evidence that would establish Whitehead's success at getting into the air would have been plans of the aircraft he built along with notes or letters documenting the progress of his aviation experiments. Whitehead, except for a few letters to *Scientific American* about his flights, left no paper trail to follow. Of course, Whitehead's supporters point out that the German immigrant was not a man of letters, but a mechanic, and the fact that he simply did not bother to document his flights does not mean that he did not actually make them.

14 In 1936, after the *Popular Aviation* article appeared, the Harvard University Committee on Research in the Social Sciences sent John Crane, a professor of economics, to Connecticut to get to the bottom of the story. Crane published his conclusions in an article in the *National Aeronautical Association Magazine* in December 1936 entitled 'Did Whitehead Actually Fly?' According to Crane, after interviewing many Bridgeport residents and Whitehead's family, he only found one person who remembered the flights and that person had a financial interest in a book that Stella Randolf was writing on Whitehead.

15 It seems impossible to establish positively from the historical record that Whitehead made the flights, but can we know if his designs were capable of flight?

16 There have been several attempts to rebuild some of Whitehead's aircraft and fly them. In the late 1980s a group studied pictures of 'Number 21' and drew up plans for an aircraft based on them. These plans were then used by the Historical Flight Research Committee Gustave Whitehead (HFRC-GV) in Germany to build an aircraft which was successfully flight tested in 1997. While the test shows that Whitehead's design might have flown, it does not prove that it actually did. Without plans drawn up by Whitehead himself, there is no way of knowing for sure if the reproduction was truly accurate. Also, the reproduction aircraft used a modern 'ultralight' engine and propeller which probably produced significantly more thrust than Whitehead's original engine/propeller combination would have had. Since engine weight vs. power was a significant hurdle for early aviators, this alone might have rendered a workable aircraft design unflyable.

← hindsight

17 Whitehead supporters point to an unusual deal made between the Smithsonian Institution and the Wright brothers' estate as one of the reasons why information about Whitehead's flights were suppressed. Though the Wright brothers are generally recognised as the first to build a successful powered aeroplane today, that was not the case in the early 1900s. The Wright brothers fought to protect their patents while other aeroplane builders tried to find either ways around the patents or ways to make them invalid. Glenn Curtiss rebuilt an experimental aeroplane designed by Samuel Langley of the Smithsonian Institution to try and show that other aircraft *could* have flown before the Wright's Flyer did. This caused a schism between the Smithsonian Institution and the Wright

171

brothers and for this reason the Flyer was not exhibited in the Smithsonian until 1948. When it finally was, it was only with the agreement that:

Neither the Smithsonian Institution or its successors, nor any museum or other agency, bureau or facilities administered for the United States of America by the Smithsonian Institution or its successors shall publish or permit to be displayed a statement or label in connection with or in respect of any aircraft model or design of earlier date than the Wright Airplane of 1903, claiming in effect that such aircraft was capable of carrying a man under its own power in controlled flight.

18 Whether without this agreement the Smithsonian would have really come to the conclusion that Whitehead flew first is purely a matter of speculation. It has, however, added to the feelings among Whitehead supporters that there has been a conspiracy not to give him his just rewards.

19 So, did Gustave Whitehead really beat the Wright brothers into the sky? This is an issue that is never likely to be settled to everyone's satisfaction. Clearly the evidence for his flights is too thin to overturn the Wright brothers' place in the minds of most historians. However, there are a lot of people who believe, and will continue to believe, that Whitehead was successful in getting an aircraft into the air several years before the Wright's Flyer left the ground at Kitty Hawk in December of 1903. It is interesting for the rest of us to consider whether the history of flight might be considerably changed if someone had thought to bring a camera to an empty field outside of Bridgeport early one morning in 1901.

[handwritten margin notes:]
Plausibility
Credibility
Reliability
Reputation
Circumstancial evidence

ACTIVITY 17.2

The following three tasks are related to the article by Lee Krystek. Complete them using ideas and concepts from this and the previous chapter.

1 Discuss and/or give short written responses to the following:

   a One of the basic criteria for judging evidence is plausibility. How plausible, or otherwise, do you find the accounts of Whitehead's alleged flights in the three quotations from *Popular Aviation* – and why?

   b Explain the objection made in paragraph 2 to the account of Whitehead's early interest in aviation. Is it a damaging objection?

   c Assess the evidence gathered by John Crane for the Harvard University Committee, using the relevant evaluation criteria. *→ craven*

   d How valuable is the evidence in paragraph 16? What would you conclude from it, and why?

   e Identify two pieces of conflicting evidence, and decide which you consider the stronger, giving reasons.

2 What do you make of the involvement of the Smithsonian Institute? What, if anything, is its significance in answering the headline question of Krystek's article?

3 Either: hold a class debate on the motion:

   The Wright brothers' place in history is questionable.

   Or: write a short speech supporting or opposing this statement.

Summary

- The purpose of this chapter was to give some detailed examples of evidence in use, and issues for critical evaluation that arise from them. In particular it illustrated how some of the *criteria* introduced in Chapter 16 can assist in evaluating evidence. These criteria included:
  - plausibility, credibility, reliability
  - reputation
  - vested interest
  - corroboration and consistency
  - circumstantial evidence.
- The concept of **selectivity** was also introduced.
- An extended example of critical analysis and evaluation of evidence was provided in the longer of the two texts.

'Therefore' text for conclusion
'Because'

End-of-chapter questions

Study the evidence in the following sources and then answer the questions that follow.

Source A: News story

The threat to humans from shark attacks is on the increase. In July 2017 tourists in Majorca came face-to-face with an 8ft blue shark. Holidaymakers on the Mediterranean island ran from the sea at one of its most popular beaches when the monster appeared. It was later captured and killed. In the same week a warning was issued that a deadly great white shark was circling the waters off the UK. Fishing expert Graeme Pullen claimed a great white had visited Hayling Island off the south coast of the UK more than once in the past two years. Reports have also just come in of two serious shark attacks near Ascension Island in the South Atlantic. A surfer was attacked when he fell from his paddle board, and a British woman was severely bitten when swimming at the same beach. It took three men to pull her ashore, one of whom, her husband, punched the shark to free her. These were the first recorded attacks by sharks at the island, but recently more sharks have been sighted closer to land, presumably in search of food.

2016 had the highest number of shark attacks on record, with 107 reported worldwide. It is obvious why. Rising water temperatures, the practice of shark-cage viewing (where the creatures are lured with bait), sea fishing excursions, and the increased popularity of surfing and paddle boarding, have inevitably brought sharks closer to our shores.

Source B: Official survey

The International Shark Attack File (ISAF), compiled by the Florida Museum of Natural History, investigated 154 incidents of alleged shark–human interaction occurring worldwide in 2016. Upon review, 84 of these incidents represented confirmed cases of unprovoked shark attacks on humans. 'Unprovoked attacks' are defined as incidents where an attack on a live human occurs in the shark's natural habitat with no human provocation of the shark. 'Provoked attacks' usually occur when a human initiates physical contact with a shark, e.g. a diver bitten after grabbing a shark, attacks on spear-fishers and those feeding sharks, bites occurring while unhooking or removing a shark from a fishing net, etc. The 70 incidents not accorded unprovoked status in 2016 included 39 provoked attacks and 7 incidents which were suspected as not involving a shark.

The 2016 yearly total of 84 unprovoked attacks was on par with our most recent five-year (2011–2015) average of 82 incidents annually. By contrast, the 98 unprovoked incidents in the previous reporting year, 2015, was the highest yearly total on record. The number of shark-human interactions occurring in a given year is directly correlated with the amount of time humans spend in the sea. As the world population continues its upsurge and interest in aquatic recreation concurrently rises, we realistically should expect increases in the number of shark attacks and other aquatic recreation-related injuries. If shark populations remain the same or increase in size, one might predict more attacks each year than the previous year because more people are in the water. But shark populations are actually declining or holding at greatly reduced levels in many areas of the world as a result of over-fishing and habitat loss.

Source C: Trend

The long-term trend in fatality rates has been one of constant reduction over the past 11+ decades, reflective of advances in beach safety practices and medical treatment, and increased public awareness of avoiding potentially dangerous situations.

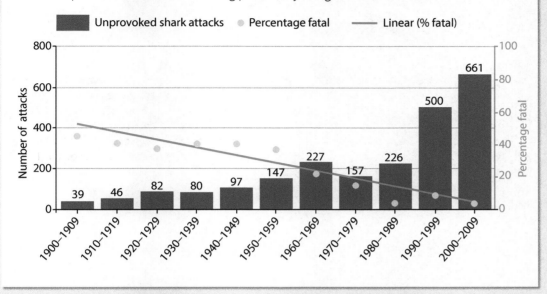

1 a What is the nature of the evidence given in the first paragraph of Source A for the opening claim that 'the threat to humans from shark attacks is on the increase'?

   b Identify two weaknesses in the evidence in the first paragraph.

   c The first paragraph ends with the sentence: 'These were the first recorded attacks by sharks at the island…' What does this add to the evidence?

   d How reliable is Graeme Pullen as a source of evidence?

   e Assess the reasons the author gives for the increase in the threat from sharks – rising water temperatures, shark-cage viewing and so on.

2 a Identify an example of consistency or corroboration between Source A and Sources B or C.

   b Identify an example of inconsistency between the sources.

3 Compare the credibility of the claims made in Sources A and B.

4 a Identify two reasons why the figure of 84 given in the first paragraph of Source B might not accurately represent the number of unprovoked attacks on people in 2016.

   b In Source B it states that 'shark populations are actually declining or holding at greatly reduced levels in many areas of the world…'
      Explain why this is not contradicted by the claim of sharply increasing numbers of shark attacks.

Chapter 18
Statistical evidence

Learning objectives

The focus of this chapter turns from information in general to statistical information in particular. Statistics are an important source of evidence in many fields of inquiry, and it is for this reason that they need to be viewed and assessed critically.

18.1 What are statistics?

A statistic is a single item of numerical data – for example, the number of students in a certain college whose second language is English, or the number of different species of trees in the world. Statistics, in the plural, are sets or collections of such items collected for a purpose, such as educational research or predicting election outcomes. 'Statistics' (as a singular noun) is also the name given to the science of collecting, analysing and evaluating data.

Statistical data must be assessed for credibility and reliability for the same reasons as evidence in general must be assessed, and by many of the same criteria:

- What is the *source* of the data; who provided it?
- What was the *purpose* for which it was collected?
- How was it collected; what was the *methodology*?
- Is it *corroborated* by (and *consistent* with) other available evidence?
- Is it relevant, plausible, informative?

18.1.1 Sources of data

The first question is crucial for obvious reasons. It is also inseparable from the second question, about purpose. People do not normally go to the trouble and expense of gathering data without a reason – to further an investigation, for example, or to confirm a hypothesis, or to justify a government policy. Unless the source of a data set is known and trusted, there is a risk of bias, whether due to vested interest, or to unscientific methods of collection and presentation. If the source is a research team and their purpose is to argue for a particular outcome, then questions regarding independence and impartiality have to be asked. This is not to say that when bias occurs it is necessarily deliberate or dishonest: researchers can unintentionally focus on evidence which supports their viewpoint or which challenges an opposing one without setting out to do so.

It is also important for critical purposes to have information about the methodology used to gather and process the data for the project in question. Suppose one such project were to investigate foreign language aptitude in a given population by conducting a survey in which a number of people were asked how many languages they could speak. As it stands this would be a crude and dubious procedure. First, we have no information about the number of people questioned, or the makeup of the sample. The sector of the community who were questioned might have had linguistic skills well above or well below the average for the population. A reliable survey needs to be accompanied by some explanation as to how such deficiencies have been guarded against.

Second, the question, 'How many languages can you speak?' is hopelessly vague and uninformative. There is nothing to indicate what level of ability counts as 'ability to speak' a language. Indeed, setting and defining such a level is notoriously difficult.

Third, some respondents might not answer truthfully, for various reasons including perhaps not wanting to appear uneducated. Last of all the evidence, such as it is, stands alone, with no mention of any corroborating evidence. It is a recognised reliability criterion for any scientific experiment or survey that it must be repeatable (with a similar outcome). This means that its findings can be confirmed by other comparable experiments; and at the same time that comparable experiments or surveys do not contradict the findings.

18.1.2 Collecting data

Statistics are basically numbers, but numbers relating to a particular population. 'Population' is the technical term for a whole collection of people or objects that fall under a particular description. Whales form a population; so do eligible voters, tomatoes, ten-dollar bills, autonomous vehicles, days since the turn of the century, species of trees in the world and so on. The number of any one of these is a statistic.

Some statistics can be obtained and verified by simply counting. The number of days between two given dates can be calculated easily enough. The number of citizens eligible to vote in the next election can be obtained from an electoral register. A count of this kind is known as a census; the term 'census data' simply means the entire number of individuals in a given population. So long as it can be shown that the counting was done carefully and honestly, census data can be taken as fact. Of course mistakes can be made, especially when the numbers are large. (Votes are often recounted for this reason.) Also, some populations are too unstable for a complete, up-to-the-minute count to be made. The world's human population is a case in point: by the time any count has been made, a large number of births and deaths will have already occurred. Nonetheless, and whatever the practical difficulties, a census is in theory a complete population count.

By contrast there are populations which are uncountable, even in theory. Future populations are an obvious example. Consider the number of votes that Party X will win in a forthcoming election. Clearly it is impossible to count votes before they are cast, and predicting the numbers in advance is notoriously difficult. The usual procedure for forecasting an election result is to ask a lot of people how they will vote when the time comes. But as experience has all too often shown, there are serious problems with this procedure:

1   There is the practical impossibility of contacting and questioning all eligible voters.
2   There is the fact voters can (and frequently do) change their minds.
3   There will always be some respondents who reply untruthfully.

18.1.3 Sampling

When census data is unavailable, the standard solution is to take a sample of the population, and to use data drawn from it as an indication of some facts about the whole population. If successful this solves the first problem listed above, though not the second or third. But it is not a solution even to the first problem unless the sample is representative of the population concerned. If it is biased or selective the sample cannot be relied upon to reflect population-wide trends or patterns. For instance, if a sample of voters contains a greater proportion of over-35s than is found in the general population, then the sample will not be representative with respect to age. This would have serious implications for the reliability of the forecast if younger voters tended to favour Party X, and over-35s Party Y. A similar risk applies if the sample contains a disproportionate number of people from one part of the country, or from a different class background. Any of these factors could undermine the prediction.

The standard way to avoid biased or unrepresentative data is to take a random sample. This is sometimes referred to as a probability sample, because it supposedly allows every member of the population a fair chance of being selected. For example, if university graduates make up 20% of all voters, then – according to probability theory – random selection should result in 20% of the sample having university degrees; and likewise for the whole range of variables in the population.

18.1.4 Sample size

Random selection, whereby each individual member of the sample is plucked out purely by chance, will not ensure representativeness for all sectors of the population, but it will increase the probability of obtaining a representative sample. There is one more (big) proviso, however: the sample must be large. The probability of the sample mirroring the population increases in accordance with its size.

Suppose you have a bag containing 20 red balls and 80 blue ones, and you pick out a ball at random – that is, without looking. There is a probability of 0.8 that the ball you pick out will be blue. If you repeat this ten times, putting the ball back each time, you will have performed a random selection. On the basis of probability the selected sample should contain 2 red balls. But in reality the outcome could be any combination – even 10 red balls in extreme cases. The possibility of such improbable outcomes decreases the larger the sample is, and increases when the sample is small. (Ten is a very small sample by any statistical standard.) If you repeat the experiment with a hundred balls, then a thousand, then ten thousand, the ratio of blue to red balls will get closer and closer to 80:20. By the same token, the reliability of the claims made on the basis of the sample increases. As a rough guide, a genuinely random sample of 1,000 items could be expected to result in a margin of error of around 5%, giving a 95% probability of a reliable outcome.

Statisticians mathematically calculate how large a sample has to be to give a reasonably reliable forecast in different kinds of inquiry. They also research the best methodologies for obtaining a truly random sample. The mathematics is complex, and is beyond the scope of this book. For most critical-thinking purposes it is enough to understand the principle involved, and to be able to recognise the most common weakness in the statistical reasoning that you encounter in the media and elsewhere. Small and/or unrepresentative samples are always defects to look out for.

179

EXAMPLE ACTIVITY 18.1

Comment critically on the following statistical claims. How reliable do you consider the evidence to be in each case?

1   A survey was conducted to assess public opinion on the recent government proposal to improve air quality by making a charge on diesel vehicles entering major cities. Around half of all vehicles on the roads currently run on diesel, but out of two thousand car drivers randomly questioned in car parks in cities across the country, 61% said they were opposed to the charge.

2   72% of retail spending is by card payment, according to a survey at the checkouts of a massive hypermarket in central France. 2 900 payments were recorded during a single day, 2 088 of which were made by card.

3   According to a recent study of the world's plants by Botanical Gardens Conservation International (BGCI) there are 60 065 species of trees in the world. A comprehensive tree list was compiled using data gathered from the BGCI network of 500 member organisations.

Commentary

The first statistic is based on the responses of a sample of car drivers to a question about charges on diesel vehicles. (Governments of several countries are planning to charge drivers of diesel vehicles in a bid to improve air quality in inner cities.) We are told that the sample was 2 000, which is a respectable size, and that it was randomly selected. Therefore, given that around half of all drivers have diesel cars, there is no reason to suppose that the sample had a bias towards those who would be financially penalised by the charge – 61% is a substantial majority, above the generally accepted margin of error for a sample of its size. But the sample was drawn exclusively from drivers questioned in city car parks, and that is not the whole population – i.e. the public at large – that the statistic is intended to represent. The outcome might be very different if pedestrians, users of public transport, parents out with their children, asthma sufferers, health workers, etc., are all proportionally represented in the sample.

There are also unanswered questions about the source of the evidence and the motives for collecting it. Likely sources are motoring organisations, who have drivers' interests at heart; or vehicle manufacturers or consortiums who would have an obvious vested interest. Such factors could have an influence on the selection and analysis of the data and/or the way the question was framed. (We should not forget the recent scandal over falsified emissions tests on some makes of diesel cars.) Reputable sources (like the BGCI in the third example) publish their identity along with their findings. If the source is not given, the reliability of the evidence is further open to question.

The second statistic is drawn from a sample of payments at retail checkouts to ascertain the proportion that are made by card (as opposed to cash or cheque). The information here is objective, unlike the previous example which concerned public opinion. It is a plain fact that 72% of the customers in the survey paid by card. The sample size was large and selection was random insofar as every payment on the day, in that store, was counted.

These are positive points. But is it safe to assume that data collected from one store, on one particular day, is representative of the retail-spending population as a whole? You will recall that a criterion of reliability for experimental or observational data is its repeatability. To test the findings from the hypermarket survey, similar samples should be taken from high-street (town-centre) shops, restaurants, bars, bookshops, music stores, street-markets and so on, to discover whether payment habits are the same across all retail outlets. Also the growing volume of e-commerce needs to be taken into account, especially as online purchases are predominantly paid for by credit or debit card. It might be argued that a hypermarket, with its enormous range of goods under one roof, is a good indicator of retail trade in general. But against this there is the fact that payments at hypermarket checkouts tend be larger than those in smaller shops, because people are typically buying in quantity. All in all, it would be unsafe to assume that the survey is either sufficiently random, or properly representative. Without the corroboration of findings from other samples, the evidence on its own must be treated with caution.

The third example is census data. It is not a sample, but a comprehensive survey of the world's plants to ascertain all and only the number of species of trees. It alleged that there were over 60 000. How do we judge such a claim? Since we as readers cannot repeat the experiment for ourselves, our main concern must be with the reliability we place on the source – or sources. Several relevant criteria were discussed in the previous chapter, in particular reputation, expertise and corroboration. The reliability of evidence of this kind obviously depends on extensive botanical knowledge, and the skill to identify and classify specimens. On the strength of its reputation it is reasonable to assume that the BGCI researchers possess the requisite expertise and that, with 500 member organisations contributing data, the findings are well corroborated.

These observations on the three surveys do not mean that the findings discussed above are necessarily right or wrong. What they are intended to demonstrate is the need for critical questioning of statistical data before rushing to general conclusions.

18.2 Trends

A trend is a pattern of more or less gradual change in a set of data. A single statistic or value cannot represent a trend, nor can a sudden leap from one value to another, though either of these can be part of a trend. When a single statistic is part of a trend we can refer to it usefully as a data point, and plot it on a graph. If a line drawn between a sequence of points can be seen to travel in a particular direction, then it represents a trend. Compare the two graphs below, giving sales figures for two businesses over the course of one year:

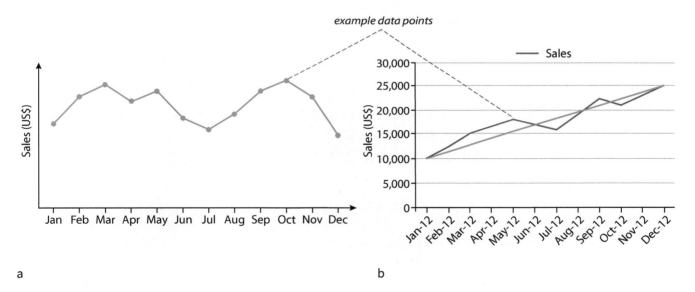

a   b

The lines connecting the data points in both graphs change direction frequently, but whilst there is no general direction of travel recognisable in graph (a), there is in graph (b), as shown by the red line. If a similar straight line were drawn on graph (a) it would give a very false impression of how sales had performed over the year.

18.2.1 Trends and predictions

Statistical trends are often used as evidence to justify predictions, and/or decisions. If a company's sales have been steadily rising over a sufficient period of time a company may feel entitled to assume the trend will continue, and make optimistic business plans accordingly. The crucial proviso, however, is in the word 'sufficient'. Making the wrong decision could result in a mountain of unsold stock if the trend changes in the near future. A trend, in this respect, functions in the same way as a sample – a sample of data points – and is open to the same critical questions about size, representativeness, and repeatability.

Like a very small sample in a survey, a very short sequence of data points is weak evidence of a lasting trend. If the company featured in graph (a) had based its forecasts on the upward trend from July to October, and planned for a bumper Christmas, it would have been in for a shock, because the data for those months was not representative of the whole year. This also emphasises the need for repeatability: a trend can only be good grounds for an important prediction if it is consistent with other relevant trends – for example, the trends in other similar companies, and/or trends over longer periods of time. Suppose graph (a) was matched with data from previous years, or repeated over several more years, and that the graph looked very similar each time. Then the company's analysts could conclude with some confidence that their sales were likely to peak in the spring and autumn, and dip in summer and winter.

> **EXAMPLE ACTIVITY 18.2**
>
> In the chart below, the top of each column marks a data point, corresponding to the number of new houses sold in the United States in that year. Joining the points does not result in a single continuous trend, but it does produce a pattern of sorts that can be interpreted and described.
>
>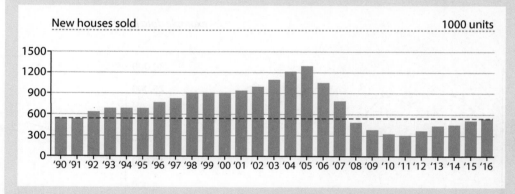
>
> Write a short paragraph describing the fluctuation in sales of new houses in the United States in the 1990s and first 16 years of the twenty-first century. What does the data provide by way of evidence for predicting house sales in the next years of the decade?

Commentary

The key word here is 'fluctuation'. The sales of house prices year-on-year were not stable nor was there a single direction of change. The broken line indicates that sales were practically the same in 2016 as they had been in 1990, but they rose and fell above and below that level by many hundreds of thousands. For the first fifteen years of the period there were small ups and downs and short periods of flat-lining. There was also a marked acceleration in the rate of increase – commonly referred to as a spike – in the five years leading up to the peak in 2005. All the same, the 15-year trend from 1990 to 2005 was relentlessly upward.

Following the spike there was an even more dramatic plunge in sales. Anyone familiar with recent economic history will understand the significance of this. In the years leading up to the 2007–2008 financial crisis, property prices in the US, the UK and many other countries rose to unsustainable levels, fuelling (amongst other things) the demand for new homes. In retrospect the bubble was bound to burst, but even the experts at the time could not (or chose not to) see it coming. Whatever the reason, the market collapsed in value, with consequences clearly reflected in the chart.

Around 2011 the downward trend bottomed out and by 2016 had returned to roughly the same rate of increase as was seen in the 1990s. Is it safe to predict that house sales in the US will continue to rise again post 2016, or that the cycle of boom and bust will be repeated? By the time you are reading this page you might be able to give an answer. But that is not really the point of the question because by then you will have the benefit of hindsight. The question is about the value of past trends as evidence for predictions. The lesson to be learnt from the chart should be clear enough: such evidence *on its own* is inherently unreliable. It has a role to play, but only if corroborated by evidence of other kinds.

It should be added that some trends are naturally more predictable that others. The rise and fall of tides can be predicted with near certainty, not just because this has always happened in the past but because we know *why* it happens as well as *that* it happens. Trends that are governed by human behaviour – like economic fluctuations – are not so fully understood. If they were, prediction could be improved.

18.2.2 Correlation

One of the reasons for studying trends and patterns in data is to identify correlations. A correlation is a measure of the extent to which two or more variables change in relation to each other. A correlation is called positive if the variables increase or decrease in line with each other. In a negative (or inverse) correlation one variable increases as the other decreases. Correlation can also be described as strong or weak, which is best understood by examples. There is a strong, positive correlation between age and height during the early years of a person's life. The trend, in other words, is to grow taller with age, not necessarily at the same rate, but more or less continually. The graph below depicts one child's development over time, correlating their age (on the horizontal axis) with their height (on the vertical axis).

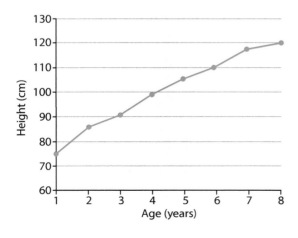

There is also a strong correlation between height and weight, not just over time, but between people of different sizes. The data points in the graph below – known as a scatter graph – represent 20 young people ranging between 1.34 m and 1.6 m in height and weighing between 28 kg and 70 kg. If there was a perfect correlation the data points would form a single straight line. But humans do not conform in that way: there are variations in the ratio of height to weight from one person to the next. We can say there is a positive correlation because the points cluster around a straight line (known as a line of best fit) which angles upwards from the bottom left-hand corner towards the top right. Because the sample is small this cannot be taken as the average weight/height ratio for the whole population. However, the cluster is close enough to a straight line to confirm that there is a strong correlation between height and weight generally – something we knew, or could have guessed, anyway.

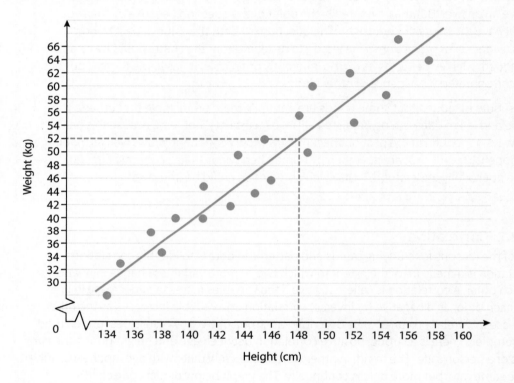

The closer the points are to a single line the stronger the correlation, whether positive or negative. If there is no recognisable line of fit, we must assume there is no correlation.

Suggest a pair of variables that would illustrate each of the examples of different patterns of data shown in the graphs below. For example, which pattern might reflect the sales of umbrellas in relation to hours of rainfall on a given day?

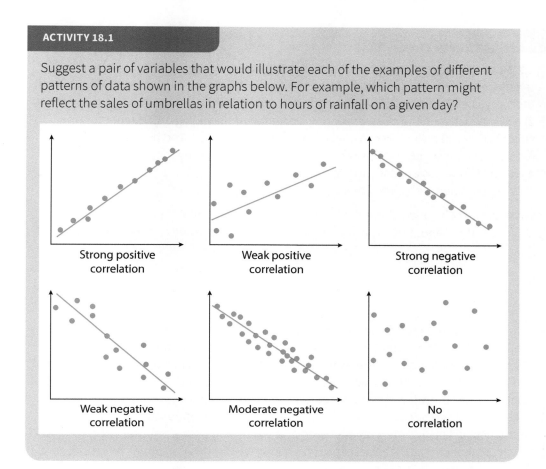

Strong positive correlation

Weak positive correlation

Strong negative correlation

Weak negative correlation

Moderate negative correlation

No correlation

18.2.3 Relations between trends

When two or more trends can be identified at the same time they may or may not be related. For instance, if seasonal air temperature is rising it can be expected that water temperature will rise accordingly. Hence we say that there is a positive correlation between the two events. Neither one *causes* the other: both have the same cause, namely the heat from the sun.

Not all correlations are positive. An increase over time in interest rates is likely to be accompanied by a reduction in borrowing and spending, again for fairly obvious reasons. Between these trends there is an *inverse* correlation, one going up as the other goes down. In this particular case it is a reasonable hypothesis that one of the factors is responsible for the other: the higher cost of borrowing usually makes people more reluctant to borrow, and with less borrowing there is less money to spend. However, the connection is not a cast-iron one or applicable in all cases: some people will continue to borrow even when interest rates are high. They 'buck the trend', as the saying goes. Nonetheless, in the population as a whole – or over a large sample – the correlation between interest rates and reduced spending is a strong one.

It is often tempting when we discover a correlation to look for a causal connection between the correlates, or to see one as the explanation for the other. (The noun 'correlate' means any one of the elements in a correlation.) Likewise it is tempting to use a statistical correlation as evidence of a causal or explanatory connection. There is an extremely important critical point to take on board here: just because two things happen at the same time, or one follows soon after the other, it does not mean that one has *caused* the other. This is even true when one thing is deliberately done with the intention of bringing about the other: it may have the desired effect, but on occasions the desired effect may just be a happy coincidence.

EXAMPLE ACTIVITY 18.3

Consider an imaginary report published by a city police authority on a five-year initiative to reduce local crime. Three trends are identified in the report: 1) an increase of 15% over the five years in the number of police officers regularly and visibly patrolling the streets; 2) a 7% reduction in the number of crimes committed (including a 12% reduction in violent crime); 3) an increase in public fear of crime – as evidenced by a survey of 1 200 residents. Of those questioned 64% said that they were growing more afraid of becoming a victim of crime (as opposed to less afraid or just the same), compared with only 46% of those questioned five years earlier.

What can be concluded about the trends and correlations identified in this 'report'? Discuss or think about this question before reading the following commentary.

Commentary

There are a number of statistical facts stated in the report. The question we are concerned with is how they are interrelated. Take the first two trends: the five-year increase in visible police patrols and a concurrent reduction in crime. ('Concurrent' means happening at the same time, or alongside, as opposed to 'consecutive' which means one after the other.) Numerically speaking there is an inverse correlation between the two trends. However, in qualitative terms (as opposed to purely numerical) a fall in crime would be seen as a *positive* outcome; a success (though evidently not enough of a success to prevent a growth in fear of crime). A rise in fear of crime, qualitatively speaking, is a *negative* outcome. But as already stated we have to be careful how we use these terms. As soon as we start talking about 'success' or positive (or negative) outcomes we are already running the risk of jumping to unsupported conclusions. There is no question about the existence of a correlation, but looking beyond that can we *attribute* the fall in crime to the police initiative? Is the report evidence that higher numbers of police on the streets has the effect of reducing crime?

The short answer is *no*. All we can conclude is that on this occasion there was a fall in crime that coincided with increased policing. The danger here is that because the increased police presence is so plausible as an explanation for the correlated fall in crime, we assume that it *is* the explanation. It is perfectly possible, however, that crime rates might have been dropping everywhere in the country during the same period and for altogether different reasons, even in cities where police numbers were being cut; so that although the two trends are matters of fact one may have had no impact at all on the other.

What about the third trend, the increase in fear of crime? Initially this might seem a negative outcome in terms of what was hoped for from the initiative. Moreover, it is a surprising fact. The natural expectation would be that better policing and a fall in crime would reduce anxiety, not raise it. Because the correlation is a surprising one, we find ourselves looking for an explanation for it, and assuming that if it fits the facts it must be the case. This too is a temptation, and one to be wary of. It is not too far-fetched to imagine that the sight of more police might have the effect of making people *more* aware of the threat posed by criminals, and this has increased their fears. But just because this *would* explain the correlation, if true, it does not mean that it *is* true.

So what can be concluded from a single initiative like the imaginary example above? The answer is: very little. Without more research and corroborating evidence the report provides little more than anecdotal evidence: a single experiment, conducted in one city and over a relatively short period of time.

The issues introduced here are discussed in more detail in the coming chapters on inference, argument, and explanation. In this section they relate to statistical evidence in particular, but they have much wider application to critical thinking in general.

18.3 Presentation

We end this chapter by looking at modes of presentation: ways in which statistical information is commonly put before the audience. One might think that data is data, and so long as it is accurate, representative, etc. it is merely a matter of preference as to how it is displayed. But how a statistic is displayed can make a big difference to the effect it has on its audience. On the positive side a well-chosen mode of presentation can make a statistic more comprehensible or digestible; but on the negative side there are ways in which essentially accurate data can create a false or misleading impression – intentionally or otherwise.

The plainest and generally the most neutral way to present a body of numerical information is in a table. Here, for example, is a table showing the weekly fluctuation in the exchange rate of the euro against the US dollar over a five-week period in 2017.

Table 18.1

Date	EUR	USD
11.3.17	1.00	1.066
18.3.17	1.00	1.076
25.3.17	1.00	1.078
1.4.17	1.00	1.066
8.4.17	1.00	1.064
15.4.17	1.00	1.061

The data from the table can alternatively be presented in visual form.

EXAMPLE ACTIVITY 18.4

Compare the next two figures. Do they represent the same, or different, information?

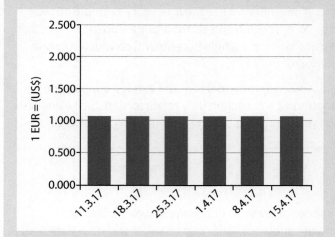

a

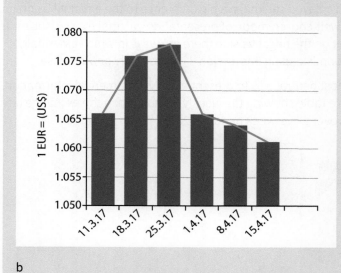

b

Commentary

Both bar charts convey the same raw data as the table in graph (a), and as each other. The difference between the two figures is purely presentational. However, that is not to say that there is no difference in the *impression* given by each one. Graph (a) suggests that the exchange rate practically flat-lined for the five weeks in question, whereas graph (b) depicts sharp fluctuations over the same period. It is easy to see why the difference occurs: it is due entirely to the range of values on the vertical axis – in other words, scale. In graph (a) the scale begins at zero, and ranges up to 2.5 dollars, rendering the 1 or 2 cent variation barely visible. The range on the axis in graph (b) is only 3 cents ($1.05–$1.08), creating a 'zoom-in' effect on the narrow range within which the rate varies.

Is one of the graphs the 'right' visualisation, and the other 'wrong'? Not exactly: both give a somewhat distorted picture. One exaggerates the fluctuations in the rate, the other registers no significant movement at all. Unless you are exchanging very large amounts of currency, a cent either way is not going to have much impact on your life, but still it is useful to know the direction in which the rate is changing, and Fig. 18.8 fails to do that. Fig. 18.9 is certainly more sensitive to variation, but perhaps unnecessarily alarmist, if used to prompt headlines such as:

EURO PLUNGES TO 5-WEEK LOW AGAINST DOLLAR

Ideally we want a happy medium: visualisation which is sensitive to variation, but not so much so as to distort or exaggerate.

18.3.1 Some problems with presentation

Sometimes the nature of the data itself makes presentation difficult. In the previous example the problem was the low level of variation, but large variations, and/or major anomalies can also make trouble. The following sales were reported by a small publishing house after its first year of trading. A total of five titles were marketed, one of which proved much more popular than the other four. They are listed in the table below as books A–E.

Table 18.2

A	357
B	488
C	361
D	580
E	16,676

EXAMPLE ACTIVITY 18.5

Examine the three graphs below, each of which is meant to depict the sales figures in the table above visually. Explain the problem with each of the visualisations.

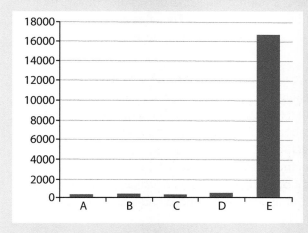

a

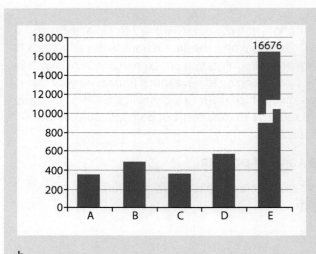

b

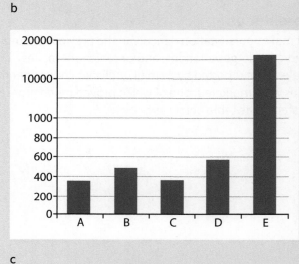

c

Commentary

In graph (a) an ordinary scale is used on the vertical axis, with a range from 0 to 20 000. This range is needed because the volume of sales of one of the books is more than 27 times greater than the next-best seller in the list. The effect is to squash the columns representing the other titles, so that the differences between them are almost indistinguishable.

The solution adopted by the next two figures is to **truncate** some of the data in one of two ways. This just means shortening, or condensing, one or more of the columns. For example in graph (b) the column representing Book E is broken, to show that there is a missing section. The actual number of sales is displayed above the column to compensate. This permits visual discrimination between the sales of the other titles, but at the cost of losing any sense of the gulf between Book E and the rest. Graph (c) has a similar purpose, but achieves it by compressing the vertical axis. Above 1 000 the intervals change from 200 to 5 000. But unless this is noticed and adjustment made in how the graph is interpreted, it could be misleading.

The message to take from this is the need for vigilance: to be aware of the purpose and usefulness of such techniques but also of their potential for abuse. Imagine a politically sensitive report on, say, funding for schools by different educational authorities. Depending on who is publishing the report, and why, there may be a motive for presenting the data in a manner that either maximises or minimises the impression created by a particular mode of presentation without actually falsifying the data.

18.3.2 Multiple trends

There are further difficulties when it comes to showing correlations between different trends in a graphic mode. Recall the earlier example of police numbers and criminal offences before and after a five-year programme to reduce crime. The first figure rose by 15%, the second fell by 7%. Without actual numbers we learn little from these statistics, beyond the fact that there was an inverse relation between the two trends. We are left with the question: 'Percentage of what?' The table below provides an answer:

Table 18.3

	Mar. 2012	Mar. 2017	% change
Police numbers	420	483	+15%
Crimes	19,002	17,672	−7%

As with the previous example, there is a large discrepancy between the numbers, making a meaningful graph difficult to construct. But in this instance it is not only the size of numbers that is different, it is what kind of set each one represents: one a number of people, the other a number of acts or events. It is, as the saying goes, like 'comparing apples and oranges'.

A common solution to such discrepancies is to use a different scale for each variable, as below. The scale corresponding to police numbers (blue) is on the left; crime numbers (red) on the right. Time, as usual, is on the horizontal axis.

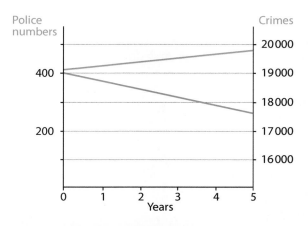

Comment critically on the presentation of the data in the graph. Does it accurately represent the statistical information in the table? Are there any respects in which you think the graph could give a misleading impression? If so, does it matter?

Commentary

The graph employs two different scales in order to depict the rising trend in police numbers and the simultaneous fall in crime. The former increases from 420 to 483, a rise of 15% as recorded in the table. The latter decreases from 19 002 to 17 672, a fall of 7%. Individually both trends are correctly plotted, but due to the choice of scales, the steepness of the decline in crime is exaggerated. In percentage terms the increase in policing is over twice that of the fall in crime, yet in visual terms it appears that the fall in crime is relatively greater. Does it matter? Yes, if the impression given by the graph has the effect of persuading the reader to draw an incorrect or overstated conclusion; and if the purpose of the report were to support the view that the initiative had been highly effective, when in fact it had a minimal effect.

Graphs and diagrams have a useful role to play in depicting trends and patterns that are hard to recognise in large and complex tables. But they can also distort data, sometimes harmlessly, sometimes to the point of falsifying evidence.

Be on guard.

ACTIVITY 18.2

Table 18.4

Country	Average income ($ per annum)	200 metres national record (seconds)
USA	30 000	18
Italy	25 000	20
Vietnam	15 000	22
Bangladesh	9000	23
Cameroon	8000	25
Honduras	6000	27

Suggest **two** explanations for the correlation revealed between national records and average income in the table.

Cambridge International AS & A Level Thinking Skills 9694 Paper 23 Q2c and source E June 2017

Summary

Following on from the discussion of evidence in general, this chapter examined some important aspects of statistical evidence. In particular it considered the importance of:

- sources of data
- collecting and sampling
- trends, and their relation to prediction
- correlation
- modes of presentation.

End-of-chapter question

Refer to Source C: Trend in the end-of-chapter questions for Chapter 17.

It shows data relating to unprovoked shark attacks worldwide.

a How does the graph in Source C support the claim that beach safety and other factors have advanced over the decades?

b Does the graph give a misleading impression of the relation between shark attacks and fatality rates? Give a reason for your answer.

Exam-style questions

1 Study the passage below and answer the questions that follow.

E4U – the energy company that's kind to the environment and YOUR WALLET!

As part of the Government's Reduce Energy Usage Scheme (REUS), E4U are leading the field in strategies to reduce CO_2 emissions and save you money.

The Government gives energy companies $170 for every household they supply, in order to help us reduce fuel bills and cut carbon emissions. We at E4U care about you so much – we want to give away even more money! E4U will pay half the cost of property insulation for every one of our customers.

According to the Government's own figures, the cost of insulating the average home is $700, so our offer represents a saving per household of $350! Once insulated, heating bills can be reduced by as much as $500 per year.

We will also give you five free energy-saving light bulbs, worth $10, that can save you $30 per year. That's an initial saving of $360 and an annual saving of $530.

a Make **three** criticisms of the data presented in the passage.

b A Government spokesman commented, 'The E4U strategy could save $890 in one year alone and shows that the REUS represents great value for money to the taxpayer.'

Is this claim supported by the evidence presented? Justify your answer.

Cambridge International AS & A Level Thinking Skills 9694 Paper 41 Q1a,b June 2013

2

Document 1

A trial at the University of Southampton in 2007 examined the effects of common additives on 153 3-year-olds and 144 8 to 9-year-olds. Some of the children were given a placebo[1]. The children's behaviour was rated by teachers and parents, plus a computerised test for the 8 to 9-year-olds. When given Mix A, a drink containing an amount of additives roughly equal to that found in two bags of sweets, children from both age groups showed significantly increased hyperactivity[2], compared to results for the placebo.

[1] Placebo - A placebo contains no medication, but the patients do not know this. A placebo often has the same effect on patients as the real medication.

[2] Hyperactivity – Behaviour characterised by over activity.

Document 2

Reported reactions per 1000 people in the UK (2005)

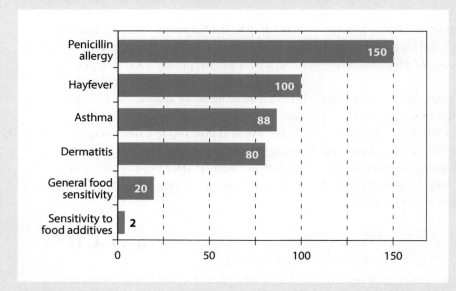

The scientists in Document C conclude that additives generally make children more hyperactive. Document D says that only 2/1000 people are sensitive to additives. Is this a contradiction? Explain your answer.

Cambridge International AS & A Level Thinking Skills 9694 Specimen Paper 2 Q2b and sources C, D 2011

Chapter 19
Uses of evidence: inference and explanation

Learning objectives

The chapters so far have been about claims, including claims that are used or understood as evidence. In this chapter attention turns to the concept of inference and the issues it raises for critical thinking.

19.1 What is inference?

The verb 'infer' means to draw a conclusion from a source of information. The noun 'inference' can be used to refer either to the *act* of inferring something, or to *what* is inferred in the process: the conclusion. If the grounds for the conclusion are sufficiently strong it can be judged that the inference is 'safe', justified or reliable. But not all inferences are safe or reliable. People can, up to a point, infer what they like from what they read or hear, whether it has sufficient support or not. The job for the critic is to decide which inferences are justified and which are not, on the basis of the available information.

The big question here is what is meant by 'sufficient'. If a flag is seen flying at half mast it would be quite reasonable to infer that someone has recently died. The word 'infer' is often used in that informal way. But this would not qualify as a safe or justified inference. There are too many possible alternative explanations – a slipped rope, a hoax, a false alarm – to name just some. None of these is as likely perhaps as the usual reason for lowering a flag to half mast, but likelihood alone is not enough to make an inference safe. In short, the sight of the flag at half mast is not a sufficient reason (or sufficient condition) for concluding that someone actually has died.

For contrast, consider the following claims:

(1) Fraud investigators have found a large hoard of banknotes, all of which have the same serial numbers.
(2) Genuine banknotes all have unique serial numbers.

If both of these claims are factually correct it can be inferred with practical certainty that the banknotes are forgeries (or at least that they are not genuine). This is more than a strong probability: it *follows* from (1) that the banknotes are not genuine.

19.1.1 Drawing inferences

In everyday life we constantly encounter texts that make claims to fact – news items, for example, like the following. It is presented without any stated conclusions or opinions: it is left to the readers to infer what they choose.

Announcement

The medical team investigating last week's outbreak of food poisoning has learned that everyone who was affected had eaten at the Bayside fish restaurant the day before reporting sick. There is a legal obligation on any establishment that may be linked to cases of food-related sickness to close for business while the matter is being investigated, and remain so until it has been given a new certificate of fitness from hygiene inspectors. The inquiry is ongoing.

EXAMPLE ACTIVITY 19.1

Discuss the above text and assume that it is a factual account. What, if anything, can reliably be inferred from the facts? Here are three possible inferences to consider:

(1)   The source of the food poisoning was the Bayside Restaurant.
(2)   Fish was the cause of the sickness.
(3)   The Bayside cannot reopen yet.

Commentary

There are three broad claims in the passage: first, that everyone who reported sick had eaten at the Bayside fish restaurant; second, that an establishment which may be linked to a case of food poisoning is legally obliged to close until it has passed an inspection; and third, that the inquiry is still going on.

So, what about claim (1)? Can it be inferred, too? Not safely. Though there are reasons for saying that the restaurant must close by law, it cannot be inferred that it caused the outbreak. If in doubt, read it again. Note, for example, that we are not told anything about the people who became sick except that they ate at the Bayside. It is possible that there were other links between them: they may have all been one big party or family who had shared other food and drink besides the meal at the restaurant, and *that* had made them sick.

Nor are we told anything about numbers involved. 'Everyone' could mean two or three, which would not provide a large enough sample to point the finger definitely at the Bayside. What is more, the statistics refer only to those who *reported* sick. There may well have been others who did not report their illness. If there were others, we do not know whether they ate at the Bayside or not. So all we really have is suspicion. Suspicion is enough to mean that legally the restaurant has to close during the investigation. It is certainly not enough to justify the inference that it was the source of the outbreak.

Can it be inferred, as in (2), that fish was the cause? Again, no. Fish restaurants serve other items besides fish. There is no guarantee that the people who were sick even ate fish. And there are plenty of other possible causes that would need to be ruled out, such as contaminated water or lack of hygiene in the kitchen. Blame cannot safely be laid on fish – or on any other particular type of food or drink – without a lot more information and evidence.

Can anything of interest be inferred from the report? The statement that comes closest is (3). Indeed, (3) is as good as stated in the text, and is therefore barely worth adding. What is actually stated in the report is that *any* establishment suspected of being associated with a food-related illness must remain closed until an inquiry is concluded, and that this inquiry is still ongoing. Since the Bayside is under suspicion – though no more than that – statement (3) can reliably be inferred. Another way to put this is that the text implies that the Bayside cannot open yet – legally, at least – or that the claim made by (3) is implicit in the text.

Note: The verbs 'imply' and 'infer' are related, but care must be taken not to confuse them in use. A text (or its author) may *imply* something, as in the example above, but it would be misuse to say the report or its author *infers* that the restaurant cannot open. Inferences are made *from* a text, not *by* it. (This is a common mistake, and you will often hear people who should know better making it, but that doesn't make it right, especially in a context like critical thinking where precision in language is important.)

19.1.2 Jumping to conclusions

Often when people read of incidents like the one in the above scenario, they go too far in what they infer, given what they know – or rather what they don't know. For example, if it was announced on the news that there had been an outbreak of food poisoning and that the Bayside had to close while there was an investigation, it would be very tempting to conclude that the restaurant was guilty.

It is particularly easy to jump to a conclusion if you are in some way biased or prejudiced in your response to the facts. Suppose, for example, you had eaten a couple of times at the Bayside, and had not enjoyed the meal. Perhaps one of the waiters had been rude, or the service had been slow. In other words you had reasons to be critical of the restaurant, but none that had anything to do with sickness. Alternatively, you may hate fish, but your friends all love it, and are always wanting to eat at seafood restaurants. You hear about a few cases of sickness and some link to a well-known fish restaurant. The opportunity is too good to miss, so you 'put two and two together, and make five'.

19.2 An example from science

Drawing inferences from observation and experiment plays a prominent role in scientific inquiry. Many such conclusions take the form of predictions. Since a prediction, by definition, cannot be regarded as fact at the time of making it, the only way to justify it or to have confidence in it is to infer it from evidence – from what is known by direct observation, or has itself been concluded from other credible evidence.

Standard view

Fact

Ice ages last for roughly 100 000 years, going by the record of the past half-million years. The warm phases in between are called interglacials. The standard view, until quite recently, has been that we are coming to the end of the present warm phase, which has already lasted just over 10 000 years. Indeed, data from Antarctic ice cores* indicated that the previous three interglacials have lasted between 6 000 and 9 000 years which, if repeated, would have seen parts of Europe, Asia and North America covered in ice since before the rise of the Roman Empire. The most recent Antarctic ice cores have revealed that the warm phase before that lasted for 30 000 years. It is known, too, that the Earth's alignment relative to the Sun during that long interglacial was similar to its alignment at the present time.

*An ice core is a sample obtained by drilling down into the ice cap. The state of the ice at different levels provides a climatic record that can extend over hundreds of thousands of years.

EXAMPLE ACTIVITY 19.2

From the information in the document above, which if any of the following can reliably be concluded?

(4) Another ice age is due any millennium now.

(5) The standard view is wrong.

(6) The present warm phase is set to last another 20 000 years.

(7) According to the recent geological record, ice-age conditions are the norm, and it is Earth's present climate which is unusual.

(8) Global warming is delaying the start of the next ice age.

Give a brief reason for your assessment of each response.

Commentary

The task here was the same as the previous one, but the text and its content are a good deal more challenging. Careful reading is needed to avoid misinterpreting the claims and implications and jumping to the wrong conclusions. We'll consider the possible inferences in turn.

The first one, (4), as well as being a bit vague, has little support from the text. If we take 'any millennium now' to mean in the next one or two – which is its natural meaning – then (4) would mean sticking with the standard view, despite the most recent findings casting doubt upon it. The standard view is that the present warm phase should be reaching its time limit; but according to the last three warm phases the limit has already been passed. The latest ice core sample also suggests that some interglacials could last as long as 30 000 years. Evidence that the Earth's present alignment with the Sun's rays resembles that of the last *long* interglacial pours even more cold water on (4). (Interestingly, even without the most recent evidence, the grounds for (4) would still be weak: half-a-million years is a blink of an eye in geological terms, and the sample of just three warm phases is too small to call a reliable trend.)

Statement (5) might seem consistent with what has just been said about (4). If we are not near the start of a new ice age, the standard view must be wrong. But there is a lot of difference between saying that an inference is unsafe, and declaring it false. (5) is a much stronger claim than anything stated or implied in the document. We *might* be near the end of a warm phase: one that is longer than the last three and shorter than the one before that. There is little or no positive evidence for such a claim; but nor is there proof that it is false. Remember the significance of strong and weak claims (see Section 15.6). A strong claim requires much more to justify it than a more moderate claim. Had (5) asserted that the standard view is now less plausible than it was, instead of plainly false, that would have been defensible.

Statement (6) suffers from the same fault as (5): it, also, is too strong. A single example of a 30 000-year warm phase, coinciding with a particular alignment of the Earth and Sun, is far from adequate to justify an out-and-out prediction that the present interglacial will also last that long. No serious scientist would go so far. It might be inferred that, even without human intervention, another 20 000 years of warmth *might be expected*. But this has a very different force compared with (6). Although it is drawing broadly the same conclusion, it expresses it in a more cautious way which would permit its author to fend off objections. To say that something 'might be expected' does not mean the same as 'It will happen'.

Statement (7) is prefaced by the phrase, 'According to the recent geological record . . .', indicating that it is not baldly stating that ice-age conditions are the norm but that this is what the geological record, as reported in the document, suggests. What is more, it is: recent ice ages (geologically speaking) have lasted between three and 17 times longer than interglacials. So glacial conditions have been the prevailing ones during that period, and it is the Earth's present climatic state that is unusual. (7) is a safe inference.

For (8) to be true it would mean that the standard view was correct after all, and/or that the trend of the last three glaciation cycles was continuing. It would also require global warming to be taking place; and to be capable of delaying the onset of an ice age. (8) is not impossible, but it would take a lot more than the claims in the document to make it true. In a word, it is unsafe.

Why do we use the words 'safe' and 'unsafe' to describe inferences? It is a recognition of the importance of reasoning carefully. What makes an inference unsafe is not just that it may be wrong, but that it may have consequences, sometimes very serious ones. Perhaps the most obvious illustration is a criminal trial, where a verdict must be reached on the basis of the evidence. A trial verdict is a particularly serious kind of inference, on occasions a matter of life or death. As the result of a faulty inference, an innocent person might go to prison for a long time. On the other hand, a not-guilty verdict passed on a guilty and violent person may leave them free to commit a further atrocity. You will sometimes hear the expression, 'That's a dangerous inference to make!'

But even if there are no obvious dire consequences, it is still important to refrain from inferring too much, or expressing an inference in terms that are too strong or too categorical. A strong or overstated inference can often be made safe or safer by *qualifying* it rather than stating it categorically (see Chapter 15).

19.3 Explanation

To explain something is to give a reason or reasons for it. As already stated, however, the word 'reason' has two significantly different meanings depending on whether it is used as grounds to infer something or given in order to explain something. In this section the focus is on the second, explanatory meaning.

> (9a) Seawater is salty. This is because the river water that drains into the oceans flows over rocks and soil. Some of the minerals in the rocks, including salt, dissolve in the water and are carried down to the sea.
>
> (9b) The river water that drains into the oceans flows over rocks and soil. Some of the minerals in the rocks, including salt, dissolve in the water and are carried down to the sea. Consequently, seawater is salty.

These are both explanations. To be more precise they are the same explanation, with slightly different wording. Typically, explanations tell us *why* something is as it is, or *how* it has come about; what has *caused* it. The explanation here consists of two reasons: the first that rivers flow over rocks and soil; and the second that the rocks and soil contain minerals that dissolve in the water. These two reasons, between them, explain a fact, the saltiness of seawater. But the saltiness of seawater is not a conclusion or inference drawn from (9a) and (9b). Most of us don't need any argument to convince or persuade us that seawater is salty. We have the evidence of our senses. We can taste it, which is a good enough reason to take it as fact.

This is the key difference between an argument and an explanation. Arguments are meant to give us reasons to believe something which we did not know, or were less sure of, before hearing the argument. Explanations work in the opposite direction: they take something that we know or just *assume* to be true, and help us to understand it. Explanation plays a very important role in science; and it is easy to see why. One of the main goals of science – if not *the* main goal – is to discover how and why things are as they are: what causes them, what makes them happen. Once we can fully explain something, such as the saltiness of seawater, we can go on to predict or infer all sorts of other related facts or phenomena.

19.3.1 The need for explanation

Explanations are particularly useful when there is something surprising or puzzling that needs to be 'explained away'; or where there is a discrepancy between two facts or observations; or where there is an anomaly in a set of facts. (An anomaly is an exception: something unexpected or out of the ordinary.) If a patient's blood pressure is being monitored, and on a particular day it is much higher or lower than on all the other days, that would be classed as an *anomalous* reading, and might well lead the doctor to look for or suggest an explanation.

Here is a fact that would seem to be at odds with (9a) and (9b) if we did not know the explanation:

River water does *not* taste salty.

We are told by the scientists that seawater gets its saltiness from the rivers that flow into it. So why can we not taste the salt in the river? Unless you know why it is the case, there appears to be a discrepancy here: if one tastes so strongly of salt, why does the other taste fresh? By analogy, if you poured some water from a jug (the river) into an empty bowl (the ocean), and then found that water in the bowl tasted salty, but the remaining water in the jug did not, you would be right to feel puzzled. You would possibly suspect that there had been some trick, since fresh water cannot turn into salt water just by being poured!

> **ACTIVITY 19.1**
>
> Give a concise explanation for the fact that rivers taste fresh and the sea salty. You may know the reason, in which case just write it down as if you were explaining for someone who did not know. If you don't know the reason, try coming up with a hypothesis; then do some research, on the internet or in the library, to find out if you were right.

19.3.2 Suggesting explanations: plausibility

In the above example the explanation is grounded on good scientific evidence. If there were any doubt about it, scientists could measure the minerals that are dissolved in rivers; they could test rainwater and confirm that it is pure, and so on. But not all facts or happenings can be explained with the same confidence, either because they are more complex, or because there is limited available data.

Science is not the only field in which explanation is needed to account for facts. Historians, for example, do not just list the things that have happened in the past, any more than scientists just list observations and phenomena. Like scientists, historians try to work out why events happened, what their causes were. For example, take the following piece of factual information:

> In October 333 BC, Alexander's Macedonian force confronted the Persian king, Darius III, and his army at Issus. The Macedonians, though more disciplined than the Persians, were hugely outnumbered. Yet, surprisingly, in the furious encounter that followed, it was Darius's massive force that fled in defeat, leaving Alexander victorious.

This is neither an inference nor an explanation. It is simply a series of informative claims; a statement of historical fact. However, it is a fact in need of an explanation because, as the text says, it is a *surprising* fact. Normally, if one side in a battle hugely outnumbers the other, the larger army wins, unless there is some other reason for the outcome. If the larger army does win no one is very surprised. No one is likely to ask: How did such a big army beat such a small one? Usually it is only when the result is *unexpected* that we want to know *why*.

With this case, as with many other historical events, we don't know for certain why or how Alexander turned the tables on Darius. But there are many *possible* explanations which, if true, would explain the outcome of the battle, against all the odds. Alexander may have used better tactics. He may have had better weapons. He may have been a more inspiring leader than Darius. The small numbers may have made the Macedonian army more mobile, easier to command. The Persians may have been tired, or sick, or suffering from low morale. They may have been overconfident because they had more soldiers and were taken by surprise by the ferocity of their enemy; and so on.

One or more of these possibilities could have been sufficient to change the course of the battle away from the foregone conclusion that most people would have predicted. We cannot say which, if any, really was a factor, less still the *decisive* factor on the day. All we can say with certainty is that there are competing hypotheses.

But we can make some valid judgements: we can assess the competing explanations in terms of their plausibility. We can ask, of a proposed explanation: would it, *if true*, have explained why the battle went Alexander's way? If the answer is yes, it is a plausible explanation, even though we cannot infer that it is *the* explanation.

Conversely, we can say that certain statements would *not* adequately explain the outcome even if known to be true. The fact that Alexander's soldiers were Macedonian is not an adequate reason, though it is a fact. It might be adequate if we also knew that Macedonians were particularly skilled or ferocious or dedicated fighters; but on its own the fact of being Macedonian does not explain their victory. Similarly, if we were told that Alexander later became known as 'Alexander the Great', that would not explain the victory. It is his victories which explain why he was called 'the Great'. Nor would the fact that Darius's soldiers fled when they realised they were beaten count as an explanation: it would just be another way of saying that they were defeated, not a reason why.

19.3.3 Don't jump to conclusions

We have seen in previous chapters that some of the worst reasoning errors come from jumping to conclusions. This is a particularly strong temptation when inferring causal explanations. Suggesting explanations is fine. Assessing their plausibility is fine. But just because an explanation is plausible it doesn't follow that it is true. If it were a fact that Darius had a huge but poorly trained army, that *could* explain the Persian defeat at Issus. But so might good training explain Macedonian victory.

Moreover, it might be that neither of these were the explanation, true or not. It might be that something quite unlikely caused the battle to go the way it did. Conceivably the battle was determined by Alexander's mother casting a magic spell, or laying a curse! This may seem fanciful and implausible. We don't really believe these days in spells and curses as real causes. But sometimes the wildest theories turn out to be correct. It is fairly well documented that in ancient times people were much more superstitious than they are today. Oracles and soothsayers were taken seriously and consulted before decisions were made; witches were burned for the evil powers they were thought to possess. Had a spell been cast, and believed, the psychological effect could have been quite potent. It might have filled one side with confidence, and/or the other side with terror.

It is not seriously suggested here that this is the explanation of the events at Issus: it is exaggerated to make the point. Plausibility is a factor in evaluating an explanation, but not a deciding factor.

19.3.4 Judging between alternative explanations

It is all very well to say that if something *were* true it would explain a fact. The mistake is to move too quickly from the discovery of a satisfying and credible explanation to the inference that the explanation *is* true. Explanations need to be evaluated just as critically and carefully as inference. In the case of explanations we are looking for the *best*. What makes one better than another?

There are two useful tests for judging the effectiveness of an explanation. One is to question its **scope**; the other its **simplicity**. These are technical concepts: the 'scope' of an explanation is a term for how *much* it can explain. Staying with ancient history for a while longer, some serious defect among Darius's troops, on that fateful October day, could explain wholly why Alexander won, without requiring any extraordinary brilliance from his enemy. Perhaps half the Persian soldiers had dysentery, or there was a mutiny. These are singular explanations which, if true, would explain a singular event. But if Persian weakness was the whole explanation, it would be difficult to explain how Alexander's elite force won so many other battles, across most of the then-known world, and against armies that frequently outnumbered them. By most accounts he was never defeated (at least until he reached India, the limit of his empire). It is highly implausible that each time there was some different, unique reason for victory.

Far more plausible is that Alexander, and/or his army, were immensely effective. We say that this explanation has 'scope', because as well as explaining the outcome at Issus, it explains countless other victories. Nor does it require his enemies to be defective: if Alexander was superior that was enough. Someone who wished to detract from his achievements might come up with a different explanation for each of his successes, always suggesting there was some failure in his opponents. But the standard historical claim, that he was an amazing general and brilliant tactician, explains much more. It also explains it more simply.

9.3.5 Beware of pleasing theories

It is very tempting to seize on an explanation that is so appealing that you want it to be true, and you therefore fail to subject it to sufficient critical evaluation.

ACTIVITY 19.2

The English word 'posh' is used to describe people who are usually wealthy, well spoken, educated, and/or have expensive tastes. Like many words, however, its origin is a mystery. It is evidently quite a new word: no record of its use has been found earlier than the twentieth century. There are various hypotheses, but linguists and historians have so far failed to come up with a convincing explanation as to why this particular word should have come into use.

One popular theory is that 'posh' is an acronym, formed from the phrase:

Port **O**ut, **S**tarboard **H**ome

This phrase, it is claimed, dates back to the nineteenth century, when people travelling to India and the Far East went by sea. Wealthy European passengers, it was said, demanded the more expensive cabins on the port side of the ship travelling east (Out), and on the starboard when returning (Home), because they were cooler in the hottest part of the day. The request was allegedly written on the tickets of these passengers using the initials only, and a similar note placed in the passenger ledger by the ship's purser. Hence the word 'posh' entered the language as an adjective for persons of wealth and position who could afford such a luxury.

It is a very satisfying, pleasing theory, and one which many people find too plausible to let go. However, there is not a shred of hard evidence for the practice. None of the tickets, for example, with the initials P.O.S.H. on them, nor the ledgers, have ever been found. None of the surviving ships' officers remembered the procedure when they were questioned in the twentieth century. No literature of the period, of which there is a lot, included description of anyone as 'posh'.

Moreover, most experts (lexicographers, etymologists and so on) dispute the hypothesis. There are other explanations offered, one of which is that 'posh' was a Romany word to do with money, and came to Britain with that meaning in the nineteenth century. No record of its modern use appears until well into the twentieth century when it was associated with 'swank' or 'dandy'. The truth is that like many slang words its origins are unknown. At any rate, the acronym hypothesis looks like being mere folk-etymology – sadly, when it is such a good story. But it serves as a useful warning. The port-out-starboard-home explanation is so plausible, and so pleasing, that once people have heard it, they want it to be true; and they are disappointed when they find out that it is almost certainly false.

Discuss the questions:

a Does the lack of evidence disprove the 'Port Out, Starboard Home' hypothesis?

b The two alternative explanations are either that 'posh' is derived from a Romany word or that it was an acronym. Which explanation is better supported by the evidence?

19.4 Inference and explanation: a case study

Three documents follow containing information and data on a topic that is often described as 'the compensation culture'. An activity and commentary follows each document. All three are then revisited as sources for exam-style questions at the end of the chapter.

Source A: How did no-win no-fee change things?

The industry surrounding large compensation claims following accidents and personal injury has attracted much media attention, with stories of millions of dollars being awarded in damages to successful claimants, and of compensation being sought for every kind of injury or loss. There has also been a dramatic increase in law firms – or 'claim management firms' that act as intermediaries – canvassing for accident victims by advertising on television, the internet or on the street. (The phrase 'ambulance chasers' is often used, disparagingly, to describe them.) People complain of getting unsolicited calls or text messages asking: 'Have you had an accident that wasn't your fault? . . .' or 'We are phoning to talk to you about your recent accident . . .', whether or not you have actually had one. Television – especially daytime television – has a high proportion of such ads.

At the same time it has become commonplace for lawyers to offer their services on a no-win no-fee basis, which allows people on low or moderate incomes to go to court with no risk of running up expenses they couldn't otherwise afford. This is also known as a 'conditional-fee agreement'. Lawyers earn nothing for unsuccessful claims but are entitled to charge up to twice their normal costs if the claim is successful. This practice, known as 'uplift', can add thousands to the bill the losing side then has to pay out.

EXAMPLE ACTIVITY 19.3

Discuss the following questions
a What can be reliably inferred from the article – and what *cannot*?
b Why might the placing of the cartoon next to the article influence the reader in what he or she infers?
c What point does the cartoon make? (Explain the joke.)

Commentary

This article has a recognisable journalistic style. It is a report, largely a factual one, on a widespread legal practice which is often given a negative press. The article itself, however, is not *explicitly* critical either of the legal profession in general, or of compensation-claim lawyers in particular. Also, it is quite careful in the factual statements that it makes. It does not say that there have been excessive claims, or claims for anything and everything, but that there is 'much media attention' on the subject, 'with stories of millions of dollars being awarded in damages to successful claimants, and of compensation being sought for every kind of injury or loss'. Even the reference to 'ambulance chasers' is a factual claim: a point about the use of the term rather than an expression of the author's own opinion. Likewise, on the subject of 'no-win no-fee' agreements in the second paragraph, the tone is predominantly explanatory, not overtly judgemental.

But the key word above is 'explicit'. The document may consist mostly of factual claims, but facts can be made to speak for themselves, especially if they are somewhat selective in the information they provide (see Chapter 17). It is hard to find a single sentence in the document which could be used to support the legal profession, and even though the author may not explicitly condemn the practice, there are several well-placed phrases that have a subtle – or not so subtle – effect on the reader, almost all of them negative. Take, for example, the word 'industry' (which from the first line suggests a large and well organised machine), or 'every kind of injury or loss', or 'canvassing for . . . victims' and 'unsolicited calls' (implying unwanted intrusion). Look, too, at the last sentence of the article: 'This practice, known as "uplift", can add thousands to the bill the losing side then has to pay out.'

These are rhetorical devices; uses of language which have the effect of influencing a reader without directly stating a viewpoint. Therefore, when we come to the main question of what can be inferred we have to be careful not to be unduly persuaded by these. The question must be answered on the basis of the evidence in the text, not the selective reporting or the colourful language. For example, you cannot infer from the information in the article that large numbers of compensation lawyers are unscrupulous, or motivated solely by self-interest, even if you happen to think that many are.

Another pictorial device, which is commonplace in journalistic writing, is the use of cartoons. The cartoon in the article is intentionally satirical – i.e. it is making fun of lawyers who specialise in compensation claims, and playing on the phrase 'ambulance chaser', which is a pejorative term (the opposite of complimentary or approving). It is a joke, but a joke that makes a point, and may well reflect the author's opinions on the topic of the article. But there is a big difference between speculating about the author's opinions and drawing reliable inferences from the actual content of the text. That is one of the first rules of critical thinking – do not jump to conclusions.

19.4.1 Popular opinion

Many people believe that there is a growing 'compensation culture', with many more claims being made for injuries – real or otherwise – than there were, say, a couple of decades ago. Many also take the view that a lot of the claims are bogus, or fraudulent, especially the infamous 'whiplash' injury, supposedly resulting from quite trivial car accidents. The writer Andrew Malleson wrote a book called *Whiplash and Other Useful Illnesses*. The content is serious, but the book's tongue-in-cheek title tells its own story – like the cartoon in Source A.

The next document is a collection of evidence, this time graphical. It consists of three bar charts (you met with several similar samples in the previous chapter). The data is from an official questionnaire conducted among 509 randomly selected adults in or around 2010.

Source B: Survey

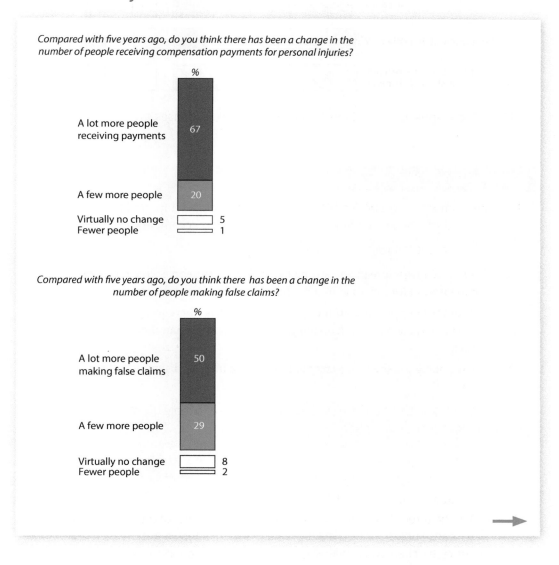

Compared with five years ago, do you think there has been a change in the number of people receiving compensation payments for personal injuries?

%

A lot more people receiving payments — 67

A few more people — 20

Virtually no change — 5
Fewer people — 1

Compared with five years ago, do you think there has been a change in the number of people making false claims?

%

A lot more people making false claims — 50

A few more people — 29

Virtually no change — 8
Fewer people — 2

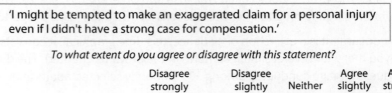

To what extent do you agree or disagree with this statement?

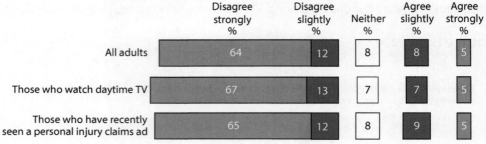

	Disagree strongly %	Disagree slightly %	Neither %	Agree slightly %	Agree strongly %
All adults	64	12	8	8	5
Those who watch daytime TV	67	13	7	7	5
Those who have recently seen a personal injury claims ad	65	12	8	9	5

Note: The graphs do not include 'Don't knows', blank responses, etc.

EXAMPLE ACTIVITY 19.4

Take some time to think about and/or discuss the question below, and those that follow in the next activity, before reading the commentaries that accompany each.

Which, if any, of the following inferences are supported by the information in the graphs?

(a) There was a widespread and strong belief that more people were receiving compensation for personal injuries than there were five years earlier.

(b) 87% of those responding to the survey believed that there were more people receiving payments for personal injury compensation than there were five years earlier.

(c) Claims being pursued for personal injury have increased significantly in the past five years.

Assume that the data is accurate, and that the sample of people questioned is representative of the population.

Commentary

The data in the three charts concerns public opinion. The first of the three claims is therefore clearly supported by the data. (As a matter of interest, it is the conclusion that the real-life researchers came to themselves.) Only 1 in 20 people thought that there had been no change. Well over half thought that the change was substantially in favour of more people receiving payments. This indicates a 'widespread and strong belief', and makes the first statement a safe conclusion. The question of whether the sample was representative need not concern you, as you were told to *assume* that the figures are accurate and well researched.

Statement (b) is a more direct interpretation of the data, and simple arithmetic shows that it too is a safe inference.

$\longrightarrow$

Statement (c) is more complex and more interesting. It would seem reasonable to argue that if there are more people receiving payments, there are more claims being made. But ultimately the inference rests on the assumption that there really *are* more payments being made; or, in other words, that the widespread belief expressed by those questioned is correct. It is this step which is the problem: reasoning from the evidence that most people believe something, to the conclusion that it is true or probable, is faulty reasoning.

Source C: Magazine feature

How did no-win no-fee change things?

Ten years after the introduction of no-win no-fee agreements, the UK Compensation Recovery Unit reported that the number of cases registered to the unit had remained relatively stable. In 2000/1 there were 735,931. The number in 2007/8 was 732,750.

For example, clinical negligence cases notified to the unit fell from 10,890 in 2000/1 to 8,872 in 2007/8. Accident-at-work cases fell from 97,675 in 2000/1 to 68,497 in 2007/8. Only motor accident claims have risen rapidly, rocketing from 403,892 cases in 2004/5 to 551,899 cases in 2007/8.

In its 2006 report on the 'compensation culture', the Constitutional Affairs Committee heard evidence that personal injury claims had gone up from about 250,000 in the early 1970s to the current level, but that the introduction of no-win no-fee had coincided with this levelling off.

Lawyers dispute the claim that no-win no-fee inevitably leads to more frivolous claims and more cases generally. They explain that the lawyer acts as a filter, knowing that every case that doesn't succeed is a financial loss to the firm.

EXAMPLE ACTIVITY 19.5

Consider the explanation reportedly given by the lawyers in the last paragraph of Source C. What is it explaining? How plausible do you find the explanation?

Commentary

Lawyers, we are told, dispute the claim that no-win-no-fee arrangements cause there to be more claims, and in particular more frivolous claims. Why this needs explaining is that the expectation would have been that the number of claims would rise once people found that they could make claims without costs to themselves in the event of their case failing. Even if they had a weak case, with a low probability of success, claimants would have nothing to lose. Instead it is evident that the number of claims had 'remained relatively stable', despite the introduction of no-win-no-fee ten years earlier.

$\longrightarrow$

The explanation offered by the lawyers is that they themselves 'filter' the claims, so that frivolous ones do not get taken on. They do this because those cases cost the firm money, since there would be no reward at the end of it, and the lawyers and other staff would still have to be paid. Is this plausible? On the face of it, yes. Lawyers would be in a position to anticipate which claims were likely to succeed and which to fail, and losing money would be a strong disincentive for taking on those with poor prospects. It is also a simple explanation: it doesn't require any complicated or questionable assumptions. Nor is there any evidence in the short text that is not covered by the explanation; no loose ends. Last of all, it is quite hard to think of an alternative explanation that is as plausible, or more so – though you may have thought of one, in which case it would be relevant to suggest it.

These are the main questions that you need to answer when evaluating proposed explanations. In this instance the answers are generally positive.

Summary

- The verb 'infer' is similar in meaning to 'conclude'.
- A safe (or reliable) inference is one that has strong support from some or all of the available evidence, and does not assume more than the evidence provides.
- To be safe an inference or conclusion must be more than just plausible or reasonable. It must follow from the claims made in or by the text.

- Some claims require explanation.
- Explanations should be evaluated according to their
  - plausibility
  - scope
  - simplicity.

End-of-chapter questions

The following questions relate to the evidence provided by the three sources in this chapter.

Gives reasons for your answers where appropriate.

1 Can the following conclusion reliably be drawn from the information in Source A?

'The introduction of conditional fee agreements has made compensation for injury available to a much wider public.'

Give reasons for your assessment.

2 **a** Assuming that the majority view represented in the cartoon is correct, would it follow that there has been a change in the number of people making *false* claims?

  b In connection with graph (b), explain why the evidence provided by the respondents may be less than reliable.

3 **a** Suggest an inference that can reliably be drawn from the data in graph (c).

  b Identify and explain a potential inconsistency between the data presented in graphs (b) and (c).

  c Can it safely be concluded, from the information in Sources B and C, that public perception regarding false or exaggerated compensation claims is mistaken?

4 Explain why law firms and claims management firms might need to advertise.

5 Assess the support (if any) that is given by the documents to each of the following claims.

  a More lawyers now handle compensation claims than in previous decades.

  b No-win-no-fee is more advantageous to lawyers than it is to their clients seeking personal injury compensation.

  c The virtue of no-win-no-fee agreements is that no one loses out.

6 Identify an anomaly in Source C and suggest a plausible explanation for it.

7 Form your own conclusion about the rights and wrongs of compensation claims and support it with reasons and evidence from the three documents.

Exam-style question

Study the information and answer the questions that follow.

High blood cholesterol is a major cause of heart disease. In the 1980s, research suggested that supplementing your diet with oat bran may help to lower cholesterol levels more than wheat bran, which was previously seen as the healthy choice. The media publicised these findings, and soon people were consuming all kinds of oat bran foods, whether they liked them or not.

Research Group A

In 1990, an article was published in a prestigious medical journal, which concluded that oat bran had only about the same cholesterol-lowering effect as wheat bran. The study was undertaken by subjecting 20 volunteers, many of them young, healthy dieticians with low or healthy cholesterol levels, to a controlled diet of oat bran. The media widely publicised the conclusion as assured results, and the implication that the public had nothing to gain by preferring oat bran to wheat bran was widely believed. However, many medical professionals were not convinced by Group A's results.

Research Group B

A series of 10 trials was then undertaken by researchers of Group B. Their sampling consisted of 84 middle-aged volunteers with borderline to high initial cholesterol levels. They were given randomised diets of wheat bran or oat bran ranging from 6 g to 16 g daily. Results showed that there was a 5% decrease in cholesterol in the oat bran group, beyond the decrease shown by the wheat bran group.

a Make **three** criticisms of the study as reported by research Group A.

b Based on the information from both research studies, draw **one** precise, credible inference about the effects of oat bran on cholesterol levels that would be consistent with both studies.

Cambridge International AS & A Level Thinking Skills 9694 Paper 41 Q1 November 2012

Chapter 20
Identifying argument

Learning objectives

This chapter introduces the major topic of argument. It examines standard and non-standard forms of argument, and argument in the sense of dispute. Activities in the chapter include identifying arguments and their components, and first steps in analysis and evaluation.

Argument = Claim supported by evidence

Reading through this chapter and attempting the activities will help you identify an argument, in the critical thinking sense, and the key components of an argument: one or more reasons and a conclusion. In this coursebook a more specialist word is generally used instead of 'reason': 'premise', which has a very similar meaning, as this chapter explains.

Cambridge International

If you are preparing for Cambridge International AS & A Level Thinking Skills, you will find that the questions in those examinations use the term 'reason' rather than 'premise'.

This chapter also introduces the concept of soundness for evaluating argument. Cambridge International do not use the term 'soundness' for this purpose and will not test you on it.

20.1 Recognising an argument

In logic an argument is defined as a set of sentences, one of which – the conclusion – is claimed to follow from the others which are its premises. Premises are reasons given to support or justify a conclusion. To say that a conclusion 'follows from' one or more premises (or reasons), is just to say that *if* the premises are true, the conclusion must also be true. If it is judged that both these conditions are met – the premises are true and they justify the conclusion – then logicians (people who study logic) can say that the argument is sound.

In natural, real-life contexts, arguments are typically used to persuade the audience of the truth or the rightness of a claim or point of view, by giving supportive reasons. Take the following very simple example:

(1)   The tide is out, so we can get to the island.

We can imagine the circumstances in which someone might put forward this argument. The speaker wants to persuade one or more companions that it is possible and/or safe to cross to an island that is usually cut off by the sea. The reason the speaker gives is that the tide is out.

The argument consists of two claims – a premise and a conclusion – joined by the word 'so'. 'So' is one of several words and phrases which are used to mark the conclusion of an argument. Others include: 'therefore', 'thus', 'consequently' and 'for this reason'. Because drawing a conclusion is very similar to inferring (see previous chapter), these words are often called inference indicators (or just **argument indicators**). What the author (or proponent) of this argument is doing is inferring *from* the observed state of the tide *that* the island can be reached. That is what makes (1) an argument.

Note: a proponent is someone who propounds, i.e. puts forward, an argument.

To judge whether or not (1) is a good argument two criteria must be met. First, it must be true that *if* the tide is out the island truly can be reached. This, as stated above, is what it means for the conclusion to follow from the reasons. If it does, the argument can be approved as **valid**. If this condition is not met, then it could be the case that the tide is out, but the island is still beyond reach, which would make the inference unsafe and the argument **invalid**. Second, the tide must actually be out. Only then can the argument be judged sound.

These are quite technical points, which may be unfamiliar to some readers. Here they are introduced briefly, but they will be revisited at various points in the coming Chapters 22–24.

20.2　An example from history

Until a few hundred years ago it was generally believed that the world was flat. This was a natural belief to have because the Earth's surface *looks* flat. But people had also observed (and been puzzled by the fact) that ships sailing away from land appeared to get lower and lower in the water, as if they were sinking, and appeared to rise up again as they approached land. Some argued – from this and other observations – that the Earth's surface could not be flat, but was curved. They drew this conclusion because if the Earth were flat, a ship would just appear to get smaller and smaller until it was too small to see. Expressed as an argument the reasoning went like this:

(2)　　If the Earth were flat, ships sailing away from land would appear to get smaller and smaller until they disappear. Instead they appear to drop out of sight after a few miles. Therefore the Earth cannot be flat.

This argument consists of two premises, corresponding to the first two sentences, and a conclusion at the end indicated by 'therefore'. However, when we refer to something as an argument, that does not necessarily mean the *text*. The text expresses the argument, but the argument *itself* – like any other claim or assertion – could be expressed in other ways without being a different argument. For example:

(2a)　　The Earth cannot be flat *because*, if it were flat, ships sailing away from land would appear to get smaller and smaller until they disappeared. Instead they appear to drop out of sight after a few miles.

In this version of the argument the sentences are in a different order, with the conclusion at the front and the reasons (premises) following. But they have the same *logical* function as they do in (2). Notice, too, that as the sentences are reversed in (2a), a different connective is needed, i.e. one that identifies the reasons. In this case the proponent has used 'because', but could have just as well used 'since'. These words can also function as argument indicators, but in a different way.

There is a third option which is to use no connective or indicator at all.

(2b)　　The Earth cannot be flat. If it were flat, ships sailing away from land would appear to get smaller and smaller until they disappeared. Instead they appear to drop out of sight after a few miles.

You will often find natural-language arguments without argument indicators, simply because the context and sentence meaning make it clear which sentence is the conclusion and which are the premises.

20.2.1 The form of an argument

In each of the examples above, the argument is expressed differently. But it is still the same argument, with the same reason and same conclusion. Because there are many ways in which an argument can be expressed, it is convenient to have one standard or regular form for setting arguments out. The standard form of argument can be represented by the schema:

R1, R2, . . . Rn ; C

in which 'C' stands for the conclusion and 'R' reason. (Use 'P' for 'premise' if preferred.) As you can see (2) is already expressed in a very standard form, with its sentences in the same order as the schema. (2a) and (2b) are variant forms, but still very recognisable as argument texts. Some arguments, however, are less obvious, and need to be extracted from the text and reconstructed to show their argument form.

The customary way do this, both in logic and critical thinking, is to place the reasons (premises) in a list, and to separate them from the conclusion by a horizontal line. So, with some abbreviation, you could set out argument (2) as follows:

(2.1) R1 If the Earth were flat, ships sailing away would appear to get smaller . . .
      R2 But they appear to drop out of sight . . . .

      C The Earth cannot be flat.

Reconstructing an argument to give it this standard form helps to make the reasoning clear, and assist with its subsequent evaluation. It also gives the critic a convenient way of referring to the components of the argument. Instead of having to write out a premise or conclusion each time it is mentioned, the labels can be used instead. For example:

R1 and R2 are given as reasons for C.

It may seem a lot of trouble to go to when an argument is as brief, and as recognisable, as (2). But with more complex reasoning, which you will encounter as you progress through the chapters, this kind of formal reconstruction is a valuable tool.

20.2.2 Argument and dispute

Of course, not everyone has to accept an argument when it is put to them. Sometimes, even when you have given your reasons, people may still disagree with your conclusion; or they might challenge the claims you have given as reasons. This may have been quite common hundreds of years ago when the first 'round-earthers' set out to persuade sceptics that the world was spherical.

(3)   **Kris:**   Did you know that Earth is a huge ball hanging in space?
          Bart: Don't be ridiculous. The Earth is flat. Can't you see that?
          Kris: It can't be flat. If you just let me explain—
          Bart: There's nothing to explain. Just use your eyes.
          Kris: I am using my eyes, and they tell me the Earth is round. Look at that ship. Soon you will only see the top of the mast. That wouldn't happen if the Earth was flat.
          Bart: (*in a lowered voice*) Well let me tell *you* something. If you go around talking this kind of nonsense, someone is going to lock you up and throw away the key. Or worse.

Kris:	But just listen—
Bart:	No, you listen. The Earth is flat, and so is the sea.
Kris:	It's round.
Bart:	Flat. F-L-A-T, flat!
Kris:	ROUND . . .

Texts (2) and (3) are both examples of argument, though in different senses of the word. This is due to the fact that in English the word 'argument' has two distinct meanings, as seen in the following dictionary definition:

argument (noun)
1 a reason or reasons supporting a conclusion; a case made for or against a point of view.
2 a debate or dispute, especially a heated one; disagreement, quarrel, row.

As you can see, example (2) is an argument of the first sort. It can be called a **reasoned argument** to distinguish it from mere dispute. Example (3) is quite obviously an argument in the second sense – a dispute, bordering on a quarrel. There is very little reasoned argument going on in (3). Kris tries to explain his position, but his opponent shouts him down. The two speakers are mostly just exchanging opinions, without giving any serious reasons to back them up. There is no single conclusion to which the text as a whole is leading.

Interestingly, the English language is unusual in giving these two senses to the same word. In Spanish, for example, *argumento* has the reason-giving sense; the disputational sense is given by *discusión*, *controversia* or *disputa*.

However, it would be wrong to think that the two meanings of 'argument' are completely unrelated. As stated at the beginning of the chapter, arguments typically exist to persuade, and it is clear that in a dispute like (3) each of the participants is trying to change the mind of the other. For (2) there is no such context available, but the most likely context would be some real or imagined debate. Why else would its proponent feel any need to give reasons or evidence to support the claim? Arguments in the reason-giving sense occur typically in the face of opposition, i.e. in the context of dispute or disagreement.

Moreover, most arguments of the disputational kind have some elements of reason-giving in them. Even in (3), which is predominantly a quarrel, both participants draw upon the evidence of their senses (i.e. sight) to support their differing conclusions. Bart says that anyone can see the Earth is flat; that all you need to do is use your eyes. Kris responds that his eyes tell a different story, and tries to explain by bringing in the evidence of disappearing ships.

If you wanted to represent Bart's contribution to the dispute as a standard argument, you could summarise it as follows:

(B) R The Earth looks flat. (You can see that.)

_____

C The Earth is flat.

No one today would rate this a good argument. Though the premise is true – the Earth does look flat – the conclusion is false. However, in the fictional dispute between Bart and Kris it was not known that the Earth was spherical. Nobody had sailed round it or seen it from space. But even without that knowledge it can still be seen that Bart's argument is invalid because the evidence – though true – does not justify the inference from R to C. In general,

217

the premise that something looks to have some property – flatness, roundness, etc. – is not a sufficient reason to conclude that it has that property. Appearances can be deceptive. A stick looks bent when part of it is under water but that does not mean it is bent. The same goes for the apparent flatness of the Earth. The surface of any sphere with a circumference of 40 000 kilometres will look flat to someone on the surface. That does not make it flat.

To accept (B) as a valid argument it would have to be assumed that things are just the way they look. Since we can't assume that, we have to reject Bart's reasoning.

20.2.3 Analysing and evaluating argument

We have seen then that an argument consists of reasons (premises) that are offered in support of a conclusion. In a good argument the reasons do justify the conclusion. In a poor one they do not. Evaluating argument means distinguishing good examples from bad ones. Much of the remaining content of this book is about the critical evaluation of reasoned argument. Here is a first taste.

EXAMPLE ACTIVITY 20.1

We have established that Bart's argument (B) is a bad one. Once the solitary premise and conclusion are identified it is very easy to see that the grounds are inadequate. But not all arguments that you hear will be as simple or as obviously defective as (B).

Compare (B) with the argument Kris attempts in the course of the dispute:

(K)   I am using my eyes, and they tell me the Earth is round. Look at that ship. Soon you will only see the top of the mast. That wouldn't happen if the Earth was flat.

Is (K) a good argument, or not? Is it better than (B)? Would it persuade you that the Earth's surface was curved if you had previously believed it was flat?

Commentary

(K) might seem like a reasonable argument, because we now accept that the Earth is roughly spherical. But, as we also know from history, arguments like (K) – or (2), which makes the same point – were not enough to convince the general public straight away. People needed more reasons if they were going to give up a belief that had persisted for centuries. Judged critically it becomes clear that (K) has much the same weakness as (B) because, like (B), it also argues from appearances. If the flat appearance of the Earth does not mean that it *is* flat, then can we be sure that the *appearance* of ships dropping out of sight does not prove, on its own, the surface of the Earth is curved. It could be an optical illusion; some kind of mirage perhaps. It isn't a mirage: it is perfectly true both that ships appear to sink and that the Earth's curvature is the reason. But today we know that fact *independently* of the argument. The single reason given in (K) does not, on its own, establish its conclusion.

Find a short argument published in a newspaper or magazine or on the internet. Copy it down and underline its conclusion.

20.2.4 Strengthening reasoned argument

For an effective argument we usually need more than one reason, or a single piece of circumstantial evidence. Imagine you were sent back in time several hundred years and had to convince people that the Earth was not flat. What would you take with you: pictures from space; stories of people who have sailed round the world? These would seem like a good start. Armed with such evidence, you could supplement (2) and thereby make it stronger, for example:

(4)   Ships appear to sink lower and lower in the water the further they are from land. But they cannot actually be sinking, or they would not come back. Also, sailors have proved that if you set off in one general direction, for example east or west, and keep going, you eventually arrive back where you started from. These facts show that the Earth cannot be flat. Besides, photographs have been taken from space that show the Earth's curvature.

Here four reasons are given in support of the conclusion. The conclusion is introduced by the phrase: 'These facts show that' – another way of saying, 'so' or 'therefore'. Three of the reasons are given first; then the conclusion; then a further, seemingly indisputable premise. So the structure of the argument could be depicted as follows:

(4.1) P1 Ships appear to sink as they sail away.
       P2 They can't actually be sinking or they wouldn't come back.
       P3 Ships can sail in one direction but return to their starting point.
       P4 Pictures from space show the curvature of the Earth.

       C The Earth cannot be flat.

Obviously (4) is a much stronger argument than (2). Whether it actually convinces its audience will still depend on their willingness to accept the evidence. But *if* they understand and believe the claims you are making, then it would be irrational of them not to accept the conclusion also.

Of course, the 'if' is a big one. In all probability the audience from that time would *not* accept your claims because they would not understand them. What could 'pictures from space' mean to a fourteenth-century fisherman? They would lock you up or declare you mad (or both), and carry on believing what they had always believed, and could see with their own eyes: a flat Earth surrounded by flat sea.

This is why 'claim' is the right word for the statements that appear in arguments. Some of the claims made in an argument may be known facts, but others may be forecasts, suggestions, beliefs or opinions. Claims may also be *false*. It is perfectly possible to construct an argument from false claims, either out of ignorance, or to misinform the audience. We hear all too much of this practice these days under the heading of 'fake news'. (That is probably what people hundreds of years ago would have suspected you of doing, as they slammed the dungeon door.)

ACTIVITY 20.2

Think of a suitable conclusion that you could add to the following to make it into an argument:

Police forces the world over face a dilemma. On top of dealing with murders and other major incidents, they have to divide their limited time and finite resources between tackling minor crimes such as shoplifting and street robbery, and traffic offences such as speeding or careless driving. Of course, the consequences of speeding can be as bad or worse than the theft of a wallet or a mobile phone. They can be fatal. But there is a big difference of another sort. The thief intends to do harm and to deprive people of their rightful property, whereas any harm that is done by a car driver, however serious, is usually accidental.

20.2.5 Grammatical note

It was noted in Chapter 14 that claims can sometimes have the form of rhetorical questions, or other sentence types such as instructions, or exclamations. When interpreting and analysing an argument in which one or more of the sentences is not a statement, but is making a claim nonetheless, it is good practice to transform it into a statement. For example, when Bart says; 'Can't you see that?' he is not really expecting an answer as one would to a normal question. He is effectively saying: 'You *can* see that (the Earth is flat)'. And he is making the same point when he uses the grammatical command: 'Just use your eyes'. The reason why we should interpret premises as claims, statements, or assertions is that ultimately we are assessing their truth, and the only expressions that can *literally* be true or false are statements.

20.2.6 Identifying arguments

Before an argument can be analysed and evaluated it must first be established that it *is* an argument. This can be harder than it sounds if the argument is expressed in natural language, and in a non-standard form; and if the context in which it is embedded is a longer text of which argument is only a part. It is also made harder if the argument is a poor one. In a good argument the conclusion can be seen to follow from the reasons. In a bad argument it does not follow – or at least it does not follow convincingly. Establishing that some piece of text is an argument then comes down to deciding whether or not the author *meant* or *intended* one of the claims to be a conclusion, and the others to be reasons for it. Judging an author's intention, from a text alone, is not a very exact science!

Matters are made easier if the conclusion or reasons are marked by indicators – 'therefore', 'so', 'since', 'because', etc. However, these connectives have other functions in the language besides signalling argument. They occur frequently, for example in explanations, but in other expressions too. Just finding two sentences joined by 'so' or 'since' does not automatically identify a reasoned argument. Think of the words of the song:

But *since* you've been gone
I can breathe for the first time . . .

There is no argument here. 'Since' in the song means '*ever* since', which is different from the meaning it has in front of a premise. For another example, compare,

(5)   Julia is ambitious; so is her daughter.

With

(6)   Julia is ambitious so her daughter will be, too.

There is no argument in (5). The word 'so' in that context means 'also', not 'therefore'. But with very little change (6) is a simple argument, an inference from Julia's alleged ambitious nature to a prediction about her daughter. The point to take from this is that although the argument indicators can help to identify possible arguments in a text, it cannot be assumed that wherever the words occur they have that function.

Besides, as observed earlier in the chapter, there are plenty of examples of natural-language arguments which contain no connectives. An argument may be expressed by a plain sequence of statements (or claims), yet obviously not every sequence of claims is an argument. There it is no argument here, for example:

(7)   Photographs from space show the Earth's surface as curved. The curvature does not show when a photograph is taken from ground level.

Being able to identify arguments means being able to distinguish confidently between argument and non-argument. It is not always as straightforward as it might seem.

20.2.7 The 'therefore/so' test

Despite what was said just now about such connectives having multiple meanings, they do at least provide a useful test for *ruling out* some sets of sentences as arguments. The test is performed by inserting 'therefore' or 'so' between the sentences and asking: does the resulting expression make sense? If it does not make sense, then there is no argument. Here is the test applied to (7):

- Photographs from space show the Earth's surface as curved. *Therefore* the curvature does not show when a photograph is taken from ground level.
- The curvature does not show when a photograph is taken from ground level, *so* photographs from space show the Earth's surface as curved.

Neither of these makes sense. So (7) is not an argument. Unfortunately it is less informative when the result is positive: if inserting 'therefore' or 'so' or 'since' does make sense it does not automatically mean that the resulting expression is an argument. The usefulness of the test is in eliminating non-arguments, leaving the others as possible arguments.

The same test can be applied to the next example, only as there are more claims there will be more rearrangements to try out.

(8)   Completed tax forms and payments must be received by 31 July. Late payment may result in a fine not exceeding $100. Your payment did not reach the tax office until 12 August.

'Therefore' text for conclusion

There are three possible configurations of the sentences, using 'so' or 'therefore':

- Completed tax forms and payments must be received by 31 July. Late payment may result in a fine not exceeding $100. *Therefore* your payment did not reach the tax office until 12 August.
- Late payment may result in a fine not exceeding $100. Your payment did not reach the tax office until 12 August. *So* completed tax forms and payments must be received by 31 July.
- Completed tax forms and payments must be received by 31 July. Your payment did not reach the tax office until 12 August. *Therefore* late payment may result in a fine not exceeding $100.

In each rearrangement the attempt to use an argument indicator sounds unnatural, which indicates that none of the sentences is the *kind* of claim that could follow from the others in the way that a conclusion follows from reasons.

EXAMPLE ACTIVITY 20.2

Using the 'therefore/so' test, and the definition of an argument as reasons given for a conclusion, decide which of the following could be interpreted as arguments.

For those that are arguments, identify the conclusion and note what kind of claim it is.

Lastly, discuss how well supported you think the conclusion is, given the reasons.

(a) The Tokyo train leaves at 4:24. It can take up to 40 minutes to get to the station if the traffic is bad. We should leave for the station by 3:40.

(b) Raisa is the only person with a key to the safe. The police are bound to treat her as a suspect. The money went missing when she was in the building on her own.

(c) You are likely to get a fine. Completed tax forms and payments must be received by 31 July and people who miss the deadline are usually fined $100. Your payment did not reach the tax office until 12 August.

(d) From the fifteenth century, European sailors reached the lands of the east by sailing west. Those who sailed on and survived eventually arrived back in Europe. When they claimed they had sailed around the world, few people believed them.

(e) There are only three possible causes of the leak in your system: the pump could be worn, a hose could be split or one of the connections could be loose. I've checked the hoses and tightened all the connections, but the machine still leaks.

Commentary

(a) can be understood as an argument. The conclusion, which is at the end, is a recommendation. This also is a useful clue: recommendations are often accompanied by reasons. Here there are two: the time of the train's departure and the possibility of a 40-minute journey to the station. If they are both true, then clearly they justify the conclusion.

$\longrightarrow$

(b) The same applies: the conclusion is a prediction that the police will (definitely) suspect Raisa, firstly because she is the only key-holder, and secondly because she was alone in the building. The argument is perhaps not quite as solid as (a). Do police *always* treat people as suspects in these circumstances? The words 'bound to . . .' make the conclusion a very strong claim. Even if both premises are true, there may be other factors – CCTV footage for instance – that show Raisa was nowhere near the safe, and therefore make it less than definite that she will be treated as a suspect. Nonetheless, it is a safe interpretation of the text to read it as an argument – good or bad.

(c) is also an argument. The conclusion is another prediction (of sorts). You could also have described it as a statement of probability: 'You are *likely* to get a fine.' The reasoning for the conclusion is that payment did not reach the tax office until 12 August, together with the second sentence which establishes that the payment was late and that late payment *usually* results in a fine. The argument is quite sound, mainly because the conclusion is a fairly weak claim. If fines are *usual* for lateness, then a fine is *likely*.

(d) is not an argument. None of the three sentences makes sense with 'therefore' in front of it, e.g. 'From the fifteenth century, European sailors reached the lands of the east by sailing west. Those who sailed on and survived eventually arrived back in Europe. *Therefore* when they claimed they had sailed around the world, few people believed them.' The connective that makes most sense is 'but', not 'therefore'. None of the claims is a conclusion drawn from either or both of the other two; and it is the same whichever order the claims are placed in.

(e) is not an argument either – at least not an explicit one – because, as in (d), none of its actual sentences is a natural conclusion. However, (e) does *point towards* a conclusion, even though it is not stated. In fact there is really only one conclusion that you could draw from (e) – that the pump must be worn – because both the other possibilities are ruled out. What we can say about (e) is that it is not a complete argument. It is left to you (the reader or listener) to draw a conclusion – though in this case it leaves you in little doubt as to what the conclusion would be if the author had meant (e) to be an argument. We could say therefore that (e) is an implicit argument, or that it has an implicit conclusion.

223

ACTIVITY 20.3

Explain in your own words why the 'so/therefore' test is useful but not the last word when identifying arguments.

20.3 Identifying arguments in dialogue

Earlier in the chapter there was some discussion of arguments in the disputational sense. Read the following passage – preferably aloud with a partner, taking a part each – and then answer the question that follows.

SCENE: a table for two in a restaurant

Anita: What are you going to have?

(*Sound of a mobile phone*)

Bara: Just a minute. I've got a message.

Anita: Not another!

Bara: I need to answer it.

Anita: Why don't you just switch it off? Restaurants are places for conversation. They're so antisocial, those things.

Bara: (*texting at the same time*) You wouldn't say that if you had one. You'd be on it all the time.

Anita: I wouldn't even want one as a gift.

Bara: Yes, you would. I'll give you my old one.

Anita: Keep it. I'm better off without it. In fact the whole world would be better off if the wretched things had never been invented.

Bara: How do you work that out?

Anita: Well for a start you can't sit anywhere quietly any more without having to listen to one end of someone else's shouted conversation. Secondly, they're a health risk because they pour out microwaves that cook your brain. Thirdly, they distract drivers and cause road accidents. So, like I said: they do more harm than good.

Bara: You just can't say that. No one thinks they are a health risk any more. They don't distract drivers unless the drivers are stupid enough to have them switched on in the car. Not everybody shouts into their phones, and not everyone finds them irritating. They help people to keep in touch. They save lives in emergencies. They access information when you need it. What more do you want?

Anita: (*shouting*) I'm sorry, but people *do* shout into them. They don't even know they're doing it. And they do use them when they're driving, whatever the law does to stop them. If someone smashed into you because she was reading a text message, you would soon change your tune.

Bara: Hang on, you're blaming an inanimate object for what people do with it. Of course there are always some idiots who misuse stuff. It's like guns, isn't it? Guns don't kill, it's the people who fire the guns. You're making the same mistake.

Anita: I'm not making a mistake. The machines *are* to blame. I agree, a gun can't kill you until someone fires it, but you can't get shot either if there are no guns to do it with. And people couldn't be distracted by their phones when they're driving if there were no mobile phones. And you wouldn't still be sending that text and spoiling our lunch.

Bara: That's just silly. You've lost that one.

Anita: No I haven't.

Bara: You have. You're just old-fashioned, so you can't see the value of the new technology.

Anita: I'm not old-fash—

Bara: Be quiet, and let me finish this message. I'll be quicker if you just stop talking.

EXAMPLE ACTIVITY 20.3

Is the conversation above just a quarrel, or is there reasoned argument going on here as well? If there is, identify some examples of arguments propounded by one or other of the participants.

Commentary

Overall, this conversation is a quarrel, and parts of it are no more than exchanges of opinion, laced with mild insults. But in the course of the exchange there are examples of developed, reasoned arguments as well, coming from both sides.

The clearest example is Anita's first long paragraph. This is practically a standard argument, with three numbered reasons and a conclusion signalled by 'so'. Bara responds with a counter-argument. This gives three reasons which challenge or contradict Anita's claims, then two further reasons (the value of keeping people in touch and of saving lives in emergencies) to support a position which is the complete opposite of Anita's. Bara's conclusion is expressed by the first sentence of the paragraph: 'You just can't say that.' In other words: 'It is not true that mobile phones do more harm than good' (as Anita has just asserted). In natural-language arguments, conclusions may not always be spelled out in full, as they are in a standard argument. Expressions such as 'Yes', 'No' and 'You're wrong!' can be understood as conclusions, if it is clear what they refer to, and they are supported by reasons.

In the three paragraphs that follow we see Anita and Bara each trying to reinforce their arguments with further reasons and objections. Then, as their tempers begin to fray, they go back to mere quarrelling and personal remarks.

In some textbooks the impression is given that critical thinking is concerned only with arguments in the standalone, reason–conclusion form, and not with argument in the sense of dispute. But as suggested earlier, we miss something important about the practical meaning and purpose of argument if we ignore the most obvious context in which it occurs. Much of our reasoning – perhaps all of it – arises in or from differences of belief or opinion. An argument that the Earth is *not* flat makes practical sense only if someone – past or present – thinks that it is flat, or needs proof that it is. A defence of the use of mobiles phones is unlikely to be called for unless there is understood to be some opposition or objection to it.

20.4 Constructing your own reasoned arguments

So far we have looked at the elements of reasoning and how they work together to form arguments. We have also considered criteria that can be applied in deciding whether reasoning is good or not. If you want to improve your skills as a critical thinker, it is important that, when you produce your own reasoning, you aim to apply the same standards as you would when assessing other people's reasoning.

The next three activities are designed to help you start writing your own reasoned arguments. However, you should also remember that working through the activities and questions in this coursebook is not the only way to develop as a critical thinker: you can apply critical thinking skills and techniques whenever you are attempting to present a point of view, either verbally or in writing.

ACTIVITY 20.4

Think back over what you have learnt up till now about good and poor reasoning. As a group, discuss what you think makes reasoning persuasive. Can you identify any writers or speakers who you think are persuasive? Is it their use of reasoning that is persuasive or is it something else?

ACTIVITY 20.5

Think of one or two reasons that could be used to support each of the following claims, making them into arguments.

(a) It is wrong to charge foreign students higher fees than other students.

(b) Private cars with fewer than four occupants should be banned from city centres.

(c) The stars of football, baseball and other popular sports deserve every cent of the millions that they are paid.

ACTIVITY 20.6

Use newspapers or the internet to find a current issue that interests you. Write your own short argument for or against a conclusion in the form, 'The Government should ...'

Your argument should contain at least three reasons as well as the conclusion.

Follow the steps below to help you develop your argument.

1 Clearly state your conclusion. (You can use argument indicators and you could put your conclusion either at the beginning or at the end of the argument.)

2 Make sure your reasons link to your conclusions.

3 Decide whether you should make your conclusion stronger or less strong. (If it is less strong, it may link more closely to your reasons.)

Summary

The topic of the chapter was argument.

- An argument was defined as a complex construction in which a *conclusion* is claimed to follow from stated *reasons* (alternatively referred to as *premises*).
- A good argument was defined as one in which the premises are true and follow from the reasons, meaning that if the reasons are true then the conclusion cannot be false.
- Standard and non-standard forms of argument were examined, with examples.
- Argument indicators were discussed as means of identifying and testing texts for the presence of argument.
- The distinction between reasoned argument and a mere dispute was discussed.
- The critical activities of simple analysis and evaluation were introduced.
- The activity of writing reasoned argument was introduced.

End-of-chapter questions

1 For each of the following short texts, decide whether or not it is an argument. If it is an argument, say which claim is the conclusion.

(a) Since the last earthquake in California, engineers have been investigating what happens to man-made structures during a large seismic event. They were surprised that a section of the Bay Bridge, which connects Oakland to San Francisco, fell like a trapdoor. They also discovered that in some of the older double-decker freeways, the joints that connect the lower column to the upper column may be suspect.

(b) The public should not expect the safety of drugs to be guaranteed by animal testing. Aspirin, which is a safe and effective painkiller for most humans, is fatal to the domestic cat. Penicillin poisons guinea pigs. These examples show that different species react to drugs differently.

(c) If more cash machines start making a fixed charge for each withdrawal, people who withdraw small amounts will pay more in the long run than those who make larger but fewer withdrawals. People with low incomes tend to make smaller withdrawals, but are more willing to look for machines that don't charge.

(d) Short-range air travel may be cheap but it makes no sense. Flying is responsible for ten times more carbon emissions than rail travel. And it is immeasurably more stressful for passengers. Also, trains take you to the heart of a city, not to some far-flung airport.

(e) You will be lucky if you get to see even one solar eclipse in your lifetime. The phenomenon occurs only when the Moon crosses between the Earth and the Sun. This happens roughly once a month, but because the Moon's orbit is angled differently from the Earth's, it is usually too high or too low in the sky to pass right in front of the Sun. Even when this does happen, every eighteen months or so, it is only visible in certain parts of the world, different every time.

2 Which one of the following is an argument? Why are the others not?

(a) Although some people think that microwave radiation from mobile phones may damage the user's brain, no hard evidence has been found of harmful effects on health. 'Hands-free' kits are supposed to make the phones safer because the user does not need to hold the phone as close to their head.

(b) Land animals such as tortoises often spread to small islands aboard ships. However, the tortoises on the Galapagos Islands must have arrived by some other means. The first people to visit the Galapagos found tortoises already there.

(c) In most countries cyclists are not legally required to wear a helmet, in the way car drivers are required to wear a seat belt. This inconsistency in the law persists despite the growing number of road accidents in which a cyclist is injured or even killed.

Exam-style question

Human beings are amongst the most significant predators on this planet and have been since they evolved from humanoids. Early humans, however, were not themselves the hunters, but were hunted down by the large cats. As a result humans moved out of the forests and developed weapons, such as spears, to protect themselves. They also began to develop the social ways of living that are typical today and early forms of language. So it is obvious that the threat from predators in fact had positive impacts on the development of the human species.

State, using the author's words, the conclusion of the above argument.

Chapter 21
Analysing argument

Learning objectives

Following on from identifying argument, this chapter makes an in-depth study of analysis and interpretation, paving the way for critical evaluation.

21.1 Critical assessment

Assessing arguments consists of three main activities:

- identifying the argument
- analysing structure
- evaluating the reasoning.

These are distinct tasks, but there is inevitably some overlap between them. You had an introduction to all three in the previous chapter, with particular focus on identification. We come now to *analysis*.

21.1.1 Unpacking an argument

In general 'analysis' means the close examination of a complex object or system in order to get a better understanding of what it is by identifying its parts. The main component parts of an argument are its conclusion and supporting premises, and it is partly by recognising these that we identify arguments in the first place. (Already, therefore, there is an overlap between identification and analysis.)

The opposite of analysis is **synthesis**. An argument is a synthesis of reasons and a conclusion – and sometimes of other elements as well. The analyst separates out these elements in order to uncover the structure or the argument and to present it in a standard form (see Chapter 20). Logicians sometimes refer to this as 'unpacking an argument', or extracting it from the text in which it is found. Sometimes the argument is the whole text; sometimes just a part.

In a standard argument the component sentences are all statements. In theory there is no limit to the number, though in practice the number of reasons given for a single conclusion would rarely exceed six or seven. However, more complex arguments can contain multiple steps or stages, each with its own set of premises and conclusion. We shall come to some examples of these later in the chapter.

The simplest kinds of argument have one or two reasons followed by conclusion, and no other content besides these. In practice such arguments don't really need analysing, as their structure is plain enough already. It is for larger, complex structures that analysis comes into play, and has most benefit. In this book we are starting with simple examples and will build up to more challenging ones.

> **EXAMPLE ACTIVITY 21.1**
>
> Here is an example of everyday reasoning, with a familiar theme: one person trying to persuade another to hurry:
>
> (1)   The train doesn't leave until 4:24, but we need to leave within ten minutes if you want to catch it. It can take up to 40 minutes to get to the station when the traffic's bad, and it's 3:30 now.
>
> How would you reconstruct this argument in a standard form?

Commentary

The first task is to identify each of the claims that comprise the argument and to separate the reasons from the conclusion, using a schema like the one shown in 20.2.1, or one that serves the same purpose. Notice that in (1) there is no argument indicator, such as 'so' or 'because'. That is because none is needed. It is obvious which of the claims is the conclusion even though it is not at the end: it is *because* of the time, the distance and the traffic that there is a need to hurry, not the other way round. On that interpretation, (1) can be reconstructed as:

> (1.1) R1 The train leaves at 4:24. (Factual claim)
> R2 It can take 40 minutes to get to the station. (Estimation claim)
> R3 It's 3:30 now. (Factual claim)
> _____*therefore*_____
> C We need to set off within ten minutes (if you want to catch the train).

Also notice that there are more claims in (1) than there are sentences. The first two reasons are connected by 'but' to form a single compound sentence, one of which in this case is the conclusion. The other two reasons are connected by 'and' to form a second sentence. The job of analysis is to identify each of the individual *claims*, which may not coincide with the number of sentences in the text. So, in standard form, the reasons and conclusion need to be listed separately, with the conclusion last.

Logically 'but' means the same as 'and', in that both R1 and R2 have to be true for the whole compound sentence to be true. 'But' has a different meaning from 'and' in the original text. But as far as the *reasoning* is concerned all that matters is that the train leaves at 4:24 *and* that the journey can take 40 minutes. Nor does it really matter logically *why* the journey to the station sometimes takes 40 minutes: it is sufficient that it sometimes does. So, when you are analysing an argument, it is often unnecessary to include every detail.

On the other hand, not all detail is extraneous: some is essential. For example, the conclusion of (1) is incomplete without the phrase: '. . . if you want to catch the train'. If the person being addressed does not mind which train he or she catches, then there is no *necessity* to set off within ten minutes, and the conclusion doesn't follow from the reasons. Where possible analysis abbreviates a text, but nothing essential can be left out. Sometimes, for clarification, analysis of the argument may require adding some detail.

21.1.1 How individual premises function

There is more to the task of analysis, even of simple arguments like (1), than merely listing premises. We also need to know how the premises relate to each other in the support they claim for the conclusion.

In some arguments the reasons function independently of one another, each giving support in its own right. If one premise is taken out, or found to be false, it doesn't fatally affect the argument because the other, or others, may still be sufficient. The argument may be a little weaker for the loss of a premise; but like a plane with two or more engines, the failure of one does not necessarily cause it to fall out of the sky.

There are other structures, however, in which the reasons work together, in combination: they are in other words **interdependent**. This is more than just an interesting detail. It is an important factor when we come to evaluation. In an argument with interdependent premises, both or all of them are necessary for the conclusion to follow. If one is omitted, or found to be false, the conclusion cannot be inferred from the other (or others) on their own.

In (1) the reasons are interdependent. It is the train time *together with* the time it can take to get to the station *and* the time it is now that justifies the conclusion. If any of these three reasons turned out to be unwarranted, then the argument would fail. For example, if the train were not due until 5:24, then the other two premises, on their own, would not establish the need for setting off at 3:40. Or if R2 is an exaggeration, and it *never* takes 40 minutes to get to the station, leaving in ten minutes would not be necessary. The remaining premises would be true, but the conclusion would not follow from them. (If you want to check this, try crossing out each of the premises in turn and see the effect it has on the argument.)

21.1.2 Mapping structure

The structure of argument (1) can be represented diagrammatically, for example like this:

The single arrow shows that it is the combination of all three premises that leads to the conclusion.

But not all simple arguments have this structure. For contrast, look at the next argument.

(2)   *Counter- claim*
        Short-range flights may have become cheap, but rail travel makes a lot more sense. Flying is responsible for ten times the carbon emissions of rail travel per passenger/km, and twice as much stress. What is more, trains take you to the heart of a city, not to some far-flung airport.

EXAMPLE ACTIVITY 21.2

Reconstruct (2) in standard form, and comment on the structure of the reasoning: how the premises relate to the conclusion.

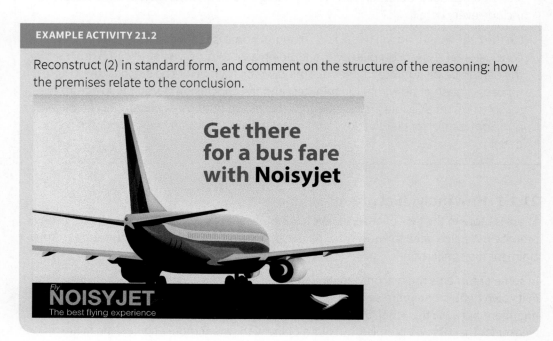

Commentary

The conclusion is the first sentence. It is followed by three separate, independent claims. These are:

(2.1) R1 Flying is responsible for ten times the carbon emissions of rail travel.
R2 Flying is twice as stressful (as rail travel).
R3 Trains take you to the heart of a city, not to some far-flung airport.

_____

C Rail travel makes a lot more sense than short-range flights.

Superficially (1) and (2) share a similar form: three premises plus conclusion. But there the similarity ends, for in (2) there is no _inter_dependence. Each premise stands alone and offers a separate line of reasoning to the conclusion. In the case of R3, for instance, the inference that rail travel makes more sense is made on the grounds that trains, unlike planes, take passengers right into a city centre. Actually, this premise is not entirely true: some airports have mainline railway stations, or an express link to the nearest city centre. But true or not, R3 is not essential to the argument, and nor do the other premises depend upon it for their joint support. So, even if you decide that R3 is not a justified reason, you can still argue that rail travel makes more sense on the basis of lower emissions (R1) and less stress (R2).

To represent the structure of (2) diagrammatically, you need three separate arrows for the three independent reasons. For example:

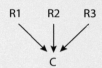

Indeed, (2) can be interpreted as three arguments, rather than just one. All three share the same conclusion, but each one is a separate line of reasoning. For this reason, and in keeping with the diagram, this form of argument is sometimes referred to as **convergent reasoning**.

Note that the first part-sentence, 'Short-range flights may have become cheap', is not a reason. In fact it is not part of the argument at all. The fact that flying may be cheaper would, if anything, be a reason for choosing to fly, so obviously it does not support the conclusion. What it does is show why an argument is needed. The author is saying: 'OK, there may be a financial reason for going by air, but look at these other reasons for travelling by train.' In other words, this opening clause puts the whole argument into the context of a potential debate: 'Which is better: plane or train?'

3 independent reason

Convergent reasoning

21.2 Mixed arguments

In arguments with more than two premises there may be some that function independently, and others that combine forces.

EXAMPLE ACTIVITY 21.3

Try rewriting the following argument in a standard form, and explaining its structure in words or by means of a diagram:

(3)   Rajinder cannot be trusted to keep a secret. He was the only person apart from me who knew about Jed and Jill getting engaged. I haven't said a word to anyone, yet now the news is all round the college. And he spread another story about Jill that I told him in confidence.

Commentary

Once again the first sentence is the conclusion, but this time it is supported by four or five reasons (depending on how you choose to analyse the sentences).

(3.1)   R1   Rajinder was the only person apart from me who knew about Jed and Jill getting engaged.

R2   I haven't told anyone.

R3   The news is all round the college.

R4   Rajinder spread a story that I told him in confidence.

C   Rajinder cannot be trusted to keep a secret.

The first three reasons depend on each other. Obviously, if I had told several people, or if others had known besides Rajinder, it might not have been Rajinder who was to blame; and if the news hadn't spread there would be no reason to suggest Rajinder had told anyone the secret. R4, on the other hand, does not have to be true for the conclusion to follow from the other three. Therefore, although R4 adds strength to the argument, it is logically detached from the other reasons: an additional reason for inferring that Rajinder cannot be trusted.

As a diagram:

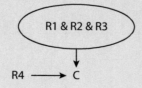

Don't worry if you have structured the sentences a little differently. For example, some people might prefer to treat R4 as two reasons: R4, Rajinder spread the story; and R5, I told it to him in confidence. These two reasons would of course be dependent on each other, so the alternative analysis would be:

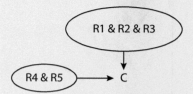

You will find, as you work on more complex arguments, that there can be some differences in the way an argument is analysed. That is because analysis is ultimately interpretation, and different interpretations can be found for the same text. The more complex the text, the more room there can be for differing interpretations – though some apparently simple arguments can also present a challenge.

So, if your way of reconstructing an argument is not exactly the same as the one suggested in the book, this won't necessarily mean that yours is wrong. What is important is that you recognise the conclusion and the main reasons, and that you are satisfied that you understand the argument and can explain it clearly. Analysis helps you to be clear, but it should not be a straitjacket. Sometimes in discussion your interpretation will be challenged by others. If so be prepared to defend yours, but also to listen to what other critics have made of the text: you may have missed something.

235

21.3 Complex arguments

We have now seen how reasons – independently or in combination – support a conclusion. In every case so far there has been just one conclusion. But in some arguments there may be more than one conclusion. One or more of the reasons may lead to an **intermediate conclusion**, which then leads on to a main or final conclusion. Intermediate conclusions, together with their supporting reasons, constitute **sub-arguments**. There may be two or more sub-arguments within the larger argument.

Here is an example:

(4)   In some parts of the world, cars are still driven on the left side of the road. This can result in accidents involving drivers from other countries who are used to traffic being on the right. Pedestrians are also at risk from looking the wrong way before crossing the roads. Cities would be safer, therefore, if in all countries the rule were the same. Since countries where the drivers keep to the left are in a minority, those countries should change over to the right.

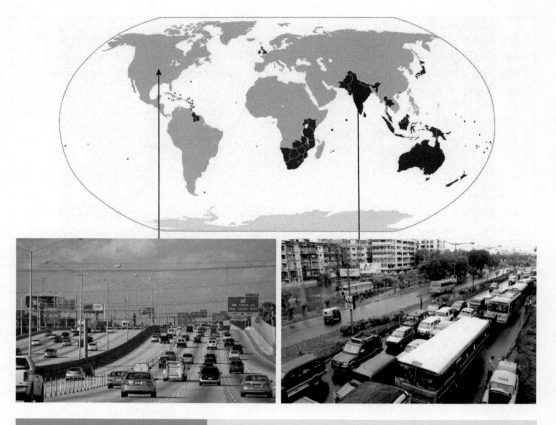

EXAMPLE ACTIVITY 21.4

Identify the two argument indicators in the above text, and use them to give an analysis of the argument.

Commentary

With the help of the two connectives, 'therefore' and 'since', you will have had no difficulty identifying two conclusions:

> C1   Cities would be safer if in all countries the rule were the same.
> C2   Countries where drivers keep to the left should change over to the right.

The first of these, C1, is drawn from two reasons:

> R1   Driving on the left can cause accidents involving drivers from other countries.
> R2   Pedestrians are also at risk from looking the wrong way.

The second conclusion then follows from the first, making a two-stage argument from R1 and R2 to C1; and from C1 to C2.

→

To put it another way, we have a sub-argument, (R1 & R2) → C1, and a main argument, C1 → C2. This means that C1 functions as both a conclusion (of one argument) and a premise (of the other). Hence we call C1 the intermediate conclusion (IC), and C2 the main conclusion (MC – or just C).

However, you may have noticed that within the final sentence there is another reason that directly supports the main conclusion, namely that countries where drivers keep to the left are in the minority. As this is a premise we can call it R3.

What would you say if you were asked whether R1 and R2 count as reasons for the *main* conclusion? Yes and no: they are reasons for the intermediate conclusion, and support the main conclusion indirectly through the intermediate conclusion. You could say that R1 and R2 are 'reasons for reasons' (for the conclusion). C1 is therefore a *direct* reason for the main conclusion. So is R3. This distinction between direct and indirect reasons – like the distinction between sub-arguments and main arguments – is very important, as you will see when we come to evaluating this argument and asking whether the reasoning does adequately support its conclusions.

21.3.1 Background information: context

You may also have wondered what to do with the first sentence: 'In some parts of the world, cars are still driven on the left . . .' You possibly listed it as a reason. This is not exactly wrong: it is *because* there are drive-on-the-left countries and drive-on-the-right countries that some accidents occur. But there is another way to look at this which also makes good sense. The first sentence can be understood as the background information, or **context**, for the argument. It is because of the diversity of traffic rules that there is an argument to be had.

Neither interpretation would make your analysis wrong; nor would it make any difference to an assessment of the success or failure of the argument. In the interpretation that follows we have chosen to call the first sentence context; but if you prefer to call it a reason, you can amend the analysis yourself. As stated earlier, there is often room for different interpretations. As long as you can defend your analysis, and it makes good sense of the text, you are entitled to give a different slant.

21.3.2 A full analysis

(4.1) **Context:**   In some parts of the world, cars are still driven on the left.

   R1   This can result in accidents involving drivers from other countries.
   R2   Pedestrians are also at risk from looking the wrong way.

   ───

   IC   Roads would be safer if in all countries the rule were the same.
   R3   Countries where drivers keep to the left are in a minority.

   ───

   C   Drive-on-the-left countries should change to the right.

21.3.3 Descriptive analysis

Lists of sentences, like the one above, are not the only way to present an analysis, and sometimes they are not the best. A short paragraph interpreting the text as an argument can be as effective, and may sometimes give you more flexibility than a fixed format. This is especially useful if you have to deal with unusual arguments, which you will from time to time.

Example (4) could be analysed in the following way:

(4.2) The fact that in some countries cars are driven on the left, and the claim that this can cause accidents, each lead (separately) to the conclusion that roads would be safer if all countries did the same. This, together with the fact that there are many more drive-on-the-right countries than left, then leads to a final (main) conclusion that the drive-on-the-left countries should change to the right.

Complex arguments like this, where one argument links into another, are often called 'chains of reasoning'. The diagram shows clearly why this metaphor is used.

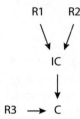

Study this argument carefully and make sure you follow the steps, or links. It is important to understand how the conclusion of one argument can also be a reason for a further conclusion. It is also very important to be able to distinguish between the main conclusion (C or MC) in an argument and any intermediate conclusions (IC), especially as this pattern of reasoning is very widely used.

ACTIVITY 21.1

Analyse the following argument to show the main and intermediate reasons and conclusions. Also separate and label any background information or opposing views which are there as a target for the argument.

The quest for alternative, renewable sources of energy has led to the development of wind turbines to generate electricity. Many people living close to these turbines complain about the noise they make and see them as spoiling the landscape. But the most obvious objection to them is that in periods of calm weather, they don't generate sufficient electricity. Demand for electricity is so high that we cannot possibly rely on a source of energy which will fluctuate in its production. We need to generate power every day of the week, which is why the construction of wind turbines, with their uneven output, is a pointless exercise.

EXAMPLE ACTIVITY 21.5

Here is another argument that exhibits a chain of reasoning. Analyse it using some of the techniques discussed in the last example. Then look at the suggested analysis that follows.

(5)   We should not rush headlong into large-scale recycling projects without
C
carefully weighing the gains and the losses. Recycling used materials may
IC1
in the long run prove uneconomical. The cost of collecting up and sorting
R1
rubbish, plus the cost of the recycling process itself, often makes the end
product more expensive than manufacturing the same product from raw
materials. This extra cost has to be paid by someone: if it is not the consumer,
R2
then it is the taxpayer in the form of subsidies. Nor is recycling always the best
IC2
solution environmentally. The high levels of energy required for processing
R3
waste can cause pollution. This can also add to global warming.
R4

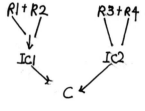

Should → suggestion/recommendation

R1 + R2   R3 + R4
  ↓   ↓
 IC1   IC2
      ↘   ↙
         C

Commentary

This is a more complicated argument to unpack than the last one because the reasons and conclusions are in a different order, and there are no argument indicators to mark the conclusions.

The main conclusion is the first sentence: 'We should not rush headlong . . .' There are two direct reasons for reaching this conclusion. The first is that recycling may be uneconomical. The second is that it may harm the environment. Each of these has its own supporting premises, making each one an intermediate conclusion leading to the main conclusion.

It was for you to decide how best to extract and display the argument. As a minimum requirement, however, you should have identified the main conclusion, and noted the two distinct sub-arguments leading to the main conclusion. Here is a suggested analysis:

(5.1)   R1   The cost of recycling often makes the end product more expensive than
             manufacturing the same product from raw materials.
        R2   This extra cost has to be paid by someone: if it is not the consumer, then it
             is the taxpayer in the form of subsidies.
        _____
        IC1 (*from R1 & R2*) Recycling used materials may in the long run prove
             uneconomical.
        R3   The high levels of energy required for processing waste can cause pollution.
        R4   This can also add to global warming.
        _____
        IC2 (*from R3 & R4*) Recycling is not always the best solution environmentally.
        _____
        C   (*from IC1 & IC2*) We should not rush headlong into large-scale recycling
             projects.

239

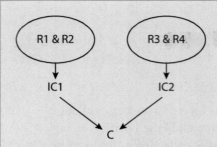

In this example the diagram really helps to show the complex argument structure. There are two separate lines of reasoning and therefore two arrows leading to the conclusion. If you took away one of the lines, say (R3 & R4) → IC2, you would still have an argument for C. It would not be as strong because it would present only the economic reasons for not rushing into recycling, not the economic *plus* the environmental reasons. So, if the sub-argument leading to IC1 were found to fail, there would still be an environmental argument to fall back on.

21.3.4 Reported or 'embedded' arguments

Very often in the media, arguments are reported, rather than being expressed in direct speech. Another way of saying this is that an argument may be embedded in a report or article or piece of research. Argument (5) was expressed above in direct speech, but originally it appeared in the following way:

(6)   An environmental consortium has advised against rushing headlong into large-scale recycling projects without carefully weighing the gains and the losses, pointing out that recycling used materials may in the long run prove uneconomical. 'The cost of collecting up and sorting rubbish', said their representative, 'plus the cost of the recycling process itself, often makes the end product more expensive than manufacturing the same product from raw materials'. This extra cost, she went on, has to be paid by someone . . .

Strictly speaking this is not an argument: it is a report of an argument, made by someone other than the author of the report. The author of the report is not arguing for or against large-scale recycling projects; and we have no idea from the report alone whether he or she agreed or disagreed with its premises or its conclusion, at the time of writing.

Nonetheless, there is an argument embedded in (6), and it can be extracted, analysed and evaluated like any other argument. Instead of being asked to respond to the report-writer's argument, you would be asked to respond to the consortium's argument, as it is represented by the report. To extract the argument, all you have to do is transpose the reported speech back into direct speech, at which point it should have the same standard form as (5).

21.4 More about context: counter-assertions and counter-arguments

As already noted, extracting an argument from the original text and listing the reasons and conclusions can leave you with parts of the text which don't seem to fit either description. In fact they don't seem to belong to the argument at all. In some cases there are parts that even appear to oppose the author's reasoning.

Here is an example:

(7)   Top women tennis players used to grumble that their prize money was less *Counter-claim* substantial than that paid to top male players in the same competition. They argued that they were being unequally treated. But the disparity was entirely justified **C** and should never have been abolished. Male players just have more prowess than women. They need to win three sets out of five to take the match; the women only **R** two. They have to play harder and faster, and expend far more energy on court than **R** the women. But most of all, if the best woman in the tournament played any of the **R** men, there would be no contest: the man would win.

How do you classify the first two sentences of (7)? Are they part of the argument? If not, how should they be interpreted in relation to the argument?

Commentary

The short answer is that the first two sentences are extra to the argument, though not to the text. They are a necessary part of the text because without them the argument would not make much sense. (Try reading the passage without them and you will see this for yourself.) But they are neither reasons nor conclusions of the argument itself. In fact, they really belong to an opposing argument – the women's successful argument for equal prizes, not the author's case for retaining the differential.

These opening sentences – that is everything preceding the word 'But . . .' – are the **counter** to the actual argument. The purpose of the writer's argument is to *respond* to the women's alleged claim of unfairness and inequality. Another way to put this is that the first two sentences place the argument in a context. Or you could say that they introduce the argument, or provide relevant background information. Any of these labels would do.

A **counter-claim** is a reason, or a statement of something, that opposes or challenges the writer's claim or argument. Likewise, a **counter-argument** is an argument included in the text that opposes the writer's own argument. The writer responds to the counter-claim (sometimes called a counter-assertion) to support, or strengthen, their own argument.

You should note that the approach we are using in this book is the traditional understanding of counter-assertion and counter-argument. Some critical thinkers take the view that the first two sentences of (7) (that top women tennis players used to grumble) are the **target** of the writer's argument, which the writer then counters with his or her own counter-assertion or counter-argument (about the women's case for equal prizes). The approach in this textbook is the approach that you will meet in examinations such as Cambridge International A Level Thinking Skills.

> (7.1) **Counter-claim**: Top women tennis players used to complain about the
> inequalities of prize money.
> *But . . .*
> R1   Men have to win three out of five sets; the women only two.
> R2   The men play harder and faster and use more energy.
> R3   Any of the men would beat the best woman.
> _____
> IC   The men have more prowess.
> _____
> C   The disparity was justified and should not have been abolished.

21.4.1 The value of analysis

The text of an argument, and the argument itself, should not be confused. To do so is what is known as a 'category mistake'. Argument texts and arguments themselves are different *kinds* of objects. For one thing, the same argument can be expressed, reported or described in an indefinite number of different ways, each a different text. For critical purposes it is useful to think of analysis as a process of *extracting* the argument from the text by identifying the reasons and conclusion of which it is composed.

Thoroughly analysing an argument is the surest way to obtain a clear understanding of its meaning and structure. It also provides the best platform for responding to the argument critically. When you see its constituent claims laid out for inspection, and the links between them, it is much easier to spot strengths, weaknesses, gaps, and so on which may not be at all obvious when the argument is wrapped up in ordinary, everyday language.

ACTIVITY 21.2

a   Extract the tennis coach's argument from the following report.

b   Identify its conclusion, premises and counter-claims (if any).

A top tennis coach has reacted angrily to calls for a ban on grunting, directed in particular at the women's game. Players who emit a loud explosive sound each time they hit the ball have been accused by some of putting opponents off their game. The coach opposed a ban by saying that grunting is a natural and unstoppable accompaniment to sudden effort, and that making competitors play in near-silence would reduce the power of their shots, placing an unfair handicap on some but not on others. Some players can control grunting, others can't, she said, adding that it is not just a female thing. Some of the men grunt almost as much as the women.

ACTIVITY 21.3

Refer to the End-of-chapter questions in Chapter 20. Analyse the short arguments in questions 1b, d, e and 2b.

ACTIVITY 21.4

Write a reasoned argument leading to each of the conclusions below.

Ways to construct an argument can vary, and you should always select a structure which suits your argument. You can refer back to Activity 20.6 for hints on writing your own arguments. One approach could be to use two of the following:

- reason
- evidence
- example
- intermediate conclusion.

(a) Therefore, you should go on holiday to Florida this year. (Pick a different destination if you prefer.)

(b) So, everyone should learn to cook while they are at school.

ACTIVITY 21.5

Swap one of the arguments you wrote for Activity 21.3 with another student's argument. Re-write their argument to include a counter-assertion. You should respond to that counter-assertion.

Note: Counter-assertions and counter-arguments are often indicated by phrases such as, 'It is often said that …', 'It cannot be denied that …', 'Experts say that …', 'On the other hand …' or 'It can be argued that …' Responses to counter-assertions often begin with words such as, 'However' or 'But'.

Summary

This chapter has covered the topic of argument analysis in considerable detail. The following were among the most salient points:

- Analysis means extracting an argument from a natural-language text and identifying its constituent parts – principally the reasons (premises) and conclusion.
- Reasons can function interdependently (i.e. in combination), or independently.
- Complex arguments may consist of chains of reasoning leading to intermediate conclusions which in turn lead to the main conclusion.

- Often an argument will be embedded in a report, and needs to be extracted from the text by converting it into direct speech.
- Some sections of a text may not be reasons or conclusions: they may just introduce or provide a context – sometimes in the form of a counter-claim or counter-argument.

End-of-chapter question

The South Pole must once have been much warmer than it is today. Scientists have recently discovered some three-million-year-old leaves preserved there in the ice. Despite their age, they are so undamaged, and preserved in such fine detail, that they could not have been carried there by wind or sea. Therefore, they can only be from trees that once grew there. The leaves belong to a species of beech tree that grows only in warm or temperate regions; and beeches do not evolve quickly enough to adapt to changes in climate.

a Using the exact words from the passage, identify the main conclusion.

b Using the exact words from the passage, identify the intermediate conclusion.

c What **two** reasons are given in support of the intermediate conclusion of the passage?

Exam-style question

It has become fashionable in the UK for people to have wooden floors instead of carpet in their homes: this trend is regrettable.

Wooden floors present a considerable noise problem for residents living in rooms below. Carpet absorbs the noise made when people walk around. These noise-reducing qualities make carpet a far superior floor covering to wood.

Wooden floors lack the protective quality of carpet in the event of a child or elderly person falling over. Serious, even fatal, injuries can result when contact is made with a hard surface. Using carpets would eliminate this risk and so relieve the pressure on health services.

Many long-established carpet manufacturers have gone out of business because of the fashion for wooden flooring. This has resulted in many people losing their jobs in such businesses. Therefore there is a harmful effect on the economy as a result of the declining popularity of carpet.

Wood is an increasingly scarce resource. Rainforest depletion is exacerbated by the demand for tropical hardwoods such as mahogany and teak. In contrast, carpets are traditionally made of wool from sheep, which is a renewable resource. The environment would benefit from a shift back to carpets as the floor covering of choice. Old hippies may go on about using natural materials such as wood and saving the planet but their position is inconsistent.

Some people have argued that carpets are not good for people with allergies as they harbour creatures such as dust mites. However, the increase in allergic conditions such as asthma has not been reversed by the rise of wooden flooring. Moreover, modern synthetic materials such as polypropylene can be used in carpet manufacture, rather than wool. In fact, 99% of the fibre used in carpet manufacture in the US is synthetic. The supposed advantages of wooden floors for those with allergies are illusory.

a Using the exact words from the passage as far as possible, identify the main conclusion.

b Using the exact words from the passage as far as possible, identify three intermediate conclusions.

Cambridge International AS & A Level Thinking Skills 9694 Paper 23 Q3a,b June 2017

Chapter 22
Interpretation

Learning objectives

This chapter takes a further look at the principal elements of an argument, before moving on to the task of argument evaluation.

22.1 Elements of an argument

To recap: an argument can be identified by its parts: a conclusion and one or more reasons given for the conclusion. But how do we recognise a conclusion in an ordinary-language text; likewise how do we single out the reasons? There are not different kinds of sentence with a distinctive grammatical form, one for expressing premises and the other for conclusions. Practically any sentence can be a reason or a conclusion. In fact, as you saw in the section on complex argument (21.3), the same sentence can be an intermediate conclusion from one set of premises and, in the same text, a premise for a further conclusion.

The fact is, 'conclusion' and 'reason' are relative terms, like 'employer' and 'employee' (an analogy suggested by the logician, Aaron Copi). A person can only be an employee in relation to an employer, and the same person can be either or both in different circumstances. The same goes for reasons and conclusion, in different contexts.

Compare:

    (1)   The tide is coming in, so the causeway will soon be covered with water.
    (2)   The causeway will soon be covered with water, so we can't get to the island.

The conclusion of the first argument is identical in meaning and expression to the premise of the second. No further analysis is required for either text, since they are both standard arguments, and the conclusion flagged in each by the inference indicator 'so'. But as you have seen, connectives like 'so', 'since' or 'therefore', though useful as clues, do not always indicate arguments: they have other functions besides. Therefore, it is important to double-check your analysis by taking the meanings of the sentences into account as well. For example, it is the rising tide in (1) which is given as a reason to believe that the causeway will soon be covered with water, not vice-versa.

Besides, many arguments have no explicit indicator words, because it is assumed that the meanings of the sentences will identify their role in the argument without explicit markers. Unfortunately, however, it is not always clear without additional contextual information which sentence is which in all cases. Take the following putative argument (putative means 'supposed' or 'assumed'):

    (3)   Tax rises are not vote winners. Every time a government has raised taxes in the last four decades, their poll ratings have fallen.

This is a good example of the kinds of difficulty interpretation can pose. Either of the two sentences could be understood as a reason for the other, depending on whether you interpret (3) as an argument or as an explanation. The first sentence might be taken as a reason *why* tax-raising governments slip in the polls; or the slip in the polls may be taken as grounds or evidence for the claim that tax rises are not vote winners. However, *if* (3) is understood as an argument, there can be no doubt which sentence is the conclusion:

    (3.1) R   Every time a government has raised taxes . . . their poll ratings have fallen.

          C   Tax rises are not vote winners.

Of course, this does not mean that the second sentence couldn't be given as a premise, in a different argument. Suppose I were to reason as follows:

(4)   The government won't raise taxes this close to the election. Tax rises are not vote winners.

Here it is perfectly reasonable to interpret the second claim as a reason from which to infer the first claim:

(4.1) R   Tax rises are not vote winners.

        C   The government won't raise taxes . . .

ACTIVITY 22.1

Identify the reasons and conclusion in the following argument, and comment on the grammatical form of the sentences.

> Just look at the statistics and see for yourself how crime has been rising over the past few years. Could there be any clearer signal that the current soft approach to offenders isn't working? Either the courts get back to zero-tolerance and harsher sentencing, or we face defeat in the war on crime.

EXAMPLE ACTIVITY 22.1

In examples (3) and (4) there was a single premise only, and a single conclusion. In the next passage there is more work to do.

(5)   Most spoken languages come in many different accents and dialects. They also contain colloquial, even slang, expressions that vary from region to region, or class to class. The only way to learn a foreign language properly is to go and live in the country where it is spoken. Classroom teaching, or books or DVDs, cannot give students the necessary exposure to the variations and subtleties of everyday speech.

Which sentence is the conclusion of argument (5), and why?

Commentary

Your discussion should have led you to see that the conclusion is the last-but-one sentence: the claim that the only way to learn a language properly is to go and live in the country where it is spoken. The author is claiming this on the grounds that spoken languages have many 'variations and subtleties' – such as dialects and colloquialisms – *and* that school language lessons cannot give students the requisite exposure to these features.

Remember that what we are primarily concerned with here is identifying the conclusion. We are not yet evaluating the argument or responding to it. But although analysis and evaluation are separate activities, there is inevitably some overlap between them, just as was seen between identifying and analysing arguments. For a claim to be recognisable as a conclusion we have to be able to say that there is *some* level of support given by the claims we identify as the reasons, even if it is not entirely convincing support.

The difficulty comes when there is more than one possible way to interpret a text as an argument. How can we be confident that in (5) the penultimate sentence really is the conclusion for which the author is arguing, rather than, say, the last sentence? Might the author not be saying that *because* of all the dialects and colloquialisms that are found in spoken languages, school lessons cannot give students the exposure they need to learn a language properly?

Well, the author might be saying this. Critical thinking is not mind-reading. But nor is it just guesswork. What we should be asking, when we analyse a piece of text as an argument, is not what the author might have been thinking, but which interpretation gives us the best or most persuasive argument. Another way to ask this is: Which interpretation makes the best sense *as an argument*? It is for this purpose that the 'therefore/so' test can be a useful (though not foolproof) procedure.

Compare:

(5.1) The only way to learn a foreign language properly is to go and live in the country where it is spoken. *Therefore* classroom teaching, or books or DVDs, cannot give students the necessary exposure to the variations and subtleties of everyday speech (dialects, slang, etc.).

with:

(5.2) Classroom teaching, or books or DVDs, cannot give students the necessary exposure to the variations and subtleties of everyday speech (dialects, slang, etc.). *Therefore* the only way to learn a foreign language properly is to go and live in the country where it is spoken.

The difference is quite clear. (5.2) not only makes better sense than (5.1), it is a better argument. In fact it makes better sense *because* it is a better argument. The best interpretation that we can place on (5) is that the first, second and fourth sentences are being presented as grounds for the third. Abbreviated, and in standard form, we have:

(5.3) R1 Spoken language has different accents and dialects.
R2 There are also colloquialisms and slang.
R3 Classroom teaching, books and DVDs cannot give requisite exposure (to these).

_____*therefore*_____

C The only way to learn is to go and live in the country.

You may have wanted to say that R3 is an intermediate conclusion from R1 and R2. However, R3 does not so much follow from the previous two claims as *join with them* to support C. The structure then would be:

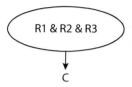

ACTIVITY 22.2

Suggest a conclusion which could be drawn from the following report.

Some students in a San Francisco art school were told they were about to see an example of prize-winning modern art and were then shown a photograph of a pile of discarded drinks containers. It was nothing more than garbage, but the students took it quite seriously and agreed that it was worthy of an award.

22.1.1 The principle of charity

The principle of charity says we should interpret a supposed argument in a favourable way – that is, as a good argument rather than a poor one. Note that despite the name, this doesn't mean being kind or generous to the author. All it means is that we should assume that the author is a rational individual who understands the difference between good and bad reasoning in broadly the same way as we do. So, if we have in front of us a text that could be understood as 'X therefore Y', or as 'Y therefore X', and we can see that X is a good reason for believing Y, but Y is not as good a reason for believing X (or no reason at all), then on the principle of charity we should accept the first interpretation and not the second.

This also helps explains why there is often some overlap between analysis and evaluation. We are not just looking for a list of sentences that can be called an argument (however bad), but one which goes some way towards being a *good* argument. By the same token, if a piece of text makes much better sense as a *non*-argument than as an argument – a simple report, for example, or an explanation – we should not just assume it is a bad argument, but look for a more charitable interpretation.

We shall return to this important principle when we discuss evaluation and refutation in Chapters 24–26.

22.1.2 Arguments with multiple conclusions

The procedure is the same for longer and/or more complex arguments, except that you may have to repeat it for each of the sub-arguments, or steps. Also you have to distinguish main conclusions from intermediate conclusions. The procedure is the same as identifying a main conclusion. You ask: 'Which claim follows from which? or: 'Which makes better sense as a reason for the other?'

EXAMPLE ACTIVITY 22.2

Look at the next example and identify, using the author's words, the main conclusion.

(6) Parents naturally tend to think that, because they are older and more experienced, they know better than their children. They consequently assume that their judgements and decisions are the right ones. But in many ways children are much cleverer than their parents give them credit for. They frequently display problem-solving skills that their parents do not possess; and they are more adventurous in their thinking, if only because they are less afraid of making mistakes. Parents should pay closer attention to what their children have to say, and allow them to make more decisions for themselves. Apart from anything else, this would help to relieve many unnecessary family tensions.

Commentary

The passage starts by claiming that parents tend to think they know best and consequently assume their decisions and judgements are the right ones. This has the look of an argument already, but it is clearly not making the author's own point. For, like the tennis argument in Chapter 21, the opening sentences are followed by the word 'But', signalling an opposing view. What parents think is therefore just the introduction or the counter-claim that the writer will argue against.

The author's own argument stems from the claim that children are often wiser than parents think, supported by observations about their problem-solving skills, and so on. Then comes the recommendation that parents should pay children more attention and allow them to make more decisions. This also looks as though it could be a conclusion – recommendations often are – but the question you need to ask is whether it *follows from* the claim that children are wiser than their parents think, or *supports* it?

Clearly it follows: the passage is not saying (nor would it make much sense to say) that parents should pay closer attention to their children, and therefore children are wiser than their parents think. So, a fair analysis would be:

(6.1) **Counter-claim:** Parents naturally tend to think that . . . they know better than their children, etc.

But . . .

R1 Children frequently display problem-solving skills that their parents do not possess.

R2 They are more adventurous in their thinking.

IC In many ways children are much cleverer than their parents give them credit for.

R3 Paying closer attention etc. would help to relieve family tensions.

C Parents *should* pay closer attention to what their children have to say, and allow them to make more decisions for themselves.

ACTIVITY 22.3

How would you interpret the following short passage? Is it an argument, and if it is can you identify the conclusion and the premises? If it is not an argument, state why not.

No one has anything to fear from giving the police random stop-and-search powers so long as they have nothing to hide. If you are carrying a knife or gun or stolen goods, then of course it's a different story. Opponents of the bill to grant the police more wide-ranging powers can only be helping to protect the guilty.

ACTIVITY 22.4

Analyse each of the following arguments, using one or more of the methods discussed in this chapter.

(a) When cities become congested with traffic, the usual solution is to make a charge for bringing a car into the centre. This works, but it is wrong to do it, because it discriminates in favour of those who can easily afford to pay. The less well-off in society are penalised so that the rich can enjoy the luxury of clear streets. Therefore congestion charges everywhere should be abolished. A system of rationing car use should be introduced instead, allowing each driver into the city just once or twice per week. Then everyone benefits equally.

(b) Train fares differ enormously, with the most expensive always applying when people have to commute to and from work, and when the trains are most crowded. Some call this a cynical and unfair policy because it exploits the fact that commuters have to travel then, and will pay whatever is charged and put up with the over crowding, because there is no alternative. But it is perfectly fair, as well as necessary, to do this. For one thing it is simply market forces at work. For another it is the only way the system can function at a profit. During off-peak periods people are travelling from choice and would not travel at all if there were no cheap fares. But the cheap fares would not be economical for the transport companies unless they can be subsidised by high fares at peak times.

251

22.1.3 Reasons for conclusions

When we say a conclusion follows from certain premises, we mean that it follows *logically*. If the conclusion does not follow from the premises, then even if the premises are true, the conclusion might be false, and the argument invalid. A logically sound argument is one in which the premises *are* true and the conclusion *does* follow. That is why, in a good argument, the premises are *reasons* for believing, or agreeing with, the conclusion, and they are recognisable by that relation.

In logic the term 'premises' is preferred over 'reasons'. In critical-thinking textbooks it tends to be the other way around. This is because critical thinking is a less formal subject than logic. In this book we have used both words, and up until now treated them as having roughly the same meaning when used in connection with arguments. However, there are differences which sometimes make one term more appropriate to use than the other. 'Premise', being the more formal word, is defined by its position in an argument – literally meaning 'placed before' – whereas a reason is identifiable more by its meaning: what it *claims*. Logicians often work with symbols rather than sentences. In an argument such as:

A & B therefore C,

'A' and 'B' represent *premises*. But nothing about these letters makes them recognisable as *reasons* for 'C'. You would have to know what 'A' and 'B' stand for – and 'C' too – before you could recognise the first two as grounds for believing C.

22.1.4 Relevance

For one thing, a premise cannot be understood as a reason for a conclusion unless it is *relevant* to the conclusion. Suppose someone tried – not very plausibly – to argue that:

(7)   Sea water is salty, so Mars is a planet.

The premise of this 'argument' is true, and so is the conclusion. But knowing that sea water is salty gives no reason to believe that Mars is a planet, since the two claims are completely unrelated. In (7) the second claim is known as a non-sequitur, meaning it does *not* follow from the premise in any natural sense of the word, even though both claims are true. Nor, for that matter, does the saltiness of water *explain* why Mars is a planet.

Compare with the following argument:

(8)   Mars is a planet since it orbits the Sun.

Its orbiting of the Sun is grounds for the claim that Mars is a planet. If someone did not already know that Mars was a planet, (8) would give them a reason to believe it (provided they know that planets are objects that revolve around suns).

22.1.5 Incomplete arguments

As stated at the beginning of the chapter, claims can only be recognised as reasons (in the premise sense) in relation to a conclusion. Sometimes, however, a text will appear to be building up to an argument but without coming to any recognisable conclusion.

For example:

(9)   If airlines did not deliberately or carelessly oversell tickets there would always be enough seats to accommodate every booked passenger. Yet often there are not enough seats. In a much-publicised incident recently, a randomly selected passenger had to be physically dragged from a plane shortly before take-off because there were insufficient seats to accommodate all booked passengers and crew, and because no one had agreed to give up their seat voluntarily.

EXAMPLE ACTIVITY 22.3

Is this an argument, and if so what is its conclusion? You should apply the principle of charity when you answer.

Commentary

The passage can be read as a critical comment on airline booking practices, in particular overbooking and its consequences, with an extreme example of an unfortunate victim of the overselling. What might tempt the reader to suppose it is an argument is that it is openly judgemental, even to the point of calling the practice 'deliberate' or 'careless'. Moreover it appears to give reasons, and cites a serious incident that has resulted from it. The problem is that none of the claims follows from the others in a way that could be demonstrated by inserting 'therefore'. Thus although the tone is argumentative, and the topic controversial, the text expresses no explicit argument.

If we apply the principle of charity, there is an alternative way to read (9). If you are satisfied that there is an unmistakable conclusion to which some or all of the claims in the text lead, then we could say that (9) was a set of premises with an unstated, but nonetheless implicit, conclusion.

Identifying an unstated conclusion is similar to asking the question: 'What can be inferred from . . . ?' But for an unstated conclusion the connection needs to be stronger: the rest of the text must clearly imply the putative conclusion.

Is there such an inference that can safely be drawn from (9)? Yes, if we interpret it as follows:

(9.1) R1   If airlines did not . . . oversell tickets there would always be enough seats for every booked passenger.

Yet . . .

R2   . . . often there are not enough seats.
R3   Recently a passenger had to be dragged from a plane, etc.

C   (*implied*): Airlines do deliberately oversell tickets.

The claim that we are calling an unstated conclusion (C) follows obviously from the reasons. In fact, R1 and R2 are sufficient grounds on their own: R3 is really an embellishment – evidence that corroborates R2. Why we can feel confident in interpreting (9) as an argument – as opposed simply to a story or report – is that it is a good argument. Better than that, it is a *valid* argument. If R1 and R2 are true, then C is true. It is therefore compliant with the principle of charity, mentioned earlier, which requires that we put the best interpretations on what we read and hear, rather than a weaker or less plausible one.

22.2 The need for caution

(9) is very obviously an implicit argument. But there is a danger in taking sets of claims to be arguments when there may be other more charitable interpretations.

Consider the following short statement:

(10) The suspect was at her desk at 3 p.m. on the afternoon of the murder. But no one reported seeing her again until after 4 p.m. That was ample time to get to the scene of the crime and back.

There is no explicit conclusion here: just three claims, related by subject matter, but otherwise unconnected. There is a natural temptation to interpret (10) as an argument, because it seems to point towards a conclusion – or number of conclusions – regarding the evidence against the subject. (The very fact that the subject is named as the *suspect* adds a bias to the text in that direction.)

What can be inferred from (10)? Obviously not that the suspect is guilty: that would be far too strong. Nor can it be safely inferred that the suspect has no alibi. Indeed, there is no conclusion that can be drawn from (10) that isn't either invalid or uninformative (i.e. more or less stated). You could infer, for example, that the crime scene was less than half-an-hour away from the office, by some means of travel; but that is effectively repeating the information in the third sentence of the text. It is not so much a conclusion as a restatement, and the resulting argument would be trivial; not worth saying.

What about inferring that the suspect could have, or might have, visited the crime scene? Or, in other words, that it is *possible* she was there? That is weak enough to be a safe conclusion, but so much so that again it adds nothing to what is stated already. Anyone *might* have committed the crime unless there is some proof that they did not. If it is possible that the suspect is guilty it is equally possible that she was not. These are statements of the obvious, not worthwhile conclusions.

The upshot of this is that it is implausible to interpret (10) as an argument, because it would be a pointless or invalid argument. The charitable interpretation is that (10) is simply an item of potential evidence that with the sufficient corroborating evidence could be relevant to the building of a case. No rational, fair-minded person would offer (10) as an evidence-based argument, as it stands.

These examples and activities are illustrative of the importance of the principle of charity, mentioned earlier in the chapter. The principle – sometimes referred to as a **maxim** – is this: interpret a text in such a way as to make it plausible and credible. Applied to identifying and interpreting arguments, this means asking: What is the best argument that can be extracted from this text without distorting the meaning? It also means that if no interpretation can be found that would be a rational or effective argument, then some other description should be considered for the text (for example, explanation, information or opinion).

Summary

This chapter examined in more detail the two main components of argument: reasons (premises) and conclusions, and the importance these have in interpreting texts as arguments.

In particular it discussed:

- reasons as premises versus reasons as explanations

- identifying the main conclusion of a complex argument
- identifying arguments with unstated conclusions.

The chapter also discussed the application of the principle of charity to the procedure for identifying and interpreting arguments.

End-of-chapter questions

1   Concern about the effects on the environment of certain chemicals currently in industrial or agricultural use has led to calls for more thorough research into their safety. But legislation to prohibit potentially harmful substances cannot wait for more research to be completed. We know enough about past mistakes to be forewarned. Much of the harm to wildlife and humans is long term, and the disturbing results we see today reflect the chemical environment of up to 40 years ago. Thousands more chemicals have been released into the environment since then. It will be argued that delays in licensing new and beneficial chemicals is costly for business and the economy. But when it comes to human and environmental protection, that is a cost that must be accepted.

   a   Identify the main conclusion of the text.
   b   Explain the function of the first sentence.
   c   Identify an intermediate conclusion.
   d   Identify a counter-assertion.

2   The law that requires drivers and passengers to wear seat belts, and punishing them if they do not, is an example of the state interfering in matters where individuals should be free to exercise choice. It is not like drunken driving which has been made an offence in order to protect others. The law about seat belts exists simply to protect the car occupants themselves, and consequently should never have been passed in the first place. It is like having a law against hang-gliding or extreme skiing, which are both very dangerous, but which people are, quite rightly, free to pursue if they wish. Alternatively, it would be like fining anyone who stepped outside on a sunny day without first plastering themselves in an approved brand of sunscreen, for fear that they will be exposed to harmful UV radiation. It is true that wearing seat belts can prevent a serious or even fatal injury in the event of a car crash. But according to medical experts UV radiation can be a serious health hazard. The point is not that one risk is greater than the other, but that it is not the business of lawmakers to decide how we should live our lives.

   a   Identify the main conclusion of the text.
   b   Identify an intermediate conclusion.
   c   Identify the counter-claim.

Exam-style question

Briefly analyse Jasper Smitt's argument in Source A below by identifying its main conclusion, intermediate conclusions and any counter-assertions.

Source A: Don't bother about how far your food has travelled

Environmentalists have argued in recent years that we should source our food locally and cut down on the 'food miles' involved in getting food from producer to consumer. This is yet another example of the enthusiasm of such tree-huggers for futile gestures to save the planet from global warming. Throw your food mile calculator in the bin!

Only 2–4% of the 'carbon footprint' associated with food (i.e. the amount of CO_2 emitted into the atmosphere) comes from transporting food. What matters is how food is produced and not where it is produced. The yield per hectare of products like lamb and apples from places such as New Zealand is far higher than in most other countries. This means that the carbon footprint of rearing sheep or growing apples locally is likely to be far higher than it is in places like New Zealand. So although the food miles are less, the carbon footprint isn't.

Buying food locally does not help save the planet. The foodstuffs that are exported worldwide come in refrigerated container ships. A modern ship emits 10–40 g of CO_2 per metric tonne of freight per kilometre travelled. This compares with 500 g for an air cargo plane. This means that the environmental impact of transporting food is far less than that of transporting air freight.

In buying food that is exported from all over the world we are merely following the norm in a global economy. People do not necessarily try to buy locally produced phones or televisions, so why should they suddenly adopt a different mode of behaviour when buying food? It is ludicrous to single out food products for special treatment.

Some people suggest that, by eating only seasonal foods – those that grow naturally at certain times of year – one can avoid eating any imported food. However, this is not a good reason for being concerned about food miles. Some countries do not have seasons. People in such countries need to import food from elsewhere to achieve variety in their diet.

There are those who frown upon purchasing food from other countries. However, you need not feel guilty about eating food from thousands of miles away. You are not going to save the planet by eating locally produced food. You will be saving the jobs of people who produce such food in other countries. So there is really no need to start growing your own vegetables.

Jasper Smitt

Cambridge International AS & A Level Thinking Skills 9694 Paper 41 Q2 November 2015

Chapter 23
Assumptions

Learning objectives

The focus of this chapter is the role of unstated assumptions in arguments, and the importance these have for the procedure by which we interpret and analyse the texts of many arguments.

Reading through this chapter and attempting the activities will help you identify unstated assumptions in reasoning. Assumptions are often seen as a missing step, or reason, in an argument and identifying them is a key part of analysing the structure of an argument.

Cambridge International

Section 23.1.5 Deep-seated assumptions; principles is for general interest and discussion and is not part of Cambridge International AS & A Level Thinking Skills.

23.1 The meaning of 'assumption'

An assumption is a claim or belief that is accepted as true, even if it hasn't been proven or justified. 'Presumption' has a similar meaning: something presumed to be true without necessarily having any firm grounds.

Sometime what it is assumpted it is debetable.

We often assume (presume) something just because there is no reason *not* to believe it. Suppose, for example, I have five banknotes in my wallet, each for 20 dollars. I have come by them in the normal way, so I *assume* they are genuine – as anyone would unless there were some particular reason to think otherwise. It is perfectly rational to make this assumption because the vast majority of banknotes we receive are genuine. Yet I know, as well as anyone else, that some banknotes in circulation are not genuine; they are counterfeit. Therefore, although my assumption is a reasonable one, it is not entirely justified; nor entirely *safe*. Under most circumstances it will be true but in some it may be false.

This is the general meaning of 'assumption', deriving from the verb 'assume'. An assumption differs from an *assertion* in that an assumption doesn't have to be stated – although it can be. In order to make an assertion I have to say something explicitly. But I can make an assumption without saying anything, or even consciously thinking it. In fact, in the example above, I would probably give no conscious thought whatever to the genuineness or otherwise of the notes in my wallet, unless or until someone questioned it. My assumption that they were genuine would be evident in my behaviour: for example, taking the money out to pay for something without a second's thought. You could say that the assumption I was making was *implicit* in my behaviour – including my surprise if I discovered the assumption was wrong.

We can see therefore that an assumption can be *explicit* (stated) or *implicit* (unstated). In critical thinking, however, 'assumption' usually means a reason that the writer has not explicitly stated. To make it clear that this sense of assumption is meant, the term **unstated assumption** is often used in critical thinking.

Identify the unstated assumption

Take the following standard argument:

(1)   The technology for detecting forgeries has improved in recent years. Unfortunately, the skills and techniques of the forger are more than keeping pace. So we are going to see ever-increasing amounts of counterfeit money in circulation.

The conclusion (C) is the last sentence; and the middle sentence is the premise (P). (The first sentence is really just context.) So, it is argued, C follows from the claim that forgery is improving faster than detection. There are no stated grounds for that claim; in that sense its truth is merely assumed. It could be exaggerated or even false. Ultimately we have to take P on trust.

Strong claim which is hard to defend.

But there is more to be said about example (1). For even if we assume that P is true, it is insufficient to establish the conclusion. C is a strong claim, predicting categorically that we will see increasing amounts of forged money in future. That follows from P *only if* the skills and techniques of the forger continue to advance ahead of detection; or, alternatively, if the technology for detection does not catch up in the foreseeable future. The fact that forgery is outstripping detection at present does not mean the balance won't change. By drawing the conclusion that we are 'going to see ever-increasing amounts of counterfeit money', the author is assuming more than he or she is saying. And because these unstated assumptions about the future are extremely questionable, (1) is not a valid or reliable argument.

23.1.1 Assumptions as hidden premises

Another way to think of unstated assumptions is as missing, or hidden, premises. They are premises because they are necessary for the success of the argument. They are hidden because they are unstated. In the example above, there was at least one hidden premise that was unwarranted, making the argument as a whole unacceptable. But unstated assumptions need not always be detrimental to an argument.

Here is another case to consider, on the same topic:

(2) These banknotes all have the same serial number, so they are fake.

Is this a sound argument? Yes and no. For anyone who knows that no two banknotes have the same serial number, it is safe to infer from the evidence that the notes in question are fake. With a true premise, and a conclusion that follows inescapably from the premise, the argument is sound. However, its soundness depends on a fact that is not stated explicitly, in this case because it is rightly assumed to be common knowledge, and needs no saying. If it were not common knowledge that all genuine banknotes have unique numbers, the single premise would not be enough to justify the conclusion.

To make the point, compare (2) with the following argument:

(3) These 20 dollar banknotes all have six stars in the bottom left hand corner, so they are fakes.

This argument has the same form as (2), and the same conclusion, but because its premise is different it requires a different assumption to be made in order for the conclusion to follow from the premise. The assumption is that genuine 20 dollar notes do not have six stars in

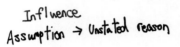
Influence
Assumption → Unstated reason

the corner, for if that is not true then the conclusion doesn't follow. In this case, however, the assumption is not common knowledge – indeed, it isn't even true, so the argument is unsound.

In effect both (2) and (3) have a hidden premise: 'hidden' because it is unstated. Another term that you will sometimes see is suppressed premise.

In standard form, (2) can be represented as follows:

(2.1)	R (*stated*)	These banknotes all have the same serial number.
	A (*assumed, unstated*)	Genuine banknotes all have unique serial numbers.
	C	These banknotes are fake.

You could do the same with (3).

Between them these three examples illustrate a very common feature of natural argument: the omitting of one or more assumptions that are necessary to the logical soundness of the argument but are left to the audience to presume. When it comes to evaluating an argument it is obviously very important to recognise when an argument relies on unstated assumption (or missing premise). If the assumption is false or in doubt the effect on the argument is the same as it would be if one or more of the stated premises is false or in doubt. In (3) the missing premise is false; in (1) it is in need of verifying; in (2) it is a known truth. (Indeed it is arguably true by definition, since 'serial number' means one number in a series.) The three arguments stand or fall accordingly.

Assertion is wrong
↓
Claim is unsound

Interestingly, (2) could have been argued as follows, by stating the assumption and omitting the stated fact:

(2.2) Genuine banknotes would have different serial numbers, so these notes are fake.

Again the single premise makes sense as a reason for the conclusion only if it is assumed that some of the banknotes in question have the same number. In (2.2) this is not stated, but only because it does not need to be. Indeed, without it the argument in (2.2) wouldn't even make sense.

23.1.2 Ascribing implicit premises

Remember that, under the principle of charity (22.1.1), we start from the presumption that the author of an argument is as rational as we are, and would not have left out a crucial premise through carelessness or stupidity, but would have meant it to be taken as read. That is why, when we interpret the argument and subsequently evaluate it as sound or unsound, we ascribe (i.e. add in) the missing piece or pieces to complete the reasoning. We don't just dismiss the argument as incomplete.

However, this does not always have the effect of showing the argument in a good light. Sometimes identifying a hidden premise can show what is wrong with an argument. Applying the principle of charity, as noted in the previous chapter, should not be confused with being kind to the author: it is better to think of it as making the best sense of what the author is claiming.

23.1.3 Identifying unstated assumptions

In the examples we have examined so far it would be very difficult not to recognise the unstated assumptions. But with longer and more complex arguments it can require careful and thorough analysis. Consider, for example, the following passage:

(4) In the days before the arrival of the internet, publishers and booksellers effectively controlled what people read, since very few would-be authors could afford the high financial risks of publishing themselves. The internet has changed all that, with Facebook and Twitter leading the charge. Now anyone can express their views publicly, or distribute information, at little or no cost, and without the tyranny of censorship.

Those who are fearful of the internet should therefore stop worrying about its dangers and acknowledge that, on balance, its growth is in the public interest, not against it. For, almost at a stroke, it has given us freedom of information on a scale that could never previously have been imagined.

Handwritten margin notes:

 How to identify assumptions!.
① Is it relevant?
② Does it support conclusion?
③ Has the idea stated but using different words?

Handwritten annotations on passage: "C" above "should therefore", "IC/R" below "freedom"

EXAMPLE ACTIVITY 23.1

Analyse the above argument so that you are clear about its reasons and conclusion. Then decide whether it contains any unstated assumptions. Here are four suggestions to consider:

(a) There are some reasons to be worried about the internet.

(b) Freedom of information is in the public interest.

(c) The internet is here to stay.

(d) Everyone has the right to publish their opinions. *β*

Commentary

In simplified form the argument runs as follows:

(4.1) R   Now anyone can express views publicly or distribute information at little cost.

IC   The internet has given us freedom of information on an unimaginable scale.

C   Those who are fearful of the internet should . . . acknowledge that its growth is in the public interest.

The first two sentences of the passage can be interpreted either as background information or as additional reasons to supplement the sub-argument, from R to IC. Either way the main argument is from IC to C. This step works only if we assume that freedom of information is itself in the public interest, since that is the reason given for saying that the internet benefits the public. If it could be shown that on balance freedom of information is *not* in the public interest – i.e. that it did more harm than good – then the argument would be considerably weakened. Suggestion (b) above plainly expresses this assumption; so, out of the four, it is the right answer.

None of the other claims is required by the argument, even if they are suggested or indirectly implied. The first, for example, is something that the author apparently acknowledges, given that he says that we should *stop* worrying. But it is not essential to the conclusion for which the author is arguing. It is just a passing remark. His argument would be no less sound if there were *no* reasons to worry: i.e. if (a) were false. If anything it would be stronger. So clearly (a) is not an assumption required for, or helpful to, the argument.

(c) is not implied at all. According to the author, the internet has brought with it freedom of information and expression. But that does not mean that it will continue to do so, or that other technology will not replace it.

You might have been tempted by (d). It may seem reasonable to assume that freedom of expression etc. is an entitlement, and so it may be. But the argument here is that the freedom of expression afforded by the internet has benefits that are in the public interest, not against it; and that therefore it should not be feared. To draw that conclusion it is not necessary to assume that such freedoms are a *right*. (d) claims more than is required for the argument; it goes too far.

ACTIVITY 23.1

Study each of the following short arguments and say which of the suggestions below it are unstated assumptions. (There may be more than one.)

(a) 'Fran will hate this book because it's non-fiction, not a novel. Worse still it's all about mountain-climbing.'

    (i)   Fran hates non-fiction.

    (ii) Fran hates mountain-climbing.

    (iii) Fran likes novels.

(b) Nashida is claiming compensation from her former employers on the grounds that she was forced to leave her job. The employers are saying that they did not actually dismiss Nashida. However, they do admit that they altered the terms and conditions of her job. The law allows that, if employees are forced to accept changes in their working conditions that mean they would suffer as a result, and for that reason only they choose to leave, then their entitlement to compensation is the same as if they had been dismissed. Therefore, Nashida's claim should be upheld.

    (i)   Nashida would have suffered as a result of the changes to her job.

    (ii) Nashida had done nothing to deserve dismissal.

    (iii) Nashida would not have left if the job changes had been favourable.

    (iv) Nashida had no choice about the changes that were made to her job.

23.1.4 Deliberately suppressed premises

Sometimes a key premise is omitted from an argument, not because it goes without saying, but because it suits the author to leave it out, perhaps because it is a questionable assumption and the author may prefer not to draw attention to it by making it explicit.

To see an example in which this might be the case, we return to the argumentative text you first encountered in Section 21.4 about prize money in tennis. Here it is again:

> (5)   Top women tennis players used to grumble that their prize money was less substantial than that paid to top male players in the same competition. They argued that they were being unequally treated. But the disparity was entirely justified and should never have been abolished. Male players just have more prowess than women. They need to win three sets out of five to take the match; the women only two. They have to play harder and faster, and expend far more energy on court than the women. But most of all, if the best woman in the tournament played any of the men, there would be no contest: the man would win.

This argument has two steps. The first step, or sub-argument, is clearly intended to establish that the men have more physical prowess than the women. It gives three reasons for this claim, including the explicit assumption that any of the men in a major tournament would beat even the best woman. Let's assume firstly that these claims are true and that they do show that the men have greater tennis-playing prowess. The next step – the main argument – is that *therefore* the differences in prize money were fine, and should not have been abolished.

It is here, in the main argument, that a crucial premise has been left out. For it raises the question: *why* should this difference in physical prowess determine the prize money? And that question in turn shows us what is being smuggled into the argument. For the argument only succeeds if it is justified to say that prize money should depend on prowess, and so, in turn, on factors such as power and speed. Suppose the women were to object that these factors are irrelevant, and to argue that *their* game is actually more entertaining than the men's and attracts as many, if not more, of the spectators and television viewers. If the women bring no fewer fans, and no less money into the sport, they should have no less reward than the men get for their brute force!

Superficially (5) looks like a reasonable case, until you look below the surface and see what is being assumed. The fact is there are many criteria which could be used to determine prize money. The author of (5) relies on just one: one which, of course, favours the men, and therefore suits his own argument. This might also explain why the author has omitted to add, in so many words, that 'muscle' should be the decider. Since he has no grounds to support that assumption it was prudent not to state it openly, and thereby invite an obvious and justifiable challenge.

Whether or not the omission was intentional makes no difference. Either way, it is a serious inadequacy in the argument, simply because the unstated assumption is unwarranted.

23.1.5 Deep-seated assumptions; principles

In some arguments, such as (4) or (5), what is assumed is a matter of opinion. In the case of (4) the author evidently believes that freedom of information is important. The very fact that it is assumed rather than stated suggests that the author takes it as a given. You can imagine someone questioning the assumption after seeing websites that encourage violence, racism or gross indecency, yet still holding on to the deep, underlying view that restricting freedom is a worse option.

Many arguments make assumptions based on strong, unshakable beliefs, strict laws, political leanings, or shared cultural attitudes and loyalties that we grow up with and keep for a lifetime. Realising when an argument rests on assumptions which we take more or less for granted, and rarely question, is an important part of critical thinking and intelligent debate.

Read the following passage and discuss one or more major assumptions underlying the argument. Consider too how someone might oppose this argument.

(6) After a much-publicised legal battle, Harvey and Hanah Steinberg watched with satisfaction as a family of travellers was forcibly escorted off the corner of their 12 000-hectare estate where the group had been living in a mobile home for 18 months. Not before time. It had taken four appeals and cost the Steinbergs a small fortune in legal fees, but justice had prevailed in the end. The travellers claimed they were following a nomadic way of life going back thousands of years, but their ways show no respect for private property or the rule of law. They did not have the landowners' permission, and they did not pay rent. The Steinbergs therefore have nothing to be ashamed of in prosecuting the trespassers, and the court did the right thing in ordering their eviction.

Commentary

The deep assumptions in this passage are about property rights. The author clearly presumes that property owners, like the Steinbergs, have the right to choose who can and cannot stay on their land; and just as clearly assume that travellers have no comparable rights to live the life they choose if it means infringing property laws. There is also an assumption that trespassing is not only illegal (which in this case is a fact), but wrong (which is a value judgement). Without this assumption it would not follow that the Steinbergs had 'nothing to be ashamed of', or that the court did the 'right' thing – as well as enforcing the law – by ordering the eviction.

The fact that the author assumes all this rather than stating it, or offering any argument for it, indicates that he or she simply takes it for granted, and no doubt expects that many if not all readers will do the same. In the culture to which the author belongs there are laws that protect property and punish trespass, and the majority accept such laws because it is in their interests to do so. Laws that prevent travellers from setting up home wherever they like also prevent them from moving into *your* house or setting up camp in your front garden. Consequently, people who own or rent homes of their own tend to accept such laws, and assume they have some moral justification, even if at times they seem harsh. The author does not see any need to spell all this out or argue for it. For him or her it 'goes without saying'.

But because a deep assumption is not an explicit part of an argument doesn't mean it cannot be challenged. Not every social group adopts the same attitudes to private property as the author. There are people who choose to live, or would prefer to live, nomadic lifestyles without permanent homes, who might start from the entirely opposite assumption that *no one* has the right to own a piece of land and keep others from using it, especially a large estate like the Steinbergs'. Many people seriously question the assumption that trespass is morally (and not just legally) wrong, or that trespass laws are just laws, or that anyone needs 'permission' to set up a home where they choose. One might argue that the Steinbergs showed a complete lack of

$\longrightarrow$

265

compassion in prosecuting the family: that they used their money and power to evict underprivileged people, of minority ethnic status, for no obviously good reason other than exercising their legal right. Some might say that the Steinbergs have *everything* to be ashamed of, and certainly much more to be ashamed of than the travellers.

How you evaluate and respond to an argument like this depends very much on your own political and cultural assumptions. But whichever side you take on the issues, you will not have dealt critically with the argument unless you have recognised and given thought to these assumptions as well as the explicit premises.

Summary

This chapter focused on assumptions. An assumption, under the ordinary meaning of the word, is a claim or belief that is presumed true, without necessarily being warranted or justified.

The following points were also explained:

- The premises of many arguments are assumptions.
- Not all assumptions are explicitly stated: some are implicit (hidden, suppressed) premises.

- An assumption can be considered a missing step in a piece of reasoning.
- Where an unstated assumption is identified it should be included in the analysis of the argument.
- An unstated assumption that is questionable constitutes a weakness in reasoning, because if the assumption is rejected, so is the conclusion.
- Some assumptions reveal the writer's deep-rooted beliefs or attitudes.

End-of-chapter questions

Identify one unstated assumption that is required for each of the following arguments.

(a) The internet has brought many advantages. It is a wonderful source of knowledge and, used intelligently, it provides for a healthy exchange of views. But history will prove that the internet is a far greater force for harm than for good. Its great flaw is that the information on it is not, and indeed *cannot be*, regulated. Anyone can access it and anything can be published on it, freely and at little or no cost.

(b) Police forces often have to divide their time between tackling rising street crime such as theft and assault, and chasing car drivers for offences such as speeding. When it comes to a straight choice, street crime should always come first. It could be said, of course, that the consequences of speeding can be far worse than the theft of a handbag or mobile phone. But the important difference between the two offences is that in one there is intention to harm the victim or deprive them of their property; whereas in the other any harm that is done, however serious, is usually accidental. Therefore, criminals who assault and steal are more of a threat to law and order than those who commit traffic offences.

(c) Graffiti arouses strong feelings in people. Some hate the sight of it; others think of it as a legitimate art form and celebrate it as popular culture. But it is not art; it is a crime. It is against the law to deface property without the owner's permission, and even with the owner's permission it is prohibited on outside walls where it is in public view. In short, graffiti is vandalism – no more, no less.

(d) Many people today think that museums should be like private companies, concentrating only on activities which are profitable. In this way, it is seen as acceptable for museums to ignore the unfashionable or less popular parts of our history. The proper function of museums, however, is to provide a balanced picture of our history. Therefore, we must ensure that they are subsidised by the state rather than having to worry about being profitable.

(e) What is the difference between history and poetry? It can't be that history isn't written in verse. A historian could write history in verse and it would still be history. In fact, many histories have been written in verse over the centuries. No, the difference between the two is that history deals with fact – it tells us what happened – while poetry deals with human feelings and emotions. For this reason, poetry is more important culturally than history.

Exam-style questions

1 Refer to Source A in the exam-style question for Chapter 22. Identify any unstated assumptions in Dave's argument.

2 Write your own short reasoned argument to support or challenge the claim:

The money spent on putting a man on the moon should have been used to improve the lives of poor people.

Chapter 24
Evaluating argument

Learning objectives

This chapter moves on to examine the third of the main tasks that comprise critical assessment: evaluation.

This chapter looks at the skills of evaluating argument. It discusses weaknesses in reasoning, including common flaws.

Cambridge International

If you are preparing for Cambridge International AS & A Level Thinking Skills, you should bear in mind that the exams will not include the term 'soundness'. You will be expected to evaluate reasoning, which will mean identifying flaws and weaknesses and assessing their impact on the strength of the argument. The term 'flaw' will be used rather than 'fallacy'.

Section 24.7 explains two forms of argument: affirming the antecedent and denying the consequent. These will not be assessed, but are included to help you understand the flaws affirming the consequent and denying the antecedent, both of which you will need to be able to identify.

Evaluating reasoning will not usually mean questioning whether claims are true or not, unless they very obviously appear to be unreasonable.

24.1 Strong and weak arguments

To return to the points made at the start of Chapter 20, a good argument satisfies two crucial rules:

Rule 1 is that the reasons should be true, as far as it is possible to judge. We cannot trust an argument that is based on false premises. If we know that one or more of the premises is false, we must reject the argument.

Rule 2 is that the conclusion must follow recognisably from the reasons, meaning that *if* the reasons are all true, the conclusion cannot be false. An argument that satisfies Rule 2 is called a valid argument. (Note that the validity of an argument can be judged without knowing whether or not the premises are *actually* true.)

→ Deductive argument

An argument that passes both these tests is said to be **sound**. An argument that fails one or both of them is unsound. Interestingly we use the same words to talk about structures like boats or buildings, and more abstract objects such as ideas, advice or plans. When you describe something as sound, what you are saying about it is that it is safe, reliable, free of faults. You would not call a boat sound if it had a hole in it and sank ten minutes after setting off from the shore. You would not call a plan sound if it led to a disaster. And you don't call an argument sound if it leads to a false or dubious conclusion. Nor do you call an argument sound if you know, or have reason to believe, that one or more of its premises is false.

→ Sound argument
  ↓
Justified + Claim is true

24.2 Flaws

Another word that is used to describe an unsound argument is 'flawed'. A **flaw** is a fault. There are two main ways in which you can find fault with an argument. You can challenge the truth of one or more of the reasons; and/or you can show that, whether the reasons are true or not, the conclusion doesn't follow from them. Arguments that are unsound for this second reason are said to contain 'reasoning errors' or 'flaws in the reasoning'. They are also called 'fallacies'. A **fallacy** is a flawed line of reasoning. Because it is very often not possible to know the truth or otherwise of the premises, most of the critical evaluation of arguments focuses on the reasoning, and whether or not it is flawed or fallacious.

Reasons is unaccurate, weak will be weakened.

Fallacy equal to the wrong logic of argument

Note: The word 'fallacy' is often used casually to mean a false or mistaken *claim*. For example, after 1912 a person might have said, 'It was a complete fallacy that the *Titanic* was unsinkable.' In critical thinking, and in logic, 'fallacy' is never used that way. A fallacy is always a defective argument.

It is important not to confuse the two issues of truth and validity. An argument can have true premises and a true conclusion and still be flawed. However, if the conclusion is known to be true there is no real need for an argument. Arguments are typically required for claims that are disputed or in doubt; or controversial in some way. So, what you are doing when you evaluate an argument is to ask whether believing the premises would commit you to believing the conclusion. If not, then the argument is invalid, and therefore also unsound. That question can be settled without your having to know the truth of the premises.

EXAMPLE ACTIVITY 24.1

Read the following argument and decide whether or not the reasoning is flawed. If it is flawed, explain what you think the flaw is.

(1)   The outstanding success of Amulk's company, which was launched against the advice and without the support of bankers, business consultants and financiers, just goes to show that one person's vision can prove all the experts in the world wrong. Anyone thinking of setting up in business should therefore trust their own judgement, and not be influenced by the advice of others.

Commentary

First we need to analyse the argument so as to identify the conclusion and the reasons. Then we need to ask whether or not the conclusion follows from the reasons, according to Rule 2.

The conclusion is the second sentence. The first, longer sentence is the reasoning given in support of it. On inspection we can see that this long sentence really contains three claims rolled into one. So a full analysis of it would be:

(1.1) R1   Amulk's company is/was an outstanding success.
       R2   It was launched against the advice of bankers . . . etc.

       IC   One person's vision can prove all the experts in the world wrong.

       C   Anyone thinking of setting up in business should trust their own judgement, and not be influenced by the advice of others.

We don't know whether or not the two initial reasons, R1 and R2, are true, but we'll assume that they are. There is no reason to believe they are untrue. If they are true then it does seem that IC is also true; for if Amulk's company really *was* such a success, and the bankers and others all advised against it, then it seems fair to say one man's

→

success (Amulk's) can prove the experts wrong. It means assuming that the bankers and others are 'experts', but we can let that pass. So we can accept that the first stage of the argument is sound.

The big question is whether the main conclusion follows from the intermediate one (IC). This time the answer is 'No'. Even if everything we are told is true, we cannot conclude from this one single example of success, or from this one misjudgement by the 'experts', that anyone setting up in business should ignore expert advice. It would be a crazy conclusion to draw and a reckless thing to do. It would be like arguing as follows:

> (2) Beth passed all her exams without doing any work. So anyone taking an exam should stop studying!

Not studying may have worked for Beth, just as ignoring expert advice worked for Amulk, but that doesn't mean it will work for anyone else, let alone everyone.

It is easy enough to see that (1) and (2) contain a serious flaw in the reasoning, one that makes the conclusion unreliable. It is also easy to see that it is the same kind of flaw in each case, even though the contexts are different. But what exactly is the flaw? How do we identify it?

24.2.1 Generalisation

(1) and (2) are both examples of common flaws: 'rash' generalisation and 'sweeping' generalisation. Another more technical term is 'generalising from the particular', i.e. from a single example or instance, or one of a small number of instances.

A **rash generalisation** is one that is based on inadequate evidence. → General claim / Not enough evidence

A **sweeping generalisation** is one that does not allow for exceptions to the generalisation. → Only possiblities

Sometimes it can be difficult to decide if a generalisation is rash or sweeping. They may appear very similar. Look again at (1). The writer has concluded from the success of Amulk's company that anyone thinking of setting up in business should trust their own judgement and not be influenced by the advice of others. So, the writer has used some evidence, but it is insufficient to support the conclusion. This is a rash generalisation based on inadequate evidence.

(2) contains the same flaw: the fact Beth passed all her exams without doing any work is not sufficient evidence to conclude that anyone taking an exam should stop studying.

Now look at (3) below.

> (3) Three people fell through the ice last winter when they were walking across the lake. No one should ever think of walking on frozen lakes.

(3) is flawed for the same reason as (1) and (2). Its conclusion is too general to draw from one, or even three, particular pieces of (anecdotal) evidence. In the right conditions it is perfectly safe to walk on frozen lakes, and people do it regularly. What happened to the three unfortunate people who fell through the ice was no doubt caused by the conditions being unsafe at the time. But it doesn't mean, as (3) concludes, that it is never safe to walk across a frozen lake anywhere.

Now read this claim:

> (4)   A law that infringes the freedom of the individual is never acceptable.

Here the word 'never' indicates a sweeping generalisation. The writer might have gone on to argue against a particular law that, for example, required people to wear seat belts in cars. Most societies accept laws designed to protect people even though some people would consider that those laws infringed their individual freedom.

24.2.2 Insufficient reasons

What is wrong with (1), (2) and (3), in general terms, is that in each argument the reason is insufficient or inadequate – i.e. not strong enough – to support the conclusion. In all three cases the argument goes too far, or claims too much.

A useful metaphor for an argument is a see-saw, or balance arm, with reasons on one side and the conclusion on the other. If the conclusion is too strong, or asserts too much, the reasons may not have sufficient 'weight' to support it. For an argument to be strong the reasons must outweigh the conclusion. In (4) they don't even counter-balance it. They are insufficient.

Here we see again why the distinction between strong and weak claims (Chapter 15) is so important in evaluating arguments. Flaws occur when weak claims are given as reasons for strongly worded conclusions. 'No one should ever think of walking on frozen lakes', is not just strongly worded: it is rash, and therefore invalid as a conclusion.

In the next example there is a complete change of tune.

Very strong claim →

> (5)   People cross this lake every year from November through to March. The ice can be anything up to a metre thick. People drive cars across it. I've even seen bonfires on the ice at New Year and folk sitting round having a party. So there is no risk of anyone ever falling through in the middle of February.

EXAMPLE ACTIVITY 24.2

Assuming the reasons are true, do they support the conclusion?

Commentary

This is another example of rash generalisation: grounds being inadequate or insufficient. Even if you add the weight of all four of the premises together, the conclusion is not supported by them. The fact that people have done various things on the ice in the past, and come to no harm, does not mean there is never going to be a risk in the future. In fact, if some scientists are right about global warming, what has been observed about frozen lakes up until now may not be very reliable evidence in years to come. On many lakes the ice in February may become thinner and less safe in the future – just like the reasoning in (5)!

24.3 Describing flaws and weaknesses

It is one thing to recognise that an argument is unsound; it is another to be able to explain what the fault is – or what the faults are, as there may be more than one. If asked to describe the flaw or weakness in (5) you could give either of the following responses:

It assumes that what has been true in the past remains true now, or in the future.

Or, more specifically,

It assumes that because people have walked on the ice safely in February in the past, it is always safe to do so.

Alternatively, you can name the weakness, if it is of a common enough type to have a name. Many have. The type of weakness exemplified by (5) is known as an 'appeal to history', or 'appeal to the past', 'to tradition' or 'to precedent'.

Appeals to precedent are not always weaknesses. Much legal argument, for instance, is based on precedent in the interests of fairness and consistency. How one person is treated by the law 'sets a precedent' for future cases: if convict K was sentenced to five years for a certain offence, it would be unjust for J to get seven years for the same offence, and so on. But appealing to the past as a guarantee of how things will remain or turn out in the future is generally regarded as unreliable.

The following is a classic example of an appeal to history:

(6)   In 1914 and again in 1939, when the two world wars broke out, there were no weapons of mass destruction on the scale there were after 1945. In particular there were no nuclear weapons. After the war, and during the so-called Cold War, the possession of ever-more-deadly nuclear armouries by the two major powers coincided with a period of non-aggression between them. Clearly the chilling promise of mutually assured destruction (MAD) was an effective deterrent, then and now. Consequently we should continue to maintain a stockpile of nuclear weapons as a safeguard against another world war which could destroy the human race.

EXAMPLE ACTIVITY 24.3

Discuss the above argument. Is it a sound argument or does it contain a weakness? Try to decide, giving reasons for your evaluation.

> **Commentary**
>
> This is a well-known line of argument, and there are many versions of it. The core of the argument is that, since nuclear weapons have kept the peace so far, we should continue to stockpile them to prevent a future catastrophic war. For some people this is a persuasive argument; the claims made in it are broadly true, and it seems reasonable to infer that if some policy has been working well it should be kept in place.
>
> Notice that the question you were asked was a closed and semi-technical question. It wasn't whether you found the argument persuasive, or whether you agree with its conclusion. Those are quite subjective questions, and open to personal opinion. It is not the job of a book on critical thinking to advise readers on *what* to think about such big and contentious issues. What *is* its job is to give the reader the tools for evaluating other people's argument fairly and critically. So even if you rate (6) as a good argument – insofar as it supports a conclusion you agree with – you should also have recognised that it is not without a weakness, starting with the very same weakness that was identified in example (5). Just because, historically, the possession of nuclear weapons has not led to a nuclear war, there is no guarantee that this will always be the case. The future is uncertain; the appeal to history as evidence for predicting the future weakens the argument.

24.4 The classic fallacies

Error in reasoning →

A fallacy is a flawed argument. It is also the word often used for the flaw itself. We can say that (5) *is* a fallacy, because it is a flawed argument. But we can also say that it *commits* a fallacy, or has a fallacy in it. Some fallacies appear over and over again in different arguments. The best-known examples were discovered and classified centuries ago, and many have Latin names. They are often referred to as the *classic* fallacies, for that reason. In the remaining part of this chapter a range of these will be introduced and explained, with examples where necessary.

Note: The following fallacies are also very often referred to as **informal fallacies**, to distinguish them from the fallacies in formal or symbolic logic. They are informal in the sense of belonging to informal reasoning, or informal logic – i.e. natural-language arguments.

24.4.1 *Cum hoc*

With this —— → Therefore sth is true

As well as the weakness of the appeal to history, there is a flaw lurking in (6). It is known as the *cum hoc* fallacy, or in full: *cum hoc ergo propter hoc*, meaning literally: 'with this, therefore *because* of this'. The fallacy is in assuming that because a long period of peace has accompanied the era of nuclear weapons, one has been the cause of the other (or at least the explanation for the other). The author of (6) goes further by attributing the cause to the deterrent effect of the nuclear threat. This may be a plausible hypothesis, but there is no evidence that it is the causal explanation. All we have is the claim that:

> . . . the possession of ever-more-deadly nuclear armouries by the two major powers *coincided* with a period of non-aggression between them.

From this alone it cannot safely be inferred that:

> . . . the chilling promise of . . . (MAD) was an effective deterrent, then and now

as the author argues in support of the intermediate conclusion.

24.4.2 *Post hoc*

A closely related flaw is the one known as *post hoc ergo propter hoc* (usually shorted to *post hoc*). The difference is chronological; the fallacy lies in the assumption that just because two things happen in close succession, the earlier one is the cause (or explanation) of the second. The absurdity of this assumption can be illustrated if we imagine someone opening an umbrella just before it starts raining, and then arguing that opening the umbrella made it rain! Of course, there are many situations in which one act or event does cause another. If a tree falls into the road and a driver swerves to miss it, it is perfectly reasonable to infer that the falling tree caused the driver to swerve. The fallacy is not that there is never a causal connection between two consecutive events, but that a causal explanation cannot and should not be *assumed*, even if it looks quite reasonable. In fact, it is when a causal explanation looks quite plausible that the fallacy is most dangerous, because it is then that people are most likely to jump to a *post hoc* conclusion that may be false.

> → No cause and relationship
> After this _ → therefore

We saw a paradigm example in the chapter on Inference (Chapter 19). We are told that a number of people ate at a certain restaurant and reported sick the next day, with food poisoning; then that the restaurant closed. It is natural enough to suspect that eating in the restaurant caused the people to be ill. People often justify such assumptions by saying that there is no other explanation; or that it is unlikely to be merely a coincidence. But on reflection there often are other possible explanations. Anyway, coincidences *do* happen, and coincidence cannot be ruled out as a possible explanation.

24.4.3 Causal flaw

These two flaws – *cum hoc* and *post hoc* – are both species of a more general reasoning error known variously as the 'causal flaw', 'false cause', 'mistaken cause', 'cause–correlation fallacy' or as confusing correlation with cause. A correlation – as you may recall from Chapter 18 – is any observed connection between two claims or two facts, or between two sets of data or trends. For instance, if there were an observed upward trend in violent crime in a city, over the same time period as a spike in the sales of violent computer games, it would be right to say there was a correlation between the two trends.

> → Cause-correlation fallacy

It would also be tempting to conclude that the games were at least a factor in causing the actual violence to increase. Many people make this inference, and not unreasonably, since a significant number of computer games have violent content. It is perfectly justified to claim that if such games did turn out to be a cause of violent crime it would be no surprise, and it would help to explain the trend in a convincing manner. But the plausibility of an explanation does not make it true. It can be posited as a reasonable hypothesis (see Chapter 18), but not necessarily a safe inference.

The inference in (6), and in the Bayside Restaurant example, also exhibits the cause–correlation fallacy. 'Cause–correlation fallacy' is just a different and more general name for the same flaw in the reasoning. One could say that there was a correlation between diners at the restaurant and the people reporting sick, on which to base a plausible hypothesis. But to infer the Bayside's responsibility for the sickness from the data alone would be fallacious. Arguments or inferences that assume causal connections from correlations alone are generally considered flawed.

ACTIVITY 24.1

Find or construct an argument that exhibits a causal flaw. Then try to construct a sound argument based on a correlation or coincidence.

24.5 Recognising and explaining flaws

There are many other classic fallacies and reasoning errors besides those discussed so far. They have names like 'slippery slope' or 'restricting the options' or *argumentum ad hominem*. The names are useful labels for cataloguing common mistakes, but more important than knowing the names is understanding what is wrong with the reasoning. You can identify a flaw without giving it a name, by describing it in your own words. Merely giving it a name does not necessarily demonstrate understanding, either of the reasoning in which the error occurs, or the error itself. If you do identify a flaw by name, it is therefore good practice to accompany it with a short explanation. For example:

The author commits a *post hoc* fallacy by concluding, without additional evidence, that the cases of sickness were caused by having eaten at the Bayside.

Several more classic fallacies now follow for reference.

24.5.1 Equivocation

Sometimes an expression is misused, or used in a purposely confusing or ambiguous way. This is also known as equivocation, especially when the same word is used with different meaning in the same argument. It may result from ignorance or it may be a deliberate ploy to mislead. Supposing someone reasoned:

(7)   The average family has 2.4 children. Since the Bell family is about as average as you can get, the Bells must have either two or three children.

The arguer would be guilty of equivocation and the argument would be fallacious because it depends on the two uses of 'average' being the same when clearly they are different. This is a transparent example, used to illustrate a point, and most people would see through it. But used cleverly or subtly, equivocation can be harder to recognise.

ACTIVITY 24.2

Write a short evaluation of the following argument, identifying and explaining the equivocation that makes it flawed.

No one passing through an urban environment these days can fail to notice the eyesore that is graffiti. Though it is illegal, some big names in the art world have expressed the view that graffiti is a legitimate form of art. But that is absurd. The fact is that spraying or daubing paint, artistically or otherwise, on someone else's property without their permission is a crime, and by definition no act can be both criminal and legitimate.

24.5.2 Conflation

'Conflation' means confusion, so it has something in common with equivocation. Where conflation leads to flawed reasoning is when two quite distinct concepts are treated as though they are the same. If you argue that someone who has been charged with an offence is innocent because he didn't know it was an offence, you are guilty of conflating innocence with ignorance. Under the law ignorance is not innocence, and claiming ignorance is no defence.

You can see a fairly obvious example of conflation in the following example:

> (8) You are wrong to criticise people who lack ambition. Take your own father who chose a career that would never bring him wealth or status. He didn't want those things and didn't value them. Surely you don't despise him.

Actually there are two examples of conflation here: first, conflating ambition with a desire for wealth and status; second, conflating being critical with despising someone or something.

24.5.3 False dichotomy / restricting the options

These are two names for the same fallacy. A dichotomy is a division into two parts or options. By analogy think of the fork in a road, which obliges the traveller to go either north-east or north-west. People often speak of the dichotomy between thought and action; clearly these concepts are distinct. But it would be wrong, and in fact absurd, to say that people cannot think and act. That would be to create a false dichotomy, or to restrict someone's options, to either thinking or acting when a third option was obviously available. A similar restriction of alternatives can be found in the following example:

→ Restricting the options

> (9) When you go into business you can either adopt ethical practices or you can make a profit. Herbco has declared itself to be an ethical company, so if you want to see good returns, you really need to invest your money somewhere else.

On the face of it this looks like sensible advice, given the two premises. If it really is true that you have to choose between ethics and profit – and it often is – then surely it is not a very good plan to invest money in an ethical company if your aim is just to get a good return.

But the speaker here is restricting the options to just two, and assuming that there are no others. Yes, you *can* choose between ethics and making a profit, as the first premise says. But you don't *have* to choose between them unless they are the only choices. By drawing the conclusion that it does, argument (9) clearly makes the assumption that it is a straight choice between ethics and profit with no other options. But it is not a straight choice: Herbco could operate ethically *and* make a profit – for example, if it suddenly became very fashionable to buy goods produced by ethical companies.

24.5.4 *Ad hominem* / personal attack

This Latin phrase (short for *argumentum ad hominem*) means arguing 'to the person' (literally 'to the man'). It occurs when a speaker chooses to challenge the holder of an opinion, or opponent in a dispute, rather than challenging the claim or argument itself. It is a common flaw. Take the following reader's letter to a newspaper. It is a blatant example of *ad hominem* argument:

→ Attacking person rather then arguement

> (10) Sir, the Treasury Minister wants to introduce a pay-freeze for two years on the dubious grounds that this will save the economy from overheating and causing serious long-term problems for everyone. This is a nonsensical claim, from a minister who only last year voted for an increase in the pay of everyone in the government, including, of course, herself.

24.5.5 *Tu quoque* / counter-attack

This flaw has some similarity to *ad hominem* insofar as it often involves a personal element. Literally the phrase means 'you too', or more descriptively: 'you did (or said) such and such yourself'. The charge may be true, but it is a flaw when it is used as an objection to what may be a valid point. For example:

Attack others →

(11) **Tom:** It's wrong for someone to jump the queue for hospital treatment because they can afford to pay for it.

Joe: Come off it. You sent all your children to private schools.

Whatever you think about the rights or wrongs of Tom's claim about private healthcare, Joe's objection is irrelevant to its evaluation. It may make Tom out to be a hypocrite, or selective, or inconsistent; but as far as his statement is concerned, it should be judged on its ethical or political merits alone. As an attempted counter-argument Joe's *tu quoque* is a fallacy.

Note that despite its name a *tu quoque* can be expressed in the third person:

(12) It's wrong for the Opposition to call this bill a 'stealth tax' when they themselves introduced all sorts of taxes by the back door. What was that if not stealth?

As with the previous example, (12) might be grounds for saying that the Opposition are being inconsistent; but on the question of whether or not it is right to call the bill in question a stealth tax, it again is entirely irrelevant. If it is a stealth tax – i.e. a hidden or disguised tax – then it's correct to call it that, regardless of whether the previous government did it too.

24.5.6 Straw man

A straw man is an easy target. It gets its name from the straw-filled sacks that soldiers and archers used to set up for target practice. The straw man flaw is found in arguments between two or more people, when one distorts or misinterprets an opponent's argument to make it is easier to challenge. The following exchange between two people in a modern art gallery contains an obvious straw man.

(13) **Jay:** Emptying a sack full of rubbish on to a wooden floor is not art. There is nothing of value in it, nothing thought-provoking, nothing engaging, nothing that requires any skill or talent to create. Just calling it 'conceptual' doesn't make it art. It's not a magic wand.

Kay: That's nonsense. Art doesn't have to be pretty. Nor does artistic skill apply only to painting or sculpture. Your argument misses the point because it fails to acknowledge that art is also about ideas.

> **EXAMPLE ACTIVITY 24.4**
>
> Identify the straw man in this exchange, and explain what is fallacious about it.

278

> **Commentary**
> The fallacy is quite simply that Kay is not responding to Jay's actual argument. First of all, Jay clearly includes a reference to ideas in his argument by saying that the exhibit in question is not thought-provoking. Second, he makes no claim that art can only take the form of painting or sculpture. Third, he does not criticise the exhibit for not being pretty. So, not only does Kay fail to respond to Jay's actual argument, she instead attacks a misrepresentation of it. It is she who misses the point, and shoots at a straw man.

24.5.7 Circular argument

An argument is fallacious if it assumes what it is effectively going to conclude. A circular argument starts and finishes with more or less the same claim. For example:

(14) Competitive examinations, with their intensive programmes of study, have a lot of critics but they have an indispensable role to play in the educational system. Exams are a means to an end. Assessment provides the goals and the motivation needed by the student to obtain good grades. Without the prospect of assessment at the end of the course the student can lose sight of these goals. Exams, whatever their deficiencies, are essential to success.

What is difficult about analysing this argument is that it does indeed go round in a circle. It begins with the basic premise that examinations are indispensable as a means to an end, and returns to the same claim with its conclusion, namely that examinations are essential. There is a further example of 'circular argument' in the claim that exams are necessary because they provide the motivation needed to get good grades.

24.5.8 Begging the question

Begging the question can be quite a difficult flaw to understand. It does not help that it seems very similar to circular argument and that the name is far from self-explanatory.

Begging the question means assuming the truth of what you are arguing for; focusing an argument on an uncontroversial aspect of an issue while stipulating or assuming the key point. Consider this very short argument:

(15) It is wrong to kill people and therefore the death penalty is immoral.

The claim that it is wrong to kill people is uncontroversial. The conclusion, that the death penalty is immoral, is based on this claim being true. A good argument in support of a conclusion offers independent evidence or reasons to believe that conclusion. If the writer assumes the truth of part of the conclusion, then the reasons are not independent. For example:

(16) Affirmative action to remedy discrimination is never be fair or just. You cannot put one injustice right by committing another.

ACTIVITY 24.3

Explain the flaw in the reasoning in the argument.

Charging motorists will not solve the growing problem of traffic congestion in city centres. For this reason local authorities need to find alternative ways to reduce car use. If they do not succeed there will come a time when traffic in major conurbations simply comes to a standstill. It is clear therefore that congestion charges are not the answer.

24.5.9 Slippery slope

The colourful name, together with the following example, should make it clear what this fallacy is:

(17) Chewing gum should be banned, like it is in Singapore. The streets there are not only free of all those sticky grey patches, but of litter of any kind. The trouble with chewing gum is that it doesn't end there. Young people – and not only the young – see the disfigured pavements, and it blunts their senses. They smoke in doorways and strew the ground with cigarette ends. Kids grow up thinking 'Why should I care? What's the point of me taking my litter home or looking for a waste bin?' Soon the streets are littered with discarded food trays, empty cans, broken glass, shopping trolleys; and the walls are covered in graffiti. It breeds a culture of hostility and violence, and before you know it you have gangs roaming your neighbourhood . . .

And all because of chewing gum! This example is exaggerated to make the point. But people do argue, sometimes quite sensibly, that comparatively minor issues can develop into major ones with serious consequences. This line of reasoning becomes fallacious, though, when it goes too far, and/or when it makes the assumption that the chain of events is inevitable or unstoppable. That is the reason for the name, 'slippery slope'. The idea is that once you are on a certain course, you keep going all the way to the bottom.

24.6 Appeals

As we saw earlier in this chapter, one way in which arguers often seek to persuade their audience is by *appealing* to various emotions, e.g. fear, or to tradition, authority, popularity etc. None of these is necessarily a weakness, but it can be if it is the *only* line of reasoning. Take the following rather obvious example of an appeal to popularity:

(18) Most people in the audience thought that Sheena was the best dancer, so Sheena should have won the top prize.

No thoughtful person would accept this as a conclusive argument, yet appeals like this are often put forward as serious arguments and can be persuasive if not critically challenged. Of course, (18) is a valid argument if it is added, or assumed, that the general public are the best judge. The weakness of (18) is that the appeal to popularity is the only argument, unsupported by any other reason for the judgement.

Another related case is appeal to the fame or importance or rank of a person as grounds for their point of view. For example,

(19)   The Governor of the World Bank thinks that income inequality is unsustainably high. Therefore something must be done to redistribute wealth ...

Even if you are in complete agreement with the Governor's alleged opinion and the author's conclusion, you cannot take the first as sufficient grounds for the second. It is a naked appeal to the authority or title of one person. The most that could be said for the premise is that it gives some support to the case for redistributing wealth, but on its own (19) is a feeble argument.

EXAMPLE ACTIVITY 24.5

Discuss and comment critically on the appeal (or appeals) made in the course of the following argument and counter-argument.

(20)   Our two villages take part in a song festival every year at the start of spring. Our songs are meant to insult the residents of the other village, and vice-versa. It's all in fun, but there are people who find the custom offensive, and it is high time therefore that festival was replaced with something more polite and respectful. People are more sensitive now than they were in the past. Also, there is a risk that tempers might get out of hand and someone will get hurt.

(21)   Oh, come on! No-one's ever been hurt at the song festival. Why should they now? It's been going for five centuries. You can't stop it now with all that tradition behind it. These things need preserving; they're part of the culture.

Which, if either, argument 'wins' in your view?

Commentary

These two arguments consist mostly of appeals, which could be described in a number of ways. The first is an appeal to *offence*: the assumption is that if some people find a practice upsetting or not to their liking, then it should be discouraged or proscribed for that reason. It is followed by a rather weak appeal to *fear* or *danger*.

The second speaker responds with an appeal to *history*: (a) it hasn't happened before so it is unlikely to happen in the future; (b) it's what we have always done so we should continue to do it.

Which of the arguments, if either, you consider stronger is for you to decide.

24.6.1 Multiple flaws

The slippery slope argument exhibits another flaw as well – one with which you are already familiar in various forms. (17) assumes that there is a causal connection between, first the chewing gum on the pavement, then the litter, and finally and much less plausibly the hostility and violence. It is another example of confusing a correlation with a cause. The correlation is between the signs of an uncared-for environment and the anti-social behaviour. There are plenty of sociologists who would agree that they are related. But there are no grounds for the assumption, implicit in (21), that it is the litter that causes the behaviour. It is just as likely – in fact a lot more likely – that it is the other way round. Or that both have a common cause – say poverty or unemployment, or a number of factors combined. So, even if you think it would be nice to get rid of chewing gum, this argument – that it will lead unstoppably to near-anarchy – doesn't justify banning it.

24.7 Conditions and conditionals

Another important concept in critical thinking is that of a *condition* (see Chapter 19). The idea of a condition is a familiar one in everyday life. Conditions of sale, for example, may allow the buyers to return a purchase within a set period if they are not satisfied with it. People are permitted to drive a car on public roads *on condition* that they hold an appropriate licence. Students applying for a place in a college or university have to meet the entry requirements – 'requirement' is another term for 'condition'. Yet although the concept of a condition is so familiar, it can be quite complex, and often leads to misunderstandings and reasoning errors.

Let's say you have been offered a place in a college of your choice if you score 70 in the entrance exam. In other words, scoring 70 is a condition of entry to the college. This might sound quite plain and straightforward. But it is actually deeply ambiguous. For there are three ways of interpreting a condition of entry, and how you interpret it can make a lot of difference to the consequences.

24.7.1 Necessary and sufficient conditions
Conditions fall into two broad categories according to whether they are:

1 necessary

2 sufficient.

A necessary condition is one that must be met in order for some outcome or other to be obtained. If scoring 70 or more in an entrance exam is a *necessary* condition, and you score 69 or less, you will not get in. However, if scoring 70 is a necessary condition *only*, then achieving it still might not secure you a place. The exam might be followed by an interview to choose the best students from all those who scored 70 or more. This condition would make good sense in circumstances where there is a lot of competition for a limited number of places. Under such a condition a score of 70 would be defined as 'necessary, but not sufficient' – which could be quite a shock if you had scored 80 and still been turned down!

Alternatively, a score of 70 might be set as a *sufficient* condition. If that is the case, and you do score 70 or more, you are accepted, and that is the end of it. There are no other hurdles to clear. When you state that a condition is sufficient that doesn't mean it is also a necessary one. For example, there may be a second chance for anyone who scored 60 or more to be interviewed, and to gain a place that way, so that as well as those who automatically qualify by exam there are others who may qualify by exam plus successful interview. This condition would make good sense in circumstances where there are more places than there are strong applicants.

There is, of course, a third way of applying the condition, and that is to make it necessary *and* sufficient at the same time. This would mean that you get in if you score 70 or more and don't get in if you score 69 or less. This is not such a viable condition in the context of college admissions, since it allows no flexibility. If the entry conditions were both necessary *and* sufficient a department could end up with fewer students than it has capacity for, or with more than it can cater for.

24.7.2 Conditional statements

Conditionals – that is, statements that stipulate conditions – typically contain the word 'if', or 'if' followed shortly after by 'then'. They are also known as **hypothetical** statements (or **hypotheticals**). For example:

(22)   If Mia scored 70 or more, then she has a place.

Note that (22) is not an argument; it is a complex statement or claim. It would be an argument if it were expressed as follows:

(23)   Mia scored more than 70 and therefore she has a place.

The difference is that in (23) it is claimed categorically that Mia scored more than the required mark, whereas in (22) it is hypothetical; it remains a possibility. In both cases, however, getting 70 or more is presented as a *sufficient condition*. It may also be a necessary condition, but the sentence doesn't tell us whether or not it is. To express necessary conditions you may need to employ other words such as 'not', 'only' or 'unless'.

EXAMPLE ACTIVITY 24.6

In practice there are many ways of expressing different conditional statements. Here are five more examples. For each one, say whether scoring 70 or more is a necessary or a sufficient condition, or both:

(24)   You will be offered a place only if you score 70 or more.

(25)   If you don't get 70 or more you won't be offered a place.

(26)   You will be offered a place if and only if you score 70 or more.

(27)   If you get 70, you are in.

(28)   Unless you score 70, you won't get a place.

Commentary

In (24) and (25) the pass mark is a necessary condition. Look at them carefully and you will see they say the same thing. However, neither of them says whether there is any other requirement, such as an interview or a medical or even some residential condition, such as living in the country or town where the college is. All (24) and (25) assert is that 70 is the minimum requirement, which is yet another way of saying that it is necessary for admission.

(25) sets a necessary and sufficient condition. It is an abbreviation (or 'contraction') of two statements: 'You will get in if you score 70 or more' and 'You won't if you don't'.

In (27) the condition is sufficient: it doesn't say whether it is necessary as well. Compare it with (22).

(28) obviously states a necessary condition but, unlike (24) and (25), it emphasises that scoring 70 is not also a sufficient condition.

24.7.3 The logical form of conditionals

A conditional is a complex statement that is true or false *as a whole*, independently of whether the parts of it are true or not. (You were introduced briefly to complex claims, including conditionals, in Chapter 15). Consider the following example:

(29)   *If* nothing is done about climate change (then) many parts of the world will soon be submerged.

This statement consists of two shorter sentences (or *clauses*), connected by 'if' or 'if ... then'. The *if*-clause is called the **antecedent** because logically it comes before the *then*-clause. The *then*-clause is called the **consequent**, because it follows logically from the antecedent. If the antecedent is true, then the consequent is true too.

Note that in natural language the order of the clauses can be reversed without altering the *logical* relationship:

(29.1)   Many parts of the world will soon be submerged if nothing is done to reverse climate change.

This logical relation holds whether the conditional is expressed like (29) or (29.1), and whether or not the word 'then' is included.

24.7.4 Hypothetical reasoning

Conditional claims are extremely valuable tools for our thinking and reasoning. Without them we would not be able to consider claims *hypothetically* – that is, before knowing whether or not they are true. Another term for this is **suppositional** reasoning. In (29) what the speaker is effectively saying is:

(29.2) Suppose we do nothing about climate change, parts of the world will be submerged.

Or

(29.3)   Suppose we were to do nothing about climate change, parts of the world would soon be submerged.

None of the claims above mean that nothing *will* be done about climate change. Nor do any of the claims mean that parts of the world *will* be submerged in the near future. The only claim that is being made is that this will (or would) happen *if* we do (or were to do) nothing; or that this will or would be the *consequence* of doing nothing.

A conditional claim can even be made when the *if*-clause (antecedent) is known or acknowledged to be false. The technical term for such a claim is **counterfactual** (or **counterfactual conditional**). Historians are fond of posing counterfactuals in order to speculate about how the world might have been if events in the past had been different. For example:

(30)   If General Lee had won the Battle of Gettysburg in July 1863, the American Civil War would have been prolonged.

This is a conditional statement which may very well be true as a whole – it is certainly plausible – even though the antecedent is false: Lee, as is well known, lost the battle.

24.7.5 Affirming the antecedent

Consider the following deductive argument:

(31) If Mia scored 70 she will be admitted. Mia did score 70, therefore she will be admitted.

What is important here is that this argument is valid. In real life no one bothers with arguments as trivial as this. A natural way to express it would something like:

(31.1) Mia scored 70 so she's in.

This is an argument of sorts but not a valid one as it stands. What makes it sound is the unstated assumption (see Chapter 23) that *if* someone scores 70 she's in. Without that assumption the conclusion of (31.1) doesn't follow from the premise.

The form of (31) – which logicians call *modus ponens* (MP) – is one of the most basic rules of logic. Remembering the Latin name is not so important as understanding the more descriptive one: **affirming the antecedent**. The antecedent, as already noted, is the *if*-clause in the conditional premise. Affirming just means claiming; so by claiming the antecedent you affirm it and draw the consequent as the conclusion.

Note that in natural language the *if*-clause is not always the first part of the sentence. The conditional premise in (31) could be expressed as: 'Mia will be admitted if she scored 70.' The logical antecedent is still: 'she scored 70'. Note, too, that in natural language there are alternative ways of expressing 'if' or 'if … then' – for example:

'so long as …; provided that …; assuming that …'

24.7.6 Affirming the consequent

What happens if instead you affirm the consequent, and still conclude the antecedent? For example:

(32) If Mia scored 70 she's got a place. She has got a place, so she (must have) scored 70.

This has the outward form of deduction, but it is not a valid argument. If you recall the discussion earlier, a condition can be sufficient without also being necessary. In the present case there may be more than one way to get a place in the college. Therefore (32) is a flawed argument, an example of the formal fallacy known as **affirming the consequent**.

ACTIVITY 24.4

Comment critically on the following deductive arguments. Which if any are invalid, and why? Which if any are valid, and why?

(a) If the tide is out we can get to the island. We can get to the island, so the tide must be out.
(b) We can get to the island if the tide is out. The tide is out, so we can get to the island.
(c) So long as she's on form Katya will win the race tomorrow. She is on terrific form, so she will win tomorrow.
(d) If the car has worn tyres it is on the road illegally. It is on the road illegally, so it has worn tyres.

24.7.7 Denying the consequent

Another important argument contains premises that are *denied* – i.e. claimed not to be true – in order to draw a negative conclusion. For example:

(33) If it's dark it is dangerous to be out. But it's not dark, so it's not dangerous to be out.

This is a valid form of argument. Its Latin name is *modus tollens* (MT); its descriptive name is **denial of the consequent**.

24.7.8 Denying the antecedent

As you may know or have guessed there is an associated flaw described as **denial of the antecedent**. It is a very common reasoning error, and it can be harder to spot than affirming the consequent. Here is an intentionally obvious example, to make the point:

(34) If nothing is done about climate change, sea levels will rise. But something is being done, so sea levels will not rise.

By saying that something is being done, the second premise denies the antecedent of the first (conditional) premise, and concludes from that that sea levels will *not* rise. The flaw in this particular argument is that even if both the premises are true the conclusion may still be false: it doesn't follow from the negative consequence of doing nothing, that *not* doing nothing would have any better consequence. But it is not just the details of this example which make the argument invalid: any argument with this underlying form is a flaw.

This is quite hard to understand at first. Study the two examples (33) and (34) carefully and be sure that you are clear as to why one is valid and the other not. Then proceed to the activities below.

ACTIVITY 24.5

Three more short arguments follow. Say which of them, if any, are valid, giving reasons for your evaluation.

(a) If you were bitten by a poisonous spider, you would already have a red, swollen wound. This wound is red and swollen, so obviously you were bitten by a poisonous spider.

(b) If that were a spider-bite, you'd need to see a doctor. But it isn't a spider-bite, so you don't need a doctor.

(c) If this specimen is a black widow spider it would have had a coloured, hourglass-shaped mark on its abdomen. Since there is no mark on its abdomen, it is evidently not a black widow.

ACTIVITY 24.6

Assess the soundness of the following argument.

If the vice-president were guilty of corruption, as you say he is, he would be in prison, not on an official state visit to South America. He is not in prison. In fact he is in Chile right now and is flying on to Argentina tomorrow, and he will not be back until next week. Therefore he is not corrupt.

24.8 Confusing necessary and sufficient conditions

We have looked in some detail at conditions and conditional (hypothetical) statements because some of the most serious flaws in arguments come from confusing them.

EXAMPLE ACTIVITY 24.7

Critically evaluate the following two arguments. What role do necessary and/or sufficient conditions play in the reasoning?

(35) If, as alleged, the government minister has a business interest that he has not declared, he would have certainly been forced to resign. Last night he did resign, so there must be truth in the allegation.

(36) A government minister would not resign over an allegation of undeclared interests unless there was some truth in it. The fact that he has resigned means that there is some truth.

Commentary

There are various ways in which you could find fault with the first argument. You could say, for example, that it assumes, without justification, that the minister's reason for resigning was the undeclared business interest, whereas he might have resigned for some other reason altogether. Another way to explain this is that although the discovery of undeclared interests would be sufficient to force the minister's resignation, it is not a necessary condition, since (as already observed) something else might have forced it. The underlying argument in (35) is as follows:

(35.1) R1 If the minister has undeclared interests, he would have had to resign.
R2 He has resigned.

C He must have an undeclared interest. (The allegation must be true.)

The argument in (35) is clearly unsound.

(36) does not make the same error. The first premise states a necessary condition: it is equivalent to saying that a minister would resign only if the allegation were true; or that if a government minister resigns over such an allegation, then it must bear some truth. Therefore, since the minister has resigned, the inference can only be that there is some truth in the allegation. The reasoning in (36) is solid.

Summary

This chapter introduced the idea of argument evaluation, and in particular what can go wrong with arguments: some of the common flaws that occur in natural-language arguments were considered, including:

- causal flaw
- equivocation and conflation
- restricting the options

- *ad hominem*
- *tu quoque*
- straw man
- begging the question
- the slippery slope
- affirming the consequent
- denying the antecedent.

287

End-of-chapter questions

1   Identify and explain a flaw in the reasoning in each of the following arguments.

   a   Recent research suggests that, contrary to popular belief, the firms that are making the most money tend to have the least happy workers. Therefore firms which impose conditions that make workers less happy can expect a rise in profits.

   b   The best-selling author, Farrah Lavallier, died at the age of 98, just before finishing the 35th book of her distinguished literary career. Critics were in almost unanimous agreement that it was as sharp and witty as any she had written. Clearly she had all her faculties right up to her last days. She also left a diary that revealed, among other things, that she had never done a stroke of physical exercise in her entire life. She was fond of joking that if she walked once round her study, she needed to sit down for a rest. So, if a long and productive life is what you want, you should forget about jogging or joining a gym. Save your energy.

   c   Just look at the statistics and see for yourself how crime has been rising over the past few years. Could there be any clearer signal that the current soft approach to offenders isn't working? Either the courts get back to zero-tolerance and harsher sentencing, or we face defeat in the war on crime.

2   Explain the weakness in the following argument.

Scotland's famous Loch Ness monster is as much an object of fascination for nonbelievers as for believers. In fact, the nonbelievers probably spend far more time trying unsuccessfully to disprove the existence of the creature than we believers do in gathering evidence that it exists. What is more, they have all the benefits of modern science and technology at their disposal, so that if there were an alternative explanation for the evidence, someone would have come up with it by now. So the odds are that there is something very much alive down there in the depths that the scientists can't account for. Anyway, what is so surprising about a large sea creature? The oceans are full of them.

3   Name and explain the flaws in each of these two arguments.

   a   The dinosaurs obviously became extinct because of some catastrophic event such as a large meteorite or dramatic change in the climate. This would mean that they did not disappear gradually over several centuries or millennia, as was once thought, but that they were wiped out practically overnight. This being so, the cause of their extinction must have been a sudden event. A gradual process could not have such dramatic consequences.

   b   Developing countries cannot be criticised for their growing energy consumption and carbon footprint. After all, the richest economies have plundered the Earth's resources for two centuries, and have not put their own houses in order yet.

Exam-style questions

Read the document below and answer the questions that follow.

Freedom of expression is not a human right

The intentions behind the United Nations Universal Declaration of Human Rights were good, but the Declaration should not have identified 'the right to freedom of opinion and expression' as a fundamental human right.

The well-known American judge, Oliver Wendell Holmes, stated in 1919, 'The most stringent protection of free speech would not protect a man in falsely shouting "fire" in a theatre and causing a panic.' This influential example shows that unrestricted freedom of speech can cause a great deal of harm. Rather than defending freedom of expression, law-makers have a moral obligation to limit it, for the sake of public safety.

In many countries, reports of hate speech and incitement have increased since laws protecting human rights were passed. It is therefore impossible to deny that belief in the right to freedom of expression encourages intolerance and discrimination based on race and religion. Fear of those who are in any way different from ourselves lurks just below the veneer of our apparently civilised attitudes and behaviour. Only legal restrictions on free speech prevent this fear from erupting into hatred and violence. History shows that reducing this protection by even a little releases unstoppable forces of evil, which lead inevitably to discrimination, persecution and eventually genocide. It is unthinkable to allow that to happen. So we must abandon belief in freedom of expression as a fundamental human right.

The rights to security of person and freedom from discrimination are more important than the alleged right to freedom of expression. Because the expression of offensive opinions threatens those rights, it should not be allowed. The Declaration was intended to ensure that nothing like the Nazi persecution of the Jews and other minority groups could happen again, but the first step which led to that persecution was the unconstrained utterance of offensive opinions about certain categories of person.

Supporters of freedom of expression often claim that religion should not be protected from verbal attack. But religious beliefs are precious to those who hold them, and it pains them to hear those beliefs mocked or denied. So any principle which would allow the free expression of anti-religious sentiments is seriously flawed.

Another form of protection which governments owe to their citizens is protection from slander and libel. These forms of defamation are illegal in all civilised states – any state which failed to prohibit them could not truly claim to be civilised. So individual freedom must not extend to making untrue and unfair comments about other people. One of the least admirable traits of human nature is our readiness to believe and pass on with embellishments anything we hear to the detriment of our relatives, friends, colleagues and neighbours.

In several recent high-profile cases, officials with access to state secrets have believed that they had a moral duty to reveal them, because they showed evidence of corruption and abuse of power. But the freedom of speech of people in such positions of trust must be drastically curtailed. Governments must be free to prevent people with access to national secrets from putting the safety of the realm at risk by revealing them.

Political Commentator

1 Briefly analyse Political Commentator's argument in the document: *Freedom of expression is not a human right*, by identifying its main conclusion, intermediate conclusions and any counter-assertions.

2 Give a critical evaluation of the strength of Political Commentator's argument in the document: *Freedom of expression is not a human right*, by identifying and explaining any flaws, implicit assumptions and other weaknesses.

Cambridge International AS & A Level Thinking Skills 9694 Paper 42 Q2, Q3 June 2017

Chapter 25
Constructing argument

Learning objectives

In this chapter the third key critical thinking task of constructing further reasoned argument is explored.

25.1 Further argument

Previous chapters have examined the key critical thinking tasks:

- identifying argument
- analysing argument
- evaluating argument.

Critical thinking is not concerned solely with applying certain criteria when scrutinising other people's arguments. It is equally important to apply the same standards when you produce spoken or written material that contains reasoning.

In Chapter 21 the task of creating your own very simple arguments was introduced. This chapter will build on that to develop your ability to produce more complex arguments and to create further argument.

Constructing further argument is the final key critical thinking task. It involves responding to a text by presenting a reasoned case for or against the claims made in that text.

Previous chapters have looked at use of evidence, examples, counter-assertion or counter-argument and hypothetical reasoning. This chapter will introduce use of analogy. All of these elements can strengthen your argument if they are used appropriately. However, it is important to remember that introducing these elements into an argument is not a guarantee that the reasoning will be strong: used inappropriately or ineffectively, the reasoning will be weakened.

25.2 Using analogy

A powerful form of reasoning is arguing from analogy. An analogy is a comparison. For example, suppose you are arguing about what it is to be a good leader, and how a good leader should behave towards the people he or she has been chosen to lead. One approach is to compare the nation-state to a family, so that being a ruler is analogous to being the head of a family. If we accept this broad analogy we can draw certain conclusions from it. An obvious conclusion is that a ruler does not merely have authority over the citizens but also a duty of care towards them, just as a parent has a duty of care towards his or her children. If you want to say that an authoritarian but uncaring parent is a bad parent (as most people would) you are also committed to saying that – by analogy – a purely authoritarian ruler is a bad ruler. This kind of reasoning is what is meant by argument from analogy. It stands or falls on whether the analogy is a fair one or an unfair one; and that is what you as the critic have to decide.

But what is a 'fair' analogy? Obviously the two things being compared are not exactly the same, or you wouldn't need to draw the comparison. What an analogy does is to say that two things are alike in certain relevant respects. In the analogy above, the role of a ruler is being likened to that of the head of a family. There is a difference in that the citizens are not the ruler's own offspring or close relatives, and of course there is a difference in the size of the 'family'. But by using the analogy for the argument you are not suggesting that the two roles are exactly the same: only that they are sufficiently alike – in the relevant respect – for the same kind of duties and responsibilities to apply.

Most people would probably agree that the nation–family analogy was a fair one if it were used to support the conclusion that rulers should not treat their citizens more brutally or unjustly than they would their own children; or simply that rulers have a 'duty of care' similar in certain respects to that of a parent. If, on the other hand, the argument was that a good ruler has to treat every citizen like his or her own child, that would be taking the analogy too far. In other words the fairness of an analogy depends upon the use it is put to in a particular argument.

It is important to remember, whether you are evaluating reasoning or creating your own, that using an analogy may be either a strength or a weakness. A good, relevant analogy can strengthen an argument, but a poor analogy – one in which the comparison is between things that are not sufficiently similar – is generally a weakness in the reasoning.

25.3 Constructing further argument

You will probably have ideas of your own on many issues you have read, not only whilst following a course in critical thinking but in arguments you encounter in the media and elsewhere on a daily basis. Analysing and interpreting the arguments of others helps you to engage with the issues in a critical way; it also helps you to form your own views and to support them confidently with reasons, evidence, and well-constructed argument that recognises, and has an answer to, opposing views.

As with any argument, you are entitled to agree or disagree with the author. Accordingly, your own argument will either add further support, or challenge the author's claims and reasons. Even if you have a pre-formed view, be sure to weigh up the grounds for both sides before proceeding with your argument. It may lead you to revise or modify your position; but even if it does not, it will help to make your response a critical one, and not simply an expression of opinion.

Source A: The thrill of the chase

In crowded cities across the country there has been a growing number of crashes as a result of police officers pursuing stolen cars. Tragically, many of these high-speed chases end in death, not just of the car thieves but also of innocent bystanders or other road users. The police should be prohibited from carrying out these car chases. If someone dies as a result of police activity and the fatal weapon is a gun, there is rightly a huge outcry. But if it is a car, that seems to be accepted as an unavoidable accident.

The police say that they are not putting the public at unnecessary risk, because their policy is to stop the chase when the speed becomes too high and therefore unsafe. This merely emphasises the stupidity of carrying out the chases. Either the policy is adhered to, and the car thieves escape, or the policy is ignored, and injuries or deaths result. Not only is it obvious that this policy is ineffective – otherwise the crashes would not have happened – but it is also easy to understand why.

The police officers will find the chase exciting, since it is a break from routine, and gives them the chance to feel that they really are hunting criminals. Once the adrenaline is flowing, their judgement as to whether their speed is safe will become unreliable. Car chases can be huge fun for all the participants.

Moreover, those police officers who are trusted to undertake car chases are the most experienced drivers who have had special training in driving safely at high speed. The car thieves, however, are almost all young men with very little driving experience. By the time the police driver judges that his speed is unsafe, he will have pushed the pursued driver well beyond his limit of competence. The police may say that if they

→

were not allowed to chase car thieves, this would encourage more people to commit more of these crimes. Would it be so terrible if this did happen? Surely saving lives is more important than preventing thefts of cars, and the police would be more profitably employed trying to catch serious criminals, rather than bored and disadvantaged young men who steal cars for excitement. In any case, there are other ways of stopping stolen cars. For example, a certain device has been developed which can be thrown onto the road surface in front of the stolen car in order to bring it safely to a halt. And sometimes the chases are unsuccessful – the car thief succeeds in evading the police, abandons the car, and escapes.

EXAMPLE ACTIVITY 25.1

Identify the main conclusion of the argument in Source A and the main grounds that are given for it.

Commentary

The conclusion is in the first paragraph, where the main argument is set out.

> C   The police should be prohibited from carrying out these car chases.

The main grounds that the author gives are that many high-speed car chases of stolen cars end in death. The rest of the article consists of additional supporting arguments and responses to potential objections.

EXAMPLE ACTIVITY 25.2

An analogy is used in the first paragraph of Source A. Identify the two things that are being compared, and assess how successful the analogy is in the context of the argument.

Commentary

The comparison is between deaths resulting from the police action of chasing stolen cars and deaths resulting from police action involving a gun.

In order to give support to the argument, the analogy has to compare things that really are similar in ways that are relevant. It also has to be true that there should be an outcry if police action resulted in deaths from firing a gun. The author clearly assumes that there should, by using the word 'rightly' when drawing the analogy.

The similarities are fairly obvious. Guns and car chases both kill. And if things go wrong, both of them kill innocent bystanders as well as criminals and suspects. It is often said that a car is potentially a lethal weapon and this is very much the analogy that is being drawn here. Is it a fair analogy? As far as the consequences go, yes, it seems very fair.

→

Why should we disapprove of a shooting accident, but shrug our shoulders at a driving accident, just because the 'weapons' used are different?

But there are dissimilarities, too, and they cannot all be brushed aside. A gun is designed to be a weapon, whereas a car is not. Also, when a gun is fired by a police officer it is with the intent to kill or wound someone, whereas generally the driver of a runaway vehicle kills by accident. Of course, this doesn't make an accidental death arising from a police car chase any less painful for the bereaved relatives. But it does explain the attitude to which the author is objecting: the attitude that 'if it (the weapon) is a car, that seems to be accepted as an unavoidable accident'.

Does the analogy successfully support the argument? Not entirely. Although the similarities seem quite striking, they are undermined by significant differences. A gun is primarily a weapon; a car is primarily a vehicle, and becomes a weapon only if it is misused. Also, if you place too much weight on this analogy, where do you draw the line? Do you want to say that any police action that results in tragic accidents should be banned, whatever the instrument – batons, riot shields, water hoses, tear gas . . .? If we completely disarm the police of all 'potentially lethal weapons', how can we ask them to protect the public from criminals who could harm them? It is a genuine dilemma, and it cannot be solved by judging all actions by their sometimes tragic consequences.

25.3.1 Writing a further argument to support or challenge a claim

Further argument goes beyond evaluation: it is your opportunity to be creative and put some of your own ideas on the table, either supporting or challenging the conclusions in a text.

Further argument is not any argument: it must relate directly to the text you are working on. It is not a chance just to set off on some line of your own that happens to be on a related topic. You would get no credit in an exam if you read the article 'The thrill of the chase' and then wrote about the justice system, or government spending on policing. There may be issues that connect these topics to the argument about police car chases, but they are not central issues. Your further argument must be for or against the claim stated in the question. Otherwise it is just a digression.

ACTIVITY 25.1

Refer to Source A: The thrill of the chase.

Write a reasoned argument to support or challenge the claim:

The police should be prohibited from carrying out high-speed car chases.

25.3.2 Preparing a reasoned argument

The task of *preparing* a reasoned argument, for or against a particular claim, and with reference to multiple sources, can be broken down into a number of steps, for example as follows. (It is not the only workable procedure. You can adapt it or experiment with others.)

Step 1 Identify the issue or debate to which the target claim belongs.

Step 2 Decide on the side you propose to take, at least provisionally – you may change or modify it after the next step.

Step 3 Extract from the documents the supposed facts, evidence, opinions, and supporting reasons you consider most relevant, and list them. It is a good plan to list these under headings such as 'for', 'against' and 'neutral', in relation to the target claim. Also think about how you will assess them critically. Reconsider Step 2 if necessary.

Step 4 Map out your argument in note form: the main argument and supporting arguments corresponding to paragraphs. Include the counter-claims or counter-arguments that you intend to include, and the way in which you plan to respond to them.

This last step is the one referred to in Chapter 21 as 'synthesis', as it takes the individual items of information, and assembles them into a single, structured argument.

This procedure may seem like a lot of work but it is worth the time. Also, the more practice you have the less time it will take. The secret is in knowing how much or how little to extract from the documents. Be selective: look for the most relevant, most interesting points and avoid repetition. This is especially important if you are working against the clock – in an examination for instance. Assuming you have one hour at most to complete the whole task, you cannot afford more than ten to fifteen minutes on preparation – important though preparation is. To prepare for an exam-length assignment aim for just three or four pieces of supporting evidence or relevant information, and one or two opposing arguments to respond to. Any more than this and you will have no time to comment critically on the items and develop your own arguments around them. It is the quality of the argument, not the quantity of information, that will earn you credit. One of the most common faults in student essays is underdevelopment.

Last but not least, keep to the point. If the task is a question, answer it; if it is a statement, either defend or oppose it. Don't take it as an invitation to stray on to a related issue that interests you more, or that you know a lot about. Of course you can and should introduce one or two relevant ideas of your own, based on personal knowledge or experience. But the key word is 'relevant'.

ACTIVITY 25.2

Taking no more than 15 minutes, use the procedure in Section 25.3.2 to prepare a further argument defending or opposing the following claim. Refer to the passage 'Freedom of expression is not a human right' at the end of the previous chapter.

People who use their freedom of expression to cause harm should be punished.

Once you have a good idea of the shape of your argument, discuss it with others or with your tutor and amend it if need be. There may be important points in the document that you have missed and/or some that you have included which are less effective or less relevant to the line you have chosen to take.

Summary

This chapter has built on earlier chapters to develop the skill of constructing further reasoned argument to support or challenge claims. It has also introduced the tool of analogy.

Exam-style questions

Read the passage and answer the questions below.

Intelligent life on other planets

People have often speculated as to whether there is intelligent life on other planets in the Universe. Science fiction has given us lots of examples, but as yet we haven't found any evidence of such life. Astronomers are making attempts to detect signals from outer space. If they were to detect such signals, that would tell us that something, or somebody, somewhere was trying to get in touch with us. However, despite their detailed, daily sweeping of the sky, no such signals have ever been found.

Those who argue that intelligent life has developed in many places beyond Earth often use the 'evidence' of UFOs (unidentified flying objects) to support their claim. However, these people are simply gullible: they believe that any stray light in the sky is a UFO. Though there are many cases of unexplained sightings of objects, they cannot be said to be evidence of our being visited by other intelligent life.

Given that the Universe is so vast, one would expect to find that, amongst the millions of galaxies with their billions of stars, life had developed on countless planets. But this is the problem: the huge distances between us and other planets that might have intelligent life will prevent any useful communication, let alone dialogue. Radio signals can take thousands of years to get here, so that by the time we get them, the senders will have given up waiting for a reply. Either nobody is there or nobody is listening. It is a waste of time and resources to keep listening and looking for signs of other intelligent life forms.

A huge amount of money has been, and still is being, spent on programmes designed to explore the solar system and beyond. When healthcare systems cannot finance some people's treatment on the grounds that the benefit doesn't justify the cost, we should stop space research programmes. The money should be spent on more worthwhile projects, such as improving the environment of our own planet.

Passage adapted from OCR AS Critical Thinking Paper 2, May 2004

1 Identify, in your own words or the author's, the main conclusion of the argument.
2 Identify an intermediate conclusion.
3 Identify one counter-claim that recognises there might be two sides to the argument.
4 Assess the argument by:
   - explaining two possible flaws in the reasoning
   - identifying two assumptions that must be made.
5 Paragraph 4 contains an example of reasoning from analogy.

   Explain the reasoning. Assess whether it is a weakness or a strength in the argument, giving your reasons.
6 The eminent physicist Stephen Hawking said that, 'We are running out of space and the only places to go to are other worlds.'

Write a reasoned argument to support or challenge the following claim:

Humans will eventually need to leave Earth in order to survive.

Chapter 26
Longer texts

Learning objectives

In this chapter the lessons of the previous chapters are extended and applied to two longer passages containing reasoned arguments and other persuasive writing.

26.1 Introduction

The sample arguments that have been discussed up to this point have been relatively short. Their purpose was to focus on particular concepts – evidence, assumptions, flaws etc. – and on the range of skills that make up the tools of critical thinking. These same concepts and skills apply to the analysis and evaluation of longer and more complex arguments, two of which are examined in the pages that follow.

Source A is an argument about criminals who become celebrities.

You should read the article twice, once for general meaning, then again for more detail, before moving on to the activities and accompanying commentaries. The biggest difference that you will encounter with this longer passage is that it is likely to contain several stages, or sub-arguments – often corresponding to the different paragraphs – leading to a main conclusion. It is also likely that a proportion of the text will be contextual material that is not directly part of the argument but is there to give relevant background information, that the author can use as a counter-argument to be refuted (see Section 21.4). You may also find opposing views, challenges and potential objections. that the author acknowledges and responds to with counter-arguments.

As you read, look out for these different elements in the text, and make a mental note of the contribution they make to the argument as a whole. Most of all, try to locate the main point that the author is driving at – the overall conclusion.

Source A: Time to get tough

It is an established legal principle, in almost all parts of the world, that convicted criminals should not profit from their crimes, even after serving their sentences. Obviously offenders such as fraudsters and armed robbers cannot be allowed to retire comfortably on the money they made fraudulently or by robbing banks.

But the law does not go far enough unless it also applies to the growing number of notorious criminals who achieve celebrity status after their release from jail. Ex-convicts who become television presenters, film stars or bestselling authors often make big money from their glitzy new careers. But they would never have had such careers if it weren't for their crooked past.

The producers, agents and publishers who sign the deals with celebrity criminals protest that the money does not come directly from a convict's previous crimes, but that it is a legitimate reward for their redirected talent, and for the audiences they attract. But the producers and others take a big cut of the profit, so of course they would say something like that. The truth is, a notorious gangster needs no talent to attract an audience: their reputation is enough. Therefore, whether the income is direct or indirect, it is still profit from crime.

It is often objected that once a person has served a sentence, they should be entitled to start again with a clean sheet; that barring them from celebrity careers is unjust and infringes their rights. This is typical of the views expressed by woolly-minded liberals, who are endlessly ready to defend the rights of thugs and murderers without a thought for their victims. They forget that the victims of crime also have rights. One of those must surely be the right not to see the very person who has robbed or assaulted them, or murdered someone in their family, strutting about enjoying celebrity status and a mega-buck income. Moreover, victims of crime do not get the chance to become chat-show hosts, or star in crime movies, because being a victim of crime is not seen as glamorous.

So, if the principle of not benefiting from crime means anything, all income, direct or otherwise, should be confiscated from anyone whose criminal past has helped them to get rich. After all, no one is forced to become a big-time crook. It is a choice the individual makes. Once they have made that choice the door to respectable wealth should be permanently closed. It's the price they pay. If would-be criminals know they can never profit in any way from their wickedness, they might think twice before turning to crime in the first place.

EXAMPLE ACTIVITY 26.1

Read Source A and then answer the following questions.

a State the main conclusion of the argument, using the author's words.

b Identify two intermediate conclusions which support the main conclusion.

Commentary

When seeking the main conclusion, first look for a likely candidate – perhaps some recommendation or prediction or verdict – and ask yourself if the other parts of the argument are recognisable reasons for making such a claim. Be careful, however, not to settle for the first sentence that looks like a conclusion, as it might be one of a number of intermediate conclusions leading to a further or ultimate conclusion. Take, for example, the sub-argument in the second paragraph. Its conclusion is that:

> C1   . . . the law does not go far enough unless it also applies to . . . criminals who achieve celebrity status after their release from jail.

The two sentences that follow are clearly meant as reasons for this conclusion:

> R1   Ex-convicts . . . make big money from their glitzy new careers.
> R2   . . . they would never have had such careers if it weren't for their crooked past.

But the argument does not end there. In the third paragraph there is a further line of argument leading to the conclusion that:

> C2   . . . whether the income is direct or indirect, it is still profit from crime.

Moreover there is a third, plainly signposted conclusion at the start of the fifth paragraph:

> C3 . . . if the principle of not benefiting from crime means anything, all income, direct or otherwise, should be confiscated from anyone whose criminal past has helped them to get rich.
>
> The question is, which if any of these arguments is *supported* by the others – or, in other words, which *follows* from the others? It should be fairly obvious that the answer to that is C3. It is *because* the law does not go far enough, and *because* profit is profit, whether direct or indirect, that the author argues for the confiscation of all income. It does not make good sense to argue from C3 to either of the other two claims: C1 and C2 are intermediate conclusions which, together with numerous other reasons, given in the fourth and fifth paragraphs, lead finally to C3.

26.1.1 Context

Look again at the first paragraph of Source A – where does it fit in, and what is its function? It introduces the 'established legal principle' and provides two examples of unacceptable income that nobody could really argue with – profit from fraud and from bank robbery.

You might want to interpret this as part of the argument on the grounds that without the principle, the argument wouldn't really make a lot of sense. In a loose sort of way it does support the conclusion that profit from crime should be confiscated. But on reflection this is not the best and clearest interpretation of its function, since the author's argument is not really about the rewards from fraud and bank robbery. In fact, it is more or less taken for granted that the direct rewards of these crimes should be forfeited if the criminal is convicted. No supporting reasons are given and none are needed. The *real* argument begins with the word 'But . . .' at the start of the second paragraph. Reading it that way, the first paragraph is more of an introduction than a direct part of the reasoning.

26.1.2 Counter-assertions and counter-arguments

A common feature of longer and more complex arguments is the inclusion of counter-assertions and counter-arguments. (Responding to a counter-argument is also known as **rebuttal**.) Two can be found in the third and fourth paragraphs respectively. They are clearly flagged by the words 'protest' and 'object(ed)', but also from the fact that they obviously challenge rather that support the author's conclusions.

Why should an author include in the text a challenge to their own conclusions? Doesn't that weaken the argument? No, on the contrary it strengthens it because it shows that the author has an answer to the challenge. Imagine you were in a debate and it is your turn to speak. Even before the opposition have their chance to raise an objection, you have anticipated it and responded to it. It is sometimes called a *pre-emptive* move: seeing off an objection before it has been made.

Take the first counter-assertion, in the third paragraph, which the author attributes to the producers, agents and publishers. The objection is that the money ex-convicts make from acting, writing, presenting and so on is due to their talent and comes only indirectly from crime; not directly, like the money from fraud or bank raids. The author rejects this with the following rebuttal:

R1   (Producers etc.) take a big cut of the profit, so . . . they would say something like that.

R2   . . . a notorious gangster needs no talent . . . their criminal reputation is enough.

IC   (Indirect income) is still profit from crime.

A second counter-assertion that the author anticipates and rebuts (in the fourth paragraph) is that ex-convicts have the right to start again on release from prison. This is dismissed as a 'woolly-minded' argument, and as one that ignores victims' rights and feelings.

Note: When a rebuttal of a counter-assertion or counter-argument is considered successful it is termed **refutation**, from the verb **refute**. If you *show* an assertion to be false, or a counter-argument to be unsound, then you can claim to have refuted it. Unfortunately, people often use the term 'refute' loosely to mean reject or deny – for example: 'I totally refute your argument'. In critical thinking contexts it should not be used in that way.

26.1.3   Main conclusion

In the latter part of the fourth paragraph, and then in the fifth paragraph, several more reasons are given in direct support of the main conclusion, which can be paraphrased as follows.

R1   Victims of crime also have rights (e.g. to be spared seeing their attackers as celebrities).

R2   Victims of crime don't get the chance to be celebrities.

R3   Criminals make a choice (they are not forced into crime).

R4   The price for that choice should be that the door to respectable wealth be closed.

R5   If would-be criminals know they will never be able to profit from their crime, they may think twice before choosing to be criminals.

MC   (Therefore) all income, direct or otherwise, should be confiscated . . .

26.1.4   Mapping the structure

We have now extracted, or 'unpacked', the argument by identifying the main components, which are:

- context
- main conclusion
- intermediate conclusions (from sub-arguments)
- counter-assertions or counter-arguments and the writer's response to them.

26.1.5   Summarising arguments

The ultimate aim of all these analytical techniques is to develop a good eye (and ear) for argument: to recognise common patterns of reasoning and to be able to summarise these clearly. Here is a short sample summary of the reasoning in Source A. (Note that this is more than a mere paraphrasing of the text: it is an analysis of the argument.)

The author begins by stating the principle that crime should never pay, but adds that that the law does not go far enough in applying it. It is not enough, he says, to prevent direct financial reward: it should apply equally to indirect profit from celebrity status, book sales etc., on the grounds that these derive from a 'crooked past'. From this he concludes that 'if the principle of not benefitting from crime means anything, all income, direct or otherwise, should be confiscated from anyone whose criminal past has helped them to get rich.'

The main reasons supporting this conclusion are, first, that criminals choose their lives and the price of that choice should be that 'the door to respectable wealth should be permanently closed'; and second that this might deter others from turning to crime in the first place. In addition, the author cites and rebuts two counter-assertions against his argument: (1) that criminal celebrities benefit from their own talent; and (2) that it would be unfair to deny criminals a second chance after completing their sentences. The response to the first is that no talent is required: reputation is enough. The response to the second is that victims of crime don't have these opportunities, and that effectively their rights are infringed by the rewarding of those who have harmed them.

It can be seen from this analysis that longer arguments are made up of steps or strands that work together to support the author's main conclusion, or point of view, that he or she is arguing for. This is often referred to as a **chain of reasoning**: the various steps and sub-arguments are the links that make up the whole. There is an old saying that 'a chain breaks at its weakest link'. This is just as true of chains of reasoning as it is of ordinary physical chains. The converse of it is that for an argument to be sound all the links must be strong. So as well as assessing the argument as a single entity, we need to examine the various parts as well, once we have identified them.

26.2 Evaluation

Analysis identifies the various parts of an argument: the main and intermediate conclusions, and the reasons that are given in support of them, any counter-assertions or counter-arguments and the author's response to them. This is not an end in itself: its purpose is to lay the ground for evaluation. Critical evaluation is only as good as the analysis that has been made of the argument. If you seriously misinterpret the argument, the evaluation will carry no weight: it will be a 'straw man'. (See Chapter 24.)

The question the critic now has to address is how strong or otherwise the support given by reasons is for the conclusion. This means assessing the whole argument and its parts, and identifying any flaws or weaknesses that may detract from them.

Straightaway we can pass over the first paragraph as mostly introductory, and move straight to where the argument really begins, in the second paragraph. The second paragraph draws the intermediate conclusion that the principle of non-profit doesn't go far enough and should apply to ex-criminal celebrities (as well as former fraudsters, bank robbers and so on).

EXAMPLE ACTIVITY 26.2

Review the reasons that are given in the second paragraph of Source A. Are they adequate support for the main conclusion? Are they convincing?

303

Commentary

The reasons given are that these celebrities often make big money *and* that they would not do so if they had not been criminals in the past. Provided you accept that both statements are true, then they do give support to the suggestion that the law needs extending, which paves the way for the main conclusion (in the fifth paragraph) that such income should be confiscated. For if it is a fact that some people do profit from having been law-breakers – and for no other reason than being law-breakers – then the principle referred to in the introduction is (arguably) being broken.

The big question is whether the reasons *are* both acceptable, especially the second. The first claim is fairly obviously acceptable because it is a known fact that ex-convicts who become presenters, film stars and so on do make big money. It could easily be checked and figures produced to support it if anyone doubted its truth. But what grounds has the author got for the second reason, i.e. that these celebrities 'would never have had such careers if it weren't for their crooked past'? Certainly none that are stated. It is an unsupported claim, which the author is expecting the reader to accept, or to take on trust.

As you have seen in previous examples, many – probably most – natural-language arguments rest on certain implicit assumptions beyond the stated reasons. This is certainly the case in the second paragraph: there is a gap in the reasoning – an obvious further reason that would have to be true to make the argument sound. Potentially such gaps are weaknesses, especially if what is being assumed is untrue or even questionable.

EXAMPLE ACTIVITY 26.3

What is assumed in the second paragraph of Source A in addition to the stated reasons? Is it a weakness in the argument?

Commentary

By claiming criminals would not succeed as celebrities if they did not have that notoriety it has to be assumed that they lack the talents that other celebrities have, and could not have achieved similar levels of fame or success as law-abiding citizens. Without this assumption you cannot accept the conclusion simply on the strength of the given premises. But since the reader has no good reason to accept this, it is a potential weakness in the argument.

It could even be said that the need for this assumption constitutes a weakness, if it is considered to be an unjustified assumption. Recall, from Chapter 24, that a common reasoning error is the restriction of options to just two – also known as a false dichotomy. Does the author make that mistake here? Is he assuming that a person either has talent or has a criminal reputation; that he or she cannot have both? If so, then arguably there is a flaw in the argument.

Either way – whether we call it a restriction of the options or a questionable assumption – it is safe to say there is a weakness in the argument at this point.

26.2.1 Response to the counter-argument

The author is evidently well aware of the potential weakness in the second paragraph. That is no doubt why, in the next paragraph, he anticipates and rebuts this objection. The objection, as he puts it, is that celebrity wealth does not come *directly* from crime, but from 'redirected talent'. The author counters this, firstly by suggesting that the producers, agents etc. have a vested interest in making this supposed defence of their clients; secondly by claiming that gangsters need no talent: their criminal reputations are all they need. And he concludes from these claims that the income from becoming a celebrity is nonetheless profit from crime, whether it is direct or indirect.

EXAMPLE ACTIVITY 26.4

How successful do you think the author's response is to the counter-argument in the third paragraph of Source A? Does it meet the objection? Is there a weakness in the reasoning?

Commentary

The author provides a robust response to the counter-argument, but it would be wrong to give it too much credit. It does not completely sweep away the objections; and it doesn't give any grounds to justify the author's assumptions. We'll take the second reason first. This is simply that the ex-convicts in question do not need any talent. Even if it is true, the fact that someone needs no talent to become a celebrity does not mean that he or she *has* no talent – say, as a comedian, or actor or poet. This remains a mere assumption, and one that is easily contested, for there clearly have been ex-criminals who have won acclaim for achievements other than criminal ones.

The first part of the reply is no better. In fact it is no more than an insinuation. The author wants us to believe that the producers and others are all motivated by profit, and would therefore say whatever was needed to justify their 'cut'. It doesn't answer the actual claim that ex-convicts may have talents as well as notoriety. There is also a fresh assumption here, namely that the only people who claim that ex-convicts have talents are producers, or others who have a vested interest. In reality there may be many people, with *no* vested interest, who would also agree with the objection.

This part of the argument clearly commits the fallacy of *argumentum ad hominem*, (see Chapter 24) meaning an attack on the person rather than his or her reasoning. What makes it a flaw is that the argument about redirected talent could be considered valid, even if the person who is making it is supposedly motivated by self-interest. If the people who have succeeded in becoming celebrities do have talent, then the objection is a strong one. You cannot make an argument or objection go away just by discrediting those who may use it – though you will find that it is a commonplace debating strategy.

What you can legitimately say is that if the only support for some point of view comes from an obviously unreliable source and from no other, then we ought to treat it with some suspicion. But that is a very different matter from saying, as the author does in this case, that because certain people 'would say something like that' the substance of what they say must be false.

EXAMPLE ACTIVITY 26.5

Another counter-argument follows in the fourth paragraph of Source A. Critically evaluate the reasoning in this paragraph, identifying any assumptions and/or flaws that it contains.

Commentary

You probably picked up straight away that there was another *ad hominem* argument here. The claim that a concern for the rights of ex-convicts is 'typical of . . . woolly-minded liberals' is obviously directed at the person rather than their argument. However, the author does go on to say why such concerns are misplaced, and here the argument is much stronger. Thus if you ignore the *ad hominem* part of the paragraph you are still left with two or three reasons that do respond to the counter-argument, and (if true) also support the author's own argument. These are the claims that:

- victims also have rights, one of which is the right not to see those who hurt them enjoying wealth and celebrity
- victims don't get the same chances (of celebrity) as ex-convicts.

These are persuasive points. You can easily imagine how frustrating and insulting it would be for someone who has been attacked or robbed to later watch the person responsible hosting a television show, or seeing his or her bestselling autobiography serialised in the newspapers or made into a successful film. The victim might be forgiven for thinking, 'Some of that fame has been achieved at *my* expense. The criminal gets the money and I get nothing. What is more, I am not a celebrity because no one is really interested in my injuries or losses, only in his wickedness.'

But, however persuasive you may find it, is this reasoning sound? Are there any assumptions hidden behind the strong language? Arguably, yes. For a start you would have to assume that there really is a 'right' of the kind the author claims for the victim. People have rights not to be harmed by others, but those rights are dealt with by the courts when they hand out sentences. Once the sentence has been served, is there really a continuing right for the victim never to see the criminal doing well? Arguably, no.

What the author is asking us to accept in this paragraph is that allowing criminals to exercise their rights to a fresh start is unfair to their former victims. But this requires another major assumption. It is the assumption that if victims and criminals both have rights, the victim's rights should come first. Without this assumption there are no grounds for the conclusion; for if, as the author claims, an ex-convict has the same rights as anyone else, then it is hard to see how the author can claim that the victim should have some special right over the criminal. This is a potential weakness in the argument.

26.2.2 The conclusion

So we come to the last paragraph, which consists of the conclusion and a further set of direct reasons. It has two strands. One is that people freely choose to become criminals and that if they make that choice they should be barred from future ('respectable') wealth. The other is that if people thinking of becoming criminals know they will be effectively outlawed in this way they may have second thoughts about turning to crime at all.

EXAMPLE ACTIVITY 26.6

As you did with the earlier steps in the argument, comment critically on the reasoning in the last paragraph of Source A.

Commentary

This is the strongest part of the argument. It places the responsibility for becoming a criminal firmly on the individual, and suggests, reasonably enough, that if that individual then faces having his wealth restricted, he has no one to blame but himself. Opponents of the argument cannot say that the criminal has not been warned. The argument is strengthened further by the claim that this may also deter people from crime, which is arguably the best reason for punishment.

But here, too, there are certain questionable assumptions. One is that people tempted by crime would even *think* about becoming legally rich and famous, far into the future. And if they did, would they care that they might be prevented from doing so? Probably not. Another is the assumption that people *freely* choose their lives; that no one is ever drawn into bad ways by their upbringing, or the influence of others or through knowing no better. Without the assumption that there is truly free choice, it would be harsh to say no one should ever be given a second chance.

26.3 Power of persuasion: rhetoric

If you read this piece of text casually, and uncritically, it is easy to be impressed by the argument. Your first reaction might be: yes, many criminals *do* profit from the fact that they have done wrong and become well known because of it; and this does seem unfair to the law-abiding majority. But, as we have seen, the argument is not necessarily as sound as it may at first seem: there are a number of hidden assumptions and common flaws in the reasoning, when you come to consider it critically.

Part of the persuasiveness of this argument comes from the language the author uses to press his case. Look at two of the phrases used in the second paragraph: 'glitzy new careers' and 'crooked past'. Both help to build up a picture of something both cheap and nasty. It may indeed be cheap and nasty, but to simply call it that is not a reasoned argument. In the next paragraph we are told that a 'notorious gangster' needs no talent, reinforcing the negative impression that is being created of the convict-turned-celebrity.

We call this ingredient of the text **rhetoric**, to distinguish it from the plainer reasoning. Authors use rhetorical devices of various kinds to embellish their arguments, to make them more persuasive. There is nothing wrong with this: it is not illegitimate to express an argument in a forceful way, provided there is an argument to embellish. When rhetoric is misused is when there is nothing else but strong words, and there are no substantial grounds underlying it. Don't make the mistake of picking out a colourful phrase and labelling it as a flaw or weakness just because it employs a rhetorical device. Do, however, be on guard against authors who employ *empty* rhetoric: colourful language to camouflage weak or non-existent argument. (Journalists, politicians and some courtroom lawyers are among the worst offenders!)

Of course, the impression that the author's language creates might be the *right* impression: one that accords with fact. Many of the ex-convicts that the author has in mind may be thoroughly unpleasant, untalented people; and the celebrity they gain may be shallow, 'glitzy', and the rewards undeserved. But that should not blind you to the fact that well-chosen language can heavily influence the way you respond to an argument; that there is always a danger that the *reasoning* can take second place to emotions or sympathies. And if that happens you are not responding in a critical way.

We also saw, in the fourth paragraph, how potential opponents of the argument are dismissed as 'woolly-minded'. According to the author they are 'endlessly ready to defend the rights of thugs and murderers without a thought for their victims'. And we are presented with the image of these same thugs and murderers 'strutting about enjoying . . . a mega-buck income'. The language leaves us in no doubt which side the author is on. But more than that, the author wants to manoeuvre us into a kind of trap, where the only choice seems to be between defending the bad guys or supporting their innocent victims – the false dichotomy discussed earlier.

A critical approach reveals that this argument is strongly biased when it comes to describing the different groups of people involved. There is no concession that there may be some ex-convicts who have genuinely turned their backs on crime, who have real talent as actors or writers, and who do what they can to put right the harm they have caused. Does the author include such people in the same category as those whom he describes as 'strutting about' in their 'glitzy new careers'? The fact is we don't know, because he has conveniently – and no doubt deliberately – left them out of the picture.

26.4 Verdict

So do we rate this as a good argument, or a poor one – overall? That final verdict is left to you. You will probably agree that it is quite a persuasive argument, but that it has weaknesses as well as strengths; and that it makes some claims and assumptions that are, at the very least, questionable. Whether or not these are enough to make you reject the argument, you must decide. You will have the chance to do so shortly.

Be careful, however, that in making this decision you are not just saying whether you agree or disagree with the author's opinion or conclusions. You could quite reasonably think that the conclusion is right but that the argument is poor. Alternatively, you might think it is a strong and compelling argument, but, for reasons of your own, disagree with its conclusion. This is the most difficult position for a critic to be in. If you really find the argument compelling, and you do not dispute its premises, then rationally you should accept its conclusion, even if this means changing a previously held view. If you still reject the conclusion, you need to be able to say where the argument fails – and that can be quite hard to do if it is a persuasive argument.

Summary

In this chapter, an extended argument has been scrutinised, drawing on lessons learned in previous chapters.

The main point that was added was that in longer texts the structure of the argument is naturally more complex, requiring both an overview of the reasoning as a whole, and attention to the component parts – usually, but not always, paragraphs.

The activities and commentaries addressed all three of the components of critical thinking:

- analysis (including interpretation and explanation)
- evaluation
- constructing further argument.

End-of-chapter questions

Read this argument and answer the questions that follow.

Some people think that they have the solution to the supposed increasing danger of shark attacks. Their answer is to go on the offensive and kill the enemy before it can kill them. Not only have officials in some coastal communities taken steps to exact revenge on the individual fish responsible for particular attacks, many are intent on ending the protection great white sharks have been under for almost two decades. Ending the protection would give the green light to unrestricted slaughter of this iconic creature, which may already be an endangered species.

The International Union for Conservation of Nature has described the great white as 'vulnerable', but that didn't deter the Minister for Fisheries in Western Australia from campaigning a few years ago to legalise shark-hunting as a way of reducing numbers. No doubt he had an eye on the economic implications, which cast doubts on the grounds for his argument. He was quoted in the press as saying that a rash of fatalities in that region was a cause for great alarm, adding: 'It won't be helping our tourism industry, and those people who want to come here to enjoy an ocean experience will be turned away because of this situation.'

To be fair, a flurry of high-profile incidents had raised public concern and made big headlines all over the country. One involved a gruesome, fatal attack on a young surfer, with the shark then turning on another who tried to help. The news coverage and minister's campaign naturally stoked up a lot of feeling. Not all of it, however, was directed at the sharks. There were those – including many swimmers and surfers – who quite rightly understand that the ocean is not just their playground. It has other inhabitants, too, and they have rights.

Moreover, compared with many other hazards, sharks don't actually pose much of a risk. Fatalities on the roads of Western Australia are 36 times the number killed by sharks, even in a bad year – and that is normal, not unusual. As several people have observed, you are in far greater danger driving to the beach than you are when you are in the sea. It's like being happy to travel to the airport in a taxi, but being afraid to fly. Most people fear the wrong things, and for the wrong reasons. Fear is not always rational.

Besides, no one has to swim or surf in waters which sharks are known to frequent. If we choose to enter their territory it must be on the understanding that we are the intruders, not they. Sharks do not come ashore and attack people in their homes. If that sounds silly, it just goes to show how absurd it is to try to empty the ocean of these great creatures so that we can feel a bit safer when we go there to play. If we lift the ban on killing great whites, because they are inconvenient to have around, what next? Lions? Tigers? Polar bears? Slaughter every species that has big teeth or sharp claws and very soon we will have nothing but other humans, and furry pets, to share the planet with – along with all sorts of man-made instruments of destruction and pollution that pose far greater threats. If we want to live longer, and share the world we live in, there are far better ways to go about it than by hunting down great white sharks.

Questions:

1 Identify, using the author's words, the main conclusion of the argument.

2 Identify three intermediate conclusions.

3 Identify one counter-assertion and the author's response.

4 Name and explain a possible flaw in the reasoning in paragraph 3.

5 Identify and explain a weakness in the reasoning in paragraph 4.

6 Paragraph 5 contains an example of what is known as argument from analogy. Explain the reasoning. Assess whether it is a weakness or a strength in the argument, giving your reasons.

7 Identify and explain what is wrong with the slippery slope argument in paragraph 5.

8 Write your own reasoned argument to support or challenge the following claim.

> 'Non-human animals have the same rights as humans.'

You are advised to take some time planning your answer. You will not receive credit for merely repeating ideas from the passage.

Exam-style questions

Questions 1 and 2 refer to Sources B to E.

1 Give a critical evaluation of the strength of E Rainbow's argument in Source B: *Meat-free future*, by identifying and explaining any flaws, implicit assumptions and other weaknesses.

2 'Everyone should adopt a meat-free diet.'

Construct a reasoned argument to support or challenge this claim, commenting critically on some or all of Sources B to E and introducing ideas of your own.

Source B: Meat-free future

It was reported recently that the Ancient Egyptians were vegetarians. Analysis of tissue from a mummy has shown that they might have had an almost entirely vegetarian diet. It is often said that protein from meat is needed to build muscle and that fish is 'brain food'. However, if the evidence is true, the Egyptians seem to have achieved great things without resorting to eating animals.

The most obvious reason for giving up meat is that killing animals is morally wrong. How often have you looked at a baby lamb and thought, 'How cute!', only to order a kebab later that same evening – and throw away the salad! It is strange that people seem comfortable watching a family film about a talking pig and then eating bacon for breakfast. Critics often reply smugly that vegetables need to be killed in order to eat them, but animals are not vegetables, they are different. Even the most committed meat-eaters would agree that we should not eat intelligent life forms. The brain is the seat of intelligence so, by their own logic, we should not eat anything that has a brain. If the Ancient Egyptians could do it, so can we. We should cut meat from our diets completely.

Many animals reared for food suffer intolerable cruelty during their lives – the process of stunning before killing does not always work and some religions insist on slaughtering techniques that seem cruel in the extreme. It is strange that none of the meat apologists ever volunteers to be kept in a pen all their life, be stunned by a large electrical current and then killed as soon as they reach adulthood!

A vegetarian diet improves your health. Heart disease is the biggest killer in the Western world. Most heart disease is caused by eating too much saturated fat, almost all of which comes from eating animals. Beef, pork, lamb, milk, cheese and eggs all contain large amounts of this killer fat. Despite claims to the contrary, plants can provide most of the vitamins and minerals needed for a healthy diet. Indeed, consuming the anthocyanins contained in many berries is associated with an ever-growing list of health benefits: reducing cancer and high blood pressure are just two examples. Most scientific studies show that vegetarians live longer than regular meat-eaters.

Already there are over 7 billion people in the world, many of whom are starving. The population of the world has been increasing exponentially for over 100 years and will continue to do so. If we continue as we are, we face widespread famine. Meat production is very inefficient: many more people can be fed from an acre of vegetables than from an acre of land used for livestock. Widespread conversion to a meat-free diet is our only hope to avoid mass starvation.

The number of vegetarians is on the increase. In the UK alone, 12% of teenagers described themselves as vegetarian in 2012. The figure was 6% in 2000 and less than 0.5% in 1960. Since the mid-1800s there has been a rapid year-on-year increase in the number of books written about vegetarian cooking or vegetarianism in general. An increasing number of celebrities are adopting a vegetarian lifestyle. Even Lisa Simpson (the most intelligent of the fictional Simpson family) gave up meat after meeting Paul and Linda McCartney. The future is vegetarian.

E Rainbow

Source C: Becoming vegetarian 'can harm the environment'

Adopting a vegetarian diet based around meat substitutes such as tofu can cause more damage to the environment, according to a new study.

It has often been claimed that avoiding red meat is beneficial to the environment, because it lowers emissions and less land is used to produce alternatives. But a study by Cranfield University, commissioned by WWF, the environmental group, found a substantial number of meat substitutes – such as soy, chickpeas and lentils – were more harmful to the environment, because they were imported into Britain from overseas.

The study concluded: 'A switch from beef and milk to highly refined livestock product analogues such as tofu could actually increase the quantity of arable land needed to supply the UK'.

The results showed that the amount of foreign land required to produce the substitute products, and the potential destruction of forests to make way for farmland, outweighed the negatives of rearing beef and lamb in the UK. An increase in vegetarianism could result in the collapse of British farming, the study warned, causing meat production to move overseas where there may be less legal protection of forests and uncultivated land. Meat substitutes were also found to be highly processed, often requiring large amounts of energy to produce. The study recognised that the environmental merits of vegetarianism depended largely on which types of food were consumed as an alternative to meat.

Donal Murphy-Bokern, one of the authors of the study and former farming and science coordinator at the Department for Environment, Food and Rural Affairs, told a newspaper, 'For some people, tofu and other meat substitutes symbolise environmental friendliness, but they are not necessarily the badge of merit people claim. Simply eating more bread, pasta and potatoes instead of meat is more environmentally friendly'.

Lord Stern of Bradford, the climate change economist, claimed last October that a vegetarian diet was beneficial to the planet. He told a newspaper, 'Meat is a wasteful use of water and creates a lot of greenhouse gases. It puts enormous pressure on the world's resources. A vegetarian diet is better'.

Liz O'Neill, spokeswoman for the Vegetarian Society, told a newspaper, 'The figures used in the report are based on a number of questionable assumptions about how vegetarians balance their diet and how the food industry might respond to increased demand. If you are aiming to reduce your environmental impact by going vegetarian then it is obviously not a good idea to rely on highly processed products, but that does not undermine the fact that the livestock industry causes enormous damage'.

The National Farmers' Union said the study showed that general arguments about vegetarianism being beneficial to the environment were simplistic.

The Telegraph

Source D: Comments on a social media site responding to criticisms of people who eat meat

Many people wrongly assume that the increase in vegetarianism in recent years has been due to the advertised health benefits of a vegetarian diet – berries good, beef bad. However, the increase in vegetarianism happened around the same time that large numbers of children began watching cartoons of talking animals. This, and the ubiquity of furry, cuddly animal toys, is the real cause of the 'vegetarian explosion'. Early-life exposure to fictional animals with human characteristics has led to a belief among the general population that animals are small furry people so we should not eat them! Maybe now we are seeing children's animated films about talking cars and vegetables this worrying trend might be reversed.

■ Whassupdoc

'Turkeys wouldn't vote for Christmas', right? Wrong! There are millions of turkeys on farms all over the world. If people did not eat turkeys there would be, at best, a small population roaming free in North America, and, at worst, they could be extinct. If I was 'Chief Turkey' I would be pleased that there is a tradition of Christmas turkey in Britain and Thanksgiving turkey in the US. Turkeys, like other domesticated birds that we eat, flourish because humans look after them. Christmas will ensure that turkey genes are passed on to generations of turkeys for years to come. Being a domesticated animal has been a very successful evolutionary strategy for many species. Those animals that tasted good, and were tame enough for humans to easily keep, benefited from assured continuation of their genetic heritage. The wild cousins of these domestic animals have struggled to survive, with many succumbing to extinction. Wild horses are rare, domestic ones are common.

■ Otis

Source E: Chart appearing on a news report about a Swedish fast food restaurant that had begun publishing the carbon footprint of the food it serves on the menus

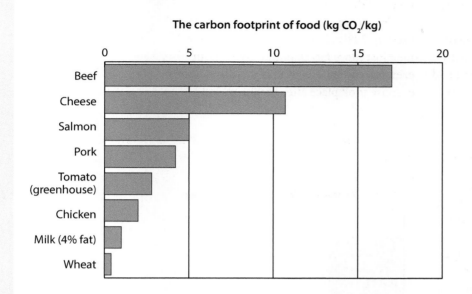

Adapted from Cambridge International AS & A Level Thinking Skills 9694 Paper 42 Q3, Q4 and sources 1, 2, 4 (part) and 5 June 2016

313

3 Study the evidence and answer the questions that follow.

Source F: News report

Early morning exercise can be bad for your health, according to researchers. They have discovered that the body's immune system cannot cope with intense exercise first thing in the morning. Their research suggests that evening is the best time to exercise.

The researchers, at the Sports Science Department at Brunel University in West London, examined the levels of cortisol, a stress hormone that can suppress the immune system, in fourteen British competition swimmers with an average age of 18. The swimmers performed their practice routines at 6 a.m. and 6 p.m. on different days. Tests revealed cortisol levels were lower (that is, better) in the evenings. In addition, levels of antibodies in the blood that help fight off infection were down sharply in the morning, causing swimmers to be at greater risk of picking up infections.

Source G: News report

The afternoon is the best time to exercise if you want to avoid injuries. Body temperature is at its highest between 4 and 5 p.m., which makes muscles warm and flexible and therefore less likely to be hurt. Strength output is 5% higher at around mid-day than at other times of day. Anaerobic performance, such as sprinting, improves by 5% in the late afternoon, while endurance is approximately 4% higher in the afternoon.

However, although afternoon exercise is best from a physiological standpoint, research also shows that people who exercise in the morning are more likely to stick to it than those who take their exercise later in the day.

Source H: News report

Exercising before breakfast is better for you than exercising afterwards, according to new research by scientists at the University of Glasgow.

The research was based on a sample of ten overweight men who did not normally undertake any exercise. The experiment had three stages. First, the men performed no exercise then ate breakfast; a week or two later, they walked briskly for 60 minutes before eating breakfast; in the third stage, they did the same walk after breakfast.

On average, exercising before breakfast used up 298kcal more energy (and so the men lost more fat) than the day without exercise, compared with only 216kcal if the exercise took place after breakfast.

Source I: News report

Many trainers advise that you should eat something before engaging in heavy exercise, but researchers in Belgium have now discovered that exercising before eating is better, especially if you are trying to lose weight. For six weeks, 27 healthy young men ate a diet high in sugar, fat and calories. A third of the men ate the unhealthy diet and did no exercise. The other two-thirds used exactly the same exercise routine, but half of them exercised before breakfast and the other half exercised after breakfast. In addition, those who exercised before breakfast drank only water during their exercise, but the group which exercised after breakfast consumed energy drinks while exercising.

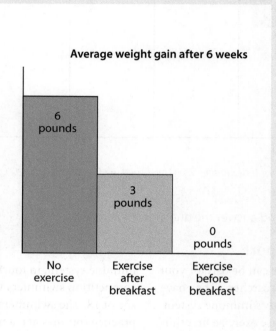

Average weight gain after 6 weeks

- No exercise: 6 pounds
- Exercise after breakfast: 3 pounds
- Exercise before breakfast: 0 pounds

a Suggest **two** reasons why the findings from Source F may not apply to everyone.

b Source F recommends exercising in the evening, whereas Source G says the afternoon is the best time. Give **two** reasons why these research results do not contradict one another.

c Suggest **two** weaknesses in the support given in Source I for its claim that 'exercising before eating is better, especially if you are trying to lose weight'.

d 'The best time to exercise is the time most convenient to yourself.'

To what extent do you agree with this claim? Write a short, reasoned argument to support your conclusion, using and evaluating the information provided in Sources F–I.

Cambridge International AS & A Level Thinking Skills 9694 Paper 21 Q2 June 2015

Chapter 27
Multiple sources

Learning objectives

In this final chapter you will examine and respond to a range of authentic documents dealing with a central theme. The eventual objective is to construct your own reasoned argument, making appropriate reference to the sources at your disposal.

27.1 Introduction

Any form of serious inquiry involves working with multiple sources. It is not enough to read one argument or article and assume that it is the last word on the subject under discussion, especially if it is a controversial subject. You might find a particular argument persuasive, and feel satisfied that its conclusion is justified, yet it is still important to balance this against opposing claims and arguments, and evidence that could be used to support a different point of view altogether, possibly one that you had not seriously considered. Even if you are not persuaded to change or modify your own opinion, you will be better equipped to make a strong case for your own position.

In this chapter, six documents are considered, all dealing with the problem of the growing use of performance-enhancing drugs in sport. The first is an argument for zero tolerance entitled 'Say No to Cheats'; the others take different, or in some cases neutral, positions.

27.1.1 Analysis and synthesis

This chapter, like the previous one, requires you to do the bulk of the work by engaging with a set of activities – some, but not all of them, followed up by commentaries. The activities can usefully be divided into two kinds, distinguished by the terms **analytic** or **synthetic**. Analysing is a task with which you are already familiar: breaking something down into its component parts so as to understand what it is and how it operates. We analyse arguments by identifying the reasons, conclusions and other features, and observing how they relate to one another. We then use the analysis to evaluate the reasoning.

Synthesis can be thought of as the opposite process: it involves bringing together various different elements – texts or parts of texts, items of evidence, and so on – and forming them into a coherent whole. This might be an assignment essay, a presentation, or a report at the end of a research project. It has many applications, including the critical task of constructing a reasoned argument.

Do not think, however, that synthesis is unconnected with analysis and evaluation: on the contrary it *incorporates* these skills. A developed argument will not only refer to items of information, evidence, claims and inferences, it will also *assess* them for their reliability, plausibility, and so on – all the qualities, in fact, that you have been studying under the heading of 'critical thinking'.

After the six documents is a mixture of analytic and evaluative tasks, and questions that compare and combine some of the material. These culminate in an assignment which draws the strings together into a synthetic whole.

The activities can be approached individually or through group discussion, or both.

27.2 The documents

Read through the documents quickly to gather a general impression of the content. You can return to them in more detail when you come to the activities. In some of the texts there is a certain amount of technical detail and terminology which you may not be familiar with. The use of dictionaries or reference sources is permitted.

Note, however, that in an examination any such terms would be avoided or explained, as for example in the footnotes to Source C.

Source A: Say no to cheats

The governing bodies who control international sport are right to ban the use of performance-enhancing drugs (PED) and to operate their policy of zero tolerance against athletes who break the rules. There is more than enough medical evidence to establish that many of the substances that sports stars are tempted to use to increase their strength and stamina are extremely harmful to their health. Permitting their use, or turning a blind eye to it, can have tragic long-term consequences, as many former athletes have discovered to their cost.

Young people are natural risk-takers and are often reckless about their own futures. That, coupled with the huge rewards that can be won by reaching the top in their chosen sport, will often drive them to disregard medical advice and think only of the gold medal, or the big sponsorship deal, or the glory of competing for their country. Those who regulate the sports have a duty of care over these men and women. To stand by whilst they harm themselves would be grossly irresponsible.

But there is another reason why the use of drugs in sport cannot be tolerated. The purpose of sport is to discover who is the best. The only way to achieve that is to start with a level playing field and for every competitor to have an equal chance of winning. You can't say who is best if some competitors are cheating by stealing an advantage. Therefore, if drugs can be driven out of sport, we will once again know who the real champions are.

It is sometimes argued that drugs give no more of an advantage than other perfectly legitimate practices, such as following special diets and taking dietary supplements, which can also boost an athlete's performance. So can the latest hi-tech equipment and clothing, computerised training programmes, physio- and psychotherapies, and so on. Is that not cheating?

No. There is all the difference in the world between eating certain foods and taking drugs because drugs, unlike foods, are banned substances. Any athlete who wants to can take advantage of a special diet or the latest equipment and training techniques. But only those who are willing to break the rules can benefit from taking drugs. Anyway, if you start saying that drug-taking is fine because it is no different from energy-giving food you would end up having to allow athletes to run races with jet engines strapped to their backs.

One more thing: if the top athletes get away with taking drugs, the young people for whom they are role models are far more likely to do the same. For their sake too, the pressure on the cheats must never be relaxed.

Source B: Performance-enhancing drugs: A new reality in sports?

Alexander Rodriguez (Baseball), Lance Armstrong (cycling) . . . These athletes made headline news because they covertly used pharmaceuticals to improve performance, commonly known as doping. A-Rod and Lance aren't alone. They just represent the most recent and very public scandals. By doping, athletes violate the World Anti-Doping Agency's (WADA's) regulation forbidding use of pharmaceutical products in competitive sports. WADA's World Anti-Doping Code includes drug lists describing what is not acceptable – and what is – in a number of sports. The National Collegiate Athletic Association (NCAA) also publishes a list of banned performance-enhancing substances (PESs) annually. Table 27.1 enumerates some reasons why athletes ignore the rules.

Table 27.1

ATHLETES' DOPING OBJECTIVES
Increase strength and endurance
Aid workout/injury recovery
Alter intensity and aggression
Sharpen focus and concentration
Combat exhaustion and fatigue
Reduce weight/body fat
Relieve aches and pains
Increase muscle mass/oxygenation

Athletes and coaches will risk a great deal to obtain a competitive edge and enhance performance. How much will they risk? *Sports Illustrated* magazine interviewed a cohort of elite Olympic athletes, asking, 'If you were given a performance-enhancing substance, you would not be caught, and you would win, would you take it?'

Ninety-eight percent of athletes answered yes. When they changed the question to, 'If you were given a performance-enhancing substance, and you would not be caught, win all competitions for five years, then die, would you take it?' More than 50% still said yes.

Doping is controversial mainly because the medical community has not defined where restoration of normal function ends and performance enhancement begins. Those opposed to doping contend that it undermines the traditional principle of a level playing field and creates unnecessary health risks. Supporters maintain that medical practitioners' concerns about long-term health effects are unwarranted and that athletes who are informed about possible adverse effects should be able to make an informed decision.

Source C: Unfair?

People do well at sport as a result of the genetic lottery that happened to deal them a winning hand. Genetic tests are available to identify those with the greatest potential. If you have one version of the ACE gene, you will be better at long- distance events. If you have another, you will be better at short distance events. Black Africans do better at short-distance events because of biologically superior muscle type and bone structure. Sport discriminates against the genetically unfit. Sport is the province of the genetic elite (or freak).

The ability to perform well in sporting events is determined by the ability to deliver oxygen to muscles. Oxygen is carried by red blood cells. The more red blood cells, the more oxygen you can carry. This in turn controls an athlete's performance in aerobic exercise. EPO (Erythropoietin) is a natural hormone that stimulates red blood cell production, raising the packed cell volume (PCV) – the percentage of the blood comprising red blood cells. Use of EPO to raise PCV is endemic in cycling and many other sports, but it is illegal.

There are other ways to increase the number of red blood cells that are legal. Altitude training can push the PCV to dangerous, even fatal, levels. More recently, hypoxic air machines* have been used to simulate altitude training. The body responds by releasing natural EPO and growing more blood cells, so that it can absorb more oxygen with every breath. The Hypoxico promotional material quotes Tim Seaman, a US athlete, who claims that the hypoxic air tent has 'given my blood the legal "boost" that it needs to be competitive at the world level.'

There is one way to boost an athlete's number of red blood cells that is completely undetectable: autologous blood doping. In this process, athletes remove some blood, and reinject it after their body has made new blood to replace it. This method was popular before recombinant human EPO** became available.

There is no difference between elevating your blood count by altitude training, by using a hypoxic air machine or by taking EPO. But the last is illegal. Some competitors have high PCVs and an advantage by luck. Some can afford hypoxic air machines. Is this fair? Nature is not fair. Ian Thorpe has enormous feet which give him an advantage that no other swimmer can get, no matter how much they exercise. Some gymnasts are more flexible, and some basketball players are seven feet tall. By allowing everyone to take performance enhancing drugs, we level the playing field. We remove the effects of genetic inequality. Far from being unfair, allowing performance enhancement promotes equality.

Notes:
* The **hypoxic air machine** provides nitrogen-rich air which is thought to boost the oxygen-carrying capacity of the blood, which in turn boosts the production of red blood cells – in much the same way as the banned drug erythropoietin (EPO). (*British Medical Journal*)

Human recombinant EPO is a hormone which is administered when a patient is not producing enough EPO on his or her own.

Source D: Just for the rich?

Forget the romantic ancient Greek ideal. The Olympics is a business. In the four years before the Athens Olympics, Australia spent $547 million on sport funding, with $13.8 million just to send the Olympic team to Athens. With its highest-ever funding, the Australian team brought home 17 gold medals, also its highest. On these figures, a gold medal costs about $32 million. Australia came fourth in the medal tally in Athens despite having the 52nd largest population. Neither the Australian multicultural genetic heritage nor the flat landscape and desert could have endowed Australians with any special advantage. They won because they spent more. Money buys success. They have already embraced strategies and technologies that are inaccessible to the poor.

Paradoxically, permitting drugs in sport could reduce economic discrimination. The cost of a hypoxic air machine and tent is about US$7000. Sending an athlete to a high altitude training location for months may be even more expensive. This arguably puts legal methods for raising an athlete's PCV beyond the reach of poorer athletes. It is the illegal forms that level the playing field in this regard.

Source E: Is doping a younger issue?

Younger people are the main users of anabolic steroids in amateur sport, according to a poll for BBC Sport.

Among sports club members aged 18–34, 13% say they have taken steroids to support performance or recovery while playing. Not one interviewee aged 55 or over said they had used anabolic steroids.

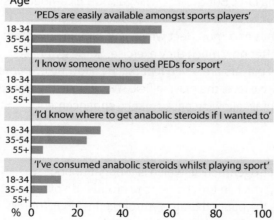

Doping in amateur sports - by age

Percentage who play each sport monthly that agree with the following

1025 British adults who were members of sports clubs, teams, or gyms were surveyed in January 2017.

Source F: Deterrence

The new code (written and implemented by the World Anti-Doping Agency (WADA)) does very little to protect innocent athletes who are sanctioned for innocuous or unintentional behaviour. When skier Alain Baxter used the wrong type of inhaler during the 2002 Salt Lake Olympics, he lost his medal and had a short ban. Should such an incident occur since 2015, it would probably conclude with a ban of between two and four years.

To appeal for a reduction, the athlete would need to risk several thousand pounds to take their case to arbitration. This discriminates against those in less wealthy sports, or who have achieved only moderate career winnings. And since the burden of proof lies with the accused, the chances of success in arbitration are slim.

This is a war in which the authorities want more power, and don't seem to mind some collateral damage. A case in point is that of the English hurdler Callum Priestley, who tested positive for clenbuterol that could have been in the food chain and was banned for two years. He retired from the sport aged 21. More such cases now look foreseeable

So is the deterrence effect demonstrable and justifiable? In recent years, the rate of detection has remained much the same, around 2% – meaning that 2% of those tested are found guilty of doping. Indeed in 2013 it reached 2.13%, slightly higher than in any previous year.

While increased deterrence is a vague possible outcome of increasing sanctions and surveillance, it is hard to imagine that it will bridge the gap between current detection rates and the reality of doping. Anti-doping policy leaders and researchers agree that 2% is a huge under-representation of the true extent of doping. Estimations of that figure vary depending on sport, country, and other factors, but globally it could be 10–20%.

The recent revelations from Russia suggest there to be significant doping sub-cultures that are not disturbed by the increasingly draconian powers of the World Anti-Doping Agency. There are still too many countries turning a blind eye to their athletes' behaviours, not conducting testing or providing sufficient education.

Deterrence is based on the fear of being caught. Athletes on a well-planned doping programme can still evade detection – think Lance Armstrong – especially in a context where anti-doping is not part of the cultural fabric of the sport. A four-year ban is a risk worth taking in such situations, especially if the motivation is a route out of poverty or where coaches and doctors are compelling athletes to dope.

There is an unintended form of inequity, where athletes operating in a highly regulated system are compelled to stay clean, knowing their competitors elsewhere are likely to be doping. And yet for those that get caught there are no second chances, no routes for redemption; the innocent are not protected in the zealous pursuit of those who are currently evading capture. In this unwinnable war, the means are not justified by the ends.

27.3 Activities

Example activities 27.1–27.3 relate to Source A.

EXAMPLE ACTIVITY 27.1

Give a brief outline analysis of the argument in Source A, identifying:

- the overall conclusion
- the main steps in the argument.

Commentary

The argument has three main lines of reasoning, or sub-arguments, which together make the case for the opening statement of the passage: that sport's governing bodies are right to ban PED and to operate a zero-tolerance policy.

The first strand of the argument is contained in the first two paragraphs. Its basic point is that the use of PED results (or can result) in self-harm and it is therefore irresponsible to permit or fail to discourage the practice. Another strand, which could be interpreted as an add-on to the first, is in the final paragraph. It is the argument that top athletes set a bad example if they take PEDs and should therefore be pressured to refrain.

The three paragraphs in between take a different line, namely that taking PEDs is cheating and confers an unfair advantage. Paragraph 3 argues for the intermediate conclusion that only by driving out drugs can we know who the real champions are. The next two paragraphs raise and respond to an often-heard objection that PEDs are not different in kind from other kinds of performance enhancement. The author claims that these arguments lead to a slippery slope whereby any kind of assisted performance is seen as acceptable.

EXAMPLE ACTIVITY 27.2

1 Re-read paragraphs 1 and 2 of Source A, and identify the reasons given in support of the conclusion.
2 What unstated *assumption* is also made here? Do you think it is a warranted assumption?

Commentary

The argument in the first two paragraphs is as follows:

R1   Medical evidence and past experience suggest that performance-enhancing drugs (PEDs) are harmful.

R2   Young athletes are reckless.

R3   To stand by while they harm themselves would be irresponsible.

IC   The governing bodies have a 'duty of care' for athletes.

C   They are right to prohibit PEDs.

We see here a very common line of ethical argument often referred to as the **argument from harm**. The underlying assumption is that if something results in harm, it is wrong and should not be condoned. This seems a reasonable argument: if you accept the truth of the premises, and there is no obvious reason not to, then a strict ban on PEDs would be a sensible policy to follow. But 'sensible' does not necessarily mean 'right', and that brings us to the big assumption that the argument makes: that athletes don't have the right to make these choices for themselves; or that the authorities *do* have the right to make the choices for them, just on the grounds of the dangers PEDs may pose to their health.

The argument from harm (or risk or danger) to the need for prohibition is often underpinned by this kind of assumption: that those in charge have the right to tell grown men and women what they may or may not do to their own bodies. Is it a warranted assumption? In general, no. Of course, authorities do on occasions impose rules for our own good or safety. Many countries prohibit the riding of motorcycles without a crash helmet, or the driving of cars without a seatbelt. But there are many other dangerous activities which we are not prevented from doing (such as mountaineering and skydiving) on the grounds that, although they are dangerous, we nevertheless have the right to do them if we want. Usually a prohibition needs other arguments beside the argument from *self-harm*, most commonly that the harm extends to others as well as oneself. For example, the strongest argument for banning smoking in public places is that non-smokers as well as smokers are affected. If the argument were only that smoking harms the smoker, it would not have anything like the force that it does have.

So the argument contained in the first two paragraphs alone looks a bit shaky after all, not from what it states so much as what it assumes. Only in the final paragraph does the author suggest that drug-use by the top performers may have a harmful influence on other, younger athletes.

The second phase of the argument introduces the **principle of fairness**. The sub-argument is that PED use is cheating, and should be prohibited for that reason in addition to the claimed health risks. Paragraph 3 concludes that if drugs can be driven out of sport we will (once again) be able to identify the 'real champions'.

323

→

There is another assumption lurking here: that there is something *specially* unfair about the use of drugs to improve performance. Why just drugs? Are drugs not just an extension of other legitimate but equally advantageous practices? Since this is an argument that has often been made – see for example Sources C and D – the author needs to acknowledge it and deal with it. In paragraph 4 she anticipates it as an objection or counter-argument, and responds to it with a rebuttal in the next paragraph.

EXAMPLE ACTIVITY 27.3

Give your evaluation of the author's reasoning in paragraph 5 of Source A. Identify any flaws that you find in this part of her argument.

Commentary

There are in fact three serious flaws that need to be looked at. These are known as the 'straw man', the 'slippery slope' and 'circular argument' respectively. Two of them relate to the last sentence of paragraph 5, namely:

> 'Anyway, if you start saying that drug-taking is fine because it is no different from energy-giving food you would end up having to allow athletes to run races with jet engines strapped to their backs.'

A 'straw man' argument, as explained in Chapter 24, is one in which an opposing argument is deliberately misinterpreted, to the point where no one would be likely to make or support it. This is what the author does here. Whether or not you used the name 'straw man', you should have noticed that in the anticipated objection there is no suggestion that drug-taking is 'fine', or that it is no different from eating food. The anticipated objection in paragraph 4 is much more reasonable than that: it merely points out that there is a difficulty in distinguishing between permitted ways of getting an advantage and prohibited ones. That does not mean that anyone raising the objection thinks PEDs should be permitted, only that the problem is not as simple as it seems.

Thus the author is arguing against an opponent who doesn't really exist. It looks as though she has scored a point, but it doesn't count because it is a 'cheap' point. You will often find this flaw in arguments. It can often be difficult to spot it and, ironically, if it's done deliberately it is cheating!

Even if there were no 'straw man' here, there is another flaw in the same sentence, namely a 'slippery slope' argument. You will recall that this flaw gets its name from the idea that once you are on a slippery slope you can't stop yourself going all the way to the bottom. In this case, the flaw is that if some PEDs are compared with legal food supplements there is nothing to stop people saying that anything athletes take or do will become acceptable.

This is obviously nonsense. The difference between special diets or training techniques and the use of certain drugs is really quite narrow. Even the experts have some difficulty drawing a line between, say, a permissible substance and an actual 'drug'. This is why the counter-argument has to be taken seriously even if you are in favour of prohibiting PEDs. The idea that athletes could use jet-propulsion is in a completely different league, and it is perfectly possible to argue for one extreme without having inevitably to slip and slide to the other.

A third flaw relates to the second sentence in the paragraph: the claim that PEDs are different from other ways of improving performance *because they are banned*, and that that is what makes their use cheating. But the main conclusion is that drug-taking *should* be banned. To say that something should be banned just because it is bad, and is bad because it is banned, is to produce a circular argument:

Conclusion:	We should ban PEDs.
	Why?
Reason:	Because using PEDs is cheating.
	Why is it cheating?
Reason:	Because PEDs are banned.

The author is arguing *for* the ban on PEDs *from* the ban on PEDs. Many of the flaws you find in arguments are due to circular reasoning. Sometimes the circularity is obvious. In others it is much more carefully disguised, and you have to be vigilant to spot it.

27.3.1 The argument as a whole

We have found a number of weaknesses, flaws and questionable assumptions in the argument for prohibiting performance-enhancing drugs. That does not mean that we have to reject the argument overall, and it certainly doesn't mean we have to reject its conclusion. Most people find the practice of taking PEDs totally unacceptable and are in full agreement with its prohibition. Most people also consider it to be cheating and believe that it harms the health of athletes.

But the converse is also true. Just because we agree with the main conclusion of an argument does not mean we have to give a positive evaluation to the reasoning. As critics we need to be able to evaluate an argument objectively whether we agree with it or not. In fact, agreeing with the conclusion can often make the job of evaluation more difficult because we are likely to be making the same assumptions and wanting the same outcome as the author.

Besides, the document we have just discussed is a *one-sided* argument. Even though it acknowledges one counter-argument, it does so in a biased way to make it easier to rebut (a straw man). So a fair-minded approach to the question, whatever your own view, must include consideration of some other claims and/or arguments.

In a real-life situation you would seek out alternative sources yourself, looking for a balance or range of perspectives. In a classroom or examination context you will usually be given a number of items to examine and compare, in this case Sources B to F. Each of the remaining activities relates to one or more of these, with further questions included in the End-of-chapter questions at the end of the chapter.

ACTIVITY 27.1

Consider and/or discuss the evidence given in paragraphs 2 and 3 of Source B. How would you describe the evidence? Also, how would you assess its credibility?

You may wish to review Chapter 16 before or after answering these questions.

EXAMPLE ACTIVITY 27.4

a Identify the main conclusion and two intermediate conclusions of the argument in the last paragraph of Source C.

b Do the intermediate conclusions support the main conclusion?

c Point out any flaws or assumptions you consider there to be.

Commentary

The argument in this paragraph lists a number of examples of inequality arising from genetic differences, and draws the conclusion that 'nature is unfair'. That is one intermediate conclusion (IC). The author then claims that 'by allowing everyone to take performance enhancing drugs, we level the playing field', and in the next sentence that 'we remove the effects of genetic inequality'. Either of these could be taken as an intermediate conclusion since they both express much the same view. Or one could be interpreted as support for the other. Putting these claims together the author then moves to the main conclusion that, 'far from being unfair, allowing performance enhancement promotes equality'.

The answers to b and c are largely interdependent. An element of judgement is also required: there is arguably a weakness in the step from nature being unfair to the IC that PEDS can eliminate the inequality. Take the author's own example, that Thorpe's enormous feet give him a massive advantage: it is hard to see how that can be levelled by any means, given that Thorpe, along with everyone else, can also enhance his performance in addition to having his genetic advantage.

On the other hand one could take the more charitable line that in conclusion the author claims only that 'allowing performance enhancement *promotes* equality.' Possibly what this weaker claim means is that some measures could be taken to level up some athletes to give them the same chances as those who start with the genetic advantage. The devil, as it is often said, would be in the detail when it came to applying such a measure.

ACTIVITY 27.2

Critically comment on the data in the bar chart in Source E.

Does it give a reliable answer to the headline question: 'Is doping a younger issue'?

You may wish to review Chapter 18 before or after answering the question.

Summary

This final chapter in the book explored the use of synthesis and analysis to evaluate reasoning and construct further argument.

The ability to synthesise information, critical comment and judgement is rightly regarded as one of the most advanced applications of thinking skills. Such skills are needed for all academic study and research, as well as for the complex demands of daily life in an age dominated by information – not all of it reliable. These are not skills that can be acquired overnight: they take practice and hard work to develop and refine. Thinking critically plays a central part in that development.

End-of-chapter questions

1 Revisit Source B.

    a How would you describe its purpose? Is it an argument, and if so what is its conclusion?

    b What contribution does the table in Source B make to the debate as a whole? To which side, if either, does it give most support, and why?

2 Assess the claim expressed by the final paragraph of Source C:

> 'There is no difference between elevating your blood count by altitude training, by using a hypoxic air machine, or by taking EPO.'

    Do you consider the claim justified? (Give your reasons.)

3 Explain the point that is made in the first paragraph of Source D by the sentence:

> 'Neither the Australian multicultural genetic heritage nor the flat landscape and desert could have endowed Australians with any special advantage.'

    How does it support the author's argument? (You may find some of the information in Source E helpful in answering this question.)

4 **a** Analyse and evaluate the argument in Source F.

    b Respond to Source F with a short argument of your own supporting or opposing the author's conclusion.

5 'Drugs have no place in sport.'

    Construct a reasoned argument to support or challenge this claim, commenting critically on some or all of Sources A–F and introducing ideas of your own.

Appendix A: Mapping of Coursebook coverage of Thinking Skills tests and qualifications

– Content is not relevant

* Content is partly relevant

** Content directly relevant

Problem Solving												
	What do we mean by a problem	Selecting and using information	Processing data	Working with models	Solving problems by searching	Finding methods of solution	Trends in data	Transforming data	Summarised data	Identifying features of a model	Necessary and sufficient conditions	Changing the scenario of a problem
Chapter	1	2	3	4	5	6	7	8	9	10	11	12
CI AS and A Level Thinking Skills[1]												
Paper 1	**	**	**	**	**	**	**	**	**	*	**	**
Paper 2	–	–	–	–	–	–	–	–	–	–	–	–
Paper 3	**	**	**	**	**	**	**	**	**	*	**	**
Paper 4	–	–	–	–	–	–	–	–	–	–	–	–
TSA[2]	**	**	**	**	**	**	**	**	**	*	*	*
(Singapore) K & I[3]	–	–	–	–	–	–	–	–	–	–	–	–
IBO TOK[4]	–	–	–	–	–	–	–	–	–	–	–	–
BMAT Section 1[5]	**	**	**	**	**	**	**	**	**	**	*	**
BCAT[6]	–	–	–	–	–	–	–	–	–	–	–	–
LSAT[7]	*	*	*	*	*	*	*	*	*	*	**	*
CCTST[8]	–	*	–	*	–	–	–	–	–	–	*	–

Critical Thinking

	An introduction to critical thinking	Claims, statements and assertions	Assessing claims	Grounds, reasons and evidence	Evaluating evidence: a case study	Statistical evidence	Uses of evidence: inference and explanation	Identifying argument	Analysing argument	Interpretation	Assumptions	Evaluating argument	Constructing argument	Longer texts	Multiple sources
Chapter	13	14	15	16	17	18	19	20	21	22	23	24	25	26	27
CI AS and A Level Thinking Skills[1]															
Paper 1	–	–	–	–	–	–	–	–	–	–	–	–	–	–	–
Paper 2	**	*	*	*	*	**	**	*	**	**	*	**	**	**	**
Paper 3	–	–	–	–	–	–	–	–	–	–	–	–	–	–	–
Paper 4	**	*	*	*	*	**	**	*	**	**	*	**	**	**	**
TSA[2]	*	*	*	*	*	**	**	*	**	**	*	**	–	–	–
(Singapore) K & I[3]	*	*	*	*	*	–	*	*	*	*	*	*	*	–	–
IBO TOK[4]	*	*	*	*	*	–	*	*	–	*	–	*	*	–	–
BMAT Section 1[5]	*	*	*	**	*	**	*	**	**	*	**	**	*	–	–
BMAT Section 3[5]	–	–	–	–	–	–	*	*	*	*	*	–	**	–	–
BCAT[6]	*	*	*	*	*	–	*	*	*	*	*	*	*	–	–
LSAT[7]	*	*	*	*	*	*	*	*	*	*	*	*	*	–	–
CCTST[8]	*	*	*	*	*	*	*	*	*	*	*	*	*	–	–

[1] Cambridge International GCE AS and A Level Thinking Skills

[2] Thinking Skills Assessment including the following pre-interview assessments for the University of Cambridge (UK):
- Economics Admissions Assessment (EAA) (problem solving only)
- Geography Admissions Assessment (GAA)
- Psychological and Behavioural Sciences Admissions Assessment (PBSAA),

[3] Singapore Examinations and Assessment Board/Cambridge International GCE Advanced Level Higher 2 Knowledge and Inquiry

[4] International Baccalaureate Diploma Programme core: Theory of knowledge

[5] Cambridge Assessment (UK) Biomedical Admissions Test

[6] Bar Standards Board (UK) Bar Course Aptitude Test

[7] Law School Admission Council (USA) Law Schools Admissions Test

[8] California (USA) Critical Thinking Skills Test

Index

Acknowledgements

The authors and publishers acknowledge the following sources of copyright material and are grateful for the permissions granted. While every effort has been made, it has not always been possible to identify the sources of all the material used, or to trace all copyright holders. If any omissions are brought to our notice, we will be happy to include the appropriate acknowledgements on reprinting.

Chapter 13 '2029: the year when robots will have the power to outsmart their makers' by Nadia Khomami, adapted from The Guardian, 22nd February 2014, © Guardian News & Media Ltd. 2008; Chapter 17 adapted from 'Gustave Whitehead: Did He Beat the Wright Brothers into the Sky?' by Lee Krystek at www.unmuseum.org; Chapter 17 uses data from The International Shark Attack File; Text and graph from International Shark Attack File, Florida Museum of Natural History, University of Florida; Chapter 27 case study 27.2.2 adapted from 'Performance-Enhancing Drugs: A New Reality in Sports?' by Jeannette Y. Wick for Pharmacy Times, 13th March 2014, © Pharmacy & Healthcare Communication, LLC ; Chapter 27 case study 27.2.3, 4 adapted from 'Why we should allow performance enhancing drugs in sport' by J Savulescu, B Foddy and M Clayton, © British Journal of Sports Medicine, BMJ Publishing Group via Rightslink; Chapter 27 case study 27.2.5 graph redrawn from data by BBC and ComRes; Chapter 27 case study 27.2.6 adapted from 'Tougher rules on drugs in sport won't help detect more doping' by Paul Dimeo (Senior Lecturer in Sport, University of Stirling) for The Conversation http://theconversation.com/tougher-rules-on-drugs-in-sport-wont-help-detect-more-doping-35404

Past examination questions throughout this work are reproduced by permission of Cambridge Assessment International Education.

Thanks to the following for permission to reproduce images:
Cover Blackdovfx/Getty Images; Inside Nora Carol Photography/Getty Images; Scott Barbour/Getty Images; AnthonyHarvie/Getty Images; US Library of Congress/Science Photo Library/Getty Images; Library of Congress/Getty Images; Tim Graham/Getty Images; Dinodia Photo/Getty Images; `Lawyer's treadmill' by Jack Corbett, used with the permission of Cartoon Stock © Jack Corbett; MirageC/Getty Images; Anton Eine/EyeEm/Getty Images; shulz/Getty Images; Sean Gladwell/Getty Images; Westend61/Getty Images; themacx/Getty Images; Juj Winn/Getty Images; Mina D La O/Getty Images; Manuel Breva Colmeiro/Getty Images; Lewis Phillips/Getty Images; Gary Waters/Getty Images; Atomic Imagery/Getty Images; pbombaert/Getty Images; Klaus Vedfelt/Getty Images; Thomas Jackson/Getty Images; oxygen/Getty Images; TEK IMAGE/Science Photo Library/Getty Images; mrs/Getty Images; Glowimages/Getty Images; loops7/Getty Images; FlowerPhotos/UIG via Getty Images; Jose A. Bernat Bacete/Getty Images; Andrea Kennard Photography/Getty Images; Richard Graves/EyeEm/Getty Images; Ilona Nagy/Getty Images